THE POLITICAL INSTITUTIONS AND THEORIES OF THE HINDUS

THE POLITICAL INSTITUTIONS

AND

THEORIES OF THE HINDUS:

A STUDY IN COMPARATIVE POLITICS

BENOY KUMAR SARKAR

GYAN

Published by

Gyan Publishing House
5, Ansari Road
Daryaganj, New Delhi-110002
Phone: 011-47034999, 9811692060
E-mail: books@gyanbooks.com

Distribution Network
gyanbooks.com
India, USA, Canada, UK, Australia

ISBN: 978-93-6780-836-8 (HB)

First Published, 1922

2nd Impression 2025

Printed at: Gyan Press, Delhi.

THE POLITICAL INSTITUTIONS AND THEORIES OF THE HINDUS
Author: BENOY KUMAR SARKAR

BENOY KUMAR SARKAR

THE POLITICAL INSTITUTIONS AND THEORIES OF THE HINDUS

THE POLITICAL INSTITUTIONS AND THEORIES OF THE HINDUS

A STUDY IN COMPARATIVE POLITICS

BY

BENOY KUMAR SARKAR

Professor, National Council of Education, Bengal,
Membre Correspondant de la Société d'Economie Politique de Paris
Author of The Science of History, Chinese Religion through Hindu Eyes,
The Positive Background of Hindu Sociology
etc. etc.

1922

VERLAG VON MARKERT & PETTERS • LEIPZIG

TO

YOUNG ASIA
THIS LITTLE BOOK
IS DEDICATED

Preface.

I.

Edward Freeman's Comparative Politics (1874) was confined to Europe. The object of the present treatise is to extend the area of investigation to Asia. The data used are Hindu, the political institutions and theories of Islam as well as those of China and Japan being set apart for separate treatment.

The methodology is indicated in pp. 5—9, 163—166. Readers will notice that the thread of argument in the author's previous writings, *Hindu Art: Its Humanism and Modernism* (1920), *Hindu Achievements in Exact Science* (1918), *Folk-Element in Hindu Culture* (1917), *Love in Hindu Literature* (1916), *Chinese Religion through Hindu Eyes* (1916) and *Positive Background of Hindu Sociology* (Vol. I, 1914, Vol. II, Pt. I, 1921) is here continued and developed only to fit in with a new order of social phenomena.

The study of institutions is based chiefly, or rather exclusively, on inscriptions, coins and contemporary reports (Authorities A). The Sanskrit and Prâkrit treatises on politics and law as well as the semi-historical epics and birth stories (Authorities B and C) have sedulously been eschewed. This "literary" material has, if at all, been used by way of illustration, especially where strictly historical evidence was not forthcoming.

The evidential value of these latter sources of information in a portrayal of *Realpolitik*, excepting perhaps that of certain sections of the *Arthaśâstra*, is as a rule very questionable. This circumstance is not adequately realized by writers on Hindu law (public or private) but will have to be grappled with from now on as a problem in indology.

The size of the book has been considerably reduced by this almost total exclusion of "literary" data. Brevity has been secured also by the avoidance of lengthy extracts and plurality of almost identical references from epigraphic tomes.

A readable account of public law, although unavoidably often shallow, meagre and halting, has been the end in view. Some of the chapters have, however, been purposely kept thin as the subject has been dealt with at some length by previous writers. And in any event the discussion is everywhere as concise and allusive as possible and is by no means exhaustive in reference.

It has been sought, however tentatively, to fill a gap in the history of mankind's constitutional and economic development. But owing to the dearth of data that might throw light on continuity the chronological treatment has not always been felt to be significant.

The "secondary" sources of information (Authorities D) have been acknowledged in the notes even where the originals have been consulted. A few borrowed references, e. g. those to some of the *Archaeological Survey Reports* could not be verified as the volumes were not available.

The treatise will serve to cry halt not only to such statements as that "the simple device by which an orderly vote is taken and the minority acquiesce in the rule of the majority as if it had been their own is found for the first time as an every day method of discussion in Greek political life" made by the neo-Hegelian Bosanquet in his *Philosophical Theory of the State* (1899, pp. 4—5) but also to such as that "the earliest form of the state known to us is the city state of ancient Greece" in Hobhouse the anti-Hegelian's *Social Evolution and Political Theory* (1911, p. 141). Indeed, on fundamental points the volume delivers a front attack on the traditional Western prejudices regarding Asia such as are concentrated in Hegel, Cousin, Max Müller, Maine, Janet, Smith, Willoughby, and Huntington.

On the other hand, the standpoint of the present undertaking is to be sharply distinguished from the trend of recent Indian researches on the Hindu constitution. Besides, on several issues, e. g. those bearing on national unification, democracy, taxation, and so forth, the facts exhibited will no doubt give a rude shock to the postulates of the political nationalists of Young India.

Many of the interpretations are necessarily calculated to challenge the conventional notions and therefore provoke a controversy. If they serve to open the questions an object of the book will have been realized.

Hindu political theory, the second theme of the treatise, does not seem to have been dealt with in its philosophical bearings by any writer in the Indian languages nor in English, French and German. The short sections of the book in which this subject is treated might easily be expanded into independent monographs. It has been aimed here mainly to suggest new lines of inquiry. Notwithstanding much work done in "private law" owing to administrative necessity it may be mentioned *en passant* that the legal *philosophy* of the Hindus is still a virgin field.

Altogether, in viewpoint and method of approach as well as in the ground covered and in conclusions this is perhaps the first comprehensive attempt at appraising, interpreting and laicizing the discoveries of *indianisme* for students of political science, and thereby introducing to the scientific world the people of ancient India as peers of the Greeks and the Romans and their mediaeval successors down to the *ancien régime*, both in constitution-making and in speculation on the state. In this endeavour the author's ally in logic is the critical technique of Abbott, Bluntschli, Brissaud, A. T. and R. W. Carlyle, Dunning, Figgis, Gomme,

Joseph-Barthélemy, Lowie, and Schömann. These investigators — political and anthropological — are all the more acceptable because the studies undertaken by most of them have hardly any reference to the Orient and are to that extent untainted by any bias so far as Oriental culture is concerned.

The invariable fallacies of such Eur-American savants — philosophical historians and historical philosophers — as deal with the facts and phenomena of the East have been discussed by the author in an essay on the "Futurism of Young Asia" in the *International Journal of Ethics* (Chicago, July, 1918). These must have to be guarded against by every student who is interested in cultural inquiries for comparative sociology.

A publication such as this could not have been undertaken previous to 1905, and nobody is more conscious than is the writer that on the strength of archaeological finds that are enriching the world's knowledge about Hindu culture from day to day many of the statements in this present study will have to be cancelled, modified or rearranged in the interest of a more "intensive" sociological interpretation.

Attention has throughout been invited to the need for more data (both epochally and regionally). But, and this perhaps is more important for political science, the logical analysis of Hindu institutions and concepts with proper orientation to Western polities and political theories should call forth serious efforts on the part of indologists in public law.

II.

The book owes its origin to the lectures which were delivered (November 1916—February 1918) at the State Universities of California and Iowa and at Clark and Columbia Universities in the United States. A paper on "Democratic Ideals and Republican Institutions in India" embodying the substance of a part of these lectures appeared in the *American Political Science Review* (November 1918) and has subsequently been incorporated as "Hindu Achievements in Democracy" in Vol. II of the author's *Positive Background of Hindu Sociology* (1921).

Part of the material contained in the present book has been written in French by the author himself for a course of six lectures on *Le Droit Public des Hindous* at the University of Paris (February—March 1921) and for two addresses, one before the Société Asiatique (April 1921) on *L'Indianisme et les sciences sociales* and the other before the Académie des sciences morales et politiques (Institut de France) on "*La Démocratie hindoue*" (July 1921). The same data have also been laid under contribution while lecturing in German at the University of Berlin (Feb. 1922) on *Politische Strömungen in der indischen Kultur*.

Thanks are due to the editors of the *Political Science Quarterly* (New York, December 1918 and March 1921), the *American Political Science Review* (August 1919), the *Modern Review* (Calcutta, March and October 1920), the *International Journal of Ethics* (April 1920), the *Vedic Magazine* (Lahore, July 1920), the *Collegian* (Calcutta, September 1920), the *Hindustan Review* (Allahabad, October 1920), the *Journal of the Indian Economic Society* (Bombay, 1921) and the *Annals of the American Academy of Political and Social Science* (Philadelphia, September 1921), — journals in which about half of the present publication appeared as articles. In each instance the material has been revised and brought up to date in regard to bibliography.

Thanks are likewise due to Professor Maffeo Pantaleoni of Rome for his interest in having the essay on gilds translated into Italian for his *Giornale degli economisti e rivista statistica* (April 1920), to M. Paul Masson-Oursel, agrégé de l'Université de Paris, for his having published in French a résumé of the chapter on constitution in the *Revue de SynthèseHistorique* (August—December 1920), as well as to the committee of the University of Calcutta on Sir Asutosh Mookerjee Silver Jubilee Volumes for their desire to have a contribution from the author, which incidentally is being availed of in the present work.

I have pleasure in acknowledging my personal obligations to the authorities of the libraries at Harvard and Columbia Universities, New York Public Library, Bibliothèque Nationale (Paris), and Preussische Staatsbibliothek (Berlin) for the courtesies received at their hands, and also to Fräulein Ida Stieler of Innsbruck, author of *Edelweiss and Alprose*, who has verified the references and done much of the library work. And for the scientific interest shown in these investigations I am grateful to Professors John Dewey, Edwin R. A. Seligman and William R. Shepherd of Columbia University, President G. Stanley Hall of Clark University, Professor A. A. Goldenweiser of the New York School for Social Research, Editor J. Mc Keen Cattell of the *Scientific Monthly* (New York), Rector Paul Appell of the Académie de Paris, Dean F. Larnaude of the Faculté de Droit, Professors Charles Gide and Charles Lyon-Caen, M. Gabriel Ferrand, Islamologist, Senator Raphael-Georges Lévy, president of the Société d'Economie Politique de Paris, Editor Rudolf Pechel of the *Deutsche Rundschau* (Berlin), Professors Walther Vogel, Alois Brandl, Eduard Meyer, Hermann Schumacher and Heinrich Lüders of the University of Berlin, and Staatssekretär Carl Becker.

Berlin, March 1922.

BENOY KUMAR SARKAR.

CONTENTS.

Preface VII
Authorities Cited XIII
CHAPTER I. Comparative Politics from Hindu Data.
Section 1. A *Yugântara* in Political World-View 1
Section 2. The Instrument of Interpretation 5
CHAPTER II. Hindu Political Development.
Section 1. The Tenacity of Monarchy in the West 10
Section 2. The State-Systems of Ancient India 13
Section 3. *Pax Sârva-bhaumica* (Peace of the World-State) 19
PART. I. THE HINDU CONSTITUTION
CHAPTER III. Hindu Achievements in Organization.
Section 1. Property and Woman in Private Law 27
Section 2. Institutional *Viriya* (Energism). 30
Section 3. Organized Charities and Utilities 34
Section 4. The Politics of Ecclesiastical Bodies (*Samghas*) 37
Section 5. *Śreṇis* (Gilds) of Peasants, Artisans and Merchants 40
CHAPTER IV. The Public Law of the Hindus.
Section 1. *Sabhâs* or Administrative Assemblies 50
Section 2. The *Sva-râj* of Rural Communes 51
Section 3. Municipal Government. 60
Section 4. Supreme Councils 67
Section 5. The Making of Laws (*Śâsanas*) 72
Section 6. The Jury System (*Ubbahika*) 81
Section 7. Deposition and Election of Kings 83
CHAPTER V. The Hindu Machinery of Imperial Nationalism.
Section 1. The War Office 87
Section 2. The Civil Service 98
Section 3. The Judiciary 107
Section 4. National Finance 111
CHAPTER VI. *Gaṇas* or Republics of the Hindus (*c* B. C. 600—A. C. 350).
Section 1. Republicanism in the Occident 137
Section 2. Three Periods of Hindu Republics 139
a) Third Period (B. C. 150—A. C. 350) 139
b) Second Period (B. C. 350—300) 141
c) First Period (B. C. 600—450) 145
Section 3. Valuation of India's Democratic Attainments 150

PART. II. THE CONCEPTS OF HINDU POLITICS.

CHAPTER VII. Hindu Literature on Politics.

Section 1. Political Speculation in Ancient India 155
Section 2. *Nîti-Śâstras* 158
Section 3. Scope and Province of *Nîti-Śâstra* 161
Section 4. Relativity of Political *Śâstra* to Politics 163

CHAPTER VIII. The Theory of the Constitution in Hindu Political Philosophy.

Section 1. The Doctrine of *Saptâmga* (Seven Limbs) 167
Section 2. A Moslem Review 169
Section 3. The *Prakriti* (People) and the State 171
Section 4. Kingship a Public Office 174
Section 5. Ministry the Pivot of National Life 176
Section 6. Right to Revolt 179
Section 7. Taxes (*Bali*) as Wages and Prices 183
Section 8. Militarism and *Machtpolitik* (*Śakti-Yoga*) 186
Section 9. Caste and Public Service 189

CHAPTER IX. The Theory of Sovereignty in Hindu Political Philosophy.

Section 1. The Theory of the State 193
a) The Doctrine of *Mâtsya-Nyâya* (The Logic of the Fish) 193
b) The Doctrine of *Danda* (Punishment, Coercion, Sanction) 197
Section 2. The Theory of Property, Law and Social Order 203
a) The Doctrine of *Mamatva* (Property) 203
b) The Doctrine of *Dharma* (Law, Justice and Duty) 205
c) The Doctrine of *Varṇâśrama* (Classes and Stages) 212
Section 3. The Theory of International Relations 214
a) The Doctrine of *Mandala* (Sphere of Influence) 214
b) The Doctrine of *Sârva-bhauma* (World-Sovereign) 222

Index

I. Indian 227
II. Oriental 234
III. Eur-American 236

AUTHORITIES CITED.

A. Inscriptions, Coins and Contemporary Reports or Chronicles (as the chief basis of institutional studies).

Archaeological Survey of India, Vols IV and VI.

Ibid, *Annual Reports*, 1903—04, 1904—05, 1907—09, 1911—12.

Arrian (*c* A. C. 130), Curtius (*c* 200), Diodorus (*c* 50), Plutarch (*c* 100), Justin (*c* 400) in J. W. Mc Crindle's *Invasion of India by Alexander*, London, 1896.

Bâṇa (*c* 620): *Harṣa-charita*, semi-historical biography dealing with Upper India, Eng. trans. by E. B. Cowell, London, 1897.

Bilhana (twelfth century): *Vikramânka-charita*, semi-historical biography dealing with the Deccan and Southern India (*Bombay Sanskrit Series*) 1875.

Coins of Ancient India by A. Cunningham, London, 1891.

Cosmas (*c* 525): *The Christian Topography*, Eng. trans. by Mc Crindle, London, 1897.

Epigraphia Indica, 1896—97, 1905—06.

Epigraphia Zeylanica, Vols I and II.

Epigraphist's Report for 1900 and 1916.

Fa Hien: *Fo-kuo-ki* (Record of the Buddhistic Kingdoms, A. C. 399—414) Eng. trans. by S. Beal, Boston, 1885.

,, Eng. trans. by Legge, Oxford, 1886.

Gauda-lekha-mâlâ (Inscriptions of the Pâla Dynasty, *c* 750—1150) edited in Bengali by Akshaya Kumar Maitra for the Varendra Research Society, Rajsahi, Bengal, 1912.

Gupta Inscriptions (*c* 350—550) ed. by Fleet for the *Corpus Inscriptionum Indicarum Series*, Calcutta, 1888.

Hiuen Thsang: *Si-yu-ki* (Record of the Western World, A. C. 629—645), Eng. trans. by Beal, London, 1885.

Hiuen Thsiang (Chinese biography of Hiuen Thsang), Eng. trans. by Beal, London, 1888.

Indian Antiquary, 1888, 1905—06, 1909.

Indian Coins by E. J. Rapson in the *Grundriß der ind-arischen Philologie*, Strassburg, 1897.

Inscriptions of Asoka (B. C. 257—240) ed. and trans. by Cunningham for the *Corp. Insc. Ind.*, Calcutta, 1877.

Ibid, Eng. trans., in V. A. Smith's *Asoka*, Oxford.

Itsing: *Record of the Buddhist Religion* (671—695), Eng. trans. by J. Takakusu, Oxford, 1896.

Kalhana (twelfth century): *Râja-tarangiṇî*, chronicle of Kashmir, Eng. trans. by M. A. Stein, 2 vols, London, 1900.

Madras Epigraphy, Annual Report, 1898—99, 1910—11.

Mahâvamso (*c* 550), chronicle of Ceylon, Eng. trans. by Turnour, Ceylon, 1837.

Megasthenes' *Indika* (B. C. 302), Arrian's *Indika* (second century) in Mc Crindle's *Ancient India* London, 1877.

The Periplus of the Erythraean Sea (Travel and Trade in the Indian Ocean by an Egyptian Greek merchant of the first century), Eng. trans. by W. H. Schoff, London, 1912.

Pliny the Elder (23—79): *Natural History*, trans. by Bostock and Riley, London, 1855—57.

Plutarch (first century): *Life of Alexander*, Langhorne's trans.

Prâchin Mudrâ (Ancient Coins) in Bengali, Vol. I, by R. D. Banerji, Calcutta 1915.

Ptolemaeus (*c*. A. C. 140): *Geography* (chapters on India and Central and Eastern Asia), Mc Crindle's trans. London, 1885.

Sandhyâkara Nandi (twelfth century): *Râma-charita*, semi-historical poem dealing with Bengal and Eastern India (*Memoir of the Asiatic Society of Bengal*, Vol. III, no I), Calcutta, 1910.

South Indian Inscriptions (*c* 900—1200), ed. by Hultzsch, Vols II and III.

B. Sanskrit and Prâkrit Texts on Politics and Law

(chiefly for studies in political theory, and subsidiarily as illustrative documents for A.).

Âpastamba (*c* B. C. 400): *Dharma-sûtra*, Eng. trans. in the *Sacred Books of the East Series* (ed by Max Müller), Vol. II.

Baudhâyana (*c* B. C. 450): *Dharma-sûtra, S. B. E.* Vol. XIV.

Bhoja (*c* 900): *Yukti-kalpa-taru*, Sanskrit text ed. by I. C. Shastri, Sanskrit Press Depositary, Calcutta, 1917.

Brihaspati (*c* 650): *Smriti, S. B. E.* Vol. XXXIII.

Brihaspati: *Sûtra* (ed. and trans. by F. W. Thomas for *Le Museon*) Brussels, 1916.

Chandeśvara: *Vivâda-ratnakara*, text in the *Bibliotheca Indica Series*, Asiatic Society of Bengal Calcutta, 1887.

Chulla-vagga (*Vinaya*), *c* B. C. 350, *S. B. E.* Vols XVII, XX.

Gautama (*c* B. C. 550): *Dharma-sûtra*, S. B. E. Vol. II.

Jimûta-vâhana (*c* 1150): *Dâya-bhâga*, Eng. trans. in Colebrooke's *Two Treatises on the Hindu Law of Inheritance*, Madras, 1865.

Kâmandaka (*c* 350): *Niti-sâra*, text in the *Bib. Ind.*, 1884, trans. by M. N. Dutt, Calcutta, 1896.

Kautilya (*c* B. C. 300): *Artha-śâstra*, ed and trans by R. Shamasastry, Bangalore, Mysore, 1915.

Mahâ-bhârata (*c* B. C. 600—A. C. 300), especially Book II (*Sabhâ-parva*) and Book XII (*Śanti-parva*), Protap Chandra Ray's edition, Calcutta, 1888—93.

Mahâ-vagga (*Vinaya*), *c* B. C. 350, *S. B. E.* Vols XIII, XVII.

Manu (*c* A. C. 150): *Smriti, S. B. E.* Vol. XXV.

Mitra Miśra: *Vira-mitrodaya*, ed. by J. Vidyasagara, Calcutta.

Nârada (*c* 500): *Smriti, S. B. E.* Vol. XXXIII.

Śukra: *Niti-sâra*, text ed. by Oppert for the Madras Government, 1882. Eng. trans. by B. K. Sarkar for the Panini Office Series, Allahabad, 1914.

Somadeva (*c* 950): *Niti-vâkyâmrita*, text in the *Kâvyamâlâ Series*, Bombay.

Vaiśampâyana: *Niti-prakâsikâ*, text ed. by Oppert for the Madras Govt., 1882.

Vaśiṣtha (*c* B. C. 150): *Dharma-sûtra, S. B. E.* Vol. XIV.

Vijnaneśvara (*c* 1050): *Mitâkśarâ*, Eng. trans. in Colebrooke's *Two Treatises*, Madras, 1865.

Viṣṇu (*c* 300): *Smriti*, S. B. E. Vol. VII.

Yâjnavalkya (*c* 350): *Smriti*, text and translation in V. N. Mandlik's *Hindu Law*, Bombay, 1880.

C. General Literature in Sanskrit and Prâkrit (for incidental references).

Aitareya Brâhmana (*Bib. Ind. Series*, Calcutta), 1895—1906.
Âpastamba: *Śrauta Sûtra, Bib. Ind.*, 1882—1903.
Atharva Veda, ed and trans by Whitney and Lanman in the *Harvard Oriental Series*, Cambridge, Mass, 1905.
Ibid, Bloomfield's version.
Avadâna-śataka, French trans. by Feer, *Annales du Musée Guimet*, Paris, 1891.
Bâṇa: *Kâdambari*, Eng. trans. by Ridding, London 1896.
Bharata: *Nâtya-śâstra*, text in the *Kâvyamâlâ Ser.*, Bombay, 1894.
Buddhist Mahâyâna Texts, S. B. E. Vols XLIX, Pt. II (Eng. trans.).
Buddhist Sûttas, Eng. trans., *S. B. E.* Vol. XI.
Catalogus Catalogorum, ed by Aufrecht, Leipzig, 1891—1903.
Dandin: *Daśa-kumâra-charita, Bom. Sans. Ser.*, 1873.
Dialogues of the Buddha, Vol. II. Eng. trans. by Rhys Davids, London 1910.
Gitâ, S. B. E., Vol. VIII.
Gopatha Brâhmaṇa, (*Bib. Ind.* 1872).
Grihya Sûtras, S. B. E., Vols XXIX, XXX.
Jaina Sûtras, S. B. E., Vols XXII, XLV.
Jâtakas, Eng. trans. in six volumes, by various scholars, ed. by Cowell, Cambridge, 1895—1907.
Kâlidâsa: *Mâlavikâgnimitra*, C. H. Tawney's trans., Calcutta 1891.
„ *Raghu-vamśa.*
Mahâ-bhârata: *Vana, Udyoga, Karṇa* and other *parvas.*
"Pali Buddhistical Annals" by Turnour in the *Journal of the Asiatic Soc. of Bengal*, 1838.
Pâṇini: *Aṣṭâdhyâyî*, trans. by Sris Chandra Vasu, Panini Office, Allahabad.
Purana: Agni, Anandashrama Series, Poona, Bombay.
Râjaśekhara: *Karpûra-manjarî* (trans. in Harvard Oriental Series).
Râmâyaṇa: *Vâla* and *Ayodhyâ kândas.*
Saddharma-pundarika, S. B. E., Vol. XXXI..
Śatapatha Brâhmaṇa, S. B. E., Vols XII, XXIV, XXVI, XLI, XLIII.
"Shabara Svami's Commentary on Jaimini's Mimâmsâ" by G. Jha in the *Indian Thought*, 1910 Allahabad.
Specimens of Old Indian Poetry, by R. T. H. Griffith, Panini Office, Allahabad, 1914.
Subandhu: *Vâsavadattâ*, Gray's trans., New York, 1913.
Sûtta-nipata, S. B. E., Vol. X, Pt. II.
Taittiriya Samhitâ, Bib. Ind., 1872.
Upaniṣads, S. B. E., Vols I, XV.
Vedic Index, 2 vols by A. A. Macdonell and A. B. Keith, London, 1912.
Viśvanâtha: *Sâhitya Darpaṇa*, trans by Mitra and Ballantyne, Calcutta, 1865—66.

D. Modern Studies in Hindu Government and Jurisprudence.

Aiyangar K. V. R.: *Considerations on Some Aspects of Ancient Indian Polity*, Madras, 1916.
Aiyangar S. K.: *Ancient India* (ch. on Chola Administration), Madras, 1911.
Ayyar V: *Town-planning in Ancient Deccan*, Madras, 1916.
Banerjea, P. N.: *Public Administration in Ancient India*, London, 1917; exposition lucid and comprehensive, more critical handling needed.

Banerjee G.: *Hindu Law of Marriage and Stridhana*, Calcutta, 1896.

Basu P. C.: *Indo-Aryan Polity during the period of the Rig Veda*, Allahabad, 1919.

Bhandarkar D. R.: *Ancient History of India* (administration), Calcutta, 1919.

Coomaraswamy A. K.: *Indian Craftsman* (gilds), London, 1909.

,, *Mediaeval Sinhalese Art* (social economy and gilds), London, 1908.

Davids T. W. Rhys: *Buddhist India* (republics and rural institutions), London, 1903.

Fick R.: *Die Soziale Gliederung im nordöstlichen Indien zu Buddhas Zeit* (gilds), Kiel, 1897.

Gibelin, E.: *Etudes sur le droit civil des Hindous* (comparative private law), 2 vols, Pondicherry, 1846.

Hindustan Review, Allahabad, May-June, 1918: Kumaraswamy K.: "Hindu Theories of State and Social Compact".

Hopkins, E. W.: *India Old and New* (gilds and land tenure), New York, 1902.

Indian Antiquary, Bombay, 1905: Shamasastry R.: "Chânakya's Land and Revenue Policy".

Ibid, July 1915: Divanji, P. C.: "Judicial Administration in India in Ante-Mohammedan Times".

Ibid, June-July 1918: V. S. Sukthankar's Eng. trans. of Jacobi's German article (1912) on the "Authenticity of Kautilya".

Ibid, 1918—19, Law, Narendra Nath: "*Vârttâ* or Hindu Economics".

Ibid, 1919, Law: "Ancient Hindu Coronation and Allied Ceremonials".

Ibid, May 1920, Divanji, P. C.: "Ancient Hindu Law of Evidence".

Indian Journal of Economics, November 1919, Balkrishna: "Economics in Ancient India".

Jolly, J.: *Hindu Law of Partition, Inheritance and Adoption*, Calcutta, 1885.

,, *Recht und Sitte*, Strassburg, 1896; summary of entire Hindu legal literature.

Journal of the American Oriental Society, 1889: Hopkins: "Social and Military Position of the Ruling Caste in Ancient India as Represented by the Sanskrit Epic.", a searching and extensive inquiry.

Journal of the Bihar and Orissa Research Society, Bankipore, 1915: Jayaswal K. P.: "Republics in the Mahâbhârata".

Journal of the Department of Letters, Vol. I (Calcutta University), 1921; Banerji, P. N.: "International Law and Custom in Ancient India".

Journal of the Royal Asiatic Society, 1916: Keith: "The Authenticity of Kautilya".

Law N. N.: *Studies in Ancient Hindu Polity* (based on Kautilya) with an essay on the "Authenticity of Kautilya" by R. K. Mookerji, London, 1914.

,, *Inter-state Relations in Ancient India*, Calcutta, 1920.

Law Weekly, Madras, April 1914: P. Nagabhushanam: "Advocacy in Ancient India".

Majumdar, R. C.: *Corporate Life in Ancient India*, Calcutta 1919; detailed account of republics; a masterpiece of archeological investigation so far as it goes; throughout awaits interpretation in the light of economic history and political science.

Matthai, J.: *Village Government in British India*, London, 1915.

Mitra, T. N.: *Law Relating to Hindu Widow*, Calcutta, 1881.

Modern Review, Calcutta, January 1912: Jayaswal: "Rituals at Hindu Coronation: Their Constitutional Aspects".

Ibid, May-July 1913: Jayaswal: "Introduction to Hindu Polity". These two essays ought to have been available in book form by this time. But all the references in Jayaswal's studies have been appropriated by subsequent writers.

Ibid, Sept. 1916—June 1918: Law: twenty one articles on "Aspects of Ancient Indian Polity"; patient and almost exhaustive research.

Ibid, Feb. 1917: Rao, G.: "Kings, Crowns and Thrones in Ancient and Mediaeval India".

Ibid, Ap.-Nov. 1918: Visvanath, L. T.: "International Law in Ancient India".

Ibid, March, 1919: Handiqui, K.: "Word *Sva-râj* in the *Rig Veda*".

Ibid, January 1920, Lal, M.: "Republican Tradition in Indian Polity".

Ibid, February 1920, Jayaswal, K. P.: "The Hindu Parliament under Hindu Monarchy".

Mookerji, R. K.: *Fundamental Unity of India*, London, 1914; a study in the theory of nationalism from Hindu texts.

„ *Local Government in Ancient India*, Oxford, 1919: intensive study of gilds.

„ *Nationalism in Indian Culture*, London, 1921.

Row, B. G.: *Ancient Hindu Judicature*, Madras, 1921.

Sarkar, G. C.: *Hindu Law*, Calcutta, 1906.

Sarkar, K. L.: *Rules of Interpretation in Hindu Law*, Calcutta, undated.

Sen, P. N.: *General Principles of Hindu Jurisprudence*, Calcutta, 1918.

Shastri, H. K.: "Fiscal Administration under Early Cholas" (Poona, 1917).

Swami, P. J.: *Warfare in Ancient India*, a pamphlet, Indian Review Office, Madras, 1915.

Transactions of the Royal Asiatic Society of Great Britain and Ireland 1828, Vol. II: Colebrooke: "Hindu Courts of Justice".

Zeitschrift der Deutschen Morgenländischen Gesellschaft, Leipzig, 1913: Jolly: "*Arthaśâstra und Dharmaśâstra*".

Ibid, 1914: Jolly: "*Kollektaneen zum Kautiliya Arthaśâstra*".

Ibid, 1914: Jacobi, H.: "Ist das Daśa-kumâra-charita gleichzeitig mit dem Kautiliya Arthaśâstra?" (reply to Jolly's *Kollektaneen*).

Zimmer, H.: *Altindisches Leben* (Vedic institutions), Berlin, 1879. N.B. Five essays on Hindu politics are announced as appearing in the *Sir Asutosh Mookerjee Jubilee Volumes* (Calcutta University, 1921). K. P. Jayaswal's book (*Hindu Polity*) is reported to be in the press. At the German Orientalists' Congress held at Leipzig (1921) Professor Stein of Prague read a paper from his forthcoming brochure (*Megasthenes und Kautiliya*).

E. Studies in Western Political Institutions and Theories (cited either for data or to indicate methodology). The standard classics are not mentioned in the list.

Abbott, F. F.: *Roman Political Institutions*, Boston, 1901.

Adams. G. B.: *Origin of the English Constitution*, New York, 1912.

„ *A Constitutional History of England*, New York, 1921.

American Historical Review, 1897: Sullivan, J. "Marsiglio of Padua and William of Ockam".

Arnold, W. T.: *Roman System of Provincial Administration*, Oxford, 1914.

Ashley, W. J.: *Surveys Historic and Economic*, London, 1900.

Atger, F.: *Histoire des doctrines du contrat social*, Nimes, 1906.

Azan, P.: *The Warfare of Today* (transl. from French by Coolidge), Boston, 1918,

Barker, E.: *Greek Political Theory* (*Plato and His Predecessors*), London, 1918.

Barker, E.: *Political Thought in England from Spencer to the Present Day*, London, 1915.

Bastable, C. F.: *Public Finance*, London, 1903.

Bluntschli, J. K.: *Geschichte des allgemeinen Staatsrechts und der Politik*, Munich, 1867.

Bluntschli, J. K.: *Geschichte der neueren Staatswissenschaft*, Munich, 1881.

Bodin, J.: *Les Six livres de la république*, Paris, 1578.

Bosanquet, B.: *Philosophical Theory of the State*, London, 1899.

Boutmy, E.: *Essai d'une psychologie politique du peuple anglais au XIXe siècle*, Paris 1909.

Brissaud: *History of French Public Law* (Garner's transl.), Boston, 1915.

Carlyle, A. J. and R. W.: *Mediaeval Political Theory in the West*, 3 vols, London, 1903—15.

Carter, J. C.: *Law Its Origin, Growth and Function*, New York, 1907.

Clausewitz, C.: *On War* (transl. from German by Graham), 3 vols, London, 1911.
Cockle, M. J. D.: *Bibliography of Military Books up to 1642*, London, 1911 (edition of 200 copies for private circulation).
Coker, F. W.: *Organismic Theories of the State*, New York, 1910.
Curzon, N.: *Frontiers*, Oxford, 1908.
Dicey, A. V.: *Law of the Constitution*, London, 1915.
Domesday Commemoration (1086—1888): Domesday Studies, Vol. I, London, 1892.
Dowell, S.: *History of Taxation and Taxes in England*, London, 1884.
Dunning, W. A.: *History of Political Theories*, 3 vols, New York, 1902—21.
Elyot, T.: *The Boke named the Governour* (Croft's ed.), London, 1883.
Encyclopaedia Britannica (11th ed.): articles on Aquinas, Capital Punishment, English Finance, Finance, Hincmar, Justinian, Roman Army, Taxation.
Fairlie, J. A.: *Municipal Administration*, New York, 1901.
Figgis, J. N.: *The Divine Right of Kings*, Cambridge, 1914.
,, *Fellowship of the Mystery*, London, 1914.
,, *From Gerson to Grotius*, Cambridge, 1907.
Fiske, B. A.: *The Art of Fighting*, New York, 1920.
Fortescue, J.: *The Governance of England* (ed. by Plummer), Oxford, 1885.
Francke, A.: *Reformateurs et publicistes de l'Europe*, Paris, 1864—93.
Frank, T.: *Roman Imperialism*, New York, 1914.
Freeman, E. A.: *Comparative Politics*, New York, 1874.
Gide and Rist: *History of Economic Doctrines* (Eng. trans., London, 1915).
Gierke, O. F.: *Political Theories of the Middle Age* (trans. from the German by Maitland), Cambridge, 1900.
Gomme, G. L.: *Primitive Folkmoots*, London, 1880.
,, *Principles of Local Government*, London, 1897.
,, *Village Community*, New York, 1890.
Goodnow, F. J.: *Comparative Aministrative Law*, New York, 1893.
,, *Municipal Government*, New York, 1909.
Greenidge, A. H. J.: *Roman Public Life*, London, 1901.
Gross, C.: *Gild Merchant*, 2 vols, Oxford, 1890.
Guizot, F. P. G.: *History of Representative Government in Europe* (Scoble's trans.), London, 1861
Gumplowicz, L.: *Der Rassenkampf*, Innsbruck, 1883.
Higginson, J. H.: *Tariffs at Work*, London, 1913.
Hime, H. W. L.: *Origin of Artillery*, London, 1915.
Hobhouse, L. T.: *Metaphysical Theory of the State*, London, 1918.
Hobhouse, L. T.: *Social Evolution and Political Theory*, New York, 1911.
Holdich, T. H.: *Political Frontiers and Boundary-Making*, London, 1916.
Holdsworth, W. S.: *History of English Law*, London, 1903.
Janet, P.: *Histoire de la science politique*, Paris, 1913.
Jenks, E.: *History of Politics*, London, 1900.
,, *Law and Politics in the Middle Ages*, London, 1898.
Joseph-Barthélemy: *Le Gouvernement de France*, Paris 1920.
Joseph-Barthélemy: *Les Institutions politiques de l'Allemagne contemporaine*, Paris, 1905.
Joseph-Barthélemy: *Le problème de la compétence dans la démocratie*, Paris, 1918.
Joseph-Barthélemy: *Le Role du pouvoir exécutif dans les républiques modernes*, Paris, 1906.
Joseph-Barthélemy: *Le Vote des femmes*, Paris, 1920.
Lalor, J. J.: *Cyclopaedia of Political Science*, Chicago, 1884.

Laski, J.: *Authority in the Modern State*, New York, 1917.

„ *Studies in the Problem of Sovereignty*, New York, 1918.

Lawrence, T. J.: *Essays on Some Disputed Questions in Modern International Law*, Cambridge, 1885.

Leach, A. F.: *Educational Charters and Documents* (598—1909), Cambridge, 1911.

Leroy-Beaulieu, P.: *The Modern State* (trans. from Fr.), London, 1891.

Leroy-Beaulieu, P.: *Traité de la science des finances*, Paris, 1912.

Lewinski, J. S.: *Origin of Property and the Formation of Village Community*, London, 1913.

Lilly, W. S.: *First Principles in Politics*, London, 1907.

Littlejohn, J. M.: *Political Theory of the Schoolmen and Grotius*, New York, 1896.

Lowie, R. H.: *Primitive Society*, New York, 1920.

Machiavelli: *Discourses on the First Decade of Titus Livius* (Thomson's trans.), London, 1883.

Mackenzie, T.: *Studies in Roman Law*, Edinburgh, 1862.

Maine, H. S.: *Ancient Law*, London, 1870.

„ *Early History of Institutions*, London, 1875.

„ *Village Communities*, London, 1876.

Maitland, F.: *Domesday Book and Beyond*, Cambridge 1897.

Maude, F. N.: *War and the World's Life*, London, 1907.

Merriam, C. E.: *History of the Theory of Sovereignty since Rousseau*, New York, 1900.

Michel, H.: *L'Idée de l'Etat*, Paris, 1898.

Modern French Legal Philosophy (Fouillée, Charmont, Duguit, and Démogue) ed. by A. W. Spencer and J. W. Winslow, Boston, 1916.

Moyle, J. B.: *Institutes of Justinian*, Oxford, 1883.

Oberholtzer, E. P.: *Referendum in America*, New York, 1912.

O'Brien, G.: *An Essay on Mediaeval Economic Teaching*, London, 1920.

Oppenheimer: *State* (trans. from German by Gitterman), Indianapolis, 1914.

Palgrave, R. H. I.: *Dictionary of Political Economy*, London, 1896.

Plehn, C. C.: *Introduction to Public Finance*, New York, 1896.

Political Quarterly, London, February, 1915. Barker, E.: "The Discredited State".

Pollock, F.: *Introduction to the History of the Science of Politics*, London, 1900.

Poole, R. L.: *Illustrations of the History of Mediaeval Thought*, London 1884.

Price, L. L.: *Political Economy in England*, London, 1891.

Ramsay and Lancian: *Roman Antiquities*, London, 1898.

Ratzel, F.: *Politische Geographie*, Munich, 1903.

Rau, K. H.: *Grundsätze der Finanzwissenschaft*, Leipzig, 1864.

Scherger, G. L.: *Evolution of Modern Liberty*, London, 1904.

Schmoller's Jahrbuch, Munich, 1921; Wilcken, U: "*Alexander der Grosse und die Hellenistische Wirtschaft*."

Schömann: *Antiquities of Greece*, London, 1880.

Seebohm, F.: *English Village Community*, 1883.

Seligman, E. R. A.: *Essays in Taxation*, New York, 1913.

„ *Shifting and Incidence of Taxation*, New York, 1902.

Sidgwick, H.: *Development of European Polity*, London, 1903.

Stockton, R.: *Peace Insurance*, Chicago, 1915.

Stubbs, W.: *Constitutional History of England*, Oxford, 1875.

Supan, A.: *Leitlinien der allgemeinen politischen Geographie*, Leipzig, 1918.

Tacitus, C.: *Works* (Oxford translation), London, 1878.

Unwin, G.: *The Gilds and Companies of London*, London, 1908.

Vierkandt, A.: *Staat und Gesellschaft in der Gegenwart*, Leipzig, 1916.

Vinogradoff, P.: *English Society in the Eleventh Century*, Oxford, 1908.
Waltham, E. L.: *Principles of War*, Vol. I, London, 1914.
Willoughby, W. F.: *Government of the Modern States*, New York, 1919.
Willoughby, W. F.: *Political Theories of the Ancient World*, New York, 1903.
Woolf, C. N. S.: *Bartolus of Sassoferato*, Cambridge, 1913.

F. History, Sociology, and Miscellaneous; Oriental and Occidental (references chiefly bibliographical, designed to set the political and cultural perspective).

Aghnides, N. P.: *Mohammedan Theories of Finance*, New York, 1916.
Asakawa, K.: *Early Institutional Life of Japan* (A. C. 645), Tokyo, 1903.
Augustine, St.: *City of God* (Dods' trans.), Edinburgh, 1871.
Banerji, R. D.: *Bânglâr Itihâs* (History of Bengal), in Bengali, 2 vols, Calcutta, 1915—19.
,, *Memoir on the Pâlas of Bengal*, Asiatic Society, Calcutta, 1915.
Beard, C. A.: *Economic Origins of Jeffersonian Democracy*, New York, 1915.
Bhandarkar, R. G.: *Early History of the Dekkan*, Bombay, 1884.
Birdwood, G.: *Industrial Arts of India*, London, 1880.
Bland, J. O. P.: *Li Hung-chang*, New York, 1917.
Boas, F.: *Mind of Primitive Man*, New York, 1911.
Bosanquet, B.: *Some Suggestions in Ethics*, London, 1918.
Brehaut, E.: *An Encyclopaedist of the Dark Age, Isidore of Seville*, New York, 1912.
Bryce, J. B.: *The Holy Roman Empire*, London, 1907.
Bury, J. B.: *History of the Later Roman Empire*, 2 vols, London, 1889.
Calhoun, A. W.: *Social History of the American Family*, 3 vols, Cleveland, 1917—19.
Cambridge Mediaeval History, Vol. II, 1913.
Cambridge Modern History, Vols VIII and XII, 1902—11.
Carr, H. W.: *Philosophy of Benedetto Croce*, London, 1917.
Chanda, R. P.: *Indo-Aryan Races*, Rajsahi, Bengal, 1916.
Compayrè: *History of Pedagogy* (Payne's trans.), Boston, 1907.
Confucius: *Great Learning*, and *Shu-king*, Eng. trans. by Legge in the *Chinese Classics*, Honkong, 1861—72.
Creative Intelligence (John Dewey's chapter), New York, 1917.
Cunningham, J. D.: *History of the Sikhs*, London, 1918.
Dawson, M. M.: *The Ethics of Confucius*, New York, 1915.
Deakin, A.: *Irrigated India and Ceylon*, London, 1893.
Depping, G. B.: *Histoire du commerce entre le Levant et l'Europe*, 2 vols, Paris, 1830.
Dickinson, G. L.: *Greek View of Life*, London, 1905.
Dill, S.: *Roman Society in the last century of the Western Empire*, New York, 1899.
Dopsch, A.: *Wirtschaftliche und Soziale Grundlage der europäischen Kultur*, Vienna, 1918.
Dubreuil, G. J.: *Ancient History of the Deccan*, Madras, 1921.
Dutt, R. C.: *Economic History of India* (modern), 2 vols, London, 1917.
Enriques, F.: *Problems of Science* (trans. from the Italian by K. Royce), Chicago, 1914.
Fazl, A.: *Ayeeni Akbari* (Gladwin's trans.), Calcutta, 1786.
Freeman, E. A.: *Chief Periods of European History*, London, 1886.
,, *Historical Geography of Europe* (with atlas), London, 1903.
Freiheitskampf der indischen Nationalisten, Berlin, 1918.
Gilchrist, R. N.: *Indian Nationality*, London, 1920.
Gomme, G. L.: *Folklore as an Historical Science*, London, 1908.

Griffiths, J.: *Paintings in the Buddhist Cave Temples of Ajanta*, London, 1896.
Guizot: *History of Civilization in Europe* (Henry's trans.), New York, 1872.
Guyot, Y.: *Causes and Consequences of the War*, New York, 1916.
Hague Court Reports, ed by J. B. Scott, New York, 1916.
Hall, G. S.: *Jesus the Christ in the light of Psychology*, 2 vols, New York, 1917.
Hardy, R. S.: *Manual of Buddhism*, London, 1880.
Havell, E. B.: *History of Aryan Rule in India*, London, 1919.
Hocking, W. E.: *Human Nature and Its Remaking*, New Haven, 1918.
Hoernle, A. F. R.: *Medicine of Ancient India*, Oxford 1907.
Howorth, H. H.: *History of the Mongols*, Vols I and II, London, 1876—88.
Hu, S.: *Development of Logic in Ancient China* (unpublished manuscript, Peking).
Huntington, E.: *Civilization and Climate*, New Haven, 1915.
„ *Pulse of Asia*, Boston, 1907.
„ *World-Power and Evolution*, New Haven, 1919.
Hussein, T.: *Philosophie Sociale d'Ibn Khaldoun*, Paris, 1917.
Ibn Khaldoun: *Mokaddemah* (*Prolégomènes Historiques* trans. by de Slane), Paris, 1862—68.
Imperial Gazetteer of India, Vols. XV, XXI.
Ibid, *Indian Empire*, Vol. II.

JOURNALS:

Collegian, Calcutta, 1915, Sastri, H. P.: "Educative Influence of Sanskrit Literature".
Hindustan Review, Allahabad, July, 1919, Sarkar, B. K.: "Comparative Literature from the Hindu Standpoint".
Ibid, August, 1919, Gupta, K. M.: "Courtesanship in Buddhist India".
Ibid, May-June 1920, Pande, H.: "The Vajji Country and the Mallas of Pava".
Indian Antiquary, 1908, Poussin: "The Buddhist Councils".
Ibid, 1913, Ghate's Eng. trans. of Bühler's German article on "Indian Artificial Poetry".
Ibid, 1918, Bhandarkar, D. R.: "Dekkan of the Sâta-vâhana Period".
Indian Review, Madras, July 1919: "The Minute of Dissent by Sir C. Sankaran Nair to the Government of India's Despatch of March 5, 1919."
International Journal of Ethics, July, 1918, Sarkar, B. K.: "The Futurism of Young Asia", to be consulted in connection with ch. 1 sec. 2 of this treatise.
Journal of the American Oriental Society, June 1910, Asakawa: "Notes on Village Government in Japan after 1600."
Journal of the Department of Letters (Calcutta), Vol. IV, 1921, Sarkar (Bejoy): "Water Transport in Mediaeval India".
Journal of International Relations, July 1919, Sarkar, B. K.: "Americanization from the Viewpoint of Young Asia."
Journal of the North China Branch of the Royal Asiatic Society, 1886, (New Series), Macgowan: "Chinese Guilds or Chambers of Commerce and Trades Unions".
Journal of Race Development, July 1912, Asakawa: "Contributions of Feudal Japan to New Japan".
Ibid, April 1919, Barnes, H. E.: "The Struggle of Races and Social Groups as a Factor in the Development of Political and Social Institutions."
Journal of the Royal Asiatic Society, 1903, Smith, V. A.: "The Position of the Autonomous Tribes of the Punjab."
Ibid, 1908, Smith, V. A.: "History of the City of Kanauj."
Le Monde Illustré, Paris, 19 Febr. 1921, M. Bourgeois: "Le Mouvement nationaliste dans l'Inde."
Modern Review, June-Sept. 1912, Maitra, A. K.: "The Stones of Varendra."
Ibid, March 1917, Sarkar, J. N.: "Oriental Monarchies."

Ibid, July 1919, Raychaudhuri, H. C.: "Lichchhavis of Vaisali."

Ibid, Sept. 1919, Sarkar, B. K.: "The Fortunes of the Chinese Republic."

Ibid, January 1920, Sarkar, B. K.: "The Political Tendencies in Chinese Culture."

The Nation, New York, Dec. 28, 1918: "Proclamation of the All-Russian Congress announced by the Chief of the Oriental Division"; Oct. 13, 1920: Programme of the Communist International.

Open Court, August 1919, Sarkar, B. K.: "Hindu View of Life."

Political Science Quarterly, New York, Dec. 1919, Sarkar, B. K.: "An English History of India."

Prabâsî (Bengali monthly), Calcutta, Vaiśâhka, 1326 (April 1919), Vedantatirtha (Vanamali): "Inter-caste marriages."

Sâhitya (Bengali monthly), Calcutta, Vaiśâkha, 1323 (April 1916), Maitra, A. K.: "Bengali Ideals."

Scientific Monthly, New York, Jan. 1919, Sarkar, B. K.: "Democratic Background of Chinese Culture."

Kincaid, C. A. and Parasnis, D. B.: *History of the Maratha People*, London, 1918.

Korzybski, A.: *The Manhood of Humanity: Science and Art of Human Engineering*, New York, 1921.

Law, N. N.: *Promotion of Learning in India by Muhammadans*, London, 1915.

Lea, H. C.: *History of Inquisition*, New York, 1888.

Lenin and Trotzky: *Proletarian Revolution in Russia*, ed. by L. C. Fraina, New York, 1918.

Letourneau, C. J. M.: *Property Its Origin and Development*, London, 1907.

Lewes, G. H.: *Life of Goethe*, London, 1855.

Lovett, V.: *History of the Indian Nationalist Movement*, New York, 1920.

Macauliffe, M. A.: *Sikh Religion*, Oxford, 1909.

Macdonald, J.: *Turkey and the Eastern Question*, London, 1913.

Mackenzie, R.: *The Nineteenth Century*, London, 1891.

Mann, H.: *Land and Labour in a Deccan Village*, London, 1917.

Mawerdi: *El Akham es-Soulthaniyah* (*Les Statuts Gouvernementaux* by Fagnan), Paris, 1915.

Mc Cabe, J.: *Peter Abelard*, New York, 1901.

,, *St Augustine and his Age*, New York, 1903.

Mc Crackan, W. D.: *Rise of the Swiss Republic*, New York, 1901.

Mencius, Eng. trans. by Legge in the *Chinese Classics*, Hongkong, 1861—72.

Metcalfe, C.: *Report of the Select Committee of the House of Commons*, London, 1832.

Mitra, R. L.: *Indo-Aryans*, London, 1881.

Möller, W. Z.: *History of the Christian Church* (Eng. trans. by Rutherford), London, 1893.

Montagu-Chelmsford: *Report on Indian Constitutional Reforms*, London, 1918.

Mookerji, R. K.: *History of Indian Shipping*, London, 1912.

Morse, H. B.: *The Gilds of China*, London, 1909.

Mukerjee, R. K.: *The Foundations of Indian Economics*, London, 1916.

Müller, F. Max: *History of Ancient Sanskrit Literature*, London, 1860.

,, *India What Can It Teach Us?*, London, 1883.

Murray, G.: *Rise of the Greek Epic*, Oxford, 1911.

Myres, F. L.: *The Influence of Anthropology upon the Course of Political Science*, Berkeley, 1916.

Nietzsche, F. W.: *Works*, New York, 1911—14.

Nizam-oul-Moulk: *Siasset Nameh* (*Traité du Gouvernement* by Schefer), Paris, 1893.

Phillimore, W. G. F.: *Three Centuries of Treaties of Peace*, Boston, 1918.

Pillai, K.: *Tamils Eighteen Hundred Years Ago*, not seen by the present author.

"R. Bhandarkar Volumes", Poona, 1920: Sukthankar's paper on the Andhras.

Rai (Lajpat): *Young India*, New York, 1916.

Ranade, M. G.: *Rise of the Maratha Power*, Bombay, 1900.

Rawlinson, H. G.: *Shivaji the Maratha*, Oxford, 1915.

Ray, P. C.: *History of Hindu Chemistry*, Calcutta, 1902—09.
Reinsch, P. S.: *Intellectual and Political Currents in the Far East*, Boston, 1911.
,, *World Politics*, New York, 1916.
Rignano, E.: *Essays in Scientific Synthesis* (trans from the Italian by Greenstreet, Chicago, 1918
Robertson, W.: *An Historical Disquisition concerning the Knowledge which the Ancients had of India* London, 1822.
Robinson, J. H.: *The New History*, New York, 1912.
Routledge: *Discoveries and Inventions of the Nineteenth Century*, London, 1899.
Rowlatt: *Report on Revolutionary Conspiracies in India*, Calcutta, 1918.
Russell, Bertrand: *Our Knowledge of the External World As a Field for Scientific Method in Philosophy*, Chicago, 1914.

Sarda, H. B.: *Mahârâṇâ Kumbha*, Ajmer, 1917.
Sarkar, B. K.: *Chinese Religion Through Hindu Eyes*, Shanghai, 1916.
,, *Folk-Element in Hindu Culture*, London, 1917.
,, *Love in Hindu Literature*, Tokyo, 1916.
,, *Hindu Achievements in Exact Science*, New York, 1918.
,, *Hindu Art: Its Humanism and Modernism*, New York, 1920.
,, *Positive Background of Hindu Sociology*, Vol. I (Non-Political), Panini Office, Allahabad, 1914 Vol. II (Political), chs. 1—11, 1921.
Sarkar, J. N.: *History of Aurangzib*, 4 vols, Calcutta (Other volumes in preparation).
,, *Moghul Administration*, Calcutta, 1920.
,, *Shivaji and His Times*, Calcutta, 1919.
Schiller, F. C. S.: *Humanism*, London, 1903.
Scott, J. B.: *Survey of International Relations between the U. S. and Germany*, New York, 1917.
Scott, S. P.: *History of the Moorish Empire in Europe*, Philadelphia, 1904.
Seal, B. N.: *Positive Sciences of the Ancient Hindus*, London, 1915.
Sewell, R.: *A Forgotten Empire*, London, 1900.
Shepherd, W. R.: *Central and South America*, London, 1914.
,, *Hispanic Nations of the New World*, New York, 1919.
Smith, V. A.: *Akbar the Great Mogul*, Oxford, 1917.
,, *Early History of India*, Oxford, 1914.
,, *Indian Constitutional Reform*, Oxford, 1919.
,, *Oxford History of India*, 1919 (See the estimate of Smith's interpretations in Sarkar's article in the *P. S. Q.* above).
Stein, M. A.: *Ruins of Desert Cathay*, London, 1912.
Taggart, F. J.: *Prolegomena to History*, Berkeley, 1916.
Taylor, H. O.: *The Mediaeval Mind*, London, 1911.
Toynbee, A.: *Industrial Revolution*, London, 1884.
Toynbee, A. J.: *Nationality and the War*, London, 1915.
Traill, H. D.: *Social England*, Vols V and VI, London, 1896.
Tucker, T. G.: *Life in Ancient Athens*, New York, 1914.
Uyehara, G. E.: *Political Development of Japan* (1867—1909), London, 1910.
Vambery, A.: *Western Culture in Eastern Lands*, London, 1906.
Vincent, W.: *Commerce and Navigation of the Ancients in the Indian Ocean*, London, 1807.
Wallas, G.: *Great Society*, New York, 1914.
Walsh, J. J.: *The Thirteenth the Greatest of Centuries*, New York, 1907.
Weir, A.: *Historical Basis of Modern Europe*, London, 1886.
Werner, E. T. C.: *Chinese Sociology*, London, 1910.
Weyl, W.: *New Democracy*, New York, 1912.

Young, A,: *Travels in France* (ed by Bethan Edwards), London, 1900.
Young, G. F.: Young, G. F.: *East and West through Fifteen Centuries*, London, 1916.
Yule, H.: *Book of Ser Marco Polo* (1254—1323), Vol. I, London, 1903.

Scholars and institutions desiring to be in touch with the advances in the world's knowledge about ancient and mediaeval India will have to regularly consult the *Indian Antiquary* of Bombay, a monthly journal of antiquities, and the Annual Reports of the Archaeological Survey of India. Nor can they afford to do without the Calcutta monthly, the *Modern Review*, which, although chiefly a political magazine devoted to the promotion of national interests and discussion of current economic and social problems, addresses itself also to the interpretation of all phases of Indian culture.

CHAPTER I.

Comparative Politics from Hindu Data.

Section 1.

A Yugântara in Political World-View.

The world is moving fast. The accepted postulates of sovereignty, nationality and democracy have been undermined by the Great War. The doctrine of the will of the people as the basis of the state is no longer to remain a pious wish of Rousseauesque philosophers. Initiative, referendum and recall are on the fair way to ring out "representative" government and inaugurate once more an era of "direct democracies". The quality of democracy itself is being powerfully affected by the advance of public ownership and municipalization, socialistic usurpation and communistic expropriation, as well as schemes for "progressive" taxation and repudiation of national debt. For, Mother Earth has commenced leavening the conventional "popular government" of the past three generations with the flesh and blood of the masses and manual workers, the real People in the human species.

Nor is constitution-making untouched by the all-round creative urge that is stirring mankind to its depths. The idealists of Young Russia have embarked on an epochmaking experiment in the manufacture of a new type of *sva-râj* (self-rule). "Functional" (occupational) sovereignty, with its corollary of sovietic (conciliar) autonomy, and ethnic (linguistic) independence with its corollary of regional (territorial) freedom, are their watch-words in economico-political self-determination. Curiously enough, the city and clan republics of ancient Eur-Asia on the one hand, and medieval gilds and feudalistic decentralization or *laissez faire*, on the other, are thus being rehabilitated to the modern conditions of wireless telegraphy, air-navigation and long-distance phones.

Naturally, therefore, the "monistic" theory of the omnipotent state, such as was conceived by philosophers from Bodin and Hobbes to Austin and Hegel, is being found to be too palpably inadequate[1] to explain the

[1] *Modern French Legal Philosophy* (Fouillée, Charmont, Duguit and Démogue), pp. XLV, XLVII, LXIII, 254, 339—344.

Realpolitik of numerous *de facto* sovereign *samûhas* or corporations that flourish within the body politic: A radical *critique* of the classical school of sovereignty is being sought in Duguit's *Les Transformations du Droit Public*. The actual federalization or pluralization of authority, i. e. the multiplicity of *imperia in imperio* in the alleged unitary state-systems of today is tending to "discredit" the state itself as an instrument of social well-being.[1] Nay, while the Lenins and Liebknechtites are but *seeking* to abolish property in order to usher in a new socio-economic order, in the enthusiasm of recent legal thought in France the state has *already* ceased to exist. And to crown all, the almost Messianic Bolshevism of November 1917, especially such as it has operated in international diplomacy and in the formulation of policy towards subject races and colonies,[2] quixotic although it may appear from the Bastille of orthodox politics, has pushed into the limbo of oblivion the messages of 1776, 1789 and 1848. Altogether, a momentous *yugântara* or transformation of the time-spirit is on in political *Weltanschauung*.

In the Orient as in the Occident, everywhere, futurists are voicing the discontent of Shelley, the arch-Bolshevist of all ages:

"The world is weary of the past,
Oh might it die or rest at last!"

The spirit of the abolition of the *status quo* is abroad. It is almost a sin today to talk of the days that are no more or wait to take a stock of the leavings of history. The greatest demand of the hour is an emancipation of the intellect from history, from tradition, from experience, from "social inheritance".

This new scepticism of "searching and impetuous souls", the Browningite faith that "men seem made for something better than the times produce", could not but have invaded the systematized bodies of knowledge nursed by academies. A revision of encyclopaedias is, therefore, the order of the hour.[3] But while all other social sciences have accordingly

---

[1] Barker's article on the "Discredited State", in the *Political Quarterly*, February 1915, pp. 107—110.

[2] Proclamation of the All-Russian Congress of Workers', Soldiers' and Peasants' Deputies, November 1917, announced by the Chief of the Oriental Division of the People's Commissariat for Foreign Affairs; see text in the *New York Nation* (Dec. 28, 1918); Lenin and Trotzky's *Proletarian Revolution*, pp. 424—426; Programme of the "Communist International" in the *New York Nation* (Oct. 13, 1920).

[3] Current tendencies in intellectual *risorgimiento* may be watched in the following among other publications: Enriques' *Problems of Science*, pp. 29—46 (critique of the methods of the special sciences), 51, 163—166, 358, 359, 361—363, 385—387; Bertrand Russell's *Our Knowledge of the External World: as a field for scientific method in philosophy*, 26—29, 236—242; Rignano's

been undergoing a comprehensive *Aufklärung* owing to the impact of "intensive" studies in anthropology, the expansion of the bounds of psychology, and the materialistic conception (that generally passes for the "economic interpretation") in history, the science of oriental lore is still in its non-age. Scholars, both in the West and the East, still take their cue from pioneer orientalists like Max Müller and Maine, and are used to interpreting the Indian "view of life" in terms of other-worldliness and pessimism, and appraising India's social, juristic, political and economic existence as but a web of archaic institutions alleged to be essentially distinct from the western. The discrepancy between the retarded growth of *indianisme* and the "geometrical" progression in the advance of other human sciences is almost as wide as that between the moral and natural philosophies of today of which Korzybski with his rigorous logic of the engineer rightly complains in the *Science and Art of Human Engineering.*

But there is no longer any reason for clinging to the over-easy generalizations of the first *corpus* of comparative studies. A scientific history[1] of Hindu Napoleons and Frederick the Greats has been rendered possible in recent years through the wealth of epigraphic data and other archeological evidence, inadequate and fragmentary though they be. New resources to be exploited by social science have been thrown open by the discovery of old books like the *Artha-śâstra*[2] of Kautilya, the Bismarck of the first Hindu Empire (B. C. 320). These have been immensely multiplied indeed by the historical researches of scholars of the two hemispheres for about half a century. And they have already borne some fruit like the one expected by Herder from his researches in the German *Volksseele.* For, that last wave of "romanticism", the nationalist movement[3] of Young India, which has won recognition as a worldforce in

Essays in Scientific Synthesis, 162—168, 197—205; Schiller's *Humanism*, preface, pp. 192—203, etc.; Dewey's "Need for a Recovery of Philosophy", in *Creative Intelligence*, pp. 5, 55—58; Hocking's *Human Nature and its Remaking*, pp. 26—28, 221—222, 225; Korzybski, pp. 15—23; Robinson's *New History*, pp. 17—18, 21, 24, 49—51, 65; Gomme's *Folklore as an Historical Science*, pp. 177—179; Boas' *Mind of Primitive Man*, pp. 17, 29, 122—123, 155—156; Wallas' *Great Society*, pp. 10, 11, 217—218, 221, 223, 225, 313, 339, 345; Hall's *Jesus the Christ in the Light of Psychology*, Vol. I, 54, 64, 154—156, Vol. II, 336—338, 358, 364—370, 702, 706, 716—731; Lowie's *Primitive Society*, pp. 432—440; Sarkar's *Positive Background*, Vol. II, pp. 1—2, 8, 12, 19, 28, 36, 45.

[1] Smith's *Early History of India* (First Edition 1904; third edition, 1914). For a general estimate of Smith's writings with especial reference to the *Oxford History of India* (from the earliest times down to 1911) see Sarkar's article on "An English History of India" in *Political Science Quarterly*, Dec. 1919.

[2] Discovered (1904), edited and translated by R. Shamasastry.

[3] Rowlatt's *Report on Revolutionary Conspiracies in India*, pp. 15—19; The "Savarkar case"

international politics since August 7, 1905, is receiving a conscious guidance and direction from the solid results of unquestionable antiquarian investigation. The sociologieal material is on the whole varied and copious enough to call for a philosophic handling, tentative albeit, in order that indology may be brought in line with the tendencies in other branches of modern inquiry.

These secular achievements of ancient India, the Hindu political institutions and theories, are virtually new data of comparative politics. But they are not calculated to pin sociology down to the past. For, comparative politics is not necrology, — the science of dead matter and tombstones, not archeology, — the study of fossils and paleontological phenomena. It is the science of *l'élan de la vie*, that one touch of Nature which makes the whole world kin. Its material is "humanistic" and thoroughly vital, as it deals with the creative endeavors of mankind, — the organizations and ideals that the human will and intelligence have invented in different lands in order to promote social happiness. And its message is equally fruitful and life-serving.

The conviction is forced upon us from a new angle that the behavioristic psychology of the races is essentially similar. Man as a political animal has responded to the stimuli of the objective universe in much the same way in the East and the West. The limits of social science are by such knowledge automatically enlarged; a phenomenal expansion of the mind is the inevitable consequence; and the prevalent notion about the Orient tends to find at last its proper place among the superficial body of unscientific *idolas*. In this wise, from an unexpected quarter, the Paracelsues of today can discover fresh reasons for finding

"No use in the past: only a scene
Of degradation, imbecility — —
The record of disgraces best forgotten,
A sullen page in human chronicles
Fit to erase."

The new "enlightenment" and Renaissance, and the *Novum Organum* of the twentieth century can acquire therefore a significant impetus from studies in jurisprudence, public law, and political philosophy from the

---

(France vs. Great Britain) in Scott's *Hague Court Reports*, pp. 275—283; Scott's *Survey of International Relations between the U. S. and Germany* (Aug. 1914 — Aprill 1917), p. 305; Reinsch's *Intellectual and Political Currents in the Far East*, 93, 105, etc.; Lovett's *History of the Indian Nationalist Movement*, Gilchrist's *Indian Nationality*, Maurice Bourgeois' „Le Mouvement National" in *Le Monde Illustré* (19 Feb. 1921), *Freiheitskampf der indischen Nationalisten*, Lajpat Rai's *Young India*.

oriental world of experience. And social science, thus reconstructed, cannot fail to have a powerful bearing on the current problems of the contemporary world. For, the acknowledgment by scientists of the basic uniformity in the mental and moral make-up of humanity is the theoretical pre-condition for a peaceful understanding of the diverse peoples. Comparative politics will thus turn out to be a most helpful ally of practical statesmanship in the amicable adjustment of relations between Asia and Eur-America. It will give birth to a new internationalism quite in conformity with this era of transvaluation of values.

Section 2.

The Instrument of Interpretation.

The term "comparative" is, however, glibly used in modern sociological parlance. But errors creep in probably almost unconsciously as soon as one proceeds to employ it. At best it is only a method; and unless used with discrimination, like statistics it can be made to prove anything one wishes to prove. In the manner of experiments in a chemical laboratory, the social comparisons should be instituted under definitely known conditions; and as in mathematics, the items to be compared should be brought to a common denominator. Obviously a hill cannot be compared with a river (except as mere terrestrial objects). Nor can mollusca be rationally compared with orchids (except as mere living bodies). Similarly, a fossil or a mummy must not be compared with organisms that can react to the environmental stimuli, nor a master be compared with a slave, — unless the basis of comparison be categorically stated and the conditions of comparison well defined.

Now, the brightest period of Occidental civilization happens to be the darkest period of Oriental. And this, again, is the epoch of the political-*cum*-industrial domination of the East by the West. In the nineteenth century and during the first years of the twentieth it may almost be said that Asia was for all practical purposes lying dead. Howsoever resentful orientals themselves may feel in regard to the prevailing albinocracy, not even the blindest idealist among them can ignore or minimize the situation. For, in the conjuncture of world politics the Orient has for quite a long period remained veritably the "white man's burthen". Asia today is indisputably a continent of slaves, *de jure*, as well as *de facto* (albeit not everywhere *de jure*). And to add insult to injury, the new life which has of late been pulsating through Asian humanity and which has created for Japan a first class rank in the concert of world-powers, is due to the inspiration furnished mainly by

Eur-America from Newton to Becquerel, from Washington and Rousseau to Mill and Treitschke. The inferiority of the Orient to the Occident in culture as well as in politics is thus from every side an established fact of modern history. The tragedy of Young Asia is complete.

Under these conditions is it possible for Eur-American scholars to evaluate past Asian achievements in science, industry, politics, art and philosophy at their proper worth? Can it be conceived that dominant races should be able to appreciate the human values in the life-processes of emasculated slaves? Here is an elementary fact in the psychology of successful nations that is chiefly responsible for the current fallacies in comparative sociology. It explains why the comparative method is yet in its infancy, at any rate, the comparison of the claims of the Orient and the Occident to have contributed to the world's scientific concepts and categories or to the building up of social and civic well-being.

Human memory, again, is very short. It does not go even so far back as one generation. It is impossible of course to call to one's mind the days of pre-steam industry. And the discoveries relating to the radium group are bidding fair to throw into the shade even the marvellous technological power of the energies that underlie contemporary life and efficiency. And yet how old are these achievements?[1] And scientifically speaking, how many are they in number? The "pragmatic" answer lies in the history of Japan. This Asian country did not take more than twenty-five years (1880—1905) to exploit the whole of western culture in order to triumph over a great European power and be invited by America to dictate terms to the vanquished foe.

Historically considered, some of these achievements are fifty years old, others seventy-five, almost none above a century. The steam engine was first applied to cotton manufacture in 1785. But it did not come into general use before the third decade of the nineteenth century. Let Americans try to visualize the life and conditions of those "Pioneers" immortalized by Walt Whitman who a few generations ago had been laying the foundations of the Middle West and the Farthest West. It is also fair to recollect the social and industrial position of Germany in the days of Goethe, the educational condition of the people of France about the time when Arthur Young was touring in that country, and the condition of the working classes and the female sex of England at the time of the Napoleonic wars.[2]

---

[1] Routledge's *Discoveries and Inventions*; R. Mackenzie's *19th Century*, pp. 181—206, 289—315, 429—432; Price's *Political Economy in England*, pp. 5—7; Weir's *Historical Basis of Modern Europe*, pp. 315—469.

[2] Chapter on "Weimar in the eighteenth century" in Lewes' *Life of Goethe*; Young's *Travels*

Coming specifically to politics, it has to be admitted that, strictly speaking, modern Europe and America do not date back earlier than 1866-1870. Europe was feudal and mediaeval almost down to that time. The political boundaries[1] were then almost as flexible as in the days of Charlemagne or the Guelphs and Ghibellins. America's freedom was threatened in the second war with England (1812), and integrity jeopardized by the Civil War, of which also her old enemy England tried to take diplomatic advantage. Nationality existed only in limited degree before Mazzini and Bismarck; the dignity of labor was not recognized before Karl Marx and Louis Blanc; "popular" parliamentary institutions were all but unknown before the first Reform Bill of England; and the right of the masses to elementary education, the sole pre-condition of a real democracy, was not really a question of practical politics in the first half of the nineteenth century.

Every student of political institutions and theories must have to remember this background of Eur-American life while trying to understand the civic and social achievements of Asians. Judged by the triumphs of today, the western people even of the first half of the nineteenth century were "unfit" for self-government. Especially was continental Europe anything but democratic, without national consciousness, and devoid of the sense of the rights of citizenship. Far worse of course were the earlier epochs.

"Then came those days," as Macaulay describes the Restoration in his *Essay on Milton*, "never to be recalled without a blush, the days of servitude without loyalty and sensuality without love, of dwarfish talents and gigantic vices, the paradise of cold hearts and narrow minds, the golden age of the coward, the bigot and the slave. The King cringed to his rival that he might trample on his people, sank into a viceroy of France, and pocketed with complacent infamy her degrading insult and her more degrading gold. The caresses of harlots and the jests of buffoons regulated the policy of the state. The Government had just ability enough to deceive, and just religion enough to persecute. The principles of liberty were the scoff of every grinning courtier and the

---

in France (Miss Bethan-Edwards' Introduction); Compayré's *History of Pedagogy* (vide Guizot's Educational Commission in 1833); Toynbee's *Industrial Revolution*, pp. 60—61; Traill's *Social England*, Vol. V, pp. 346—347, 453, 455, 601—604; Vol. VI, 69—70, 620—30; Chapter on "social movements" in *Cambridge Modern Hist.*, Vol. XII, pp. 730—731, 761—762; Calhoun's *Social Hist. of the American Family*, Vol. I, 83—127, 245—258, Vol. II, 80—101, 171—199.

[1] A. J. Toynbee's *Nationality and the War*, pp. 9—15; See "The Congress of Vienna and its Legacies" in Phillimore's *Three Centuries of Treaties of Peace*; Guyot's *Causes and Consequences of the War*, pp. 207—211, 222—226.

Anathema Maranatha of every fawning dean. In every high place worship was paid to Charles and James, Belial and Moloch, and England propitiated those obscene and cruel idols with the blood of her best and bravest children."

Nor in Louis XIV *le grand monarque's* psychology was there any respect for the rights of the people. He acted on the creed of absolutism, viz., *L'état c'est moi*. Besides, his high-handed measures at home and his unjust wars of aggression constitute a reflection on the political institutions and international morality of the times. Not less "characteristic" of occidental development are the horrors of judicial torture and inhuman penal legislation, both secular and ecclesiastical, which prevailed in Europe from the revival of Roman law in the thirteenth century to the epoch of reform initiated, at any rate in so far as the ideal is concerned, by the Italian jurist Beccaria in his *Crimes and Punishments* towards the end of the eighteenth.[1]

The scientific method consists in proceeding from the known to the unknown. Students of comparative politics ought to approach the political literature and institutions of Asia with a full knowledge of this tradition of despotism in European history. It is as unjust to compare ancient and mediaeval Asia i. e., the Asia of the Asians, with the Europe and America of the twentieth century, as to compare the latter with the Occident previous to the "industrial revolution". Unbiased investigators will find in Asian history the same struggles and tribulations through which European humanity has passed. It is impossible to mention a single institution or ideal in the Occident for which a parallel or replica is not to be found in the Orient. And no political weakness can be cited in Asia of which there is no double in Eur-America. But in order to avoid superficial analogies[2] what is required of scholars is: first, to practise scientific detachment from the conditions of life in which they are living today; secondly, to master the actual facts of political development and speculation in Asia; and thirdly, to place them in the perspective of occidental *Realpolitik* and "pious wish", epoch by epoch, area by area, and item by item.

The "superior races" of the last hundred years have been misled by their fact of success to postulate the whole development of Asian polity as nothing but an unchanging record of semi-savage, i. e., almost unpolitical or pre-political group-life, and the entire literature of oriental

---

[1] Lea's *History of Inquisition*, Vol. I, pp. 234—236; Vol. III, 300, etc. 421—423.

[2] *Vide* the sections on the "comparative method" and the "age of modernism" in the author's article on the "Futurism of Young Asia" in the *International Journal of Ethics*, July, 1918.

political thought as at best but commonplace speculation pervaded by theocratic ideas. Thus has been engendered a monumental *idola* in the realm of social science. They manage to forget that the superior races of the ancient and mediaeval world were not Europeans but Egyptians, Assyrians, Persians, Mohammedans and Buddhist-Shamanist Tartars, whether in the strength of arms or in the "more glorious victories" of peace. Down to the second siege of Vienna in 1699 it was the historic role of Asia to be always the aggressor and of Europe to be on the defensive.

On the other hand there is a class of Oriental scholars, among both Indian nationalists and leaders of the Chinese revolution, who try to demonstrate the existence of every modern democratic theory and republican institution and perhaps also of sovietic communism in the experience of ancient and mediaeval Asia. There is an attempt on their part to trace the latest Eur-American phase of the art and science of government in the teachings of Confucius and Mencius, Śukra and Manu, and in the clan-republics and village-commonwealths of the Orient.

Both these attitudes must be set aside as superficial. It is not necessary to claim extraordinary achievements for Orientals in order to prove their political *viriya* and administrative *śakti* (genius). Nor again is it permissible to read modern ideas into the "liberties" of Athens and Rome or forget the limitations of feudal and Hapsburg Europe or be blind to the two thousand years of occidental autocracy from Alexander to the end of the *ancien régime*.[1]

What is urged here is that it is unfair to compare the East in its worst and most degraded condition with the West in its best and most prosperous stage, and that it is a vicious practice to try to understand Asia such as she was as the leader of humanity's progress from the servile and degenerate Asia of today, the Asia that is facing annihilation. Justice and science require that Asia and Europe should be tried in the balance "under the same conditions of temperature and pressure", i. e., under conditions of absolute freedom and mutual respect.

Such is the instrument of interpretation that we propose to apply to the epochs of Hindu polity roughly synchronous with European development from Pericles to Dante.

---

[1] Cf. the author's "Democratic Ideals and Republican Institutions in India" in the *American Political Science Review* (Nov. 1918), pp. 581, 587—588, 592, 596, 605—606, and "Democratic Background of Chinese Culture" in the *Scientific Monthly* (January, 1919), pp. 58, 62, 65. See in this connection Montesquieu's *Lettres Persanes* (1721).

CHAPTER II.

Hindu Political Development.

Section 1.

The Tenacity of Monarchy in the West.

Modern mind, especially in the United States, is so deeply grounded in the republican ideal that scholars are invariably disposed to forget the fact that in the western world the norm of political development is to be sought not in the republic but in the monarchy, and in that, again, generally of an irresponsible autocratic character. At the threshold of a scientific study of oriental polity it is essential, therefore, for a clarification of fundamental ideas, to recapitulate the trend of Western political experience.

Americans won their independence by defeating the British. When they had to think of constructing a sovereign government, the most natural form that suggested itself to them was a *popular* polity. None of the thirteen colonies was bossed by a prince of royal blood. Their society from the very beginning had known only of councils, assemblies, courts, and clubs. A dynasty of kings was thus absolutely out of the question. Besides, in 1782 Washington, the hero of the field, magnanimously rejected, "with great and painful surprise", the crown and the supreme power offered to him by some discontented officers. The most important problem before the Yankees after 1783 was therefore not the form of government but the form of union. The republic (no matter whether democratic or otherwise)[1] was with them an accomplished fact, one of the socio-political *data*, so to speak; their sole struggle was over the nature of the federation. America's record thus really stands apart from the story of the evolution experienced by those peoples who by the term 'government' are used to mean the rule of a king.

This norm is represented by France. The French revolution followed close upon the American revolution, and was to a great extent inspired by its theories and achievements. Besides, there is an interesting coincidence between the two. Americans in the first stage of their resistance

[1] Beard's *Economic Origins of Jeffersonian Democracy*, pp. 309—316, 464, 465.

to England's control did not think of actual separation or declaration of independence. The French people likewise in their opposition to Louis XVI did not at first contemplate an abolition of the monarchy. Like the American "independence" the French republic was a second thought, an aftermath of painful necessity, and like some of the great discoveries of the world a real "accident" of history.

The revolution began in France with the conversion of the "third estate" into the National Assembly under the influence of Siéyes on June 17, 1789. The monarchy was abolished and France declared a republic by the Convention (the third revolutionary government) on September 22, 1792. But during these thirty-nine months neither the prominent leaders, Siéyes, Mirabeau, Lafayette, nor the demagogic journalists and ultra-radical "friends of the people", Desmoulins, Marat, Danton, nor even the people themselves in the thousand and one *cahiers* (pamphlets on the grievances to be redressed) ever expressed any desire to do away with the royalty as an institution. Even the "rights of man" did not include the abolition of kingship.

It was unexpectedly and virtually through friends and well-wishers of the king and the queen that royalty was abolished in France. The National Assembly's Bolshevistic short cuts with the feudal privileges and hereditary nobility had made the country too hot for the aristocratic classes. The French nobles thereupon sought refuge in the Germanistic territories. The public opinion and military support of the continent were successfully canvassed by them against the revolutionists on behalf of the old royalist regime. Eventually the Austrian emperor and the Prussian king in coalition with this "emigrant" nobility invaded France to "re-establish the liberty and honour of the most Christian king and his family and place a check upon the dangerous excesses of the French revolution, the fatal example of which it behooves every government to repress". It was this foreign invasion that led the National Assembly to declare the country in danger; and it was against this *tyrannie* of foreigners, and not against Louis XVI, that the famous *La Marseillaise* was composed.

The attempt of Austria and Prussia on France could not but be interpreted by the Convention as an underhand measure of the King himself. He was therefore tried on a charge of "treason", found guilty and executed (January 21, 1793). The same fate awaited the queen in October and on the same charge. Thus in France the abolition of monarchy was not accomplished as a matter of principle. It was a by-product of inevitable circumstances, over which the revolutionists had no control. Up to the last moment France was royalist at heart.

What, again, is the lesson of Switzerland,[1] the oldest republic of the modern world, with regard to the inception of the republican idea? In early times the Swiss peasantry and nobility lived in forest cantons. In 1291 three districts, Schwyz, Uri and Unterwalden, formed a league to defend themselves against powerful neighbours. They defeated the Austrian invader at Morgarten in 1315, and successfully fought against the laws of the Diet of Worms (1500). Freedom from Imperial interference was thus ensured by the strength of arms. The territory of the league was gradually extended by the voluntary accession of new cantons, and the complete independence of the Confederacy was acknowledged by the treaty of Westphalia (1648). The story of the Swiss republic is thus similar to that of the American. We have here republicanism developed among peoples that had never known kingship as an actual institution of social life.

Holland was a republic for a short time during the seventeenth century. But as it is now a monarchy, the experience of the Dutch does not count in modern republicanism.

The "glorious" English revolution preceded the French by a century. The people of England did not go mad over the magic name of republic. Virtually no *doctrinaire* principles guided them in the practical framing of their constitution of 1688. They replaced one king by another, but one with fetters on. Previous to this "great rebellion" there had indeed been a period when England was a republican commonwealth. But a kingless regime did not commend itself to the temperament of the English, and this in spite of the fact that they had a regicide to their credit (1649). Since the Reform Bills of 1832, 1866 and 1886, the monarchy of England has been a republic all but in name, a "crowned republic" in the words of Tennyson; but the republican form is not yet.

The principles of the American and French revolutions were advertized and sown broadcast through the long wars of the Napoleonic era (1793—1815). The years 1830 and 1848 were the years of revolutions and risings against absolutism and privilegism all over Europe. But in spite of the steady progress in constitutional ideas, checks on royalty, and the assertion of popular rights, a formal republic did not make its appearance in any European country until yesterday (March 16, 1917).[2] The third republic of Europe has been born in Russia, the quarter where it was least expected. On the whole, however, Europe seems still to be chary of losing her crowned heads. Although the expulsion of Hohen-

---

[1] Mc Crackan's *Rise of the Swiss Republic*, pp. 111—115.

[2] Lenin and Trotzky's *Proletarian Revolution in Russia*, pp. 17—23.

zollern-Hapsburg rulers by "divine right" (Nov. 8, 1918) from Germania may lead eventually to the sweeping off of monarchy from the world's stage, the restoration of Constantine in Greece (1921) still points "atavistically", so to speak, to the historic norm in European political *psyche.*

Next remain to be considered over a score of republics in Latin America.[1] Their origins are the same as that of the United States of North America. These had at first been members of the European "colonial" empires, especially Spanish and Portuguese. Subsequently they won their independence by successful wars. Like the north Americans, these Latins from Mexico to Argentina, also, had no royal family to look up to. The republic was therefore the most natural polity to them. Yet in some of these states, such as in Mexico and Brazil, monarchy was established either by the choice of the people themselves or by the usurpation of the General-Presidents. Ultimately, however, all of them have successfully withstood the dynastic ambitions of the "first citizens".

But perhaps the best example of the extreme tenacity of the monarchical idea is furnished by the history of Italian regeneration. If there is one man in Europe of the nineteenth century who by his life and work made the ideal of nationality and the idea of republic the life-blood of millions both in his own land and abroad, that man is Joseph Mazzini. The country of Mazzini, therefore, if not any others, may be expected to have realized the republican idea while its new life was being ushered into existence (1861—1870). But half the mission of Mazzini still awaits fulfillment. Italian nationality has been achieved, and Dante's and Machiavelli's dreams of a United Italy have been realized, nay, exceeded (1919) so far as southern Tirol is concerned; but Italy is not a republic yet.

In the perspective of this record of Eur-America let us place the facts of Hindu political development. We may safely begin with the inductive generalization that monarchy dies hard and that it has been almost a fetish to human beings.

Section 2.

The State-Systems of Ancient India.

In regard to oriental monarchies we have to realize, first, that Hindu states were thoroughly secular. In India, paradoxical as it may seem to pre-conceived notions, religion is never known to have dominated

[1] Shepherd's *Central and South America*, pp. 71—96, and *Hispanic Nations of the New World*, 166—195.

political history or philosophy. Politics were invariably independent of theology; nor did priests interfere in the civil administration as a matter of right, temporal or spiritual. In short, with the exception of the quasi-religious statal organization of Sikhs in the seventeenth century, Hindustan knows of no "theocracies" strictly so called. Even under Asoka the Great, Harṣa-vardhana, and Dharma-pâla, the supreme dignity of the empire as a worldly organism was not sacrificed to the personal religiosity of the crowned heads. Consequently, the struggle for "Caesaro-papism"[1] among the so-called "Byzantine" emperors, the long-drawn-out conflict between the papacy and the Holy Roman Empire, the rivalry with regard to the custodianship of the "twain keys" to heaven, the temporal sovereignty of spiritual heads, the political influence exerted by the pope through his cardinals, legates and pardoners over the internal politics of states in Western Europe, these and other facts that contribute to the complexity of occidental history are not matched in Hindu political development.

Hindu monarchs with non-Hindu officers, non-Hindu princes with Hindu ministers and generals have been the norm in India's history. The functions of priests were confined to the private religious life of the royal families and the people. Their place on state councils was relegated to the administration of social and national festivals. And the dictates of religious scriptures were placed before the mind's eye of rulers and statesmen, if at all, solely as principles of moral guidance. These may be taken to have been checks and restraints on the possible autocracy and high-handedness of the powers that be. Nothing analogous to the Church as an institution of "public law" was ever attempted by the priestcraft of the Hindu, Buddhist, Jaina and Moslem faiths, notwithstanding the efficiency of their ecclesiastical organization and occasional military activities.

With these general remarks we shall tabulate here the principal landmarks in the history of Hindu politics. Let us begin with the Maurya Empire (B. C. 323—185).[2] Its capital was located at Pâtaliputra (site of modern Bankipore) on the Ganges in Eastern India. Under Asoka

[1] Bury's *History of the Later Roman Empire* (A. C. 395—800), Vol. II, ch. XI. *Vide* the preface to Vol. I. for a discussion of the proper title. Bryce's *Holy Roman Empire*, pp. 89—120, 153—166, 204—228; Freeman's *Chief Periods of European History*, Lectures IV, and V; Lea's *His. of Inquis.*, I. pp. 213, 221, 233—236; III. 190—192, 295, 300, 515; Sidgwick's *Development of European Polity*, 223—229.

[2] See map on p. 105 of Smith's *Oxford History*. The political and administrative history for preceding three centuries may be seen in D. R. Bhandarkar's *Ancient History of India* (B. C. 650—325).

the Great the empire included the regions covered at present by Afghanistan and Baluchistan, the whole of Northern India, the Deccan, and Southern India excluding the extreme south (Chola, Pândya, Kerala, Satyaputra and Ceylon). The area and pretensions of the undivided Roman Empire at its zenith were thus anticipated by this first *sârva-bhauma* (universal) empire of the Hindus by about five hundred years. And of course Great Britain's rule in India today falls considerably short of Maurya achievement.

It should be pointed out, however, that this was the only Hindu state with jurisdiction over all India. For subsequent periods in pre-Moslem times the fortunes of the south were to all intents and purposes separate from those of the north, exactly as in Europe the story of the Eastern (or "Byzantine") empire ran independently of that of the Western. In spite of Samudra-gupta's *dig-vijaya* or conquest of the quarters (A. C. 330—350), embracing some of the southern territories in its Alexandrine sweep, and the Râṣṭrakûta (Deccan) intervention (*c* 914—916) in northern Indian politics as well as Râjendra-chola the *Gangaikonda's* (1013—1042) victories on the banks of the Ganges northerners and southerners never again came to be held together by a single administrative and military system.

Three states acquired prominence in three different parts of India after the extinction of the Mauryas. The first was the empire of the Sungas (B. C. 183—63). It served virtually to keep up the continuity of the Maurya Empire in the eastern provinces. The capital remained unchanged. Puṣya-mitra, the founder of this House, inflicted a decisive defeat on Menander, the Hellenistic invader of India (B. C. 153). The second was the empire of the Ândhras (*c* B. C. 240—A. C. 250). They were rulers of the Deccan from sea to sea with eastern and western capitals.[1] These southern emperors maintained commercial intercourse with western Asia, Greece, Rome, Egypt and China. Gotami-putra (109—135) and Yajna-śrî (173—202) are two of their most aggressive monarchs. Their rivals in the north were the Indo-Tartars or Kuṣâns (A. C. 15—226) with capital at Puruṣa-pura (modern Peshawar). This northern and northwestern power was in relations of commerce and diplomacy with the Han Empire of China and with the Roman Empire during its period of greatest extent. Kâniṣka (A. C. 78—123) of this House was the contemporary of Trajan and Hadrian. Through the Kuṣân

[1] D. R. Bhandarkar's "Dekkan of the Sâta-vâhana Period." in the *Indian Antiquary*, 1918 which must be studied, however, in the light of the new material placed by V. S. Sukthankar in the *R. G. Bhandarkar Commemoration Volumes*. For republics of this period see *Infra*, p. 141.

empire the Indian sphere of influence, political and cultural, was extended over Central Asia. Recent excavations have brought to light an underground "Greater India" from among the "ruins of Desert Cathay".[1]

Nothing is known of Northern India for a century after the epoch of the Kuṣâns, and for about three hundred years the history of India south of the Vindhya Mountains is a blank. But the next scene reveals in the Gangetic Valley the India of the Vikramâdityan Guptas (A. C. 320—550) with capital at Pâtaliputra through whom Hindu culture commenced to become a world-power;[2] as subsequently it served to help forward the Chinese renaissance of the Tang period (618—905) and thus indirectly sponsor the emergence of Japan as a civilized state. The epoch of Gupta imperial glories was synchronous with that of the dismemberment of the Western Roman Empire, but was paralleled by the period of consolidation in the Byzantine Empire from Constantine to Justinian. The age of the Guptas is in India's literary history the age of Kâlidâsa (*c* 400—460), the Virgil of the Hindu *Aeneid*, the *Raghu-vamśa* ("The House of Raghu"), and is as famous in popular tradition as that of Alexander or Charlemagne in Europe. In the language of this poet of imperial nationalism the Vikramâdityas were

"Lords of the lithosphere from sea to sea,
Commanding the skies by chariots of air."

The Gupta Empire was followed by what may be described as a diarchy like that of Ândhra-Kuṣân India. The Empire of the Vardhanas (606—647) in Northern India had its capital at Kanauj on the Ganges in the middle west. Emperor Harṣa had diplomatic touch with the Chinese Napoleon, Tang Tai-tsung. The empire of the Châlukyas (550—753) in the Deccan had its capitals at Vâtâpi (modern Badami in Bijapur) and Nasik. Pula-keśî II was paramount sovereign over India south of the Narmadâ and reciprocated embassies with Khusru II, the Sassanian monarch of Persia.

During the seventh and eighth centuries India witnessed the formation of myriads of states similar to those in Europe. In various quarters the effort to achieve hegemony gradually led to the operation of centripetal tendencies. Out of a veritable *mâtsya-nyâya* ("logic of the fish") or Hobbesian "state of nature" there eventually arose the condition of what may for ordinary purposes be characterized as a pentarchy. India's destiny remained for several centuries in the hands of five chief

---

[1] Mookerji's *History of Indian Shipping*, pp. 116—141; Stein's *Ruins of Desert Cathay*, Vol. I, pp. viii, x, 469—496.

[2] Sarkar's *Chinese Religion Through Hindu Eyes*, pp. 184—229.

nationalities. (1) Bengalis[1] of the lower Gangetic Valley became a great power under the Pâla and Sena Emperors (730—1200). Ḍharma-pâla (795—830) and Lakṣmaṇa-sena (1119—1170) are the Charlemagnes of Bengal. (2) Gurjara-Pratîhâras (the so-called Rajputs) (816—1194) of Upper India and Rajputana, celebrated in Râjaśekhara's *Karpûra-manjarî* as "world-monarchs", had their capital at Kanauj. A *digvijaya* (conquest of the quarters) was successfully undertaken by Mihira Bhoja (*c* 840—890) of this dynasty. (3) Râṣtrakûtas (750—973) of the Deccan[2] with capital at Malkhed became a power by dispossessing the Châlukyas of their dominions. Govinda III was the *sârva-bhauma* ("world-ruler") of the South. Râṣtrakûtas were replaced by Châlukyas of Kalyan (973—1190) who in their turn were expelled by Hoysâlâs of Dvâra-samudra and Yâdavas of Devagiri. (4) Cholas[3] (850—1310) of Southern India militated against Châlukyas of the Deccan and also came to measure their strength with Pâlas of Bengal. Râja-râja (985—1018) and Kulot-tûnga I (1070—1118) are the most celebrated monarchs of this House. (5) The kingdom of Kashmir[4] (*c* 650—1339) had a more or less isolated career in the extreme north. Gurjara-Pratîhâras submitted to Mohammedans in 1194, Senas in 1200, Hoysâlâs, Yâdavas and Cholas in 1310, and Kashmir in 1339. Thus came to a close the ancient period of Hindu India which furnishes the background of the present treatise.

The history of India for about sixteen hundred years from the time of Mauryas exhibits to us the picture of a gradually growing and expanding political consciousness as well as scientific and cultural development. The Hindu Alexanders, Caesars, Constantines, Charlemagnes and Frederick Barbarossas could easily challenge competition with their western peers on their own terms of *śakti-yoga* or *Machtpolitik*. It is, moreover, only fair to note that for one Justinian in Europe there were a dozen Maurices, for one Charles the Great the name of Charles the Fats was legion, and for a Frederick II, the "wonder of the world", there were myriads of Adolfuses and Wenceslauses.

Not altogether extinct, however, was the sovereignty of Hindus with

---

[1] Banerji's *Memoir on the Pâlas of Bengal*, and *Bânglâr Itihâsa* (History of Bengal, in Bengali language) Vol. I. (Hindu Period), A. K. Maitra's articles on the "Stones of Varendra" in the *Mod. Rev.* (June—Sept. 1912). *Re* the drama *Karpûra-manjarî* see Konow's translation in the Harvard Oriental Series, p. 179 (cited by H. C. Ray Chaudhuri in the Mod. Rev. Oct. 1921).

[2] R. G. Bhandarkar's *Early History of the Dekkan;* Kincaid and Parasnis' *History of the Maratha People*, Vol. I (To the Death of Shivaji). Chs. II—VI.

[3] Aiyangar's *Ancient India*, 90—191.

[4] Kalhana's *Râja-tarangini* (trans. by Stein). The *Imperial Gazetteer of India*, Vol. XV, pp.90—96.

the advent of Islam. Excluding the isolated enterprise of the Bengali Danuja-mardana[1] (*c* 1417), devoted to Kâlî, the patron-goddess of energists, there were at least four state-systems embodying independent Hindu power during the period when portions of the Indian sub-continent were members of consolidated Mohammedan empires or lesser Mohammedan states. Inevitably the first to come in touch with the new factor in Indian politics were the kingdoms of Rajputs in the Middle West.[2] Beginning in the ninth and tenth centuries, these "cognates" and "agnates" of Gurjara-Pratîhâras have continued their existence until today. The empire of Vijaya-nagara[3] (1336—1565) in the extreme south was necessarily the last to feel the Mohammedan pressure. By the middle of the seventeenth century two important Hindu reactions were provoked by the firm establishment of the Moslem as a paramount power. In the Deccan the bulwark of Hindu independence was built up by Shivaji[4] (1627—1680), the Frederick the Great of India, in his empire of the Marathas. This was continued during the eighteenth century under the Peshwas or ministers. Fragments of Maratha states still exist more or less as "feudatories" of Great Britain. The second great reaction against political Islam manifested itself in the militant nationalism of Sikhs in the Punjab.[5] Some of their kingdoms maintain themselves today in "subordinate alliançe" with the British power.

During all this period of tug-of-war between Hindus and Islam no part of India came to be subject to a "foreign power". Mohammedans were as much the children of the soil as the original inhabitants. Neither the Sultanate of Delhi (1200—1526) nor the Moghul monarchy that replaced it was in any sense the "government of one people by another". The Moghuls are celebrated chiefly through such world-figures as Akbar,[6]

---

[1] For Hindu reaction in Bengal under Ganeśa and Danuja-mardana (*c*. 1409—1442) see Banerji, Vol. II, Ch. vii, also his "Two New Kings of Bengal" in the *Arch. Sur. Ann. Rep.* 1911—12, pp. 167—170. *Re* Danuja-mardana see Bhattasali's Bengali article in *Bhârata-varṣa* (Aświn 1328, Sept. 1921).

[2] *Imp. Gaz. of Ind.*, Vol. XXI, pp. 93—103; Sarda's *Mahârâṇâ Kumbha*; *Early Hist.*, pp. 407—415; *Indian Empire* Vol. II, pp. 308—318 (*Imp. Gaz. Ind.* Series).

[3] Sewell's *Forgotten Empire*, H. Krishna Sastri's articles in the *Ann. Rep. of the Arch. Sur. of Ind.*, 1907—1909, 1911—1912; *Ox. His.* pp. 299—317.

[4] Ranade's *Rise of the Maratha Power;* Rawlinson's *Shivaji the Maratha;* Kincaid and Parasnis, Vol. I, pp. 271—277; J. N. Sarkar's *Shivaji and His Times*, Chs. XV, XVI.

[5] Cunningham's *History of the Sikhs;* Macauliffe's *Sikh Religion*, Vol. I. (Nanak), Vol. IV (Teg Bahadur), Vol. V (Gobind).

[6] Smith's *Akbar the Great Mogul*, Havell's *History of Aryan Rule in India*, Chs. XV—XX; cf. the present author's "Political Tendencies in Chinese Culture" in the *Mod. Rev.* (January, 1920).

Shah Jahan and Aurangzib[1] (sixteenth and seventeenth centuries). The Moghul period of Indian history is one of the most important epochs of civilization. For the people of India, it was an era of prosperity, material and intellectual. The epoch, known generally as the age of Indo-Saracenic renaissance, looms therefore as large in the consciousness of the Young India of today as does the age of the Vikramâdityan *sârva-bhaumas.* The policy of the Moslem states was always secular, and the personal bigotry and intolerance of some of the rulers were not more frequent than were the fanaticism and inquisitionism of Christian monarchs of contemporary Europe.[2] From Prithvî-râja and Mohammed Ghori of the twelfth century to Baji Rao and Haidar Ali of the eighteenth, Hindu and Mohammedan India can exhibit therefore as many Charles Vs, Gustavus Adolfuses, Louis XIVs, Fredericks and Peters as can the western half of Eur-Asia.

In the foregoing account no notice has been taken of autonomous city-sovereignties and independent clan-commonwealths. They were in existence off and on during the extensive ages that gave birth to Vedic literature, the *Jâtakas*, the early Jaina and Buddhist books and the *Mahâbhârata*, down to the beginnings of the Gupta Empire (*c* 350 A. C.). Some of them are described in the Greek and Latin literature on India and Alexander. These nationalities were republican in type, more or less aristocratic or oligarchic in character, and thus resembled in general features the states of ancient Greece and Rome, as well as the mercantile towns of medieval Italy and of the Hanseatic League.

Section 3.

Pax Sârva-bhaumica

(Peace of the World-State).

It is clear that political development in India was not a continuous growth. Students of history will not find in it the simplicity and unity that characterize, generally speaking, the dynastic history of Japan, or still better, of China from the days of Tsin Shi Hwang-ti (B. C. 222). We have here all the complications and intricacies of the Byzantine

[1] J. N. Sarkar's *History of Aurangzib:* Vol I (Reign of Shah Jahan), Vol. II (War of Succession), Vol. III (1658—1681); Law's *Promotion of Learning in India by Muhammadans*, pp. 139—193.

[2] For Moorish toleration in Europe during the epoch of Christian fanaticism, see McCabe's *Peter Abelard*, 227—229. Turkish liberalism was appreciated by Bodin in his days (*vide* Bluntschli's *Geschichte der neueren*); *cf.* also Toynbee's *Nationality*, p. 415, and Macdonald's *Turkey and the Eastern Question*, p. 34. *Vide* Voltairès *Lettres Philosophiques* (1734).

empire and the Caliphate.[1] The inextricable cobwebs of diplomatic intercourse that Europe witnessed in the Middle Ages owing to the rivalry among the Christian empires and kingdoms on the one hand, and their relations of intrigué with the competing Moslem nationalities on the other, repeated themselves in the military annals of Hindus also and subsequently of Hindus and Mohammedans. Nay, from the standpoint of the political centre of gravity and *status quo*, the picture of India's state-systems is as bewilderingly varied and diversified as is that of the western world from the armageddon of the Homeric epics down to the world war against Germany. Nothing short of the kaleidoscopic changes in Freeman's *Historical Geography of Europe* can therefore fitly portray the multitudinous ups and downs of "races" and "classes" in India through the ages.

The fallacy of sociologists from Bodin to Buckle, Montesquieu to Maine, and Hegel to Huntington[2] equipped as this last is with "energy-charts" and "maps of civilization", as well as of indologists from Max Müller to Vincent Smith has, however, been broadening down "from precedent to precedent". Fundamentally, it consists in their not recognizing this essential parallelism and pragmatic identity in the development of *Realpolitik* in the East and the West. As a rule, they are obsessed by the postulate of Eur-American "superiority" to, or at any rate,

---

[1] Bury's *Later Roman*, Vol. II, pp. 510—511.

[2] While not prepared to be a "monist" or "absolutist" in the conception of *Kultur-geschichte*, the present author accepts with certain limitations the general thesis as to what Bagehot would call the influence of "physics" upon "politics". A recent summary of the geographical interpretation of history is to be seen in Huntington's *Pulse of Asia* (Ch. XVIII). It will be noticed that the philosophical analysis attempted by "physicists" is invariably based on too many *assumptions* in regard to the historical data themselves, especially to those bearing on the Orient. The hemispheroidal generalizations are therefore reared on erroneous premises. Some of the worst specimens of the mal-application of the comparative method, so far as the selection of sociological facts is concerned, are furnished in the writings of Huntington. In the *Pulse of Asia* this neo-climatologist takes for granted in the newspaper style that "Mohammedanism favors immorality" (pp. 128, 232) and that Persians are "prone to lying" (pp. 364—366). The postulate of the "white man's burthen" is, moreover, the pervading philosophy of this book (p. 323) as also of his *Civilization and Climate* (pp. 35, 201, 259, 262). His appreciation of Japan in the latter volume (pp. 255—256) is accordingly explained by a corollary to the same logic, viz, that "nothing succeeds like success". From the obverse side the identical *idola* is illustrated in the chapter on the "Problem of Turkey" in his *World Power and Evolution*, which *en passant* is inspired more by political propagandism than devotion to science. A short but comprehensive criticism of the prevailing fallacies in comparative culture-history is set forth in Sarkar's "Futurism of Young Asia" in the *International Journal of Ethics* for July 1918. See also the section on "Asians *vs.* Latins and Slavs" in the author's article on "Americanization from the viewpoint of Young Asia" in the *Journal of International Relations* (July 1919) for an examination of the alleged social and cultural distinction between the oriental and European laborers in regard to their assimilability to American conditions.

difference from, the oriental races. The shortcomings of Hindu politics are thus assumed by them to be "characteristic" of India.

But any body with the sense of historical perspective must have to admit that none of the alleged failings of Hindu culture, e. g. weakness of military organization, lack of patriotism, absence of national solidarity, and so forth, are the attributes exclusively of Indian, or for that matter, of Asian *Weltanschauung*. The "southern" and "sub-tropical" climate of India and the caste-system of Hindus cannot be rationally invoked to explain socio-political and socio-economic phenomena that are almost universal and world-wide in their range. Genuine "comparative history" is the only solvent of false explanations and unscientific hypotheses.

Hellenes, notwithstanding the temperate zone of their "isles of Greece", were not more remarkable for unity than were Hindus of the time of Alexander. Nor did their character display any enviable patriotism when put to the test of Macedonian gold[1] and arms. The crushing defeat inflicted on Seleukos and Menander by Chandra-gupta Maurya (B. C. 303) and Puşyamitra Sunga (B. C. 153) respectively was not less decisive a feat of Hindu *viriya* or *parâkrama* (i. e. energism) which served to keep European military power away from India than were the victories of the Greeks over Persians at Marathon and Salamis which saved Hellas from the "expansion of Asia". The failure of Hindu nationalities before hordes of Scythians, Tartars or Huns was no worse specimen of military incompetency, social disintegration, moral corruption and political instability than was the disruption of the Roman empire by the "barbarians".[2]

The processes by which during the seventh and eighth centuries Saracens[3] made themselves masters of Sicily, Southern Italy, Spain and southwestern France and converted the Mediterranean Sea into an Asian lake do not by any means prove that the organizing ability of Christians, although they had no caste restrictions, was appreciably superior to that of Gurjara-Pratîhâras who fell equally before other inroads of Islam. Nor did East-Europeans exhibit extraordinary physical vigor and martial qualities because of the physiography of Russian snows when in the thirteenth century they had to capitulate to the avalanche

---

[1] Bury's *History of Greece*, Vol. II, pp. 303, 305—306.

[2] Dill's *Roman Society of the Last Century of the Western Empire* pp. 303—345; Bury's *Later Roman*, Vol. I, pp. 25—36; Young's *East and West through Fifteen Centuries* (B. C. 44—1453), Vol. II, pp. 131—137.

[3] Scott's *History of the Moorish Empire in Europe*, Vol. II, pp. 35—37; Young, Vol. II, pp. 567—570; *Cambridge Mediaeval History*, Vol. II, pp. 379—385.

of Buddhist-Shamanist Mongols[1] of Central Asia inch by inch as far to the interior of Europe as the Carpathian Mountains. In the fifteenth and sixteenth centuries, again, Christians of the Balkans, Greece, Italy, and Spain persisted in their antagonistic relations[2] even in the face of Ottoman invasions. Certainly they did not appear to be more alive to the fact of the common danger, and failed not less ignominiously to present a united front against the peril from "Greater Asia" than did Hindus and Mohammedans in the eighteenth century while confronting the menace from the "expansion of Europe". What, then, are the counts on which the climatological or any other "monistic" interpretation of history seeks to base the alleged distinction between the West and the East?

In order to understand the strength and limitations of Hindu politics it is essential, moreover, to realize that the historic state-systems of Europe have neither been long-lived nor built up on "national" principles such as are defined by Ratzel in his *Politische Geographie.* The classical institutions were notoriously ephemeral, and in the Middle Ages dynastic revolutions were plentiful. This discontinuity of political life was not the special feature of the imperial area alone. It affected all the provinces of Europe in the north, south, east, west and centre.

Even if we take the individual peoples like Franks, Goths, Saxons, Danes, Swedes and others and confine our attention to small territories we find the same checquered career, the same multiplicity and poly-statal heterogeneity as on the Indian sub-continent. England, because of her insular position, as Frederick List explains it in his *Das Nationale System der politischen Ökonomie*, has managed to enjoy the longest period of continuity as a "nation-state". And yet the little land of Angles, Saxons and Jutes (excluding Wales and Scotland) had to pass through the *mâtsya-nyâya* of a heptarchy and the aliendom of Scandinavian and Norman aggressions. Chronologically the next nation-state to evolve in Europe is France. And yet here, even so late as on the eve of the Revolution, notwithstanding the previous centralizing efforts of *le grand monarque* there were about three hundred and sixty distinct bodies of law,[3] in force sometimes throughout a whole district, sometimes in a much smaller area. Besides, the peace of Westphalia (1648) and the congress of Vienna (1815)[4] are standing commentaries on the absence

[1] Howorth's *History of the Mongols*, Vol. I, pp. IX—XI, Vol. II (*The so-called Tartars of Russia*), pp. 25—183; Yule's *Book of Ser Marco Polo*, Vol. I, pp. XL—XLIII.

[2] Depping's *Histoire du commerce entre le Levant et l'Europe*, Vol. II, pp. 207—214, 222—224.

[3] *Cambridge Modern History*, Vol. VIII, p. 49.

[4] Phillimore's *Three Centuries*, pp. 13—61.

of nationality-states conceived as linguistic or cultural units. It is only by the Bolshevik dismemberment of Russia (1917—1918) according to the doctrine of self-determination that nationalism has been ensured in Eastern Europe. But in Central Europe, although the Congress of Versailles (1919) sat with the object of achieving it, the creation of half a dozen German "irredentas" in foreign states has but added to the list of the world's erstwhile Alsace-Lorraines.

The sole unifying factor in medieval European development was the magic name of Rome and the halo of the Roman empire. But, in practical politics, in spite of Bury's special pleading in his *Later Roman Empire*[1] to demonstrate the existence of a theoretical unity, the name of Rome led to anything but unity in western life. Such a Rome Hindustan also had in its Pâtaliputra. Built about B. C. 450 by Udaya of the Śiśunâga dynasty the city remained the seat *par excellence* of historic empires under Mauryas, Sungas, Guptas, and Pâlas. In India, too, it was ever the ambition of powerful Charlemagnes to attempt achieving the glory of the Vikramâdityan *sârva-bhaumas*. Further, during the period from the thirteenth to the eighteenth century Mohammedan Delhi occupied the place of the older Pâtaliputra and became a second Indian Rome, at once the crown of honor and bone of contention to all *vijigîṣus* or aspiring *Siegfrieds*, whether Hindu or Moslem.

Europe has continued to be what Dante described "slavish Italy" to be, the continent of warring nationalities and conflicting ambitions. The scheme of a unified Europe (really, western Europe) managed by a universal empire, of which the chief was to be both pope and caesar, was indeed elaborated by him in *De Monarchia*. He also prophesied very often in the *Inferno*, the *Purgatorio*, and the *Paradiso*, the advent of such a Caesar-Pope, poetically called the *Veltro* (the Greyhound), the Messiah or *Yugâvatâra*, the redeemer of Europe, who would restore the ancient glory of Rome. But this Ghibelline dream of Dante's, fused no doubt with the "Italian" nationalism of the Guelphs, remained a pious wish. Besides, the ostensible continuity of that "Austrian imposture", known in history as the Holy Roman Empire, until its overthrow by Napoleon should not mislead anybody as to the existence of centripetal forces in European polity, since it is too well known that it was neither holy, nor Roman, nor an empire as one should understand it. Such pious wishes and such legal fictions of empires have their "doubles" or replicas in the *nîti-śâstras* of the Hindus and in the Moghul-Maratha achievements of medieval India.

---

[1] Vol. II, p. 539; Vol. I (preface), Freeman's *Comparative Politics*, pp. 333—335.

Let us consider now the actual boundaries of states or territorial limits of nationality in the history of European polity without being biased by the principles of Curzon's *Frontiers* or Supan's *Politische Geographie.* In terms of population and area, ancient and medieval Hindu polities present specimens and types that can well stand comparison with the contemporary western units. The Athens (including all Attica) of Pericles had only twenty five thousand "free citizens" with three hundred thousand slaves. Men, women, and children of all classes were numbered at 400,000.[1] The population of France at the time of the Revolution was under twenty five millions. At the same time England and Wales had only eight millions and a half.[2] And today the average of first class powers is between forty-five and fifty millions. Besides, there exist a score of lesser sovereignties, including the new "self-determined" states born out of the Russian Leviathan through drastic Bolshevik surgery and those carved out of the old Germanistic empires, which have to maintain themselves virtually as buffer-states, at least as theatres of intrigue, for powerful neighbours.

Now, India is as large in size as Europe *minus* the Russia of the Czars. If, therefore, in ancient and mediæval India there were as many rival nationalities in the "state of nature" as in Europe, Indian history need not be condemned,[3] as it has been done *ad nauseam*, as a horrible record of anarchy, bloodshed and internecine civil war, or barbaric raids of military adventurers. Mankind may legitimately expect within Indian boundaries (accommodating, as they do, three hundred and fifty million people) as many first class powers of the Mazzinian or Leninian pattern, lower-grade nationalities and neutralized states, with their balance of power, *entente cordiale*, and what not, as one witnesses on a continent of the same area, or peopled by the same number of men and women.

If, roughly speaking, forty or fifty million people can be conceded to be the human basis of great powers in modern Eur-America, each enjoying eternal openings to prepare for "the next war", no student of political science or international relations should shudder in the name

[1] Dickinson's *Greek View of Life*, p. 73; Tucker's *Life in Ancient Athens*, 23, 62.

[2] Traill, Vol. VI, p. 84.

[3] Smith's *Early Hist.*, pp. 356—357. The same fallacy is to be noticed in Banerji, Vol. I, pp. 225—228, 307, 308, in Banerjea's *Public*, pp. 235—239, and even in the poet Yogindranath Basu, whose recent epics in Bengali, *Prithvi-râj* (1915) and *Shivaji* (1918), are intended to be history in verse. All of them have an extraordinary conception of the importance of political unity in national life. It is evidently forgotten that the *élan de la vie* of mankind is not unity so much as freedom (*sva-râj*), be it the freedom of five thousand or of five million.

of world-peace if the same phenomena come to happen in China or India. An impossibly high ideal of unity or the *ignis fatuus* of federation that Europe has failed and refused to consummate must not be forced on the peoples of the orient. There should not be one standard for the West and another standard for the East in the ethics of political development or nationalistic upheavals. Logically, therefore, the attempt of Young Asia to organize "unities" embracing sub-continents is as absurd an anachronism in the twentieth century, pervaded especially, as it happens to be, by the pluralistic and separatistic doctrine of self-determination or *sva-râj* for culture-zones, as was the Hildebrandine project of a west-European Christendom under one theocratic monarchy.

Be that as it may, comparative sociology must have to declare that the political annals of mediæval India do not offer greater insecurity and worse absence of peace than such as were exhibited by the Welsh, Irish and Scotch wars of England, the Hundred Years' War between France and England, the wars of the Hapsburgs, the wars of the innumerable German baronies, the wars of the Italian kingdoms and cities, the English civil war, the French wars of the Fronde, the meteoric acquisitions of Sweden's Gustavus Adolphus and of the Polish Kingdom, the expansion of Turkey to the gates of Vienna, the courting of Moslem alliance by Christian monarchs against brother-christians, the annexations of Peter and Frederick, and the steady decline and fall of the Holy Roman Empire. In regard, specifically, to the relations between Mohammedan states and original Hindu states or between Mohammedan empires and their Hindu citizens or between Hindu empires and Mohammedan citizens, Eur-American historians have yet to prove, item by item, that the picture was in any way darker than was the story of the contest between Roman Catholics and Protestants culminating in the horrors of the Thirty Years' War.

So far as the ancient period is concerned, the historian has to observe that the records of Hindu imperial power are not usually marked by the accession and disappearance of dozens of puppet emperors such as were chosen and slain by the army in Rome. No generation was without its *sârva-bhauma, chakravarti*, or *châturanta* i.e. "world-ruler", whose regime was signalized by peace and security for the people. This *pax sârva-bhaumica* was the result of a well-regulated administrative machinery, and was helped forward to no small extent by remarkably long reigns, two or three of which sometimes covered a whole century. In any case no Eur-American scientist can legitimately congratulate himself on the superiority of the trend of occidental history if only he remembers a mediæval statement cited in Engelbert's *De Ortu et Fine Romani Im-*

perii.[1] "The Roman Empire", ran the opinion, "was and is always troubled by wars and rebellions; hardly ever were the gates of the temple of Janus shut; the greater number of Roman emperors have died violent deaths; and the Roman Empire has been the cause rather of disorder than of peace."

This must not be summarily dismissed as only the view of a radical anti-imperial propagandist. For, the duration and geographical extent of peace given by "Romans" were not really of a remarkable order. From the oriental platform, besides, the claim may be advanced that not more than once did European history exhibit the formation of a "unitary" state (of an "inorganic" character, of course, to use Seeley's phrase) with the size and area of the Maurya Empire (third century B. C.). This was the Roman Empire at its height during the second and third centuries A. C.[2] Even the less extensive Gupta Empire of the fifth century, the Vardhana Empire of the seventh century, and the Chola Empire of the eleventh century were barely approached by the Franco-German Empire of Charlemagne, or by the haphazard European possessions of the Spanish Emperor Charles V or by the ephemeral conquests of Napoleon.[3]

While, therefore, for purposes of comparative politics it is necessary to conclude that *pax sârva-bhaumica* or *federation de l'empire* is at least as conspicuous an achievement[4] of Hindu statesmanship as *pax Romana* of occidental, it is on the other hand to be admitted on scientific grounds that the political unity of India is, historically speaking, as great a myth as is the political unity of Europe. India furnishes but another illustration of the universal sway of *mâtsya-nyâya*, the Hobbesian "state of nature", which can lead but to pluralism, whether anarchic or well-ordered. The East has reproduced the same *Naturprozess* of Gumplowicz's *Der Rassenkampf*[5] as has the West.

---

[1] Woolf's *Bartolus*, 286.

[2] *Atlas of Ancient and Classical Geography*, pp. 16—17. *Vide* infra, pp. 133, 135.

[3] Atlas to Freeman's *His. Geo*; *Early Hist.* (maps facing pp. 284, 340); *Ox. His.* pp. 211—212.

[4] See the summary of inscriptions in Mookerji's *Fundamental Unity of India*, pp. 116—127.

[5] Chapter IV.

PART I.

THE HINDU CONSTITUTION.

CHAPTER III.

Hindu Achievements in Organization.

Section 1.

Property and Woman in Private Law.

The bed-rock of modern legal institutions is twofold. First, the individual adult is treated as an entity quite independent of the family, the village, the gild or any other corporation. Secondly, the woman is juridically a *selb-ständig* i. e. self-sufficient unit enjoying rights different from, and independent of, those of the man, even of the husband.

In Europe, and especially in America it is the "industrial revolution" (with its concomitant mobility of labor and more or less freedom of economic competition) that is chiefly responsible for the daily advancing social and political equalization. And no doubt the impact of this new democracy has powerfully influenced the foundations of organized life in Asia also, from Tokyo to Cairo.

But it is interesting to observe that even under ancient and mediæval conditions the legal sense of Hindus was akin to and approached the "modern" conscience in both these postulates of civic existence. Thus, for instance, the emancipation of the individual from the head of the family was effected very early in Hindu law. It is embodied in the institution of inheritance and partition of property *per stirpes* (i. e. per stocks) as opposed to that *per capita* (i. e. per head).[1]

A has two sons, B and C. B dies after leaving two children, 1 and 2, and C dies after leaving four, a, b, c, and d. On the death of the grandfather, A, the Hindu law of succession to A's property will keep the stocks of the two sons (B and C) separate; and one half of the inheritance

---

[1] For the relations between Manu, Vijnânesvara and Jimûtavâhana on the question of individualism in property rights see Radhakamal Mukerjee's *Foundations of Indian Economics*, pp. 20—21; Maine's *Early History of Institutions*, Lect XI, p. 328.

will be divided between the two grandchildren (1 and 2), and the other half between the four grandchildren (a, b, c, and d). This is known as division *per stirpes;* the tendency of more developed and modern law on the subject is to prefer this mode of partition.

But in less developed and in archaic or primitive systems, although not invariably, if we accept Lowie's sociology of ancient institutions, the property is divided equally between all the six grandchildren, share and share alike. This mode, or partition *per capita*, will not consider the claims of the fathers (B and C) as of any importance at all, but place the entire jurisdiction or dominion within the grandfather's will or cognizance.

But the importance of the father as an individual is recognized as greater than that of the grandfather in the matter of partitioning the grandfather's property according to Jîmûta-vâhana's *Dâya-bhâga* school of law, prevalent in Bengal since the twelfth century, which, although professedly a digest of all ancient codes, attaches special prominence to Manu (A. C. 150). The same system is followed in Vijnâneśvara's *Mitâkṣarâ*, a commentary (eleventh century) on the *Institutes* of Yâjna-valkya, (A. C. 350), another old jurist, which has authority in every part of India including Bengal.[1] Individualism was thus held in high respect in the judicial psychology of the Hindus.

Secondly, in regard to the legal status of woman, both Jîmûta-vâhana and Vijnâneśvara declare *strîdhana*[2] or "woman's special property" incapable of alienation, on the basis of older authorities. In Hindu India the husband[3] has absolutely no right to whatever a woman may have "acquired by inheritance, purchase, partition, seizure or finding", — the five origins of property in Gautama's jurisprudence.[4] Besides, when the husband dies, sonless Hindu widows[5] have for ages been entitled to enjoy the husband's property for life. But the right does not extend to alienation except under specified conditions.

---

[1] G. C. Sarkar's *Hindu Law*, pp. 27—29; V. N. Mandlik's *Hindu Law* (Texts and translations of *Vyavahâra Mayûkha* and *Yâjnavalkya Smriti*); Colebrooke's *Two Treatises on the Hindu Law of Inheritance* (*Dâyabhâga* and *Mitâkṣarâ*); Jolly's *Hindu Law of Partition, Inheritance, and Adoption*, pp. 9—30; Jolly's *Recht und Sitte*, pp. 87—92; Mitra's *Law Relating to Hindu Widow*, pp. 61—69.

[2] *Yâj*, 145; *Dâya*, Ch IV, sec I, 1, 2; *Mit*, Ch II, sec XI, 2; *Manu*, IX, 194 ("sixfold" property of woman); Jolly's *Hindu Law*, pp. 226—261.

[3] *Yâj*, 147; *Mit*, Ch II, sec XI, 31, 32. See Mackenzie's *Studies in Roman Law*, pp. 92, 93 (*parapherna*).

[4] X, 115; For "seven modes" of acquiring property *vide Manu* X, 115; cf. also *Manu*, IX, 44; Jolly's *Recht*, pp. 90—92.

[5] *Dâya*, Ch XI, sec I, 2, 3; *Mit*, Ch II, sec I, 2, 3.

"Nowhere", then, as Gooroodas Banerjee[1] remarks, "were the proprietary rights of women recognized so early as in India; and in very few ancient systems of law have these rights been so largely conceded as in our own. In certain cases *** a woman's dominion over her *strīdhana* is absolute".

The Code Napoleon and the Continental laws based on it give the wife an absolute right to only a part of her property, the *parapherna.* But the rest has to be added to the common household as *dot.* This law of *dot,* which, again, is really a continuation of the law of *dos* in the *Institutes* of Justinian, is thus less developed than the Hindu law of *strīdhana.*

The Married Women's Property Act (1886) of England is, according to Boutmy in his *Essai d'une psychologie politique du peuple anglais au XIXᵉ siècle,* essentially distinct from the Napoleonic and continental codes in so far as it gives independence to women proprietors. But even this Act falls short of the Hindu. Because, as Maine[2] explains it, not only has the Hindu woman "singularly full power of dealing with the *strīdhana,* — not only is the husband debarred from intermeddling with it save in extreme distress, — but when the proprietress dies, there is a special order of succession[3] to her property, which is manifestly intended to give a preference, wherever it is possible, to female relations over males".

One need not read into all this a conscious anticipation in India of the theory adumbrated by Mill in his *Subjection of Women.* We are not confronting here the feminism of today, i. e. the economic independence and political enfranchisement of women such as are advocated by Bebel the German socialist in his classic on *Woman.* Rather, on the whole, the mind of the Hindu in regard to Private Law was, to all intents and purposes, not much distinct from that of the European.

But first, it should be realized, however, that so far as the *paterfamilias* of the patriarchal family is concerned, the spirit of Hindu jurisprudence was not more servile than that of the early Roman Twelve Tables (B. C. 452). Secondly, the ecclesiastical law of Europe provides that the first charge of a man's property is the purchase of "masses" for his soul. And here the Roman Catholic meets on a common platform

---

[1] *Hindu Law of Marriage and Stridhana,* p. 312; cf. Gibelin's *Etudes sur le Droit Civil des Hindous,* Vol. I, p. 111.

[2] *Early History,* Lect XI, p. 334. cf. Coomaraswamy's *Mediaeval Sinhalese Art,* p. 35 for the corresponding position of the Ceylonese woman. *Vide* Boutmy's *English People* pp. 215—216.

[3] *Mit,* Ch II, sec XI, 9, 12, 13; Ch I, sec III, 8, 9, 10. But the *Dâya* law (Ch IV, sec II) is different.

the Hindu with his doctrine of "spiritual benefit",[1] according to which property is generally held to be intended for the discharge of sacrificial duties (*pinda*) for the manes of the dead.

Culturally speaking, besides, the mentality of the Hindu woman will be found to be identical with that of the Latin (French and Italian) as described in Joseph-Barthélemy's *Le Vote des Femmes*. Nay, it will be not much different from the female *psyche* of the United States in the early nineteenth century as analyzed by Calhoun in his *Social History of the American Family*.

Section 2.

Institutional *Viriya* (Energism).

Now that during the epoch of the "white man's burthen" the Hindu has been deprived of the chances for displaying an aggressive secularism except, if at all, only as a "second fiddle" to the "natural master", there has grown up a general scepticism among Eur-American scholars even as to the capacity of Hindus for organized activity and institutional achievements.[2] This occidental suspicion about the Orient has absolutely no foundation in facts. The Hindu *viriya* (i. e. energy or genius) for organization and cooperative endeavor has exhibited itself as much in the political as in the non-political spheres of social life.

(a) *Samgha* ("group-person").

One Hindu institution at least is known to orientalists. This is the *samgha* or church of Buddhist Asia. Necessarily it is as old as Śâkya the Buddha (B. C. 623—543). It has really had a longer history, since in Pâṇiṇi[3] the philologist's time (B. C. 650) *samgha* was the "generic" term for any public body, incorporated association or corporation. Its social significance was equivalent to that of the Greek *polis* (lit. city)

---

[1] G. C. Sarkar, Ch IX, pp. 311—317. For the resemblances between Hindu, Greek, Roman and Germanic laws see Gibelin, Vol. I, pp. 52—55, 85, 114, 292, 302.

[2] Smith's *Early Hist.*, pp. 357, 477; *Akbar*, 385; *Ox. Hist.*, pp. XI, XII. Majumdar's *Corporate Life in Ancient India* is a reply to the sweeping statements of Smith, as Mookerji's *History of Indian Shipping* is to the conventional theory regarding the alleged "splendid isolation" of Hindu culture.

[3] III, 3, 42; V. 3, 112—114; Majumdar, p. 90; Mookerji's *Local*, 32, 33; Bhandarkar's *Anc. His. Ind.*, pp. 141—153. For the date of Pâṇiṇi see R. G. Bhandarkar's discussion in the *Bombay Gazetteer*, 1896, Vol. I, pt. II, p. 141, *The Pos. Back. Hind. Soc.*, Vol. I, p. 69, and Jayaswal's note in the *Ind. Ant.*, May, 1918. For *polis cf.* Gilbert Murray's *Rise of the Greek Epic*, pp. 31, 79, Schömann's *Antiquities of Greece*, 91, 92, 95, 96, 121, 122, and Dunning's *Political Theories*, Vol. I, 51, 55, 56.

as popularized by the political philosophers of Hellas. The different organized bodies of the seventh century B. C. were known as *samghas* of different species.

Thus there was the *pûga* characterized as *samgha* of a special denomination. It was a corporation of men I) belonging to different social groups (*nânâ-jâtîyâh*) and (II) practising diverse (no regular or fixed) professions (*aniyata-vrittayah*), but (III) distinguished from other *samghas* by having a preponderance of economic or secular interests (*artha-kâma-pradhânâh*). Such an association was either a rural commune or a *municipium*.

A second *samgha* of the day was the *vrâta*. It was similar to the *pûga* in having the first two "properties"; but its *differentium* was indicated by the concept of *utsedha-jîvinah*, i. e., the profession of blackmailing, brigandage or hooliganism as a regular means of livelihood. The European counterpart of the Hindu *vrâta* was the order of *Ritter* or "Knights" whose exploits have received a romantic treatment in Goethe's *Götz* and Schiller's *Räuber*. The modern Bengali novelist Bankim Chandra Chatterji's *Ânanda Matha* (The Abbey of Bliss) is likewise an idealization of a similar corporation.

The *âyûdha-jîvi samgha* was a third organized body of Pâṇiṇi's days. As the name implies, it was an association of men who "lived by the profession of arms". Men proficient in military tactics used evidently to incorporate themselves into bands, and were available most probably for mercenary service. This *samgha* was therefore distinct from the *vrâta*.

The world into which Śâkya was born was thus familiar with several incorporated associations.[1] It was only a commonplace floating term of the period that Buddhist *Vinaya* (discipline, organization, government) literature of the fourth century B..C. adopted as the name of an ecclesiastical polity.

But the secular significance of the term continued to prevail as current as ever. For, about the same time the school of politics associated with the name of Kautilya[2] described all corporate bodies by Pâṇiṇi's term. In the Kautilyan category there were at least two classes of *samgha*. One class consisted of those who "lived by the science of economics" (*vârtâ-śâstropa-jîvinah*) i. e., were engaged in farming, industry, commerce or banking. To the other class belonged those with whom the

[1] Fick's *Die Soziale Gliederung im nordöstlichen Indien zu Buddha's Zeit*, pp. 172—183 (chapter on *Die Gilden der Kaufleute und Handwerken*).

[2] *Artha-śâstra*, Bk XI, ch. I.

"epithet of *râjâ* or King was a source of social existence", i. e., who were rulers by profession. In Kautilya's days, therefore, the ordinary *śreṇî* or gild was as good a *samgha* as the republic or non-monarchical body of people among whom "every person is a *râjâ*".

Thus during the period that closed with Alexander's failure in India and Chandragupta Maurya's expulsion of Hellenistic Greeks from Afghanistan Hindus were used to at least six classes of public association, viz. the *pûga*, the *vrâta*, the *âyûdha-jîvi*, the *śreṇî*, the *râjâ*, and the *vihâra* (monastery or church). While the first four would have been usually known by their special names, the common term *samgha* would have denoted the republics of the Lichchhavikas, Vrijjikas and others as well as the ecclesiastical organization of Buddhist monks.

(b) *Samûha* ("group-person").

In the later literature of political institutions the term *samgha* seems to have dropped out of general use. The most "generic" term for *polis* with the authors of the *smriti-śâstras*, at any rate, is *samûha*. In the fourth century A. C. Yâjnavalkya[1] used it generically for any corporation. *Samûhas* were known to be divided into various classes differing from one an other according to the nature of objects for which the association was instituted or the kind of persons organizing themselves into a *polis*. One of these was the *śreṇî*, i. e. gild, a second was the *naigama* (also *nigama*) or body of traders (the "gild merchant"), and a third was the *pâṣaṇḍi*, or group of socio-religious heretics and dissenters, e. g., Buddhists, Jainas and other denominations; and *gaṇa* (town) was the fourth.

The use of *samûha* as a "genus" is to be noticed in Mitra Miśra's *Vîra-mitrodaya*,[2] a commentary on Yâjnavalkya. For according to him the *pûga* is a particular class of *samûha*. It was made up of those who "lived at the same place", but belonged to different social orders, the so-called castes, and followed different professions. It was thus a territorial concept, the term for a village or town, having the same connotation as in the grammar of Pâṇiṇi. In Vijnâneśvara,[3] also, another commentator of Yâjnavalkya, *samûha* is generic, for he defines *gaṇa* to be a division of *samûha* and considers *grâma* (village) and other settled areas as belonging to this species. The same use of *samûha* is to be seen in Kâtyâyana,[4] a jurist cited by Mitra Miśra.

The *milieu* that produced the *dharma* or *smriti śâstras* (law-books) was therefore one in which at least four or five institutions, the *śreṇî*,

---

[1] II, 192.

[2] [3] [4] Majumdar, 17, 58; Mookerji's *Local*, 31.

the *naigama*, the *pâşandi*, the *gaṇa* or the *pûga* were centres of public life.[1] The common name for all of these bodies was *samûha*.

(c) *Gaṇa* (*municipium* and republic).

But it would appear that people were using some of these terms interchangeably. The same institution was being described by different names, and the same name was being given to different institutions. We have just noticed that Vijnâneśvara uses *gaṇa* where Mitra Miśra employs *pûga* to denote the identical "group-person". Both commentators were right because their common authority Yâjnavalkya[2] himself was responsible for the confusion, as he had used *gaṇa* in the sense of a town-corporation. Nârada[3] (450 A. C.), another jurist who preceded these scholiasts had also done the same. Indeed the same confusion is to be noticed in all writings on *smriti* (tradition) and *dharma* (law).[4] Kâtyâyana similarly identifies *gaṇa*[5] with *pûga* when he defines it as a *samûha* of *kulas* or families.

During the early centuries of the Christian era, the term *gaṇa* appears to have been elevated one flight up in the series of "communities". From its status as the name of a *grâma* and *pura*, the *domus* and *civitas* of mediæval European jurisdictions, it came to imply also the *regnum* of a whole people, thus giving rise to another confusion in language. In the eulogies on military triumphs or other meritorious deeds inscribed by poets of the period we find the term being used to describe the association of "self-rulers", i. e., of "poly-archal" peoples organized on the principle of *sva-râj*. Republican nationalities of the Yaudheyas, Mâlavas and others are thus known as *gaṇas* in the coins[6] and inscriptions[7] of the Ândhra-Kuşân and Gupta times. The poets of the *Mahâbhârata*[8] also described the states in which all were "equal" by the same epithet.

Neither *samûha* nor *gaṇa*[9] seems ever to have acquired the comprehensive connotation of *samgha*. But the diversity of Gierke's "group-

[1] Jolly's *Recht*, p. 136.

[2] II, 8, 187—192, 361.

[3] Introduction, I, 7, X, 2.

[4] Manu III, 164, IV, 209; cf. also Śukra, IV, v, 59—62.

[5] *Viramitrodaya*, p. 426; Majumdar's interpretation (p. 94) of Kâtyâyana's passage is untenable; cf. Mookerji's *Local*, 30.

[6] Cunningham's *Coins of Ancient India*, pp. 76—79; Rapson's *Indian Coins*, p. 15; Banerji's *Prâchin Mudrâ* (Ancient Coins), Ch. VI.

[7] Fleet's *Gupta Inscriptions*, pp. 14, 152. *Ep. Ind.* 1905—06, pp. 44—47.

[8] *Śânti*, Ch. CVII, 31—32.

[9] Note the use of *gaṇa* in Jaina literature. cf. Jacobi's *Jaina Sutras*, 113, 273, 286, 306.

persons" in Hindu public life through the ages is self-evident. The attempt on the part of grammarians, logicians, political theorists and lawyers to analyze the concept of a public body and differentiate its various species is also significant. The story of Hindu public life has therefore partially to be sought in the development of *samghas, samûhas* and *gaṇas,*[1] the different categories of what may be called the Asian *polis.*

Section 3.

Organized Charities and Utilities.

As specimens of Hindu energism in group-activity let us begin with organization in social service or welfare work. In Europe the hospital was unknown until Emperor Constantine (306—337) founded it for the first time in the fourth century A. C. But in India the first hospitals both for animals and human beings were founded at least as early as the third century B. C. by Asoka the Great.[2] And about 400 A. C. among the institutions that drew the notice of Fa Hien,[3] the Chinese scholar-saint, at Pâtali-putra, the capital of the Gupta Empire, we are told of the free hospitals "founded by the respectable nobles and landowners of the country". These were resorted to by "the poor of all countries, the destitute, cripples and the diseased", and every kind of requisite help was offered gratuitously.

Similarly Hindu public life can count in its manifold experience the founding and maintenance of *pariṣats* (academies) for the prosecution of research in the arts and sciences, as well as of educational institutions of ambitious scope and encyclopaedic character. It was in the hands of scholars who graduated from such centres of learning that the administration of government was entrusted.[4] One such institution was the University at Nâlandâ in Eastern India (Bihar), founded by Emperor Narasimha-gupta Bâlâditya (*c* 469—473). Itsing, the Chinese scholar, was an alumus of this university for ten years (675—685) in the departments of medicine and logic. The number of residents at Nâlandâ exceeded 3000, was between 3500 and 5000, at that time. The lands possessed by the University comprised more than 200 villages, the gifts

---

[1] A brochure given over to the analysis of these and other new terms in indology from the constitutional and economic viewpoints is a desideratum for comparative politics.

[2] Rock Edict II.

[3] Beal's *Travels of Fa Hien and Sung Yung,* p. 107. For the political "immunities" of a village belonging to a hospital in Ceylon *vide* p. 75.

[4] Takakusu's *Itsing: Record of the Buddhist Religion,* Ch. XXXIV, p. 177.

of kings for several generations.[1] Itsing mentions eight halls and three hundred apartments among the buildings of the institution.[2]

The Nâlandâ corporation was a residential-teaching university like the *El Azhar* at Cairo and gave instruction, room, board, and medicine free of any cost whatsoever. Hiuen Thsang was very much impressed by its architectural magnificence. "The richly adorned towers", as we read in his Chinese biography, "and the fairy-like turrets, like pointed hill-tops are congregated together. The observatories seem to be lost in the vapors of the morning and the upper rooms tower above the clouds".[3] This was the institution that inspired in subsequent years the monastery-college at Horiyuji near Nara in Japan. And it is on record that the Afghan scholar Vîra-deva was elected Chancellor here in the ninth century then enjoying the patronage of Deva-pâla,[4] the Bengali *sârva-bhauma* of Eastern India. It is obvious that for several centuries after their establishment the Universities of Bologna, Paris and Oxford[5] would certainly have envied the material endowments and international reputation enjoyed by the presidents and faculties of Nâlandâ for about seven hundred years (*c* 500—1200). The long story of this university bears undoubted testimony to the continuous and cumulative organizing ability of the race in which it flourished.

A very interesting *sâhitya pariṣat* (literary academy) of southern India was the *Sangam* of the Tamils[6] at Madura. Early in the Christian era in this Pandyan city a body of censors formed themselves into an institution to correct the abuses of literature. The third of these *Sangams* was in existence in the second century. Forty nine critics and poets were members of this association, which thus anticipated by about fifteen hundred years the French Academy founded by Richelieu (1637) in its aim at checking the growth of literary weeds. The *Sangam* enjoyed the patronage of the state for several generations. Its influence on the people may be gathered from the fact that the celebrated Tamil classic, the *Kural* of Tiru-valluvar, received the imprimatur of the academy before king Ugra-Peruvalludhi. It is interesting to note that the author himself was not a member of the association. Similarly the two other masterpieces of the Augustan age of Tamil literature, viz., the *Epic of the Anklet*

---

[1] *Ibid*, Ch. X, p. 65.

[2] *Ibid*, Ch. XXXII, 154.

[3] Beal's *Life of Hiuen Thsiang*, pp. 110—112.

[4] *Ind. Ant.*, 1888, pp. 308—309, 311.

[5] Leach's *Educational Charters and Documents* (A. C. 598—1909), pp. xxii—xxvii, 276.

[6] Aiyangar's *Anc. Ind.*, pp. 70, 337, 359, 360, 379—382.

and the *Jewel-Bell*, were submitted to the examination of this body of connoisseurs.

Pariṣads or academies, whether stationary or peripatetic, have indeed existed in India since time immemorial. Medicine, grammar, logic, chemistry, mathematics, political science, jurisprudence, almost every branch of learning has grown up in India through the clubbing of intellects. Cooperative researches have been the tradition of intellectual life among Hindus. As a result of these corporate investigations we know today only of "schools" or "systems" of thought, very rarely of the individuals who built them up through the ages. Most of the names in the annals of science and philosophy in India are those of masters or pioneers, and these again, are but pseudonyms associated with the patronymic saints or gods, the Prometheuses and Apollos of Hindu culture.

It is this collective or *pariṣadic* origin that explains why the treatises on arts and sciences in Sanskrit literature have in general the title of *Samhitâ* i. e., compilation. Mostly encyclopaedic works, as these are, they bear internal evidence of the collaboration and cumulative experience of many minds.

Individualistic ideals and ends are as a rule associated with moral, religious, and spiritual affairs in India. Yet even in this field the capacity for cooperation has been equally evident as in other spheres. Every twelve years Hindus have had a Council of Trent, so to speak, since the earliest times. These congresses of spiritual leaders, the *sanyâsins*, monks and hermits, are called *Kumbha-Melâ* after the planetary conjunction (of Kumbha) which recurs periodically. The present-day survivals of these institutions are tremendous vitalizing forces; their delegates number about 75,000, and the audience millions.

Some of the inscriptions of the ancient Gujaratis throw an interesting sidelight on the Hindu legal sense and institutionalism. India's appreciation of corporate energism will be evident from the measures that General Uṣavadâta adopted to perpetuate the benefits from his charities.[1] This great philanthropist of the Ândhra Deccan had the terms of his endowments registered by the *nigama-sabhâ* (town-corporation) of Govardhana (Nasik). And these were then inscribed on the door of the monastery. Gifts for public purposes used thus to be looked after by public bodies.

---

[1] *Early Hist. Dek.*, sec. IV.

Section 4.

The Politics of Ecclesiastical Bodies (*Samghas*).

As embodiments of Hindu institutional life we have to mention also the *vihâras* or monasteries of ancient and mediæval India. These were *samûhas* i. e., public bodies and were bound by definite rules and regulations as to election; quorum, voting, and business procedure. Students of European polity are aware that on various occasions in the West the church and the state have borrowed from each other the methods of internal administration. It would appear that in the Orient also common principles of organization have been followed by religious associations and secular institutions alike. The ecclesiastical bodies of Buddhist Asia should have thus to be treated as quasi-political corporations, even independently of the fact that in certain regions, e. g. in Tibet and Mongolia, as in Catholic Europe the spiritual head has claimed also temporal dominion over his flock.

The origins of all this institutionalism are of course to be sought in the publicity work and propaganda methods of Śâkya the Buddha himself (B. C. 623—543). Śâkya's father and brother were *râjâs* or archons i. e. presidents of the Sakiya Republic in Eastern India. It was natural, therefore, that when he fled the world and founded a *Samgha* (Order) of monks, the only constitution that he could conceive for it was that with which he had been familiar at home and in his own state. And as a matter of course he made no distinction between his own ecclesiastical order, the *Samgha*, and the contemporary republican Confederacy of the Vajjian States, when called upon to enunciate the "seven conditions of the welfare for a community".

Of these seven conditions three may be regarded as directly constitutional or political. "So long, O medicants", said Śâkya, "as the brethren meet together in full and frequent assemblies, — so long as they meet together in concord and rise in concord, and carry out in concord the duties of the Order, *** so long as the brethren honor and esteem and revere and support the elders of experience and long standing, and hold it a point of duty to hearken to their words, — so long may the brethren be expected not to decline but to prosper."[1]

In this Śâkyan constitution, defining, as it did, the type as much of an ecclesiastical society as of a secular state, e. g. a clan-republic, there are emphasized, as we see, the importance of the assembly, the

---

[1] *Mahâ-parinibbâna-sutta*, Ch. I, 6, in Rhys Davids' *Buddhist Suttas*, Vol. II, pp. 6—7. The subject was discussed for the first time by Jayaswal in the *Mod. Rev.* 1913.

need of unity, and the authority of age and experience. This last feature is such as was embodied in the primitive Indo-Aryan, Teutonic and Hellenic polities or is in evidence today in the Japanese *Genro* ("elder statesmen"). These and other principles of Śâkya's politics have all been codified in the *Chulla-vagga* and the *Mahâ-vagga*, both of which treatises may be regarded as statute-books laying down the fundamental laws and constitutions (*Vinaya*) of Asian ecclesiastical bodies.

The following is a typical picture of the method of deliberations generally observed in the Buddhist monasteries and conferences of ancient India: "Then the venerable Mahâ Kassapa laid the resolution before the *Samgha*: 'Let the venerable *Samgha* hear me. If the time seems meet to the *Samgha*, let the *Samgha* appoint that these five hundred *bhikkhus* (monks) take up their residence during the rainy season at Râjagaha. ** This is the resolution. Let the *Samgha* hear. The *Samgha* appoints accordingly. Whosoever of the venerable ones approves thereof, let him keep silence. Whosoever approves not thereof, let him speak. The *Samgha* has appointed accordingly. Therefore is it silent. Thus do I understand.'"[1]

An important feature of these monastic institutions was that no business was held valid without quorum. "If an official act, O *bhikkhus*," as we read Śâkya saying in the *Mahâvagga*,[2] "is performed unlawfully by an incomplete congregation, it is no real act and ought not be performed." Along with this caution against incomplete congregations went the injunction against "unlawful acts." In the following extract the *Mahâ-vagga*[3] mentions some of those acts that have to be ruled out as unconstitutional: "They performed unlawful acts before an incomplete congregation; they performed unlawful acts before a complete congregation; they performed seemingly lawful acts before an incomplete congregation; they performed seemingly lawful acts before a complete congregation; a single *bhikkhu* pronounced expulsion against a single one; a single *bhikkhu* pronounced expulsion against two; a single *bhikkhu* pronounced expulsion against a number of *bhikkhus;* a single *bhikkhu* pronounced expulsion against a *Samgha*". As no unlawful acts were to be permitted within the church or among the church members, Śâkya definitely laid down the rule: "Therefore, O *bhikkhus*, you ought to train yourself thus: Lawful acts which are performed by complete congregations—such acts we will perform."[4]

---

[1] *Chulla-vagga*, XI, i, 4.
[2] IX, iii, 2.
[3] IX, ii, 1.
[4] *Mahâ-vagga*, IX, ii, 4.

A breach of this ruling appears to have been committed by the monks at Vesali in 443 B. C., about a century after the death of Śâkya. They ordained, for instance, that it is permitted to a *Samgha* which is not sufficiently numerous to accomplish an ecclesiastical act by saying 'we will make the other *bhikkhus* consent when they come.' This ruling called *anumati-kappa* was challenged as illegal by the *bhikkhus* of other centres, and the case was submitted to a jury for trial. The jury decided against it.[1]

In order to ascertain the opinions of the members in regard to the topics discussed the ecclesiastical organizations made use of coloured *salâkâs* (or pins) of wood. These were the voting tickets. A *salâkâ-gâhaka* ("taker" or collector of pins) or teller was appointed by the association to explain the significance of the colours to the voters and then take the votes. In the *Chulla-vagga*[2] we find Śâkya describing the ballot and other kinds of voting. "I enjoin upon you, *bhikkhus*", says he, "three ways of taking votes, ** the secret method, the whispering method, and the open method." The secret method of taking votes is then described. "The *bhikkhu* who is the teller of the votes is to take the voting tickets of different colors and as each *bhikkhu* comes up to him he is to say to him thus, 'This is the ticket for the man of such an opinion, this the ticket for the man of such an opinion. Take which ever you like'. When he has chosen (he is to add), 'Do not show it to anybody." The *Chulla-vagga* enumerates also ten cases of "invalid" voting.[3]

As conflict of opinions is inevitable in democratic deliberations, the rule of the majority was accepted by the *Samgha* as the regular procedure. "By that *bhikkhu*, the taker of the voting tickets", we read in the *Chulla-vagga*,[4] "are the votes to be collected. And according as the larger number of the *bhikkhus* shall speak, so shall the case be decided".

All this points to the highly developed institutional sense and corporate consciousness among Hindus. And these principles of *samûha* (or public associations and corporations) were not the patents of Buddhist, Jaina or any other religious bodies but were held in solution in the general socio-economic and civic life of ancient and mediæval India. These quasi-political institutions were only drawing upon and

---

[1] Poussin's "Buddhist Councils" in the *Ind. Ant.*, 1908, p. 89.

[2] IV, xiv, 26.

[3] IV, x.

[4] IV, xiv, 24. *Re* the principle of majority *vide infra*, p. 82.

contributing to the same stream of national experience as did the economic *śreṇis* (gilds) and the political *gaṇas* (republics) or constitutional *sabhās* and *samitis* (assemblies).[1]

Section 5.

Śréṇis (Gilds) of Peasants, Artisans and Merchants.

It is well known that the "chartered liberties" enjoyed by the mediæval towns, e. g., those of the Hanseatic League, have been great formative forces in the evolution of modern states in Europe. An analysis of the municipal privileges, the *liber burgus* as they were called, brings us invariably down to the basic economic factors, viz. the gild merchant and the craft organization. Probably these units were not identical with the boroughs. Nor do they seem to have exclusively represented the vital principle of borough life. But there are no grounds for doubting that these industrial and commercial nuclei were some of the chief "characteristic elements of the municipal constitution".[2] It was these economic fraternities that had the lion's share in the government of the greatest cities like London, Paris, Cologne, Ghent and Florence.[3]

The Orient was not poor in such economic centres of civic vitality in ancient and mediæval times. Students of commercial history are generally familiar with Chinese gilds.[4] But it is not so well known that in India as in China almost every economic function from agriculture to money-lending and banking was organized into a gild.

1. *Archaeological Data.*

Epigraphic evidences in regard to the gild of peasants are practically *nil* for the time being. Cultivators' unions have only to be inferred from the general laws on the subject of "companies". Gautama[5] (*c* 550 B. C.),

[1] For analogies and interactions between civil and religious societies in the West see Guizot's *History of Civilization in Europe*, Lectures V, VI, XII. *Vide* Möller's *History of the Christian Church*, pp. 235—242, 328, 337.

[2] Gross' *Gild Merchant*, Vol. I, pp. 92, 105; Article on "Gilds" in Palgrave's *Dictionary of Political Economy*, Sidgwick's *Development of European Polity*, 238, 251.

[3] Unwin's *Gilds and Companies of London*, p. 61.

[4] Macgowan's article on "Chinese Guilds, or Chambers of Commerce and Trades Unions" in the *Journal of the North China Branch of the Royal Asiatic Society*, 1886, New Series, Vol. XXI, pp. 133—192.

[5] XI, 21.

Manu[1] (*c* 150 A. C.), Brihaspati[2] (*c* 650), Śukra,[3] all writers mention the association of agriculturists in their schedule of *śreṇis*. The association of shepherds, however, is not unknown in the inscriptions. In the eleventh century, under Râjendra Chola, the shepherds of a village in Southern India agreed to become security for one Eran Sattan, a fellow-shepherd "who had received 90 ewes of this temple in order to supply *ghī* (clarified butter) for burning one perpetual lamp". If he died, absconded, or got into prison, fetters, or chains, the fraternity bound themselves to discharge his duties.[4] The responsibility was thus considered to be a joint one by the members.

In regard to the gild merchant more inscriptions may be drawn upon. In Madras of the twelfth century under Vikrama Chola (1118), the hero of an historical Tamil poem, there was a traders' gild[5] with a membership of 500. Its activities and interests were coextensive with the South Indian Empire. In Gupta India during the fourth and fifth centuries bankers (*śreṣṭhins*), traders (*sârtthavâhas*) and merchants (*kulikas*) used to close their business correspondence with clay seals. The *nigama* or corporation of these commercial interests, with headquarters probably at Pâtali-putra, was "something like a modern chamber of commerce".[6] Such bodies working, as they did, in concert (*sambhûya*) were notorious in the fourth century B. C. owing to their attempts to "corner" the market. The problem of "profiteering" had to be tackled by the Maurya Empire especially because the union of merchants tried to raise prices so high as to yield a cent per cent profit.[7]

The gild merchant must have been in existence in the sixth century B. C. as Gautama's *Dharma-Sûtra* mentions it as one of the law-"making" or law-"declaring" bodies.[8] Still earlier, as the *Valahassa*, *Chullaka setthi*, *Supparaka* and other *Jâtakas*[9] or Buddhist "Birth Stories" narrate, maritime and land commerce used to be undertaken on the joint stock principle by companies of "five hundred trading folk", "seven hundred

[1] VIII, 40.

[2] I, Constitution of a Court of Justice, 26.

[3] IV, v, lines 35—36.

[4] Hultzsch's *South Indian Inscriptions*, Vol. II, Pt. III, cited in Coomaraswamy's *Indian Craftsman*, p. 17.

[5] *Government Epigraphist's Report*, 1916, p. 121, cited in Majumdar p. 35.

[6] *Ann. Rep. of the Arch. Sur.*, 1903—04, p. 104.

[7] *Artha*, p. 403.

[8] *loc. cit.*

[9] Majumdar, pp. 32—33; Mookerji's *Local*, pp. 45—47, 76, 77.

merchants", etc. India's experience in commercial unions is therefore at least as old as China's.[1]

The story of Hindu craft gilds may be told with more details and greater confidence. Unions of industrial experts or workingmen's gilds were conspicuous institutions of the Gupta Empire. In 465, under Skandagupta, a gild of oil-men[2] at the city of Indra-pura presided over by Jîvanta was entrusted with an endowment out of the interest of which a temple lamp was to be maintained. The terms of the deed stipulated that the removal of the corporation from its present head-quarters would not invalidate its jurisdiction over the property. Nullification of the trust might ensue only from the dissolution of the gild (or secession of some of its members). In Kumâra-gupta's time (413—455) a gild of silk weavers[3] was formed at the city of Daśa-pura. They had migrated from Central Gujarat, but part of their comrades took up other pursuits, e. g. archery and fighting, astronomical studies, and asceticism, at their new place of domicile. Incidentally it appears that the change of hereditary or caste occupations was not rare in Gupta India.

Among Gujaratis of the early Christian era under Ândhra Emperors, there were gilds of weavers, druggists (*gândhikas*), corn-dealers (*dhânyaka-śreṇis*), and oil-manufacturers.[4] Like the gilds of the Gupta Empire the Ândhra gilds also discharged the functions of banks. Moneys and real estates were received by them in perpetuity as a deposit or trust fund.[5] For the use of this property they paid to the beneficiary named in the grants interest varying from 9 to 12 per cent. In 120 A. C. two gilds of weavers[6] at Govardhana (Nasik) were entrusted by General Uṣavadâta with 2,000 and 1,000 kârṣâpaṇas. In the third century several other gilds of the same city,[7] viz. those of potters, *odayântrikas* (workers fabricating hydraulic engines or water-clocks), and oil-millers, became trustees of a permanent endowment to provide medicines for the monks of a *Samgha*. The planting of wayside trees was one of the

---

[1] Werner's *Chinese Sociology*, Table II; see the Vedic references to gilds in Mookerji's *Local*, p. 41—43.

[2] *Gup. Insc.*, p. 71; for the Gwalior gilds of the tenth Century *vide* p. 63.

[3] *Ibid*, p. 80.

[4] R. G. Bhandarkar's *Early Hist.*, secs. IV and VII.

[5] "Nasik Inscriptions" in the *Arch. Sur.*, Vol. IV, p. 102 (cited in Hopkins' *India Old and New*, p. 175).

[6] *Ep. Ind.*, 1905—06, pp. 82, 83.

[7] *Ibid*, p. 88.

objects for which a gild was similarly endowed with the income of two fields.[1]

Like the gild merchant the craft gild also must have been prominent in Maurya times. Kautilya's scheme of fleecing the "gold-lords" for the public treasury has reference most probably to the gild of goldsmiths.[2] His *Artha-śâstra* suggests, besides, that certain wards of the city should be set apart for the corporations of artisans.[3] And one of the functions of the Imperial superintendent of accounts was to record all about the customs, professions and transactions of the associations, whether of traders or workmen, rural or urban.[4]

Kautilya's idea about the establishment of gilds in the different wards of a city was but a reflex of the actual civic life of his own and previous times. For in the *Sîlavanaga* and other *Jâtakas*[5] streets (*vîthis*) are sometimes named from a particular class of artisans living in them. Even an entire village of 1,000 families was often monopolized by a single industry, e. g. smithery or timber-work.

Gilds were then prominent institutions among Hindus as early as the sixth and seventh centuries B. C.; and epigraphy traces them down to the Chola Empire. The Buddhist story books open up to us an economic India in which the various orders of manual and skilled workers were organized on the corporate basis. There were gilds of sailors, muslin-weavers, leather-workers, painters, goldsmiths, workers in war-implements, stone-carvers, and so forth.[6] In addition to the conventional "eighteen gilds" there must be mentioned also the unions or companies of traders and commercial men. For all subsequent periods since then, therefore, the law books could not but devote special attention to the gilds as economic institutions of the land. Gautama's *Dharma-sûtra*[7] was composed or compiled in the *milieu* of gilds of peasants, herdsmen, traders, moneylenders, and artisans. Gilds held a high place in the Kautilyan theory of finance as important sources of public income.[8] Authors of the third century A. C. e. g. those responsible for the com-

---

[1] See details of the five inscriptions in Majumdar, pp. 8—10. *Vide* the south Indian inscriptions in Mookerji's *Local*, pp. 89—99.

[2] p. 305. A "house of the gild" belonging to the Maurya period is described by Marshall in his article on "Excavations at Bhita" in the *Arch. Sur. Ann. Rep.* 1911—12, pp. 30, 31.

[3] p. 61.

[4] p. 69.

[5] Fick's *Soziale Gliederung*, 179—181; Mookerji's *Local*, 74.

[6] Majumdar, 4; cf. also *Râmâyaṇa Ayodhyâ-kânda*, Ch. XIX.

[7] *Loc. cit.*

[8] p. 66.

pilation of Viṣṇu's law-book[1] were living in an age when the gilds of metal workers, especially goldsmiths and silversmiths, were well in evidence in social life. Not only Manu[2] (*c* 150) and Yâjnavalkya[3] (*c* 350) but all jurists down to Nârada[4] (*c* 500) and Brihaspati[5] (*c* 650) had consequently to reckon gilds among the subjects of "private law". These public bodies were expressly mentioned in connection with crimes and punishments to which all individuals were liable according to the laws of the state. The violation (*vyatikrama*) of *sambids* (gild compacts or agreements) was accordingly important enough to demand special treatment along with the general law of contract.

2. *Samûhas as "Group-Persons"*.

But not all unions, companies or associations are "corporations". How far, therefore, it may be asked, were these *śreṇîs* (often identified with *gaṇas* and *pûgas*) of the Indian socio-economic system real gilds? To what extent did these *samûha* organizations come to be conceived and recognized by Hindus themselves as "artificial civic bodies", i. e. "aggregate individuals" with "natural corporate existence"? The book of Brihaspati (Ch. XVII) furnishes an answer to these queries. The juridical concept of a corporate person or one-in-the-many as pertaining to *śreṇîs* is quite manifest in the particulars he lays down regarding the constitution and rights and duties of *samûhas*. The older Yâjna-valkya and his mediæval commentators also leave no doubt on the point.

Gilds were governed by boards of two, three, or five persons.[6] They conducted their business in a *sabhâ*, i. e. soviet or public assembly. As corporate bodies they could make *samaya*[7] or compact with private individuals as well as among themselves, and the state had to see to it that gild compacts were enforced like all other compacts in the land.

The "power of attorney" could be conferred by them on some of their members, and these agents represented the associations in law courts or other public offices. Accordingly the funds donated by the government to a single member had to be deposited with the joint stock

---

[1] Hopkins' *India*, p. 170.

[2] VIII, 5, 219.

[3] II, 15, 187, 192.

[4] X, 5; *Vide* Gibelin's *Etudes sur le droit civil des Hindous*, Vol. I, pp. 299—310 (*Des Sociétés*).

[5] XVII, 19. Some of the gilds of Ceylon in later times are described in Coomaraswamy's *Mediaeval*, pp. 55—56.

[6] Brihaspati, XVII, 10.

[7] Nârada, X, 1—2; Brihaspati, VIII, 9; XVII, 5.

of the *samûha.*[1] In Yâjnavalkya's code anything acquired by a member of the gild while on gild business was to become common property. Eleven times the value of the acquisition was the penalty for wilful violation of this ruling.[2] According to Brihaspati any member who injured the joint stock might be punished with deportation.[3]

The agreement entered into by a gild was binding on each and all of the members. Anybody failing to perform the duties implied thereby was liable to be banished and have his property confiscated.[4] All expenditures were treated as common charges.[5] Responsibility for loans contracted by a member on behalf of the association was also common. Lastly, *śreṇis* had the "right of joint action" in relation to the state, as we have noticed in the agreement of the south Indian shepherds,[6] one of the privileges for which the European craft used to fight.

According to Kâtyâyana, an authority later than Brihaspati, cited in Mitra Miśra's *Vîra-mitrodaya*[7] and Chandeśvara's *Vivâda-ratnâkara,*[8] two commentaries on Yâjnavalkya and on other jurists new members were entitled to share equally with the old the properties of the established gild. Debts of the *samûha* were likewise to be shared by them as a matter of course. Nay, the spiritual merit, as says Mitra Miśra, accruing from charities and religious services that the gild may have undertaken in the past was believed to be beneficial to persons who were elected to membership long after the deeds had been performed. The usual mode of cooption was *sarva-sammati* i. e. unanimous approval.

Nothing illustrates better the "legal fiction" of corporations as "immortal persons" than these latter-day ideas in regard to *gaṇa, śreṇi,* and *varga.* It is clear, therefore, that Hindu *samûhas,* whether of capitalists, working men or peasants, and trade unions or commercial fraternities had the distinctive characteristics of a homogeneous "community" with common rights and common obligations, — the "real group-persons" of Gierke and Figgis.[9]

---

[1] Brihaspati, XVII, 22, 24.

[2] II, 180.

[3] XVII, 15.

[4] *Ibid*, XVII, 13.

[5] *Ibid*, XVII, 24.

[6] *Supra*, p. 41.

[7] p. 432. For schools of Hindu Law see G. C. Sarkar, pp. 28—29, Jolly's *Recht*, 31—41, and Mitra, 61—69.

[8] p. 188 (chapter on *Sambid-vyatikrama*).

[9] cf. Barker's article on the "Discredited State" in the *Political Quarterly*, Feb. 1915, p. 111. The importance of this question has not been grasped by previous authors although some of them have cited the relevant passages in other contexts.

3. *The Politics of Economic Associations.*

We shall now analyze the constitutional, political or civic immunities and liberties enjoyed by the gilds of ancient and mediæval India. This will throw light on the amount of decentralization achieved in Hindu polity. No governmental documents are available however. The only authorities are literary.

In the first place, *śreṇis* were monopolistic organizations anxious to maintain in tact their economic autonomy. We learn from Nârada that the gilds were indeed open to more than one socio-religious group or caste.[1] But generally speaking, their regulations were as exclusive in spirit as the ordinances, say, of the English hatters' craft in the fourteenth century.[2] They sought to regulate the number of apprentices and also the hours of labor.[3] On festive occasions, in street processions, and at social gatherings each *śreṇi* was represented by its own banners and buntings bearing on them the implements and emblems of the respective crafts.

In the second place, the *jetthaka* (alderman) and *setthi*, i. e., the heads of corporations were treated by kings as representatives of the people functionally divided as artisans, merchants and peasants. In pre-Maurya times, i. e. previous to the third quarter of the fourth century B. C., it was through their gilds that the people were summoned by the king on important occasions.[4] *Śreṇis* appear thus to have played an important part in the public finance. The taxes to be paid by traders and other inhabitants of the town were agreed upon by the ruler "in consultation with the heads of the gilds".[5]

Necessarily, therefore, in the third place, *mukhyas* i. e. heads, presidents or representatives of the corporations constituted, like councillors of the king, an important "estate" of the realm. At the coronation of kings, e. g. in the *Râmâyaṇa*, gilds had the right to the sprinkling or anointing ritual. Sometimes gild members occupied high state offices, as we know from the *Jâtakas*.[6] Socially, on the whole, they were "peers" of the king. As poets of the *Mahâbhârata*[7] have declared the royal ideal of manliness, kings were ashamed to return to their homeland if they were

---

[1] Hopkins' *India*, p. 174; Mookerji's *Local*, pp. 58, 61, 62.

[2] Unwin, p. 80; Palgrave's *Dictionary* ("Craft gilds").

[3] Birdwood's *Industrial Arts of India*, pp. 137—140; Hopkins' *India*, pp. 171—174, 193—196. See Nârada's rules of apprenticeship in Mookerji's *Local*, 51, 52.

[4] Rhys Davids' *Buddhist India*, p. 97.

[5] Hopkins' *India*, p. 176.

[6] Fick, p. 177.

[7] *Vana-parva*, Ch. 248, 16.

defeated in battles. For, "what would the elders of the gilds say to me", argued the kings, "and what should I speak to them in reply?" The moral control exercised by gilds on state policies may be presumed to have been of a high order. Undisputed, therefore, was their influence on public opinion.

In the fourth place, leaving aside the fact that men following the soldier's profession were often organized on the gild principle (*śreṇī-vala* or gild corps[1] e. g. the Kṣatriya gilds of Gujarat described by Kautilya) the ordinary industrial and commercial *śreṇīs* had great military importance as well. The chief reason of course was their power over the purse or the sinews of war.

Political theorists, therefore, considered it a part of the statecraft to pacify the gilds of one's own state and try to win over the elders of the enemy's gilds. The methods suggested in the *Mahâbhârata*[2] are the well known ways and means of *Realpolitik*, such as were appreciated by Philip of Macedon, Machiavelli the Italian, Walpole the Englishman, and Guizot the Frenchman. These are the corrupt practices of bribery and the sowing of dissensions among the members of corporations. Or perhaps in the language of Bolshevik economics these should partially be described as the traditional tactics of capitalism which is said to be "international" enough to seek allies even among enemy bankers.

4. *Functional Sovereignty.*

Now, *śreṇīs* had their own judicial tribunals. The craftsmen had thus the privilege of being tried by the jury of their own peers. In the matter of legal decisions, if we may take Brihaspati[3] as a narrator of actual facts, even court practice had to yield to the opinion of gilds. Corporations were "invested with the power to decide law suits",[4] and their meetings were declared to be "resorts for the passing of a sentence".[5] As such, gild courts may have had jurisdiction over cases affecting the community at large and not solely over their own disputes. But it is to be observed that the judicial system of the Maurya Empire for which alone we have some reliable evidence does not have a place for gilds as public tribunals.

Of equal importance was the legislative or law-making power of *śreṇīs*. The gilds "made" or "declared" their own laws and had their

[1] *Artha*, pp. 415, 455.
[2] *Śânti-parva*, Ch. CXLI, 64.
[3] II, 26.
[4] Nârada, I, Legal Procedure.
[5] Brihaspati, I, Constitution of a Court of Justice, 26—30.

own usages binding upon them.[1] As a rule, the state could not institute any regulations over-riding these gild customs. We learn from Manu, Brihaspati and other codifiers of laws or customs that "rules of their own profession" were recognized by the state for cultivators or peasants and farmers, artisans such as carpenters or others, artists, money-lenders, companies of tradesmen, dancers, persons wearing the token of a religious order such as the Pâśupatas, and even robbers.[2] Gautama also, the earliest of the writers, observes that peasants, traders, herdsmen, money-lenders, and artisans have authority to lay down rules for their respective classes. And in the suits brought before the state judiciary in appeal from gild tribunals, the royal judges were expected to learn the facts and rules "from those who in each class had authority to speak". The king's officers were to give legal decisions "in accordance with what were declared to be the rules in the *śreṇî*".[3]

Last but not least, the administrative *sva-râj* or "self-determination" of *śreṇîs* was practically unconditioned. They could exercise their governmental power as almost sovereign units, as *imperia in imperio*, i. e., without depending on the sanction of the state. The right of the *samûha* to punish even the *mukhya* or president is stated by Kâtyâyana as well as by Mitra Miśra[4] who cites him while interpreting Yâjnavalkya's opinion on the question. In Brihaspati's law also the gild-*sabhâ* could normally punish one of the guilty members, ostracize or even banish him, as has been pointed out above. Only, if in boycotting him the gild were "actuated by hatred" might the state "restrain" the corporation.[5] The ultra-democratic constitution of Chinese gilds was all but outdone by the *samûhas* of India.[6]

The executive, judicial and legislative autonomies[7] of *śreṇîs*, or the *laissez faire* enjoyed by these "local" bodies, must have been considerably restricted and circumscribed by the "centralizing" exploits of successful empire-builders or "nation"-makers.[8] But archaeological researches have

---

[1] *Mahâ*, *Śânti*, Ch. 54, 20.

[2] Brihaspati, I, Constitution of a Court of Justice, 26; *Śukra* IV, v, lines 35—36; Manu, VIII, 40, 41; Nârada X, 2, 3.

[3] Gautama, XI, 21, 22.

[4] *Vîra-mitrodaya*, p. 448; Yâjnavalkya, II, 187; Majumdar, pp. 12, 21, 22.

[5] Brihaspati, XVII, 18—19.

[6] Morse's *Gilds of China*, pp. 9, 12.

[7] In regard to coins issued by gilds see Banerji's *Prâchîn*, p. 18, Cunningham's *Coins*, p. 59, Mookerji's *Local*, p. 214 and Marshall's article in the *Arch. Sur. loc. cit.*

[8] All economic and political interpretation of Hindu gilds must be regarded as hypothetical until light is thrown on this important constitutional question. This aspect of the problem has escaped the notice of antiquarians.

not as yet unearthed any evidence as to the adverse effects, inevitable as they must have been, of the *śâsanas* (i. e. legislative enactments or statutes and ordinances) of *sârva-bhaumas* on the immunities of gild-soviets. It is apparent, however, that, on the whole, the *sva-râj* of Hindu *śreṇis* i. e. the "functional" sovereignty of India's old economic associations was essentially an analogue if not a replica of the *liber burgus* of mediæval Europe in so far as this latter was achieved by and dependent on gilds and crafts.[1]

[1] Goodnow's *Municipal Government*, pp. 55—61, 137; Brissaud's *History of French Public Law*, 253; Gross, Vol. I, pp. 105, 159—162; Sidgwick, p. 253; Sarkar's *Pos. Back*, Vol. II, p. 98.

CHAPTER IV.

The Public Law of the Hindus.

Section 1.

Sabhâs or Administrative Assemblies.

We shall now take up the institutions of Public Law, i. e. the political institutions proper. To begin with the *sabhâs* or *comitias.* These were of three grades: the rural, the municipal and the national, corresponding to the territorial distribution of governmental or administrative powers.

The assembly or *comitia* of the rural institutions was known simply as the *sabhâ* or *mahâ-sabhâ* (great assembly) of the *grâma*[1] (village). In mediæval times the village association came to be described in the vernaculars as *panchâyat*[2] or "government by the five" (i. e. by a body of competent men). But the term is not to be found in Vedic or classical Sanskrit literature. Nor does it appear to be used outside of northern India.

As a unit of administration the town, known as *pura,* was necessarily the nucleus of a separate institution. In its corporate capacity, i. e., as a *municipium,* the *pura*[3] went generally by two, or rather three, different names, — the *pûga,* the *gaṇa,* and the *nigama.* The *pûga*[4] was a well-known organization in the days when the Buddhist *Vinaya* literature was being compiled. Nay, Pâṇini[5] was familiar with it. The municipal corporation was thus well established in pre-Maurya times. And, of course, Manu,[6] Yâjnavalkya,[7] the later lawyers and their commentators also lived in an age when the *pûga* was the centre and basis of an institutional activity. *Pûga* was often employed as a synonym for *gaṇa,* as we have noticed above.[8]

---

[1] *Vedic Index,* Vol. I, 244—247.

[2] Sarkar's *Folk-Element,* 21, 66—67. *cf. Pânch Pyârâ* (Five Dear Ones) of the Sikh polity.

[3] *Vedic Index,* Vol. I, 538—540.

[4] *Chulla-Vagga,* V, 5, 2; VIII, 4, 1.

[5] V, 3, 112.

[6] III, 151.

[7] II, 31.

[8] p. 33.

Nigama as a term for the municipality is used in the Nasik inscriptions[1] of General Uṣavadâta in the first century A. C. It occurs also in the Casket inscriptions[2] of the second century found at Bhattiprolu in Southern India. In the fourth century Jâjnavalkya[3] also uses the term. But it is questionable if he would have employed it to denote the same institution for which he used *pûga* and *gaṇa*. In his hands, at any rate, *nigama*, seems to be specifically applied to a much limited category, viz., the corporation of traders. In any case *sabhâ* as the name of a meeting, council or assembly would stand equally for the *concilium* or *comitia* of the *pûga*, the *gaṇa*, and the *nigama*.

The conciliar element in the national, supreme, or central body of the Hindu state was known simply as the *sabhâ* in Vedic[4] times and in the poetry of the *Râmâyaṇa*[5] and the *Mahâbhârata*.[6] In Kautilya's language it was the *mantri-sabhâ* (*sabhâ* of ministers) or the *mantri-pariṣat*. *Pariṣat* is like *sabhâ* a generic term implying an assembly or association.

The *sabhâ* in each of the three stages of political jurisdiction can be taken as a deliberative or legislative body, as an executive council or committee, and even as a judicial assembly or court of justice. Unless the technical sense is clearly indicated, and except where the functions of government have been differentiated into distinct organs, the three territorial assemblies, the *grâma-sabhâ*, the *nigama-sabhâ*, and the *mantri-sabhâ* may be treated indifferently as *comitias* of the legislature, the executive or the judiciary (of the village, the town, and the nation respectively). Normally speaking, Hindu *sabhâs* are administrative or governmental councils of an all-round comprehensive character.

Section 2.

The *Sva-râj* of Rural Communes.

1. *Pre-Imperial Local Units.*

The folk-element in the Hindu constitution is for obvious reasons as old as the *Vedas*. Vedic India was for centuries a land of numerous *svarâjes*[7] or self-ruled commonwealths. Plentiful therefore as a matter

[1] *Ep. Ind.*, 1905—1906, p. 82; Bhandarkar's *Early Hist.*, Secs. IV, VII.

[2] Majumdar, p. 61.

[3] II, 192. Nârada's use of *nigama* in X, 2 seems to be identical.

[4] *Vedic Index*, Vol. I, 426, 427.

[5] *Ayodhyâ-Kânda*, Ch. C, 18.

[6] *Sabhâ*, ch. V, 30; *Śânti*, ch. LXXXIII, 6—11, 47.

[7] *Atharva*, XVII, 1, 22, 23; *Vedic Index*, Vol. II, p. 494; Handiqui's "Word *sva-râj* in the *Rig Veda*" in the *Mod. Rev.* for March 1919.

of course were the *sabhâs*,[1] *samitis*, *samsads*, i. e. the *panchâyats*, assemblies, *Versammlungen* or "soviets" of the people. All-comprehensive were the functions of such bodies, deliberative, judicial, military, and what not.

Kingship may be taken to have originated early among the Vedic institutions. But in regard to these folkmoots, which were really "direct democracies" of the people, the king's position was virtually that of a "permanent executive".

And as the whole state was conterminous with the tribe or the village, there could not arise any differentiation of functions between the central and local governments. The "nation" and the "rural commune" were convertible terms. No matter whether tribal (i. e. national) or rural (i. e. territorial), these earliest village councils of the Hindus were the counterparts or replicas of the Homeric *agoras* and the *gemots* of the Tacitean *civitas*.[2]

During the lifetime of Śâkya the Buddha and after (*c* sixth century B. C.), the initiative in local civics and politics was regularly made use of by folk-India. *Santhâgâras* or mote-halls, rest-houses and reservoirs were constructed by the villagers through cooperative efforts. Self-administration extended even to the laying out of parks and the mending of thoroughfares between village and village.

This cooperation in communal politics was not however the monopoly of men. Women also were proud to be partners in works of public utility.[3] Such was the local government in republican India in which the *dramatis personae* of the *Jâtakas* or Buddhist story-literature used to participate previous to the epoch of Maurya Imperialism (B. C. 322).

Probably the village institutions of this period were not much different from the rural communes of Vedic India. Nay, indeed, these may have been but descended from and were but continuing the traditions of those oldest units of self-rule on Indian soil.

Under Maurya, Gupta, and other imperial dynasties the government of India was extensive and complex enough to admit of a more or less rigid division between central and local functions. Institutions of rural

---

[1] *Vedic Index*, Vol. II, 426, 427, 430, 431; *Atharva*, II, 27, VII, 12, VI, 87; *Am. Pol. Sc. Rev.* for Nov. 1918, pp. 592—595, 597; Zimmer's *Altindisches Leben*, pp. 172—175; Basu's *Indo-Aryan Polity during the Period of the Rig Veda.*

[2] Stubbs, Vol. I, 26—30; Tacitus' *Germania*, II, 12; Vierkandt's *Staat und Gesellschaft in der Gegenwart*, p. 11; *cf.* the data on territorial associations in Lowie's *Primitive Society.*

[3] The stories may be read in the *Kulavaka* (no. 31), *Kharassara* (no. 79), *Ubhato-bhattha* (no. 139), *Gahapati* (no. 199), *Paniya* (no. 459) and other *Jâtakas*; *cf.* Rhys Davids' *Buddhist India*, p. 49; Majumdar, pp. 57, 176.

sva-râj were conspicuous in the Western Deccan (Mahârâṣtra and Gujarat) under the Ândhras of the early Christian era.[1] But on the solid basis of epigraphic evidence the best available picture we have of the constitution of *panchâyats* (lit. government by the five, or council of five, i. e. a body of competent men), the primary units of political life, is that in regard to Southern India[2] and Ceylon between the ninth and the thirteenth centuries.

2. *Local Government in Southern India.*

We know of forty villages during the reign of the Chola Emperor Râja-râja I (985—1013) in which the villagers as a body managed their own affairs.[3] It was in public meetings that the business was conducted. Earlier, in Parântaka I's time (907—948) we hear of a "full meeting of the great assembly, including young and old". Evidently there was a General Assembly for the entire village and this central *panchâyat* seems to have been sub-divided into several committees or sub-*panchâyats*. There was an annual committee in addition to four separate committees on gardens, tanks, gold and justice. And finally there was a committee styled *pancha-vara*. It was intended most probably for general supervision or possibly for the collection of a special tax.[4]

The local self-government ordinances of Chola India provided that members of the committees must be below 75 and above 30 years of age. The property qualification for *panchâyat*-membership was twofold. First, the person must own more than a quarter *veli* (5 acres) i. e. $1^1/_4$ acre of tax-paying land. Secondly, he must live in a house built on his own real estate.[5] The village assembly was thus not a commonwealth of all men, but a really exclusive institution, an oligarchy.

---

[1] *Early Hist. of the Dek.*, sec. VIII. Evidences of *smriti* and *niti śâstras* have been generally avoided by the present author in the study of institutions. Majumdar's references (p. 60) to Viṣṇu III, 7, 11 and Manu VII, 115, 116 are irrelevant. The village, of course, must always have been a territorial unit of administration. But the assembly of the village folk is an altogether different phenomenon which needs a separate evidence, such for instance as can be furnished from south Indian inscriptions. His references (p. 66) to Nârada X and Brihaspati XVII are not convincing, for nobody is entitled to postulate about the constitution of a rural assembly all that is known about the gild organization.

[2] Aiyangar pp. 158—191; Matthai's *Village Government in British India*, pp. 25—30; V. Venkayya's "Irrigation in Southern India in Ancient Times" in the *Arch. Sur. Ann. Rep.*, 1903—04; Majumdar, pp. 67—69, 76—79, 82—84; *South Indian Inscriptions*, Vol. III, Pt. I, pp. 1—22; Mookerji's *Local*, pp. 135—142, 210.

[3] *Arch. Sur. Ann. Rept.*, 1904—05, pp. 130, 144, 145.

[4] *Madras Epigraphy, Ann. Rep.*, 1898—99, p. 23; 1915—1916, pp. 115, 116.

[5] *Ibid*, 1909—10, p. 98; Aiyangar 169, 170, 173.

Two classes of persons were declared ineligible for membership on the committees. First are those who were members before but failed to render proper accounts. To the second class belonged those who were guilty of certain grave sins. And an important constitutional procedure excluded from membership those who had been on the committee for previous three years.

Impressive were the methods of voting and election for the constitution of the central body. "The village with its twelve streets was divided into thirty wards (the number of members is thirty). Every one who lived in these wards wrote a name on a ticket. The tickets were first arranged in separate bundles representing the thirty wards. Each bundle bore the name to which it belonged. The bundles were then collected and put into a pot and placed before the general body of inhabitants both young and old in meeting assembled. All the priests were required to be present. The oldest priest among the present then took the pot, and looking upwards so as to be seen by all people, called one of the young boys standing close by who does not know what is inside to pick out one of the bundles. The tickets in this bundle were then removed to another pot. After it had been well shuffled, the boy took one ticket out of this bundle and handed it to an officer called the arbitrator, who received it in the palm of his hand with fingers open. He read out the name, and it was then shouted out by the priests."[1] The village was governed in this way by popular "representatives".

Offices seem to have been strictly annual, and the officials were appointed, as we see, both by election and lot. The rotation of offices, provided for thereby, served as a school of almost universal education in public life and citizenship. The committee of supervision could thus become efficient in its control of the smaller committees.[2] It is interesting to observe that the female sex was not under any ban in rural civics. There was no absolute prohibition against women as such. Inscriptions furnish us with references to women members on village *sabhâs*.[3]

3. *The Content of Rural Democracy.*

Not of a trivial order were the functions and powers of the village *sva-râjes* of mediæval India. The responsibility on the shoulders of the

---

[1] Aiyangar; Matthai; Majumdar; Mookerji's *Local*, 148—164; the long inscription found at Uttaramallur is reproduced by them all.

[2] Aiyangar, 173; Mookerji's *Local*, 155—156, 160. *cf.* "*l'amateurisme démocratique*" of Joseph-Barthélemy, Infra, p. 147.

[3] Matthai, *loc. cit.* In this connection cf. the ethnographic data bearing on woman's status in Lowie.

rural folk, peasants, shepherds, artisans, craftsmen, and priests, was great indeed. In the eleventh century, the rural communes of Ceylon[1] ascertained the facts of murder and robbery and sat in session thereon. They were entitled to levy fines and inflict punishment on the criminals. And they were responsible for the execution of the statutes and decrees promulgated by "His Majesty the King in Council".

The cultivators of Ceylon used to refer all questions of common interest to the local assembly of notables and elders. Especially in connection with irrigation did they feel the necessity for joint cooperative effort.[2] The communal administration of tanks was the normal feature of village politics. Repairs of irrigation works had to be done by all landholders each according to his share, or else they were refused water. Nobody was permitted by the *panchâyat* to irrigate fresh lands unless a surplus were available. In seasons of drought the peasants could claim only limited proportions of the diminished stream. The rural authorities determined with strict justice the rotation of watering and the order in which the cultivators would be supplied with water. Breaches of the irrigation regulations and thefts of water met with due punishment from the *sabhâ*.

It can legitimately be generalized from over a dozen Chola inscriptions bearing on a Tamil village near Conjeeveram that the village *sabhâs* had in their hands full responsibility for the entire administration of the rural areas.[3] The South Indian *panchâyats* were absolute proprietors of the village lands, with rights of ownership over newly cleared lands. They had authority to fine, in case of delinquency, the "great men of the year", i. e. the elected officials of the rural commune. They "received deposits of money and grants of land for charitable purposes, and administered the trust by a board of commissioners specially appointed for the purpose from year to year". They received all the taxes and had the right to render villages tax-free, and if necessary could grant to landholders an exemption from customary dues. Sometimes an independent corporation e. g. that of temple authorities was endowed with jurisdiction over certain lands by the ordinances of the village *sabhâs*.

The *panchâyats* were also authorized to take possession of and sell the lands of persons who had failed to pay the Government dues for

---

[1] *Epigraphia Zeylanica*, Vol. I, no. 21.

[2] Deakin's *Irrigated India and Ceylon*, p. 243.

[3] Aiyangar, 163—164; Majumdar cites several new inscriptions not exploited by other writers, pp. 70—74. Note the twenty references to village assemblies serving (like gilds) as local banks (p. 73).

three years.[1] And of course local justice fell within the jurisdiction of these assemblies. Even in cases of murder they could sit in judgment, and what is remarkable, had the power to exercise discretion in meting out penalties. On several occasions the rural soviets of ancient Madras, finding that the murder was not culpable homicide, sentenced the defendants to simple fine instead of the usual capital punishment. And in order to carry out their decisions the village assemblymen did not have to refer the matter to the central authority represented by the royal officer.[2]

No attempt is being made here to give evidence in regard to the existence of "village communities"[3] in ancient India. The discussion as to whether and how far the lands were held in common and to what extent they were held in severalty is primarily of an economic character. This agrarian question of land-tenure is not to be confounded with the political administration of villages as the territorial divisions of a state. Communal proprietorship or no communal proprietorship, it is clear that the legislation of Ceylon and the Tamil Empire conferred immense powers of government on the inhabitants of the rural districts. The *panchâyats* as the "representative" *sabhâs* of the village people were very essential organs of Hindu public life. These were the principal agencies in and through which the masses could participate in the administration of the country.

4. *The Extent of Centralization.*

There is a further distinction to be noted by students of constitutional history. In spite of the manifold privileges of self-determination, the rural communes of India since Maurya times must be sharply distinguished in political status from the "direct democracies" or patriarchal commonwealths of Vedic India and the smaller village or town republics of later times. For the *panchâyats* and the like associations were no longer the full-fledged "sovereign" bodies of old, but institutions of "local government" enjoying rights and immunities only within the bounds of royal or imperial will, viz. according to the grants of charters.

---

[1] *Ibid*, 161.

[2] *Ibid*, 168.

[3] Jolly's *Recht*, pp. 93—96 (*Feldgemeinschaft*). For Vedic land tenure *vide grâma* in the *Vedic Index* Vol. I, 244, 245. The alleged existence of "village communities" in all periods of Hindu history is taken for granted in Havell's *History of Aryan Rule in India*, pp. 31, 52, 69, etc. and in Mookerji's *Local*, 2, 3, 23—25, in fact, in every writing on Hindu institutions, without any evidence. See the chapter on public finance, *infra*. pp. 116, 123. *cf. the* discussions on private property in Lowie.

The extraordinary authority which the village assemblies of Chola India possessed in regard to the distribution of rural lands was clearly defined by orders issued from the central government. Râja-râja[1] legislated from Tanjore that the land of those landholders who had not paid the taxes for three years "shall become the property of the villages and be liable to be sold by the inhabitants of those villages to the exclusion of the defaulting landholders". Now, if it was the royal will that conferred the right on the rural communes, it was also the royal officers, the *adhikârins*, superintendents or intendants that looked after the proper use of the right.

And, as a corollary, the *imperium* or autonomy of the *panchâyats*, was legally subject to the control exercised by the imperial civil service. Not few and far between was the intervention of the supreme authorities in local politics, and hence the curtailment of village liberties. In 1230 the lands belonging to certain *drohins* (enemies of the state) in a South Indian village were sold by public auction. The initiative however was taken not by the village assembly but by the king who had sent eight officers to fix the price and conduct the affair.[2] In another village a new headman was appointed by the supreme government for the specific purpose of dealing with certain persons who were *râja-drohin* (traitors to the king).[3] Sedition and treason appear thus to have been beyond the competency of the rural communes to handle. Even in far simpler matters the *panchâyats* had to feel the limits of their jurisdiction as but the lowest rungs in an administrative hierarchy. It appears that on one occasion some money ear-marked for a temple was misappropriated by the village assembly. The temple authorities appealed to the king for redress. Both parties had to appear at the capital. The king's court found the assemblymen guilty and fined them. The money was eventually restored to the temple.[4] Besides, the inspection and auditing of *panchâyat* accounts were normal functions of the Chola bureaucracy.[5]

These instances give us an insight into the amount of centralization and administrative unification achieved in Hindu India under efficient and masterful rulers. More comprehensive and far-reaching had certainly been the nationalizing consolidation brought about by the Maurya emperors, if we can depend on the financial and land measures described

---

[1] Aiyangar, 161, 162. *Vide Infra*, p. 102.

[2] *Mad. Ep.* 1910—11, p. 75.

[3] *Ibid*, 1912—13, p. 110.

[4] *Ibid*, 1906—07, p. 71.

[5] *Infrâ*, pp. 98—99, 112. *South Ind. Ins.* Vol. III, Pt. 1, no. 57.

in the *Artha-śâstra.*[1] Nay, it is difficult to believe that the *gopa* (village officer), the lowest grade member of the imperial civil service under Chandra-gupta or Asoka, left any important executive work to be administered by the rural *sabhâ* through any of its committees. Too thorough and exacting were the supervision and control imposed on the *panchâyats* by the Supreme Government. The village *sva-râjes*, those primary units of self-rule, must then have been reduced, generally speaking, to an atrophied state, the moribund condition, say, of the French rural communes under the *ancien régime* of *Richelieu.*[2] To cite a modern analogue, the *de facto* initiative and responsibility of the Maurya rural assemblies were not more real than is the sham "local self-government" enjoyed by the municipalities and district boards of British India at the beck and call of the District Magistrate.[3] It is surprising and significant, at any rate, that Kautilya does not mention even by name these local nuclei of public life, although of course his silence does not argue their total annihilation.[4]

5. *Empire vs. Village in World-Evolution.*

Since the publication in 1832 of the Report of the Select Committee of the House of Commons[5] it has become almost a piece of sanctified idealism with foreign as well as Indian writers to wail over the disappearance of the "little republics" that are alleged to have been governing

---

[1] *Ind. Ant.*, 1905, pp. 7, 8. *Infra*, pp. 105, 121.

[2] Brissaud, pp. 255—257; Goodnow's *Comparative Administrative Law*, Vol. I, 162—165.

[3] *Report on Indian Constitutional Reforms* (Montagu-Chelmsford, 1918), pp. 11, 12, 103, 104, 154, 155, 157—161.

[4] Majumdar's reference (pp. 59, 63) to Kautilya (Book III, Ch. X) hardly indicates the existence of the assembly and proves the exact opposite of what he intends to demonstrate. The Kautilyan village-headman as a limb of the imperial civil service was eminently calculated, as Tocqueville would have remarked, to destroy village democracy and not conserve it. From the standpoint taken in the present treatise Mookerji's characterization of Indian rural institutions as *sui generis* (cf.*Local* pp. 5—10, 23—25) is questionable. See Gomme's *Principles of Local Government*, pp. 35—109. Indologists who are never tired of quoting Metcalfe should note Gomme's remark that in England also the "localities" have "survived all shocks, all revolutions, all changes, and their position on the map of England is as indestructible as the country itself" (pp. 39—40). The notion as to the distinctiveness of Hindu development is due to generalizations not sufficiently founded on Occidental data down to the industrial revolution. An intimate familiarity with Greek, Roman and mediaeval Europe will bring out the fact that East and West were replicas of each other. See the comparative study of "private law" in Gibelin's *Etudes*. cf. Asokawa's *Early Inst. Life of Japan*, pp. 2—3.

[5] Metcalfe, 1832, Vol. III, App., 84, p. 331; Romesh Chunder Dutt's *Economic History of India*, Vol. I, pp. 118, 119, 141, 206, 346—348, 359, 386—388; Mann's *Land and Labor in a Deccan Village*, pp. 150, 151; Maine's *Village Communities*, pp. 122—126; Coomaraswamy's *Mediaeval*, pp. 28—29; Birdwood's *Industrial*, 135—137; J. N. Sarkar's *Moghul Administration*, pp. 22—24, 78—80.

the so-called village-communities of India even as late as the period of the declining Maratha and Moghul Empires. In the light, however, of actual history based on epigraphy, as we have seen, the real self-sufficiency and genuine autonomy of rural *sva-râjes* must have been prominent by their absence during the ascendency of *sârva-bhaumas* like Chandra-gupta Maurya and Kulottûnga the Chola-Châlukya (1070—1118).

Local self-government and national imperialism militate against each other, be it in southern Asia or in western Europe, be it under Marathas or under Bourbons. In so far, therefore, as the self-containedness and freedom of the village assemblies were facts of *Realpolitik* in the East or in the West, they are to be regarded as marks not so much of democratic independence or sovietic sovereignty of the people as of decay in imperial-militaristic pretensions and in centripetal activity on the part of the powers that be. The prevalence of rural liberties, whenever it may have obtained in ancient India, has to be explained more often by the temporary or occasional absence of the Hindu Louis XIV's than by the conscious application of *laissez faire* and decentralization in local politics as the well-reasoned statecraft of successful nation-makers and empire-builders. Or, perhaps, in certain cases the idyllic picture of autonomous village *panchâyats* as a feature of old Hindu polity should have to be taken as depicting a "survival" in mediæval times of the more primitive folk-institutions of Vedic and republican India, untouched by the Samudra-guptan careers of the numerous *vijigîsus*, Siegfrieds, or aspirants to world-dominion, and practically shunted off, like benighted Arcadias, from the main tracks of enlightenment and culture.[1] The precise amount of popular initiative and self-direction remains, however, to be worked up for the different epochs of Hindu polity. It is not safe as yet to generalize about all periods of Indian constitutional history in regard to the relations between national control and local democracy.[2]

---

[1] Traces of old rural democracy can still be detected in the administration of certain socio-religious institutions like the gilds of *gambhirâ* singers and playwrights in Bengal. *Vide* B. K. Sarkar's *Folk-Element in Hindu Culture* (references to *panchâyat, mandala* etc.), pp. 20—22, 66—68. The socio-economic study of the village in Radhakamal Mukerjee's *Foundations of Indian Economics* (pp. 441—445) is not quite correct in the references to western economic history. And it might have appeared a little bit too romantic were it not for the fact that the possibilities of the village as a political unit even under conditions of the twentieth century science and mechanics are being demonstrated in and through the Russian *Mirs*. *Cf.* Asakawa's "Contributions of Feudal Japan to New Japan" in the *Journal of Race Development*, July 1912, Gomme's *Primitive Folkmoots*, pp. 20—69, *Folklore*, 353—364 and *Village Community* 290—295, Seebohm's *English Village Community*, 437—441, and Ashley's *Surveys Historic and Economic*, 92—156, Carlyle's *Med. Pol. Theory*, Vol. III, pp. 28—29, 75. *Vide* Lewinski's *Origin of Property*.

[2] Majumdar's Ch. II (esp. pp. 55—85), full as it is of long extracts from epigraphic volumes

All the same, the hypothesis can reasonably be advanced at the present stage of inquiry that India's story would but corroborate the trend of world-evolution exhibited by ancient and mediaeval Europe.

Section 3.

Municipal Government.

We need not wait to catch a glimpse of the epic capitals like Ayodhyâ, almost an "ideal" city under Daśaratha as described in the *Râmâyaṇa*,[1] or Indraprastha (near modern Delhi) and Dvârakâ, the seaport on the Gujarat coast, of the *Mahâbhârata*[2] fame. For, information is available in regard to actual life in the cities of northern and southern India from more genuinely historical sources.

1. *Urban Culture in Hindu India.*

In Alexander's time and earlier, Taxila (to the northwest of modern Rawalpindi in the Punjab) was one of the greatest cities of Asia. The *Jâtakas* (Buddhist Birth-stories) describe it as a university town and the centre especially of *Âyurvedic* (medical) learning. Commanding as it did a strategic position in regard to the Afghan frontier it was selected as the seat of the northwestern viceroyalty of the Maurya Empire.

According to Pliny, in the first century A. C., Mâdurâ, the capital of the Pândya kingdom in the farthest south, although an inland town, was in commercial and political touch with the Roman Empire through ports on the Malabar Coast (Western). Its cultural pre-eminence was marked by the activities of the *Sangam* (Academy) of Tamil literature.

In Tamil classics of the early Christian era we have several model cities. Mâdurâ was famous for its lofty mansions and high buildings, Woraiyur for superb exellence in everything that contributes to healthy civic life, Vanji on the Malabar Coast for its commercial prosperity, and

---

which evidently have not been exhausted, is in need of a thorough revision and a more critical handling from the angle of constitutional development. Altogether, the view of rural institutions set forth by the present author is fundamentally different from the conventional attitude represented by all recent writers. The prevailing fallacy arises from an incomplete comprehension of the stages of constitutional evolution in western Europe and an inadequate analysis of the relations between the local and central governments during the different periods. The attempt at interpreting ancient and mediaeval Hindu polity in terms of recent growths in Eur-America is equally unwarrantable. A scientific interpretation of the mass of facts such as are exhibited by Majumdar and Mookerji will require a special monograph which it is not sought in this volume to undertake.

[1] *Vâla-kânda*, Ch. V.

[2] *Jour. of the Am. Or. Soc.*, 1889, 174—179.

Pukar (Kâverîppumpaṭṭinam) on the Coromandel Coast for its excellent natural harbor which secured safe anchorage for merchant vessels.[1]

In the seventh century Vâtâpi (Badami in Bijapur District) was the capital of the Châlukya Marathas. It was a city of international importance and attracted envoys from Khusru II (591—628), the Sassanian Emperor of Persia.[2] Some of the celebrated frescoes at Ajantâ in the Bombay Presidency were the handiwork of painters of this city.

One of the oldest cities of India is Tâmralipta (modern Tamluk), the seaport of Bengal. In the seventh century, in the words of Hiuen Thsang, it was situated on a bay and contained stores of rare and precious merchandise and a wealthy population. This is the port wherefrom passengers bound for China left Eastern India.

Kanauj on the Ganges in the Middle-West became the capital of Upper India first under the Vardhanas and next under the Gurjara-Pratîhâras. In the *Harṣacharita* we have a poetic picture of the city and the district from the pen of Bâṇa. Hiuen Thsang found here hundreds of institutions accommodating 10,000 scholars in Buddhist lore. The city was strongly fortified and extended for about four miles.[3]

Ujjayinî in Malwa is one of the most well-known Hindu cities. It was famous even in pre-Buddhistic times, and became the capital of the western prefecture under the Mauryas. For ages it continued to be a commercial half-way house between the cities of Northern India and the ports of the Bombay Coast which had maritime intercourse with Persia, Egypt, and the Greco-Roman world. It was from this city that Varâhamihira (A. C. 505), the astronomer of Gupta India, reckoned the longitudes of the earth.[4]

In Subandhu's romance, *Vâsavadattâ* (sixth century), we have a picture of Pâtali-putra (near modern Bankipore in Bihar). It may be taken for a poet's account for the closing days of the Guptas. We can wring out the solid fact, however, that the white-washed houses of the city were adorned with well-carved statues.[5] In Vardhana times it was only a second city of the northern empire. From the Pâla inscriptions we can to a certain extent reconstruct the military glories of Pâtali-putra

---

[1] Ayyar's *Town-planning in Ancient Deccan*, p. 16.

[2] Griffiths' *Paintings in the Buddhist Cave Temples of Ajanta*, Vol. I, p. 23, Plate V.

[3] pp. 81, 82; Smith's article on "The History of the City of Kanauj and of King Yasovarman" in the *Journal of the Royal Asiatic Society*, 1908, pp. 769, 771, 774, 782, 790.

[4] A romantic account of the city is furnished by Bâṇa in the *Kâdambarî* (Cowell's transl.); pp. 210—214.

[5] pp. 75—76.

during its last epoch of political importance, namely under the Bengali emperors.

In Pâla times the colossal boats of war on the Ganges at Pâtaliputra looked, as it were, like a range of mountains. So many in number were the dark huge elephants that the sun's rays seemed to be shut out by an extensive screen of clouds. The skies used to remain always dusky through the volume of dusts raised by the hoofs of countless horse with which the allied powers of northwestern India presented the eastern *sârva-bhauma* as tokens of friendship. Nay, the earth sank low under the steps of the infantry which the feudatory chiefs brought along with them when they came to the capital to render homage. And from their position in the high towers of the palace, the lions of gold which the kings, defeated in battles, had to surrender from their crowns were terrific enough to scare even the hare in the moon and to cause it to think of running away from its doom.[1]

The democratic spirit and militarism of some of the Punjab cities are testified to by Greek and Roman writers. Pliny's *Natural History*, and the Egyptian-Greek merchant's *Periplus of the Erythraean Sea*, both of the first century A. C., as well as Ptolemy's *Geography* (140) and Cosmas' *Christian Topography* (535) furnish pictures of the material well-being and commercial enterprise of the townsfolk especially at the sea-ports, from the mouths of the Indus to those of the Ganges, including the island of Ceylon. And the Chinese scholar-pilgrims from Fa Hien (fifth century) to Itsing (seventh century) speak of the cultural attainments as well as educational and religious charities of the public-spirited citizens in the interior of India.

But in regard to methods of city government hardly any details can be gleaned from these sources. We exclude, of course, from our present consideration the republican cities of Bihar in Eastern India described in Pali Buddhist books of the pre-Maurya epoch.

An important administrative function of cities is to be read in inscriptions of the earliest times. We hear of a city council in connection with what appears to have been a second class town in the Western Deccan under the Ândhras. The institution was known as the *nigama-sabhâ*. The municipal corporation of Govardhana (Nasik) is described as being a witness to and registrar of the deed of gifts made by General Uṣavadâta (*c* 100 A. C.) through two gilds. The town-assembly thus became responsible for the carrying out of his instructions in regard to the charities.[2]

---

[1] *Ep. Ind.*, 1896—1897, pp. 251—253; Maitra's "Bengali Ideals" in the *Sâhitya* (1916).

[2] *Supra*, p. 36.

Among the social functions of municipalities we have to note the endowment of temples out of public property. In the tenth century the city of Gwalior in the middlewest dedicated two pieces of municipal land to two divinities. And it is interesting to observe that instead of the city fathers themselves becoming the bankers they sought the cooperation of the gilds of oil-millers and gardeners with whom their gifts were invested for the permanent provision of oil and garlands.[1]

2. *Town-Planning in Tamil Territories.*

Tamil literature affords us some glimpses into the wards, streets, sewers, markets, gardens, tanks, temples and public buildings of South Indian cities. In regard to Mâdurâ we know that the streets around the palace and other streets, large and small, straight and crooked, were provided with *puri-mams* (dust receptacles). Such receptacles were built of bricks and were plastered over with white lime. There was one *purimam* at either end of each street.[2] There was a deep ditch around the walls of the fort. Into this ditch was received all the drainage water of the city.[3] "Red light districts" were segregated for public women with separate parks, baths and gardens.[4]

At Kâverip-pumpattinam the foreign (Roman) merchants were housed near the sea-coast. This was intended for the facility of collecting duties from them. Customs officials sealed the goods with the "tiger stamp" of the state. The removal of goods from the docks was forbidden until the duty was paid. The city maintained light-houses on the beach.[5]

There is an interesting account of the system of water supply for Vanji (Karur), the capital of the Chera state on the west coast. A ditch encircled the walls of the city. By a network of *tumbu* (conduit pipes) the water of the palace, public halls and private residences was conducted into the ditch. Those who could afford the expense had separate baths specially constructed for them in such a manner that water might be filled in or let out at pleasure.[6]

In Tamil books the cities of Madras are generally decribed in extent as nine miles each way or at any rate in length. The governors of urban areas paid considerable attention to drainage. Walled cities were universal like the *polises* of Greece. Hiuen Thsang[7] also noticed the "wide and

---

[1] Majumdar, p. 62.

[2] [3] [4] Ayyar, pp. 42, 44, 51.

[5] Pillai's *Tamils Eighteen Hundred Y'ars Ago*, pp. 16, 24, 26; *Ind. Ship.*, 135—137.

[6] Ayyar, p. 61.

[7] *Si-Yuki*, Vol. I, 73—74.

high walls" and "inner gates" of Indian cities. In his account the walls are mostly built of brick or tiles, and the towers on the walls are constructed of wood or bamboo. Walled towns and villages have been the rule since Vedic times.[1]

3. *Pâtaliputra, the Indian Rome.*

The municipality of Pâtali-putra, the Rome of the Hindus, was administered almost like a complex modern city. According to Megasthenes,[2] the Greek ambassador (*c* B. C. 302) to the Maurya Empire, the city fathers of Pâtali-putra were thirty in number. In their collective capacity they had "charge both of their special departments, and also of matters affecting the general interest as the keeping of public buildings in proper repair, the regulation of prices, the care of markets, harbors and temples".

The municipal corporation consisted of six divisions. Each had five members on the *panchâyatic* principle. The first jurisdiction of the city government was industrial arts. The second division looked after the entertainment of foreigners. To these the city assigned lodgings and kept "watch over their modes of life" by means of those persons who were appointed to assist them. The city arranged to "escort the aliens on the way" when they left the country, or, in the event of their dying, forwarded their "property to their relatives". Foreign visitors were treated indeed as guests of the nation. They were taken care of by the city when they were sick, and buried under government supervision if they died. Census and vital statistics constituted the jurisdiction of the third board. The City regularly recorded facts as to "when and how births and deaths occur, with the view not only of levying a tax, but also in order that births and deaths among both high and low might not escape the cognizance of Government".[3]

The fourth board superintended trade and commerce. Its members had charge of weights and measures,[4] and saw to it that the products in their season were sold by public notice. No one was allowed to deal in more than one kind of commodity unless he paid a double tax. The fifth division supervised manufactured articles which they sold by public notice. The new were sold separately from the old, and there was a fine

---

[1] *Vedic Index*, Vol. I, pp. 538—540.

[2] Mc Crindle's *Anc. Ind.*, pp. 87, 88; Abbott's *Roman Political Institutions*, 280—281, 307—309; Fairlie's *Municipal Administration*, pp. 16—17.

[3] Law's *Hind. Pol.*, pp. 106—114, cf. Abbott, 192—193.

[4] Arnold's *Roman System of Provincial Administration*, p. 209.

for mixing the two together. The sixth class of municipal governors consisted of those who collected the tithes (i. e. the tenths) of the prices of the articles sold. Fraud in the payment of this tax was punished with death.

Heavy was the responsibility of this Indian Rome's *nâgaraka* (mayor) and city council. For Pâtali-putra in the third and fourth centuries B. C. was the largest city in the world. Its territorial limits were more than four times those of Periclean Athens (*c* B. C. 430) or of Augustan Rome (B. C. 27—14 A. C.), the greatest cities of ancient Europe.

The story is well known how the first rude settlements of Romulus on the Palatine Hill were gradually extended until the so-called "wall of Servius" furnished the "city of the seven hills" with a circuit about five miles (*c* B. C. 490). Never was the area of Athens larger than this of Servian Rome. For about eight hundred years, again, the physical dimensions of Rome remained unchanged. It was in the third century A. C. that Emperor Aurelian (270—75) enlarged the city beyond its historic limits. The walls of the new city including what may be called Greater Rome measured a circuit of 18, 337 metres (about $10^1/_2$ miles). The number of towers over the walls was then 383 and there were 16 principal gates.[1]

Let us now consider the size and area of Pâtali-putra as seen by Megasthenes,[2] and the magnitude of the municipal government would be apparent at once. The city was encompassed all round by a ditch, 600 ft. in breadth and 30 cubits in depth. The ditch was meant for defence of the city as well as for receiving its sewage. The wooden wall of the metropolis was "pierced with loopholes for the discharge of arrows". It was "crowned with 570 towers and had 64 gates". In the inhabited quarters, Pâtali-putra "stretched to an extreme length on each side of 80 stadia" (about 9 miles). "Its breadth was 15 stadia (about $1^3/_4$ mile). And it was of the "shape of a parallelogram". The total circuit was therefore about $21^1/_2$ miles, i. e. slightly above the double of that of Aurelian's Rome. Verily, Hindu burgomasters must have had Atlantean shoulders to bear on them the financial burden and civic duties of two European Romes in one Asian capital.

4. *Specimens of Municipal Legislation.*

If the town governments of the viceregal capitals like Taxila, Ujjayinî, Tosali and Suvarṇa-giri and other important cities of the empire were

[1] Ramsay and Lancian's *Roman Antiquities*, pp. 10, 15.

[2] Mc Crindle's *Anc. Ind.*, pp. 66, 68.

modelled on that at Pâtali-putra, we may believe that special attention was paid by the townspeople to sanitation. The health regulations were strictly enforced. Persons committing nuisance on roads, in bathing places, near reservoirs, temples and palaces were fined one *paṇa* (25 cents).[1] One-eighth of a *paṇa* was the penalty for throwing dust on the road. Persons carrying carcasses of dead animals on public roads were fined three to six *paṇas*. And the highest fine known to the Mauryas, that of 3,000 *paṇas*, was inflicted on persons who carried dead bodies by other than fixed paths. Houseowners were bound to keep the gutter of their houses in such condition as to allow a free passage to gutter water.[2] Violation of this municipal law was likewise punished with fines. Scrupulous cleanliness of the city was thus maintained by positive law.

To protect the city against fire[3] the inhabitants were ordered to cook outside the house. The fire brigade was very elementary, however. The householders were expected to have five earthen pitchers filled with water in front of the house. Nobody was allowed to keep haystocks, strawmats etc hard by. And in case of fire able-bodied citizens were in duty bound to help extinguishing it under pain of fine. Such cooperation with the municipal authorities was demanded of the people in other spheres also. Citizens were expected to be on the look out as to whether a merchant had or had not paid the toll at the customs office.[4]

Every arrival and departure of guests had to be notified to the city police by the inhabitants. Failure was visited with a fine of three *paṇas* provided there was no thieving at night. The city kept special watch on the movements and whereabouts of hermits and ascetics. The names of spendthrifts and persons cruel in nature were entered on the municipal "black list".[5]

The city tried to protect the consumers by market laws both as regards weights and measures as well as prices. In regard to the sale of bony flesh it was the law that butchers must give towards compensation as much more meat as was equivalent to the weight of the bone. False balance was punished with a fine of eight times the value of the meat sold. "Profiteering" was carefully guarded against, as there was an official attempt to regulate the prices of commodities. The pious

[1] *Ind. Ant.*, 1905, pp. 51, 52.

[2] *Ibid*, 59.

[3] *Ibid*, 51—52.

[4] *Ibid*, 48.

[5] *Ibid*, 51.

wish was also expressed that such large profits as are ruinous to the people should be abandoned.[1]

The municipal register of the *nâgaraka* recorded not only the arrivals and departures of persons. It was a complete statistical gazetteer similar to the record books of the village-magistrate, the *gopa*, and the district-magistrate, the *sthânika*. The inhabitants were numbered as males and females. Their castes and professions were described. The number of quadrupeds in each household was noted down. Even the family budgets, the incomes and expenses of the citizens found a place in this comprehensive city directory.[2] It was on the data of all these local statistics that the national or Imperial Gazetteer of Maurya India must have been compiled by the *samâhartâ* or collector-general of the empire.

Section 4.

Supreme Councils.

We have seen that in addition to what may for general purposes be described as mass-meetings of the villagers and often as "representative" assemblies of the rural folk, ordinarily known as the *panchâyats* (or councils of the five), Hindu India was used to several other *sabhâs* or councils as organs of public administration. These were the conferences of the ecclesiastical associations (*samghas*), the agricultural, industrial and commercial *samûhas*, i. e. gilds or *śreṇîs*, and the municipal corporations of cities like Govardhana, Pâtali-putra, Ujjayinî, Taxila and so forth. The conciliar element in Hindu polity was further embodied in another important institution. This was the Supreme Council of the king or emperor.

In regard to these royal and imperial assemblies, however, no old constitutional documents or gazetteers have yet been unearthed by archaeological exploration unless the *Artha-śâstra* of Kautilya be partially treated as such. Neither the inscriptions on stone and copper plates discovered up to date nor the stories by Greek and Chinese travellers afford anything more than tantalizing glimpses into the institutions such as may have actually existed among the people.

1. *The Tamil Assemblies.*

During the early centuries of the Christian era there were "Five Great Assemblies" in the kingdoms of Chera, Chola and Pandya in southernmost India. The assembly of "people's representatives" safe-

[1] *Ibid*, 55—56.

[2] *Ibid*, 51—52.

guarded the rights and privileges of the people. The assembly of priests directed all religious ceremonies. The assembly of physicians supervised public and royal health. The assembly of astrologers fixed auspicious times for public ceremonies and predicted important events. It was thus similar to the Roman college of augurs. And the assembly of ministers attended to the administration of justice and collection and expenditure of revenue. Each of these assemblies had a separate place in the metropolis for the transaction of its business and holding its meetings.[1] All these assemblies were what we should call "national" councils, i. e., different from and higher than the village *panchâyats.*

It is not clear as to which, if any, of these assemblies looked after the making of laws. Legislation may be presumed to have been the work of the "people's representatives" who constituted the first among the five national bodies. But there is another point on which more light is needed. Whom did this body represent? What connection did these representatives have with the primary assemblies, the rural *sabhâs*? The *panchâyats* of the villages or the local soviets may be presumed to have sent up deputies to the capital in order to form the metropolitan assembly of the people.

In any case it is apparent that representation as a political device has to be counted in its elementary form among the institutions of Hindu public life. And this representative system, in so far as election implies representation, was not confined to the national, central or supreme assemblies. For, as we have noticed in a previous section, even the rural communes were, as a rule, constituted on the elective principle, and not all village or local assemblies were therefore "direct" democracies of the entire folk.

For the present, however, the Tamil "great assemblies" should appear to be the only specimens of "indirect" or representative polity on a national scale. In reality, details about supreme councils in other periods of Hindu politics are almost nil. But in Maurya India, as we can glean from Kautilya's *Artha-śâstra*, there were two Imperial Councils.[2]

2. *The Kautilyan Councils.*

The first was known simply as the *Sabhâ* or the deliberative "Council of State". It studied the "means of commencing operations" and "providing men and materials". "Distribution of place and time" was one of its functions. And it also addressed itself to the "counteracting

[1] Pillai's *Tamils*, pp. 108—114.

[2] Law's "State Council in Ancient India" in the *Mod. Rev.* for April 1917.

of disaster" and "successful accomplishment". The councillors were asked by the Emperor for their advice individually and collectively, and their opinions had to be given together with reasons.

The second was the *Mantri-pariṣat* or the *executive* "Council of Ministers". Its functions were fourfold: commencement of work not begun, completion of the work already begun, improvement of accomplished work, and proper execution of passed orders. Members of this body did not ordinarily take part in the deliberations of the "Council of State" but only looked after their respective charges. On emergency, however, they might be invited to join the Council of State. The advice of the majority (*bhûyiṣthâh*) would appear to have often been rejected by the Emperor at discretion if some other course appealed to him as more conducive to success.

The description of the councils is however given in such general terms that one wonders as to whether Kautilya was here adumbrating a theory or giving an account of the actual institutions of public law.

In the theory[1] of the constitution as expressed in the *Mahâbhârata*, *Kâmandakî-nîti*, *Śukra-nîti*, *Agni-Purâṇa*, and other treatises, the council is a very important estate of the realm. The councillors constitute, as Bharadvâja says, the "sole prop" of the state.[2] The ideal appears to have been realized to a certain extent in *Realpolitik*.

3. *The Power of the Ministers.*

In ancient Madras the orders of Râja-râja and Râjendra had to be approved of by the *Olai-nâyakam* (chief secretary) and another dignitary.[3] And it was with the approval of the viceroy and the rural *sabhâs* concerned that the Chola promulgations were registered and preserved in the record office. It was in conjunction with the Council that the kings of Ceylon[4] conferred immunities, issued decrees, and made grants. Sometimes we find the councillors making themselves into king-makers. With the "people's approval" they elected at least one historical ruler, Harṣa-vardhana, to kingship (A. C. 606).[5]

In Kashmir, as we read in the *Râja-taranginî*,[6] Pratâpâditya I was

---

[1] *Am. Pol. Sc. Rev.* for Nov. 1918, pp. 585—586. While it is possible to trace *ideas* of constitutional government in the political *śâstras*, it is not allowable, as Banerjea does (*Public*, 50—51), to describe the actual Maurya monarchy as "limited".

[2] *Artha*, Book V, Ch. IV.

[3] Aiyangar's *Anc. Ind.*, 177—178.

[4] *Epigraphia Zeylanica*, Vol. I, nos. 9, 21; Vol. II, no. 5; *Infra*, p. 75.

[5] *Si-yu-ki*, Vol. I, pp. 210—211.

[6] Books II, verses 6, 114—116, and III, verse 528.

invited by the ministers from abroad and installed on the throne. Similarly they were instrumental in crowning one of themselves, the minister Sandhimati, as Ârya-râja. The founder of the Karkota dynasty also, a man of humble origin, owed his coronation to the initiative of Premier Khankha (*c* 625).

There are, besides, several instances of the ministers remonstrating with the king against arbitrary expenditure. If Hiuen Thsang's stories are to be relied on, Asoka the Great's financial extravagance was greatly curbed by his minister Râdhâ-gupta.[1] A councillor likewise prevented Vikramâditya of Srâvasti from indulging in ultra-philanthropic schemes. His arguments[2] were thoroughly modern. "Your Majesty", as the member of the council is said to have pointed out, "indeed will get credit for charity, but your minister will lose the respect of all *** and then fresh imposts will have to be laid *** and then the voice of complaint will be heard." The power of the council is likewise evident in an event of the second century A. C. It was out of his private purse that Rudradâmana, a satrap of the Kuṣâṇ Empire, was compelled to repair the Sudarśana Lake at Girnar (in Kathiawar, close to the Arabian Sea) because of the Council's opposition to the project.[3]

As indicated above, the *Sabhâ* or *Pariṣat* as a supreme council of the state is well known in the *Râmâyaṇa*, the *Mahâbhârata* and the *nîti-śâstras* (literature on polity).[4] But as yet positive knowledge about the institution exhausts itself merely in stray references to a few premiers, financiers or minister-generals of actual history.

4. *Bourbonism in the East and the West.*

Apparently the supreme councils of Hindu polity, although "permanent" bodies, did not for all practical purposes rise above the pretensions and powers of the Frankish *Champs de Mars* and *Champs de Mai*, or the *officium palatinum* of the Visigoths and the Council of Toledo in Spain.[5] The *Sabhâ* of Hindu monarchies could not thus be anything more than a privileged oligarchy. And evolutionally speaking, it came

---

[1] *Hiuen Thsiang*, Book VIII.

[2] *Si-Yu-ki*, Vol. I, p. 106, 107.

[3] *Ep. Ind.*, 1905—1906, p. 49.

[4] *Mahâbhârata* (*Sabhâ*, V, 30; *Sânti*, LXXXIII, 47), *Râmâyaṇa* (*Ayodhyâ*, C, 18) *Satapatha Brâhmaṇa*, II, 3, 2, 3; V, 3, 1, 10. *Atharva Veda*, V, 31, 6, VII, 12, 1, 2; *Rig Veda*, VI, 28, 6, VIII, 4, 9; *J. A. O. S.*, Vol. XIII, pp. 148—151; *Śukra*, II, lines 23, 105—109, 110—113, 141—143, 145—148 (number of councillors), 220—224, 232—233 (board of three members for each department of state) etc.

[5] Guizot's *History of Representative Government*, Lect. XX, XXVI.

to discharge the functions of the democratic *agora* of the Vedic *civitas* in much the same manner as the council of the *witan* in the early English constitution inherited, as a close exclusive body, the status of the ancient Teutonic folk-moot.

The expansion of the state in area and population was responsible both in Asia and Europe, first ,for the strengthening of the monarchy, and secondly, for the gradual dwindling of the old democratic assembly of the entire people or of the majority of the masses into an aristocratic corporation of the king's ministers, advisers or councillors.[1]

England is distinguished from the rest of Europe by a continuity of democratic evolution during the Middle Ages, at any rate from the fourteenth century on, up to the "glorious revolution" of 1688. But, for over two thousand years since the destruction of Greek liberties by the "Emathian conqueror" and the final abolition of the last Hindu republics by the Gupta "superman" the world both in the East and the West knew of only one statecraft. In one word it may be summed up in Bourbonism such as was embodied in Louis XIV's dictum, *L'état c'est moi.*[2]

None of the references cited by K. P. Jayaswal in his article on "The Hindu Parliament under Hindu Monarchy" in the *Modern Review* for February 1920 can be interpreted to indicate that the *jânapada* is "an institution", viz. the *sabhâ* or assembly of the *janapada* (country) as he claims it to be. It is impossible on the strength of his evidences to attach any technical significance to the term. It denotes nothing more than "an inhabitant of *janapada*". The singular number, wherever it occurs in connection with the term, must not mislead anybody, for according to the grammatical aphorism (*jâtau ekavachanam*) the singular simply indicates "a class".

No extraordinary value is therefore to be attributed to the passage in the Hâthigumphâ inscription (165 B. C.) where the word *jânapada* occurs. The import merely is what is conventionally related of almost all Hindu kings in the epics, stories and eulogistic verses. We are to understand simply that Khâravela's work afforded satisfaction to his subjects. The passage cannot imply that "privileges" were granted to "parliament" (the "national assembly").

All such statements, whether epigraphic or literary, bespeak at best

---

[1] Jenks' *History of Politics*, 88.

[2] cf. Uyehara's *Political Development of Japan* (1867—1909), pp. 23—27. *Vide* Adams' two books on English Constitution for the "feudal contract" origin of limited monarchy. The idea that the democratic institutions of England can be traced back to old Teutonic polity seems now to be exploded.

the general democratic trend[1] of Hindu political speculation but do not by any means necessarily point to the popular, parliamentary or conciliar government of the realm. If we are asked to take the *jânapada* in an institutional (corporate or collective) sense wherever it occurs in relation with a king, or for that matter if we have to take every passage in Sanskrit or Prakrit bearing on a ruler's satisfactory performance of his duties towards the *prakriti* (people) as evidence of a legal control or even a *de facto* authority exercised by the people in administration, the entire history of Hindu India down to 1300 should have to be treated as the history of constitutional monarchy, — more radical at times perhaps than has yet been realized any where on earth. Only a postulate like this can explain how Mr. Jayaswal has been carried away from point to point until he is forced to the furthest logical consequence, viz. the sensational pronouncement at Sec. 288.

Section 5.

The Making of Laws (*Śâsanas*).

1. *Hindu Archives.*

The supreme government of the Chola Empire (900—1300) had a record office[2] as one of its bureaus of administration. It was here that every *śâsana* (or *râjnâm âjnâ* as it is called by Kautilya, i. e., "command of the state") was registered. This department was the depositary also of all official papers having permanent value. In southern India historiography must thus have received an impetus from the public registration of royal decrees and charters.

Hiuen Thsang noticed that in regard to the records of events each prefectural province of the Vardhana Empire (606—647) had its own official for preserving them in writing. The records were called *nîla-pita* (blue deposit). Good and evil events were mentioned therein, as well as calamities and fortunate occurrences.[3]

Further, we know from Megasthenes[4] that under the Mauryas (B. C. 322—185 B. C.) the city fathers of Pâtali-putra regularly kept census and vital statistics of the municipal area. Such data were compiled for every territorial jurisdiction, as is borne out by the *Arthaśâstra.* The

---

[1] *Vide* the section on the "doctrine of resistance in Hindu thought" in the *Pos. Back.* II, pp. 43—46.

[2] Aiyangar's *Anc. Ind.*, pp. 175, 177, 178.

[3] *Si-Yu-ki*, Vol. I, p. 78.

[4] Mc Crindle's *Anc. Ind.*, pp. 87—88.

gazetteer of the village was compiled by the *gopa*.[1] The *sthânika* was responsible for the district gazetteer, as the *nâgaraka* for that of the city. The imperial gezetteer was the compilation of the *samâhartâ* or collector-general from these local directories. All details from the number of males and females to the incomes and expenditures of the families were to be found in these official registers.

But, curiously enough, with the exception of certain sections in the *Artha-śâstra*[2] bearing on revenues and on crimes and punishments students of Hindu polity can hardly point to any collections of *śâsanas*, (ordinances and statutes) or statistical documents in ancient Indian archives. Semi-historical writings like Kalhana's *Râja-taranginî* (Kashmir) Sandhyâkara's *Râma-charita*[3] (Bengal) and Bilhana's *Vikramânka-charita* (Deccan),[4] all of the twelfth century, which may be likened to a certain extent to the *Shu* books of China are, moreover, few and far between. Further, in the Sanskrit literature on legal institutions no treatise has yet been discovered which can be compared to the three volumes compiled during the reign of Justinian (526—565), viz., the *Digest* containing fragments of the work of lawyers like Gaius and Ulpian of the second and third centuries, the *Institutes* drawn up by his own lawyers, and the *Code* embodying the imperial "constitutions" from Hadrian (117—138) to his own times.[5]

2. *The So-called Law-Books of the Hindus.*

The only literature available for the present is twofold. First are the *dharma-śâstras*[6] associated with the names of Manu, Yâjnavalkya, Brihaspati and others. Next come the *nîti-śâstras*[7] like the *Kâmandakî-nîti*, *Śukra-nîti* and Bhoja's *Yukti-Kalpa-taru*. For our present purpose

---

[1] *Ind. Ant.*, 1905, p. 5.

[2] Books III, IV. Kautilya defines *śâsana* as *râjnâm âjnâ*, i. e. the commands of rulers. *Vide* Law's *Hind. Pol.*, pp. 122—123.

[3] Edited by Hara-prasad Shastri (*Memoirs of the Asiatic Society of Bengal*, Vol. III, no. 1).

[4] Edited by Bühler for the *Bombay Sanskrit Series*.

[5] Mackenzie's *Studies in Roman Law*, pp. 21—27; Article on Justinian in the *Enc. Brit.*; Moyle's *Institutes of Justinian*; Taylor's *Mediaeval Mind*, Vol. II, 239—248.

[6] *The Sacred Books of the East Series*, Vols. II, VII, XIV, XXV, XXXIII. For a general account of the entire legal literature see Jolly's *Recht* (Ch. I. *Die Quellen*). In his articles in the *Zeit. Deut. Morg. Ges.* (1913, pp. 51—90, and 1914, pp. 345—347) he has pointed out the passages that the *Artha-* has in common with the *Dharma-* and *Kâma-śâstras*.

[7] Sanskrit text of Kâmandaka in the *Bibliotheca Indica* Series (English translation by M. N. Dutt); Sans. text of Śukra edited for the Madras Government (Engl. transl. for the Panini Office Series by B. K. Sarkar); Sans. text of Bhoja published by the Sanskrit Press Depository, Calcutta.

the important question is to find out how much of the laws and manners mentioned in these books constitute "law" in the Austinian sense. From this point of view it is doubtful if these so-called legal codes of India have barely even as much legitimacy or validity as the twelfth and thirteenth century compendiums of feudal customs[1] in Europe which were expressly modelled on Justinian's achievements. Neither the *Manu Samhitâ* nor the treatise of Sukra can legitimately be likened to the *Spiegel* ("Mirrors") of the Saxons and Swabians, the *Summa de legibus* of the Normans, and the *Consuetudines Feudorum* of the Lombards, or the "*Bracton-nîti*" (*De Legibus et Consuetudinibus Angliae*) of England and the contemporary *Beaumanoir-nîti* (*Coutumes de Beauvoises*) of France. The simple reason is that there is a lack of undisputed archeological proofs concerning the actual life in ancient India. Consequently it is not easy to analyze these Indian *śâstras (Wissenschaften)* and point out precisely which passages describe the conscious and positive "will" of the state (*râjnâm âjnâ*) or actual laws enforced by "sanction", which indicate merely the immemorial customs or "unwritten laws" of the land, and which others, finally, are nothing but the "pious wishes" of the Hindu Ciceros and Senecas, Alcuins and Jonases, Augustines and Isidores, those champions of *dharma* (i. e. justice and truth).

3. *Epigraphic Data on Hindu Dharma (Law).*

It is not surprising, therefore, that Henry Maine whose indology was confined mostly to the *śâstras* and the so-called "village communities" of a politically defunct India should have started the notion, since then held in reverence by Eur-American sociologists, that Hindu states were not *dharma*-enacting i. e. legislating *samûhas* but mere tax-exacting bodies or rather tribute-collecting corporations.[2] But the student of Indian epigraphy today is master of enough historical material to be able to demonstrate that for the period of over fifteen hundred years from Kautilya, the Richelieu or Bismarck of the Mauryas, to Kulottûnga, the Châlukya-Chola, the statesmen of India consciously instituted laws and modified and revised them at will. The "making" of laws in addition to the simple "declaration" of traditional usages must therefore be reckoned among the institutional achievements of the Hindus.

The inscriptions, although mainly donative in character, leave no doubt as to the legislative functions of the states. The fiat of official

---

[1] Carlyle's *Mediaeval Political Theory in the West*, Vol. III, pp. 35, 36, 42; Walsh's *Thirteenth, Greatest of Centuries*, p. 361.

[2] *Early His. of Inst.*, Lect. XIII, pp. 380—383. See *infra* (analysis of *dharma*, *danda* etc.).

proclamations is known to have often abolished old customs and introduced new usages. The new regulations were held binding within jurisdictions for which they were intended. And the state exercised its "sanction" (*danda*) or penal authority, the essence of Austinian sovereignty, in order to punish the violation of its orders and announcements.

4. *Legislation in ancient Mádras and Ceylon.*

It was a law of Râja-râja the Great by which in 986 the village *panchâyats* of southern India were anthorized to take possession of and sell the lands of the persons who failed to pay the government dues for three years.[1] The abolition of tolls that had weighed heavily upon the people for generations was likewise effected by Kulot-ţûnga's liberal legislative enactment in 1086.[2] The "positive" character of Chola legislation is manifest as much in the local government ordinances as in the cadastral and other centralizing measures.

In Ceylon the charter by which the rural commune enjoyed its liberties emanated from the state as an 'Act to confer immunities'. In the tenth century a law was passed by King Kassapa IV (963—80) "in Council" to define the privileges of a village belonging to a hospital. "Whereas it was decreed," ran the proclamation, "that boundary stones *** should be set up *** all these officers of state *** have come from the council and set up in this village a pillar." According to this bill of rights granted by royal order, enforcers of customary laws were not to enter the village. It was placed beyond the jurisdiction of headmen of districts and keepers of district records. Servants of the royal family were likewise declared inadmissible. Laborers, carts, oxen and buffaloes of the territory were not to be appropriated. It was also made into an asylum against the right of extradition. Criminals who sought refuge in the village could not be arrested.[3]

We have specimens of fiscal legislation also in Ceylonese inscriptions. From a desire that "succeeding kings should not again impoverish the inhabitants of Lamkâ by levying excessive imposts" Kirti Nissamka Malla (1153—86) ordained certain rates at which alone revenue should be collected. And since "those who labor with billhook in clearing thorny jungles for cultivation earn their livelihood distressfully" he granted them by the same Act perpetual exemption from taxation.[4]

---

[1] [2] Aiyangar, pp. 161—162, 149—150. For other Chola legislation see *supra* (the section on rural communes) and *infra* (national finance).

[3] *Ep. Zeyl.*, Vol. II, no. 5.

[4] *Ibid*, Vol. I, nos. 9, 21.

5. *The Institutes of Asoka.*

Asoka's Edicts[1] are well known to have been mainly moral or social in their scope. Some of these declarations can be scheduled as "sumptuary" regulations in a wide sense. Not all the proclamations of the Emperor-propagandist were, however, *râjnâm âjnâ* or statutes binding on the empire as a political organization. The *corpus* of Asokan rescripts had, on the whole, no greater authority on the state than are the announcements of a zealous and sincere educational missionary. Constitutionally speaking, they belong to the same category as the Educational Rescript (1890) of Mikado Mutshuito in *Meiji* Japan, or the "messages" to Congress from the Presidents of the United States.

These the people were persuaded by commissioners, magistrates and judicial officers to respect and observe. But the main body of Asoka's time to time messages was not treated as the "commands of a sovereign", the violation of which would be cognizable offence to be tried and punished by the courts of justice. All the same, a minute analysis brings out the fact that some real legislation or lawmaking is to be found in the midst of these thirty pronouncements of various sizes.

One positive law is referred to in Pillar Edict IV. (*c* B. C. 243). By it Asoka gave respite of three days to prisoners convicted and sentenced to death.[2] It was universally applicable throughout the Empire and calculated to bring about legislative centralization and uniformity. An imperial command to this effect was specially called for, because otherwise there might be a great diversity in administrative practice. And such diversity was naturally expected because of Asoka's custom of granting independence to the members of the civil service "in the award of honors and penalties" in order that they might "in security and without fear perform their duties". The Provincials' Edict likewise embodies the purport of a law by which officers in charge of the city were to "prevent unwarranted imprisonment or unwarranted torture of the citizens".[3]

Regulations in regard to *ahimsâ* or non-slaughter i. e. sanctity of animal life appear also to have been laws in the strictest sense of the term. According to Pillar Edict V (*c* B. C. 243), parrots, starlings, adjutants and other animals were exempted from killing.[4] By Rock Edict I (*c* B. C. 257) Asoka disallowed even the animal sacrifices indispensable for certain ceremonial performances.[5] The humane legis-

[1] Cunningham's *Inscriptions of Asoka.*

[2] [3] Smith's *Asoka*, pp. 148—150, 136—138.

[4] [5] *Inscr. of As.*, pp. 138, 117, 118—119.

lation was thus arbitrary and intolerant enough to curtail religious liberty, or, at any rate, the freedom of practice. When, therefore, we read the touching self-complacent note in Rock Edict IV (*c* B. C. 257)[1] in which the monarch congratulates himself on the growth of non-killing and "prevention of cruelty to animate beings" in his reign, can we not believe that the ideals of a "moralist" had indeed in a considerable degree been rigidly transformed into positive law?

Similarly in the statement recorded in Pillar Edict V (*c* B. C. 243) that "in the period extending up to my twenty sixth coronation day I have twenty five times liberated the prisoners", one may read the gist of a law on the general pardon of convicts at coronation-anniversary.[2] Further, in the report about the growth in humanitarianism among Asoka's subjects we are told by this self-conscious emperor that the thing was unknown "for many hundred years past". Here then is to be detected a change of ancient customs brought about, although not exclusively perhaps, by definite commands of the state.

6. *Code Kautilya.*

We are on more solid ground in regard to the legislation of Asoka's grandfather, Chandra-gupta,[3] the founder of the Maurya House. Megasthenes (B. C. 302) was an eye-witness to the law about the license-tax paid by merchants and the tithes on sales. A person convicted of bearing false witness suffered mutilation of his extremities. He who maimed any one not only suffered in return the loss of the same limb but his hand also was cut off. If he caused an artisan to lose his hand or eye, he was put to death.[4] The *Artha-śâstra* corroborates all these statements of the Greek. Laws of foreign trade regulating the customs duties are given in Kautilya's treatise.[5] It describes also the laws relating to the sale of lands, escheat, the royalty from mines, and the terms on which salt, a government monopoly, could be manufactured by private capitalists.

All violations of harbor regulations[6] were severely punished by the *nâvadhyakṣa* or superintendent of ships (port commissioner). The ships of pirates were doomed to destruction, as well as those bound for the

---

[1] *Inscr. of As.*, pp. 118—119.

[2] Smith's *Asoka*, pp. 150—152.

[3] *Vide* "The Law of Contract" in Law's *Hind. Pol.*, and Shamasastry's article on "Land and Revenue Policy" in the *Ind. Ant.*, 1905.

[4] *Meg.* XXVII in Mc Crindle's *Anc. Ind.*, p. 71.

[5] II, xxii, xxxv, xxxvi.

[6] *Ind. Ship.*, pp. 106, 107, 109, 111.

enemy's country. The legislation required the arrest of suspected persons, e. g. those having a perturbed appearance, those travelling without baggage, and those pretending to be suffering from disease. And the commodities of persons travelling without a pass as also of those who with a heavy load forded a river at an unusual place and time were liable to confiscation at the discretion of the harbor or port officials.

The violation of fiscal laws was generally punished with confiscation or fine. The evasion of the tax on sales was a capital offence. The punishment for false statements to census officers about age, income, expenditure, etc. might extend even to death. Offenders against sanitary and other municipal laws were punished with fines which ranged from $^1/_8$th of a *paṇa*, i. e. about 3 cents to 3000 *paṇas* ($ 750).[1]

7. *Despotism of Custom in Europe.*

The enactment of law is the most important function of modern states. This "modernism" dates however from the promulgation of the Code Napoleon.

But in the present epoch students of political science, used as they are to daily law-making and legal reforms, are apt to forget the comparative absence of "legislation" in ancient and mediæval European polity and to ignore the long ages during which the "despotism of custom" held its sway in the West.[2] When, therefore, they come in touch with the institutions of the Old Orient they are easily tempted to dwell on the "primitive" character of Asia's achievements and mark them down as distinctively "oriental". They are, moreover, misled by the paucity of reliable data into taking for granted that law-making was not practised by Hindu states at all.[3]

But now, no epigraphist and archeologist entertain any doubts as to the complex, centralized and well-differentiated machinery of imperialism wielded by the Maurya, Gupta, Pâla, Chola and other *sârva-bhaumas* (world-emperors). One might then suggest, even on *a priori* grounds, that the extensive *Weltherrschaften* consolidated through the enterprise of men of "blood and iron" were not based exclusively on moral maxims,

---

[1] *Ind. Ant.* 1905, pp. 52, 59.

[2] Jenks' *Law and Politics in the Middle Ages*, Ch. II, pp. 59, 63—64; Carter's *Law, Its Origin, Growth and Function*, p. 109; Willoughby's *Government of the Modern States*, pp. 306—308.

[3] Maine's *Ancient Law*, Ch. II, p. 22. On this point as on others Banerjea (pp. 137, 139) echoes the stereotyped notions. He misunderstands, besides, the term *droit administratif* in employing it with reference to Hindu *śâsanas*. For its technical significance see Dicey's *Law of the Constitution*, 326—346.

"declared" customs and unwritten laws like the tribal commonwealths of the earlier epochs of pre-Maurya and Vedic India.

The postulate about the "unchanging East" is indeed an *idola* of the nineteenth century. In any event, Asia was not more stationary than Europe, epoch for epoch. The dynamic process in India's legislative annals can be illustrated by the changes in the penal code from age to age.

8. *Dynamic Character of Hindu Law.*

It is undeniable that the criminal legislation of the Mauryas[1] was exceedingly severe. Lengthy was the schedule of capital offenses even under Asoka the Great, benevolent preacher though he was of *ahimsâ* (mercy to animal life) and propounder of the cult of *dhamma* (piety or duty). We have only to observe, however, that the capital list in the East was much too short when compared with that in the West.

There is nothing exclusively oriental in this barbarity of the Maurya laws. Europe's record in penal legislation down to very recent times has not been at all different from that of Asia. Let us ignore for the present the Roman XII Tables and the Christian Inquisition. The penal code of England during the seventeenth, eighteenth, and early nineteenth centuries was fostered in the same psychology and was as inhuman and Draconian as was that of India of the third and fourth centuries B. C. During George III's reign more than sixty offences were added to the list of capital crimes. In 1845 two hundred and fifty offences (including, of course, some of the most trivial, e. g. breaking a window and stealing two pence worth of paint) were punishable by death. The generation preceding this date witnessed 1400 executions among the English people for offences that have since then been removed from the capital list.[2]

In the perspective of this criminal statistics in modern Europe the India of the Gupta Vikramâdityas in the fifth century A. C. must have been a veritable utopia. For it was a land of profoundly humane legislation, almost millennial, that Fa-Hien, the Chinese traveller, found in the Hindu Empire. To say that the administration of the criminal law appeared to him milder than in China would not mean much to the modern mind. But the important point is that fines were the ordinary punishments for almost all crimes, capital punishment being all but unknown. Amputation of the right hand was the penalty for repeated

---

[1] *Artha*, Book I, Ch. iv, II, xxxv, xxxvi.

[2] Article on "Capital Punishment" in the *Enc. Brit.* Lea's *His. of Inquis*, Vol. I, pp. 234—236, 421—423, etc.; Vol. III, p. 300. For severity of the Twelve Tables and punishments in Roman law see Mackenzie, 5, 6, 351—356.

rebellion, brigandage, and so forth. But even this was resorted to very rarely; and the Chinese scholar testifies to the absence of judicial torture among Hindus.[1]

India's judicial sense did not thus stop at the findings of Kautilya recorded in the *Artha-śâstra.* Radical legislative changes embodied the new tendencies of the Hindu mind in subsequent ages; and the law-makers knew that they were deliberately breaking the traditional customs.

For the seventh century Hiuen Thsang gives the same evidence as Fa Hien for the fifth in regard to the absence of capital punishment. The offenders against the "power of the ruler", i. e. seditionists were imprisoned. They were "simply left to live or die and were not counted among men". This amounted to life-long social ostracism. Amputation of limbs or deportation was a penalty for the violation of what in Confucian ethics is known as the rules of domestic "propriety". For other offenses the punishment was a small payment of money. In the investigation of criminal cases there was no use of rod or staff to obtain proofs of guilt.[2]

Gupta and Vardhana India was thus inestimably in advance of that of the Mauryas. Nay, the modern world which has restricted capital punishment to three crimes, viz., murder, treason, and piracy (Act of British Parliament, 1861) and which liberally practises torture to extort confession is still behind the Hindu conscience of the fifth century. It was left to the Bolsheviks of Russia to revive India's ideal under the Guptas by removing capital punishment from statute books for the first time in European history.

In any case it ought to be clear to students of *Staatswissenschaft* that Hindu law (public or private) cannot be summed up in single shibboleths, whether those of Kautilya, or, as it was the custom so long, the slogans of the hoary Manu. It has changed from epoch to epoch and region to region. Besides, for the study of the legal institutions and positive laws of India the attention of scholars must have to be diverted from the so-called lawbooks[3] to the inscriptions and archeological documents. The fact that the rates of assessment on land which obtained in Maurya and Chola India[4] are entirely different from the conventional $^{1}/_{6}$th of the produce idealized in the *śâstras* is but one of

---

[1] Legge's *Fa Hien*, Ch. XVI, pp. 42—43.

[2] *Si-Yuki*, Vol. I, pp. 83—84.

[3] Jolly's *Recht und Sitte* is a comprehensive study of Hindu laws and morals based on this body of literature. See Gibelin's *Etudes*, Vols I and II, for a comparison of Hindu "private law" with that of the Greeks, Romans and Teutons.

[4] *Infra* (National Finance), pp. 115—116, 124.

many instances of discrepancy between custom and actual law which should warn the student of *Realpolitik* against depending too much on the Manu's and the Śukraś in his institutional investigations.

Section 6.

The Jury System (*Ubbahika*).

Modern liberty, both political and judicial, has, theoretically at any rate, one of its greatest corner-stones in the trial by jury. It consists in the right to be judged by one's peers. As such its origins can be traced to the primitive Frankish, Teutonic and Anglo-Saxon customs. But the definite beginnings of the institution, as it obtains in Europe, are to be sought in the Civil and Criminal Juries of England in the twelfth century. To a certain extent its crude origins are furnished also by the *Vehm-gerichte* or Fehmic Courts of the thirteenth century which were developed in the German-speaking lands (viz. Westphalia) between the Rhine and the Weser.[1] India's political experience seems, however, to furnish the first land-marks of the system among the Indo-European races.

1. *The Jury as a Hindu Institution.*

The oldest historical date for the institution of the Hindu jury is B. C. 443, a hundred years after the death of Śâkya the Buddha. The occasion was brought about by the "ten heretical practices" of Vesali which were submitted for examination to a committee of eight presided over by a judge. In conformity with a rule established by Śâkya, one Revata proposed to refer the matter to a jury. He chose four *bhikkhus* (monks) from the east and four from the west. This choice was formally approved by the *Samgha* (Ecclesiastical Council). There was added to the arbitrators, as regulator of the sittings, a monk named Ajitâ.[2]

The *idea* of the jury is therefore at least as old as Śâkya (sixth century B. C.). Evidently it was an well-established institution in the public law of his time. By advocating and adopting the system for the settlement of disputes in ecclesiastical matters this spiritual doctor gave but another evidence of his strong civic and legal sense. "If, O *bhikkhus*", said he on one occasion, "whilst the case is being inquired into by those *bhikkhus*, pointless speeches are brought forth, and the sense of any

[1] Holdsworth's *History of English Law*, Vol. I, 135, 145, 149, 156, 158; Walsh's *Thirteenth*, 368—369; Article on "Jury" in Lalor's *Cyclopaedia of Political Science*, Vol. II, 653—662. It is well known how List in his *National System of Political Economy* attaches an extraordinary importance to the jury system in its effects on the British political mentality.

[2] Poussin's "Buddhist Councils" in the *Ind. Ant.*, 1908, p. 85.

single utterance is not clear, I enjoin upon you, O *bhikkhus*, to settle the case by referring it to a jury or commission (*ubbahika*)."[1]

Not everybody could be elected on the jury. The *Chulla-vagga* mentions ten qualifications of the juror. It was held, among other things, that the *ubbahika* must be "competent to point out both friends and foes, to get them to understand a thing, get them to see it and recognize it, and able to pacify them". Secondly, the person to be chosen on the jury must be "clever in judging both as to the origin and as to the settlement of disputes". And thirdly, he must "understand legal questions, the origin thereof, the close thereof, and the way that leads to the close thereof".[2]

The method of appointing a jury was also clearly described. First, the *bhikkhu* was to be asked as to whether he was willing to undertake the office. Then some discreet and able monk was to address the *Samgha* thus: "May the venerable *Samgha* hear me ***. Let it appoint *bhikkhus* of such and such a name, and of such and such a name on a committee. This is the motion ***. The *Samgha* appoints *bhikkhus* of such and such names on a committee to settle the case."[3]

Traces of the jury system are to be detected in Maurya India. For, by a ruling of Kautilya in the *Artha-śâstra*, disputes concerning boundaries, fields and "miscellaneous hindrances" were to be decided by elders of the neighborhood. If they were divided in their opinions decision was to be given in favor of the opinion of the honest *vahavah*, i. e. the "many" or the majority.[4] There is here an anticipation of the Grand Assize of Henry II by which the claimant to disputed lands could demand the nomination of four knights of the neighborhood. The Kautilyan principle is also the same as that of the Assize of Northampton by which the property due to heirs was determined in the identical manner.

2. *Hindu Ideas about the Jury.*

The institution could not but influence the political thinking of the philosophers. Śukra and other writers on the theory of the constitution

[1] *Chulla*, IV, 14, 19.

[2] *Ibid*, IV, 14, 19.

[3] *Ibid*, IV, 14, 20.

[4] The interpretation of *vahavah śuchayah* (*vide* the *Artha*, Bk. III, Ch. IX) in Jayaswal's "Introduction to Hindu Polity" in the *Mod. Rev.*, June 1913, is more accurate than that in Shamasastry's translation (pp. 214—215). For the law of the majority see also Śukra, I, lines 732—733. Bosanquet is certainly more chauvinistic than philosophic when he naively makes the statement that the principle of the majority is "found for the first time as an everyday method of discussion in Greek political life" (*Phil. Theory of State*, pp. 45). cf. *Pos. Back*, II, p. 19.

have therefore naturally been the spokesmen of the philosophy that underlies the English Assizes and the Fehmic Courts of Westphalia. The principle of trial by one's peers is thus stated in the *Śukra-nîti*:[1] "The foresters are to be tried with the help of foresters, merchants by merchants, and soldiers by soldiers." Śukra lays down also the principle of local judges for local cases in the following terms: "In the village the cases are to be settled by persons who live with both parties, i. e. by neighbours. Those persons are the best judges of the merits of the case who live in the place where the two parties stand, and where the disputed matters and grounds of quarrel exist."[2]

In Hindu thought merchants[3] appear to have been in high demand as qualified to serve on the jury. Their strong commonsense was evidently their chief merit, or perhaps they were likely to have legal knowledge. In the *Śukra-nîti* even the audience at a court of justice is regarded as part of the jury. In regard to the man who happens to know the law we are told that "one can speak, whether appointed or not, because he speaks the voice of God who knows the law".[4] And we are also asked to entertain respect for the layman's commensense view of the case. For, an extremely radical view is adumbrated by Śukra when he declares that "either one should not come to the court or should speak truthfully. That man is a sinner who keeps silence or utters falsehood".[5]

Altogether, then, in Śukra we have to recognize a theorist in regard to the institution of which the practical regulations had been laid down by Śâkya for his Congregation. And if in the absence of evidences from inscriptions or contemporary writings it be safe to take the passages in the *Śukra-nîti* as describing the actual judiciary in certain states of India in any period of its history, the jury must be regarded as an essential feature of the system of Hindu tribunals.[6]

Section 7.

Deposition and Election of Kings.

In England James II was deposed, among other reasons, for having violated the "original compact", Richard II as "useless, incompetent,

[1] IV, v, lines 44, 45.

[2] IV, v, lines 45—47.

[3] IV, v, 52.

[4] IV, v, lines 53, 54; see also Nârada, *Legal Procedure*, III, 2.

[5] IV, v, 55, 56.

[6] Banerjea's identification of the *sabhyas* (members of a judicial assembly i. e. assessors) with the jury (*Public Adminis*, p. 143) is not acceptable.

and altogether insufficient and unworthy", and Edward II for having broken the "coronation oath".

1. *People's Control over the Crown.*

In at least two historic instances the attitude of the Hindu mind in regard to kingship was identical. Brihadratha, the last Maurya Emperor (B. C. 191—185), was "crushed" because, as we read in Bâṇa's *Harṣa-charita* (seventh century), he was *pratijnâ-durbala* i. e. weak in keeping his coronation oath.[1]

A specimen of the *pratijnâ*, promise, vow or oath made by Kings to the people is thus worded in the *Aitareya Brâhmaṇa*:[2] "Between the night I was born and the night I die, whatever good I might have done, my heaven, my life and my progeny may I be deprived of, if I oppress you." And the *Mahâbhârata*[3] furnishes the traditional form of the oath administered to Veṇa's son Prithu in the following terms: "I shall always regard the *bhauma* (the country) as the Brahma (the highest God). And whatever is to be prescribed as law on the basis of statecraft I shall follow without hesitation, never my own sweet will." A *samaya*[4] or compact was in this way entered into by the king and the people. The non-fulfilment of the *pratijnâ* was tantamount to the violation of the compact, comparable to the feudal contract introduced in Norman England, which Adams considers to be the real origin of limited monarchy in Europe.

Another case of expulsion in Hindu history is that which resulted in the founding of the Śiśu-nâga Dynasty in B. C. 602. The populace were led to depose the reigning king, Nâgadasako the "impious", because of his parricide. Really they condemned the whole House as a "parricidal race", as another ruler of the family, Udayibhaddako, the perfidiously impious son of Ajâtasattu, had put his parent to death.[5]

Besides, in the *Mahâbhârata* the plea for the deposition and execution of the tyrant Veṇa[6] is that he was *vidharma* i. e. unlawful or unconstitutional and the "slave of wrath and malice". On these and similar

---

[1] p. 193.

[2] VIII, 4, 1, 13.

[3] *Śânti-parva*, Ch. IX, 106, 107.

[4] *Ibid*, LXVII, 17, 24. The "feudal contract" theory is the special feature of Adams' *Origin of the English Constitution* and *A Constitutional History of England*. cf. Carlyle, III, 39—40.

[5] *Mahâvamso*, Ch. IV, p. 15. See the stories in the *Râja-taranginî*, *Supra*, pp. 69—70.

[6] *Sânti-parva*, LIX,94; Jayaswal's "Constitutional Aspects of the Rituals at Hindu Coronation" in the *Mod. Rev.*, January 1912; Law's "Ancient Hindu Coronation and Allied Ceremonials" in the *Ind. Ant.* (1919); Basu's *Indo-Aryan Polity*.

grounds Vedic India also was used to the expulsion of rulers. The story of *aparuddha* or expelled kings is familiar to the readers of the *Brâhmaṇas* and *Samhitâs.*[1]

2. *The People as King-makers.*

Nor as regards title to kingship has the political psychology of Asians been at variance with that of Europeans. Succession to the mediaeval German Empire was determined, as a rule, by election. In France none but the immediate successors of Charlemagne were elected by the people. And in the history of the English Constitution election has been almost as important as the hereditary principle.

Now, while hereditary succession was the rule in Hindu polity, the history of India can exhibit several authentic instances of popular election. The latest is that of Gopâla (*c* 730—40), the son of a successful soldier, who was "made by the *prakriti* (the people) to accept the throne".[2] Eventually he became the founder of the Pâla Empire of Bengal and Eastern India. Harṣa-vardhana (606—47) became Emperor of Upper India through election by ministers and magistrates in an assembly presided over by Premier Bhandi "the distinguished".[3] On that occasion the people's approval was "shown in their songs".

Rudra-dâmana (*c* 125—150) acknowledged his claim to the crown in the Satrapy of Western India because of election by "all the orders of the people".[4] And Śiśunâga's Dynasty was set up, as we have seen, as the result of a mass movement. The city mob,[5] infuriated at the parricide of Nâgadasako, and desirous of gratifying the whole nation, "unanimously installed in sovereignty the eminently wise minister bearing the historically distinguished appellation of Śiśunâga" (B. C. 603). Further, the *Mahâbhârata* records the tradition that Kuru[6] was elected king by "all the people" because he was *dharmajna* i. e. proficient in law, and that the "people of the cities and villages" prevented Devapi's accession to the throne because he had *tvagdoṣa* or skin-disease[7] (leprosy) and installed Śântanu the youngest son.

3. *Succession determined by Vox Populi.*

Even in the election of the heir-apparent the people of India had a voice, at least in the epics. We read in the *Mahâbhârata* that on several

[1] Atharva Veda, III, 3, 4; *Śatapatha Brâhmaṇa*, XII, 9, 3, 3; *Taittirîya Samhitâ*, II, 3, 1.
[2] Banerji's *Memoir*, p. 45.
[3] *Si-yu-ki*, Vol. I, pp. 210, 211.
[4] *Ep. Ind.*, 1905—06, 43.
[5] *Mahâvamso*, p. 15.
[6] *Âdi-parva*, XCIV, 49; *Journal of the American Oriental Society*, 1889, pp. 137, 139, 143.
[7] *Udyoga-parva*, CXLIX, 23.

occasions the revolts of the folk brought about a modification in the choice of a crown-prince. It was only with the people's consent secured after a fracas that Yayâti could instal his younger son, Puru, as crown-prince against the technically rightful eldest son Yadu.[1] And Dhrita-râṣtra was compelled by the people's protests to elect his nephew as heir-apparent instead of his unworthy son.[2]

Such "democratic" settlements of crown-princeship, described also in the *Râmâyaṇa*[3], may be taken to have anticipated (in theory, at any rate, as long as evidences from the strictly historical sources are not forth-coming) the recorded instances in the procedure of mediaeval Europe. The *Ordinatio Imperii* of Lewis the Pious in 817 is the document that provided for the partition of his dominions between his sons. In accordance with its provisions, after the ceremonial fast of three days his eldest son Lothair was elected by Lewis and the whole people to be his colleague in the empire. Then "with common counsel" it was decided to give the younger sons, Pippin and Lewis, the title of kings and to allot to them certain lands by definite *capitula*. These were considered and then "confirmed by Lewis and all his faithful subjects".[4] Now, if Megasthenes' observations be of any value, the *Mahâbhârata* or the *Râmâyaṇa* ideal was not the mere fine frenzy of poets. For, says the Greek ambassador, *vox populi* was consulted by the responsible officers in determining succession on the failure of heirs, and the regulating principle was merit.[5]

[1] *Âdi-parva*, LXXXV, 22.
[2] *Ibid*, CXL, 23.
[3] *Ayodhyâ-kânda*, Ch. I.
[4] Carlyle's *Med. Pol. Theory*, Vol. I, p. 237.
[5] Fragment L.

CHAPTER V.

The Hindu Machinery of Imperial Nationalism.

Section 1.

The War Office.

In no branch of national life was the administrative genius of the Hindus more in evidence than in the organization of the army and the navy. It was not only in the numerous aggressive wars within the Indian continent that the efficiency of the race in generalship and as a fighting machine was put to the fire test. Hindu military might was also equally manifest when pitted against foreigners who threatened the freedom of India. From Seleukos to Menander (B. C. 305—B. C. 155) the Hellenistic Greeks of the Afghan bufferland were successfully driven back within their own folds by Hindu archers, horsemen, and elephant corps. In later times, the Huns also had to sustain severe defeats, first, from Skanda-gupta between A. C. 455 and 458, and, secondly, from Narasimha-gupta about 528.

1. *Militarism in Hindu Culture.*

Indeed the Charlemagnes and Fredericks, by whose *parâkrama* (prowess) the frontiers of India were advanced so far as to include, on several occasions, Afghanistan and Central Asia on the land side, and the islands of the Indian Ocean to the south, had their hands always full with the problem of training and equipping the soldiers and sailors. The profession of arms and the command of the fleet called forth as a matter of course the administrative capabilities of Young India from age to age, — in the northern, eastern, central, western and southern provinces. And the spirit that pervaded these disciplined forces is what came out in the fourth gymnosophist's reply to Alexander's query. Alexander asked him as to why he had persuaded Sabbas (Śambhu) to revolt. Because, as we read in Plutarch's *Lives*, said the Hindu sage, "I wished him either to live with honor or die as a coward deserves."[1]

[1] Plutarch's *Life of Alexander*.

And this was not an empty word of the philosopher cited like a maxim, as it were, from the *Mahâbhârata*. We are told by Plutarch that Alexander experienced no less trouble from the priests, preachers, and religious teachers of India than from the warriors who "used to fight for pay". It was the endeavour of the "philosophers" to fix a mark of infamy upon those princes, who, like the king of Taxila, declared for the Macedonian and became traitors to Indian independence. The free republican nations also were excited by what appear to be the learned and priestly classes, i. e., the *intelligentsia*, to take up arms against the alien invaders. Many are the Hindu philosophers who therefore had to espouse the martyr's doom meted out to them by Alexander's vindictive court-martial.

In order to appreciate the age-long militarism of the Hindus and their organization of the general staff it is necessary to have an idea of the Roman institutions of national defence and war-machinery.[1] In B. C. 225 the republic placed 65,000 soldiers on the field and had 55,000 in reserve at Rome.[2] At Trebia (B. C. 218), as Polybius writes in his *History of the Roman Conquest from B. C. 264—146*, the strength of the army was 38,400. And the largest force that the Romans are known to have mustered during their republican period was that under Scipio for the Second Punic (Hannibalian) War (B. C. 218—202).[3] On this occasion the army consisted sometimes of 18,20, or even 23 legions. A "legion" at that time was made up of 4,000 or 5,000 soldiers, and of this number about 300 or 400 constituted the cavalry.

In point of numbers the Roman armies must have been regarded as pigmy indeed or but as "pocket armies" by the generalissimos of Hindu nationalities. For, the fighting hordes maintained by the states of India appear to have always been formidable in size. A "standing army" of half a million was nothing extraordinary in military India's psychology. Among the fragmentary notices of the nations, some of them difficult to identify accurately, that we can glean from Megasthenes' stories (*c* B. C. 300) we find that the Pândyas[4] of the extreme south who were ruled by women had an army of 150,000 foot and 500 elephants. The ruler of Gujarat[4] on the Arabian Sea coast was in command of 1,600 elephants, 150,000 infantry and 5,000 horse; and the force wielded by the sovereign of the races[5] between the Ganges and the Himalayas,

[1] Greenidge's *Roman Public Life*, pp. 68—74 (Roman army according to the Servian classification).

[2] *Enc. Brit.* (Article on Roman Army).

[3] Ramsay's *Roman Antiquities*, p. 432.

[4] Mc Crindle's *Anc. Ind.* (*Meg.*, LVI), 147.

[5] *Ibid*, 138.

occupying the districts of north Bihar, north Bengal, and possibly western Assam, was composed of 50,000 infantry, 4,000 cavalry and 400 elephants.

In Plutarch's *Life of Alexander* we learn, further, that the king of Magadha (the Gangaridae and Prasii nations on the banks of the Ganges) in Eastern India was master of 20,000 horse, 200,000 foot, 2,000 chariots, and 3,000 or 4,000 elephants. Evidently this ruler was one of the "nine Nandas". The size of one of the smallest Hindu armies can be given from Pliny's *Natural History*.[1] It belonged to another people of the eastern provinces of India, viz., the Gangaridae Kalingoe, ancestors of the modern Oriyas. Their king with capital at Protalis had 60,000 infantry, 1,000 horse, and 700 elephants "always caparisoned for battle". But, as usual, in regard to most of the periods of Hindu military and naval history, authentic information is wanting about the system of discipline, salaries, hierarchy of officers and other items of the War Office, except what may be gathered from the *nîti-śâstras* and other literature on polity.

2. *The Gupta and Pâla Digvijayas.*

About A. C. 360 Hari-ṣeṇa, a *mahâdanda-nâyaka* (high grade military or judicial officer) of the Gupta Empire, composed in Sanskrit what he called a *kâvya*.[2] It was an ode, in verse and prose, in eulogy of Samudra-gupta's conquest of "all the world". That panegyric "in one single gigantic sentence", which half a century later furnished Kâlidâsa with an epigraphic precedent for his own romantic account of Raghu's *digvijaya* ("conquest of the quarters") is at present the only contemporary account of a Hindu military enterprise that has satisfactory details as to the names of nations and rulers. Hari-ṣeṇa exults over the "violent extermination" of old states, and describes how kings were "captured and then liberated" by his hero. We are told that Samudra-gupta's "officers were always employed in restoring the wealth of the various kings who had been conquered by the strength of his arms".

As might be naturally expected, in this description of the aggressor's

[1] Book VI, Ch. xxii; *Vide* also *Meg.* LVI, B.

[2] Text of the *kâvya* in *Gup. Insc.* The English translation by Fleet was corrected in Bühler's German article on Indian Artificial Poetry, and this has been Englished by V. S. Ghate for the *Ind. Ant.* (1913). *Re* the date of the composition *vide* the *Journal of the Royal Asiatic Society*, 1898, pp. 386—387. The identification of some of the regions overrun by Samudra-gupta seems to be open to question. H. C. Ray Chaudhuri says in the *Mod. Rev.* (Oct. 1921) that the Western Deccan lay outside of the sphere of Gupta conquests. He accepts the interpretation in Dubreuil's *Ancient History of the Deccan* and rejects Smith's identifications.

triumphant expeditions through kingdoms, forests, hills and rivers we read of the "blows of battle-axes, arrows, spears, pikes, barbed darts, swords, lances, javelins for throwing, iron arrows" and many other weapons that disfigured or rather "beautified", as the poet-laureate would have it, the "charming body" of Samudra-gupta with the "marks of hundred confused wounds".[1] But while the world-conqueror is portrayed as "skilful in engaging in a hundred battles of various kinds", with "*parâkrama* (strength) of his own arm for his only ally", the officer-biographer leaves us in the dark as to the Indian Napoleon's plan of campaign, methods of field organization, and administration of the army services. We can only guess the thoroughness of the military department from the fact that the extensive Alexandrine career of uninterrupted success covered no less than three thousand miles of territory and was spread over about twenty years (330—350).

Hardly anything has been unearthed as yet in regard to the Bengali legions with which Dharma-pâla started from Pâtali-putra on his Upper Gangetic Valley campaign about 783 in order to set up a nominee and protege, Chakrâyudha, on the throne of Kanauj. The adventure of this expeditionary force led to the temporary conquest of Malwa, North Eastern Rajputana, Eastern Punjab and Sindh, Western Punjab and the Northwestern frontier provinces, and parts of Afghanistan. The soldiers of Bengal were thus in a position to enjoy the waters as far to the northwest as at Kedâra in the Western Himalayas and as far to the southwest as at Gokarna in the North Kanara District of the Bombay Presidency.[2]

In the Khâlimpur copper plate inscription we have a hint that Dharma-pâla had to build a bridge of boats at Pâtali-putra. And "the manifold fleets of boats proceeding on the path of the Ganges made it seem as if a series of mountain tops had been sunk to build another causeway". The general superintendent of boats was then as in Kautilya's language known as *târika*.[3] The organization of Devapâla's extensive campaigns by which he compelled entire Northern India from sea to sea to pay tribute to Bengal is as unknown as that under his predecessor. The name of one general can be wrung out of the inscriptions, that of Somesvara, the son of the Premier, Darbha-pâṇi. For obvious reasons Bengal has always had a boat service attached to the army.

---

[1] *Ind. Ant.*, VIII, p. 31, 172; Fleet's *Gupta Ins.*, p. 12, 14, 16.

[2] Banerji's *Memoir*, pp. 51—53, 55—56; *Bânglâr Itihâsa* (*History of Bengal* in Bengali), Vol. I. pp. 167—170; *Ind. Ant.* 1892, p. 257.

[3] *Ep. Ind.*, 1896—1897, pp. 252, 253.

Under the Sena Emperors (1068—1200), as under the Pâlas, *nau-vala* (naval force) was an important arm of the military establishment.[1]

It is known among archeologists today that during the tenth century there was a series of triangular conflicts[2] between the ambitious *digvijayî* monarchs of Bengal, Upper India and the Deccan. But the military achievements of the Gurjara-Pratîhâra and Râṣtra-kûta *sârva-bhaumas* are as unillumined, so far as the details of field work, training of officers, commissariat or transport service are considered, as are those of the Pâlas.

3. *The Tamil War Office.*

The army of the Chola Empire in Southern India appears to have been divided into sections according to the kind of arms they carried, and according as they were mounted or otherwise.[3] There were the "chosen body of archers", the "chosen foot-soldiers of the body-guard", the "chosen horsemen" and the "chosen infantry" of the "right hand" (i. e. the infantry recruited from the artisan class). Among the commanders of the elephant corps we find the names of a few princes. According to the plan of cities with which early Tamil literature makes us familiar, young recruits to the army received military training in quarters specially set apart for them outside the city. Conjeeveram,[4] for instance, had an "outer city" with open spaces that were reserved for breaking the war elephants and horses. The grounds were utilized also for drill, parade and manoeuvres.

The Chola Emperors had a powerful navy. With its aid Râja-râja the Great (984—1018) destroyed the fleet of the rival Chera state on the West coast, and annexed Ceylon to his empire, which eventually embraced the whole of modern Madras Presidency, Mysore, and southern half of Orissa. The army and navy of Râjendra-chola (1018—1035) won a pan-Indian and even extra-Indian reputation on account of his numerous successful campaigns. In his time the Bay of Bengal, the Indian Mediterranean, became a Chola lake. His naval engagements brought about the conquest of "countless old islands", viz., the Laccadives and the Maldives. He crossed the Bay over to the Burman side and captured the kingdom of Prome or Pegu. His navy annexed also the Nicobar and Andaman Islands. Lighthouses were constructed at the leading ports of the Chola Empire.[5]

---

[1] *Ind. Ship.*, p. 220.

[2] Banerji's *Memoir*, p. 52, 56.

[3] Aiyangar, p. 184.

[4] Ayyar's *Town Planning*, p. 70.

[5] *Ind. Ship.*, pp. 175—177, 137; Aiyangar, 185; Ayyar, p. 15.

4. *Military India in the Seventh Century.*

Bâṇa tells us in his biographical story-book, the *Harṣa-charita*,[1] that Emperor Harṣa made his *debut* with a solemn vow. "How can I rest", declared this *vijigīṣu* (aspirant to world-conquest) of the seventh century, "so long as my feet are not besmeared with an ointment found in every continent, consisting of the light of precious stones in the diadems of all kings?" Accordingly in 606 he set out on his career of triumph; and we know from Hiuen Thsang the figures as to the strength of Harṣa's army at two dates. It was at the head of 50,000 infantry, 20,000 cavalry and 5,000 elephants that the Vardhana hero went forth "conquering and to conquer. But by the end of his first period of campaigns, continuously spread over five years and a half during which he brought Northern India to subjection, he was in command of 100,000 cavalry, and 60,000 elephants.[2] From Bâṇa's story we know, further, that Kuntala was a chief officer of the Vardhana cavalry, Simha-nâda was a *senâpati* (general), Avanti was the supreme minister of war and peace, and Skanda-gupta was commandant of the whole elephant troop.

But the powerful army of Harṣa-vardhana's formidable adversary, Pulakeśî II, the Chalukya *sârva-bhauma* of Southern India, who compelled the northerner to know the limits of his ambition, is remembered today only by the triumphant resistance that he offered from the mountain-passes on the Narmada to the aggressor's southward march (620). Hiuen Thsang mentions only that the *forte* of the Deccan Emperor lay in the elephants. The Maratha monarch had, besides, a "fleet consisting of hundreds of ships". Purî, the Lakṣmî (the goddess), i. e. the queen of the Arabian Sea, is known to have been reduced by him as the result of naval engagements.[3]

In the seventh century, probably both in Northern and Southern India, as we understand from Hiuen Thsang's general summary,[4] the military force was divided into the traditional four arms, viz. infan ry, cavalry, chariots and elephants. The elephants were covered with strong armour and their tusks were provided with sharp spurs. The chariots were drawn by four horses abreast. Two attendants drove the chariot according to the command of the leader who sat between. The general issued orders from his chariot and was surrounded by a body of guards who kept close to his chariot wheels.

---

[1] pp. 177, 180, 187, 188, 189. *Vide* the description of mobilization, pp. 199—201, 206—209. See Harṣa's vow, p. 188.

[2] *Si-Yuki*, Vol. I, p. 213.

[3] R. G. Bhandarkar's *Early Hist.*, sec. X.

[4] *Si-Yu-ki*, Vol. I, p. 82, 83, 87.

The cavalry spread themselves in front to resist an attack, and in case of defeat they carried orders to and fro. The infantry by their quick movements contributed to the defense. They carried a long spear and a great shield; sometimes they held a sword or sabre and advanced to the front with impetuosity. All their weapons were sharp and pointed.

Soldiers were levied according to the requirements of the service; they were promised certain payments and were publicly enrolled.

5. *The Deccan and the Punjab through Hellenistic and Roman Eyes.*

Previous to the rise of the Châlukyas the dominions of the Deccan had for centuries been held by the Ândhras. Like the other nationalities of India south of the Vindhya Mountains the Ândhra monarchy was a naval power with base on the Madras Coast. A large two-masted ship[1] was the device of the coins that were struck by Yajna-śrî (*c* A. C. 173—202). It was intended evidently to be an emblem of the people's maritime importance. About five hundred years previous to this date the founders of the Ândhra Dynasty had measured their strength with the mighty Mauryas (*c* B. C. 300) only to submit to their superior numbers. The Deccan army was at this time made up of 100,000 infantry, 2,000 cavalry, and 1,000 elephants, according to both Megasthenes and Pliny.[2]

From the accounts of Greek and Roman writers it would appear that in ancient times the Punjab was, what Bengal has always been, a land of navigable rivers. Like the Easterners, therefore, the Northwestern Hindus were naturally skilled in riparian warfare. The Punjab fleets were strong elements in India's opposition to Alexander. The Xathroi or Kṣatriyas[3] may be described as having been by far the most noted naval architects and shipping experts.

It was, again, the boats of the various Punjab republics that made up the fleet, 800 to 2,000 vessels strong, with which Nearchos was entrusted for the voyage down the Indus and up to the Persian Gulf.[4] It is said that 4,000 Hindu boats had been assembled on the Indus to resist the earlier invasion of India by Semiramis, the Assyrian queen, and also that in much later times Mahmud the Moslem invader had to encounter

---

[1] *Ind. Ship.*, 119; For the boundaries of the Ândhra Empire see D. R. Bhandarkar's "Dekkan of the Sâta-vahana Period" in the *Ind. Ant.* (1918), pp. 150, 151, 156; See also the studies of V. S. Sukthankar for an altogether new light on the expansion of the Ândhra dominions (*R. G. Bhandarkar Commemoration Volumes*, Poona, 1920).

[2] *Meg.* LVI; *Natural History*, Book VI, Ch. xxi—xxiii; *Ind. Ant.*, 1918, p. 70.

[3] *Infra*, p. 144.

[4] Vincent's *Commerce and Navigation of the Ancients*, Vol. I, p. 12.

the measures of national defense organized by a Punjab fleet of the same strength.[1]

6. *Defensive Measures against Alexander.*

The gallant resistance offered by the nations of India, both single and united, to the all-sweeping raid of Alexander, is obviously an important event in the annals of the Hindu army. The ancient European historians of that invasion furnish us with some figures about the troops of the various states that stood in the way of the Macedonian's penetration into the Indo-Gangetic plains. The first formidable opposition came from the Assakenoi of Afghanistan. They defended their fort at Massaga with 30,000 infantry, 20,000 cavalry and 30 elephnts.[2] The next defendant of Hindu freedom was Poros, ruler of the Punjab between the Hydaspes (Jhelum) and the Akesines (Chenub).[3]

Poros opposed Alexander with an army over 50,000 strong. At the battle of the Hydaspes (July B. C. 326) the centre of the Hindu army was occupied by 200 elephants stationed at intervals of a hundred feet from one another and probably in eight ranks. The infantry numbering 50,000 were placed behind the elephant corps, but with files pushed forward between the elephants. There were 3,000 cavalry and 1,000 chariots to defend the flanks. The *vyûha* (battle-order) of this force resembled a city, says Diodorus. The elephants looked like the towers and the men at arms between them resembled the lines of wall between tower and tower.[4]

The spirit of the Macedonians was abated, says Plutarch, by the combat with Poros, and they resolved not to proceed any further in India. It was with extreme difficulty that they had succeeded in defeating the small army of the Punjab hero. They, therefore, opposed their chief with the greatest firmness when they came to learn that the monarch of the farthest east on the banks of the Ganges was ready to fight the foreign aggressor with 80,000 horse, 200,000 foot, 8,000 chariots and 6,000 elephants.

But before Alexander could finally retire from the Punjab he had to contest his way through every inch of the lower Indus valley. Incessant and severe were his military engagements with the sturdy republics.

---

[1] Robertson's *Disquisition*, pp. 296—297 (notes). See Bejoy Kumar Sarkar's "Water Transport in Mediaeval India" in the *Journal of the Department of Letters*, Vol. IV (Calcutta 1921).

[2] Mc Crindle's *Invasion of India* (*Arrian*, XXV; Curtius, X), 66, 194.

[3] *Ibid* (Plutarch's *Alexander*, LXII), 310.

[4] *Ibid* (*Diodorus*, Book XVII, Ch. lxxxvii), p. 274.

The Agalassoi met him with 40,000 foot and 3,000 horse.[1] The most warlike of these autonomous non-monarchical nations were the Malloi or Mâlavas. At the present juncture they happened to contract an alliance with the Kṣudrakas, their sworn enemies for ages. The combined armies amounted to 90,000 infantry, 10,000 cavalry and 900 chariots.[2] During this period the shaft used by the Indian archers was three yards long. Nothing could resist their shot, says Arrian,[3] — neither shield nor breast plate, nor any stronger defence, if such there be".

7. *Imperial Armies: Hindu and Roman.*

The mind of military India quickly shook off the nightmare of Macedonian invasion (B. C. 327—324). Nay, Hindus lost no time in rising to liberate the Punjab from the yoke of Alexander's army of occupation (B. C. 322). The force that accomplished this expulsion of European garrisons from the "land of the five rivers" was the nucleus of what in a decade or two developed into the standing army "on daily pay", as Pliny puts it, of Chandra-gupta, the founder of the Maurya House of the Magadhan Empire. And when Seleukos the Greco-Syrian had to submit to the Hindu monarch and cede Afghanistan and Baluchistan to the victor (B. C. 303) the Maurya army was composed of 600,000 infantry, 30,000 cavalry, 9,000 elephants and about 8,000 chariots.[4] Excluding followers and attendants, but including the archers, three on each elephant, and two fighting men on each chariot, the whole army consisted of 690,000 men. The exact figures of the Maurya naval force are not forthcoming yet.

Let us here place the military facts from the side of European imperialism. The temporary national militias of republican Rome became a "standing army" for the first time under Augustus.[5] He bequeathed to Tiberius (A. C. 14—37) probably the largest army that Imperial Rome ever commanded. Besides the praetorian guards and three fleets it was made up of 25 legions (of Roman troops) and 25 legions of *auxilia* (i. e. soldiers furnished by foreign dependents and allies, comparable to the Imperial Service Troops of the feudatory or protected states in British India). And the total force numbered 320,000.[6] It is clear that the Maurya General Staff had the ability to drill, equip, finance and

---

[1] [2] *Infra*, pp. 143—144.

[3] Arrian's *Indika* XVI.

[4] Pliny's *Natural History*, Book VI, Ch. xxii; Plutarch's *Alexander*; *Meg*. LVI.

[5] Arnold's *Roman Provincial Administration*, 114.

[6] Ramsay, 432; Arnold, 113.

manipulate more than double the man-power of the imperial-Roman war-machine.

8. *The Maurya General Staff.*

A good percentage of the national revenues must have been ear-marked for the army and navy by the Mauryas. The fighting men were maintained, as Megasthenes[1] records, at the king's expense and were always ready, when occasion called, to take the field. And the pay was so liberal in Arrian's estimation that they could "with ease maintain themselves and others besides".[2]

The Supreme War Office of the Mauryas was administered by a council of thirty members.[3] This consisted of six boards, with five members to each. Army and admiralty formed the joint charge of one of these boards. The second board looked after supply, comprehending transport, commissariat and war service. It was responsible for the bullock trains that were used for "transporting the engines of war, food for the soldiers, provender for the cattle, and other military requisites". It had to furnish the servants who beat the drum and others who carried gongs, grooms also for the horses, and mechanists and their assistants. To the sound of the gong they sent out foragers to bring in grass and by a system of rewards and punishments ensured the work being done with dispatch and safety. Another board was in charge of the infantry. Cavalry, war-chariots and elephants were likewise entrusted to three separate boards.

There were royal stables for the horses and elephants and also a royal magazine for the arms because the soldier had to return his arms to the magazines and his horse and his elephant to the stables. The chariots were drawn on the march by oxen, but the horses were led along by a halter that their legs might not be galled and inflamed, nor their spirits damped by drawing chariots. In addition to the charioteer there were two fighting men who sat up in the chariot beside him. The war elephant carried four men, three who shot arrows, and the driver.

The naval arm of the Maurya war office was as minutely looked after as the military. The *nâvadhyakṣa* or superintendent of ships and boats dealt with all matters relating to navigation, not only of oceans but also of rivers and lakes, natural or artificial. His functions combined the supervision of fleets for riparian or maritime warfare with the administration of customs and harbor laws.[4]

---

[1] Mc Crindle's *Ancient India*, p. 85.

[2] *Ibid*, p. 211.

[3] *Ibid*, pp. 88—89.

[4] *Artha*, Book II, Ch. xxviii; *Ind. Ship.*, 104—112.

The centre of eight hundred villages in the Maurya Empire was the seat of a fortress calles *sthânîya*, if the finance minister Kautilya's directions were carried out. A fortress called *droṇa-mukhya* was constructed in the centre of four hundred villages. Two hundred villages had at their centre a fortress called *khârvâtika*. And a fortress called *samgrahaṇa* was situated at the centre of ten villages. Such is the strategic scheme of fortifications described in the *Artha-Śâstra*.[1] From the military standpoint, then, or rather from the angle of national defense, the Maurya Empire was a thorough *federation de l'empire* i. e., a centralized organization of states or provinces. And it served to furnish all future empire-builders with the prototype of a perfect system of "preparedness" that might be the solid basis of effectual *pax sârva-bhaumica* (peace of the world-state).

9. "*Peace Insurance*" *in Hindu India.*

In this Maurya achievement of imperial nationalism is to be found the nucleus of the code of duties by which Vîra-sena,[2] the commander of the Sunga fortress on the banks of the Narmadâ, was guided towards the end of the second century B. C., as well as of the military manuals that were in use among the officers of the Vardhana General, Skanda-gupta, in the seventh century A. C. The curriculum of studies in the war-academies of Bengal under the administration of General Someśvara (ninth century) must likewise have accorded a prominent place to the military institutions and practices described by Kautilya. And these were no doubt adapted with modifications to the local conditions of the Gangetic Delta by Vallâla Sena's war-minister Hari-ghoṣa in the twelfth century.[3]

For want of positive evidence it is not possible yet to single out a Gustavus Adolphus of ancient India as *the* genius of Hindu military science and art from among the score of "world-conquerors" down to the *Gangâikonda* Chola (1013—1108). Nor can any of the extant Sanskrit

---

[1] *Ind. Ant.*, 1905, p. 7. Elaborate details about Maurya military administration and Hindu ideas on the subject of warfare prevailing in the third and fourth centuries B.C. are to be found in the *Arthaśâstra*: IX. The Work of an invader: Knowledge of power, place, time etc. Time of recruiting, Annoyance in the rear, Loss of men, External and internal dangers, Persons associated with traitors and enemies; X. War: Encampment, March of the camp, Treacherous fights, Battle-fields, Array of troops; XII. Powerful enemy: Battle of intrigue, Slaying the commander in chief, Spies with weapons, Capture of the enemy; XIII. Strategic means to capture a fortress: Sowing seeds of dissension, Enticement of kings by secret connivances, Work of spies in a siege, Operation of a siege, Restoration of peace in a conquered country.

[2] *Malavikâgnimitra*, p. 7.

[3] Banerji's *Memoir*, 106.

texts on warfare and war-office be definitely fathered on one or other of the historic emperors, generals, or presidents of military colleges. But to all writers[1] on strategy, tactics, battle-array, fortification, and arms and accoutrements, whether for the *dhanur-vedas* and *nîti-śâstras*, or for the *Manu-Samhitâ* and the *Mahâbhârata*, the military and naval chapters of the *Artha-śâstra* must have been but the postulates of the science of warfare and national defense. And these every theorist had to accept as the A, B, C of his investigation on "world-peace", or as Stockton, the American militarist, would have it euphemistically, on "peace insurance".[2]

Section 2.

The Civil Service.

1. *Centralization in Tamil India.*

Each of the provinces of the Chola Empire in Southern India was under a vicerory, who was either a scion of the dispossessed royal families or a prince of the blood. As a rule, it was the near kinsmen such as uncles, brothers or sons that obtained the voceroyalty.

Even previous to Râjarâja the Great (984—1018), royal records were preserved on palmyra leaves in the office buildings at the capital. And orders promulgated from the imperial headquarters were registered in a book of documents[3] by the *mahâ-sabhâs* (central *panchâyats*) of the rural districts.

We have a few facts about the working of the Chola bureaucracy. The inscriptions point to a good deal of intervention on the part of the civil service in the affairs of the local bodies, especially in rural finance. Two imperial officials, the *adhikârin* (the magistrate) and the *senâpati*

---

[1] It must not be ignored, however, that some of the *ideas* and institutions described in the *Mahâbhârata*, the *Manu Samhitâ*, the *nîti-śâstras* and the *dhanur-vedas* may have been older than Kautilya. *Cf. Śukra-nîti*, Ch. IV, sec. vii. Note the relative proportion of the constituents of the army in lines 41—52, and the eight battle-arrays in lines 527—536; *J. A. O. S.*, 1889 (military tactics, pp. 192—219; chariots, pp. 235—262; cavalry, 262—265; Elephant riders, 265—269; weapons, 269—308). See the list of weapons in the *Râmâyaṇa* (*Vâla-kânda*, Ch. XXVII). Some of these and other literary evidences have been used in P. Swami's pamphlet on *Warfare in Ancient India*, and in Banerjea's *Public*, 196—218. But such material has been avoided by the present author.

[2] H. W. L. Hime's *Origin of Artillery*, pp. 74—85; E. A. Altham's *Principles of War*, Vol. I, p. 43; M. I. D. Cockle's *Bibliography of Military Books up to 1642*; Fiske's *Art of Fighting*, p. 47—49; Stockton, p. 203; The Hindu *Gîtâ* is cited by Maude in the introduction to Graham's translation of Clausewitz's *War*.

[3] Aiyangar, 175.

(the commandant) appear to have regularly inspected the accounts of the village assemblies. It was according to their directions that the different taxes realized by the communes were scheduled and the appropriations regulated.[1] These officers used to go out on tour of inspection through their circle, examine the rural funds, and audit the accounts. They also made allotments out of the public revenues, although of course the *panchâyats* themselves had to make the appropriations for the special purposes. On one occasion the supervisors had reasons to suspect a reduction in the expenses. The officials of the local soviet were therefore asked to "state the revenue and expenditure" "in accordance with the royal order and the royal letter". The vigilance of imperialism in the Tamil states must evidently have robbed the village *sabhâs* of fiscal autonomy.

Very rarely does the Hindu civil service seem to have been paid in money. The officials of Chola-mandala were renumerated by gifts of land or assignments of revenue.[2] Hiuen Thsang also noticed that the governors, magistrates, ministers and other officers of the Vardhana Empire (seventh century) had portions of land consigned to them for personal support.[3] For Gupta India Fa Hien (fifth century) mentions only that the royal officials did not have to fleece the people but were maintained by the state with regular salaries.[4]

2. *Nation-making under the Mauryas.*

But for the present we have more facts about the earliest epoch of Hindu imperial polity than for any others. Under Asoka the Great (B. C. 269—232), as we gather from the Edicts, the Maurya Empire was divided for administrative purposes into at least four viceroyalties. These were intended for what may conveniently be called the northern, eastern, western and southern prefectures. A *pucca* "imperialist" was this Asoka, a fully self-conscious *chakravarti* or *sârva-bhauma*. The "problem of the empire" was a serious concern to him; and he set before himself the definite task of maintaining "uniformity in administration and penal procedure"[5] throughout a territory, the dimensions of which were hardly to be attained in the annals of "haughty Rome" or by the ephemeral Napoleonic empire at its height (1808—1812). The viceregal staff and

---

[1] *Ibid*, 165.
[2] *Ibid*, 184.
[3] Beal's *Si-Yuki*, I, 87—88.
[4] Legge's *Fa Hian*, XVI, pp. 42—43.
[5] Pillar Edict IV.

office organization in each prefectural province were accordingly modelled on those of the Emperor himself. Believer as he was in Ŝâkya's *appamâda* (energism and strenuous exertions),[1] Asoka was personally in charge of the home government comprising the capital and the central regions.

The imperial executive of the Mauryas consisted of eighteen departments.[2] Each of these departments was helped by a board or boards of advisers. Uniformly with the six divisions of the municipal corporation of Pâtali-putra and the six divisions of the War Office, these boards of the Executive were constituted on the literal *panchâyatic* principle of the village assemblies; i. e., there were five members on each board.

The Maurya civil service superintended the rivers, measured the land "as was done in Egypt", says Megasthenes, and inspected the sluices by which water was let out from the main canals into their branches so that every one might have an equal supply of it. The forest officers among them had charge of the huntsmen with the power of rewarding or punishing them according to their deserts. Taxes were collected by these authorities, and the occupations connected with land, e. g. those of wood-cutters, carpenters, blacksmiths and miners, fell within the scope of their supervision. Construction of roads was one of their important functions, and in this connection it is reported that pillars were set up at every ten *stadia* (i. e. a little over one mile) to indicate the by-roads and the distances.[3]

3. *The Domesday Surveys of the Hindus.*

The principle of centralization that was observed in the management of the army and the navy was manifest also in the administration of public finance and other branches of civil government. The village was, as we have seen, the unit for purposes of military organization. It was the unit for revenue and police purposes as well. The member at the lowest step in the bureaucratic system was known as the *gopa*. This magistrate-collector was placed in charge of five or ten villages and was ultimately responsible to the *samâhartâ*, the collector-general. As the rural limb of the imperial civil service, it was the duty of the *gopa*[4] to maintain the boundary marks not only of villages, but also of fields, gardens, roads, pasture lands, assembly halls, irrigation works, cremation grounds, charitable houses, temples, groves and bathing places.

---

[1] Minor Rock Edict I.

[2] *Artha*, I, Ch. viii, xv; II.

[3] *Meg*. XXXIV.

[4] *Artha*, Book II, Ch. xxxv; *Ind. Ant.* 1905, p. 5.

He had personally to supervise the transactions of gift, sale or mortgage of lands and other properties of the villagers. He used to keep a register giving in detail the number of souls living in each house. The people were classified by him according to castes and occupations such as agriculture, pasturage, trade, arts, manufactures, manual labor and menial service. This census[1] and vital statistics was all-inclusive. It was applicable also to slaves, quadrupeds, and birds maintained in each household. And, of course, in the same register the *gopa* had to note not only the amount of taxes and tolls that each house had to pay to the government, but also the probable dues in working men and fines.

These comprehensive inquiries made by the village officer of the Maurya Empire could be copied *in toto* in Europe over thirteen hundred years later. The items of information which William the Conqueror needed for his *Domesday Book* (1086) in order to get a complete idea of the "geldable" (taxable) resources of England were identical with those mentioned by the Hindu Richelieu. "What is the name of this manor?" as the *Inquisitio Eliensis*[2] or the *questionnaire* of the Norman Duke who wanted to prevent in English society the disruptive tendencies of continental feudalism proceeds, "Who held it in the time of King Edward? Who holds it now? How many acres are there? How many ploughs belong to the lord of the manor? How many belong to the villeins, cottars, slaves, freeman, and sokemen? How much woodland is there? How much meadow? How much pasture? How many mills and fisheries are there? How much has been added to or taken away from the estate? How much was the estate formerly worth? How much is it worth now? How much has or had each freeman or sokeman there? Could it be made worth any more?" There was nothing distinctively Occidental in the queries. These had been anticipated by the political genius of Asia.

Moreover, a curious chronological coincidence is to be noted between the East and the West. In 1086, the very year of the English Domesday inquiry, a second survey of the Chola dominions was instituted by Kulot-tûnga I. the Chola-Châlukya.[3] On the occasion of this re-survey the tolls were abolished, but in certain cases we notice an enhancement of the rates. The re-adjustment was evidently in high request as some lands had been over-assessed in the previous settlement which was organized by Râjarâja about a century previous to this date. The first

[1] Law's *Hind. Pol.*, pp. 106—114 (Census).

[2] *Domesday Commemoration* (1086—1886): *Domesday Studies*, Vol. I, pp. 7—8; Maitland's *Domesday Book and Beyond*, p. 24.

[3] Aiyangar, 144, 149—150, 176; *Epigraphist's Report* for 1900, sec. 25, p. 10.

survey (*c* 986) was so minute that accuracy was guaranteed to $\frac{1}{50,000}$ th of a square inch.[1] There were two kinds of assessment. One was known as "calculated" (i. e. according to previous surveys) the other as "settled" (i. e. according to the actual yield). It was by this Instrument of Râja-râja that the village assemblies were authorized to take possession of lands whose owners failed to pay the government dues for three years. It may be observed here, in passing, that the dues were collected in kind, or in gold or in cloth.

4. *Roads and National Unification.*

Census and cadastral survey were thus normal processes in the Hindu machinery of imperial nationalism. Among the agencies by which the civil service contributed to the establishment of *pax sârva-bhaumica* (peace of the world-empire) we must also mention the roads, both strategic and commercial. These were deliberately laid out by the bureaucracy in order to bring the different parts of the empire within easy reach of one another. One such imperial thoroughfare was the grand trunk road all along the Coromandel coast (Eastern) covering about 1200 miles from the banks of the Mahânadî in Orissa to Kottaru near Cape Comorin at the southern tip of the Indian peninsula.[2] It was constructed by Kulot-tûnga (1070—1118) specifically for the extensive campaigns that he undertook in the north and the south. As bulwarks of his vast empire he, moreover, planted agricultural colonies along this road. Really of a military character were these plantations, as the territories were allotted to the army officers who occupied the settlements at the head of the forces at their command.[3]

It is evident that in the annals of imperial Rome nobody was a greater administrative genius than the Châlukya-Chola monarch of the early twelfth century. And Kulot-tûnga, "the highest in the family", was but continuing the tradition of the first *sârva-bhaumas* of India, the Mauryas, whose civil engineers had constructed a magnificent highway from Pâtali-putra to the Afghan frontier, a distance of 10,000 *stadia* (over 1,100 miles).[4] Besides, in an account of the achievements of the Hindu civil service we must not omit to mention the monumental irrigation works that signalized the "developmental functions" of Indian states

---

[1] Aiyangar, 175—177.
[2] *Ibid*, 188—189.
[3] *Ibid*, 143.
[4] Arrian's *Indika*, III.

from at least the time of Megasthenes' observations, — in Kashmir as in Ceylon, in Gujarat as in Madras.

5. *Administration of Irrigation Works.*

Kashmir[1] had always given small produce, as Kalhana writes in the *Râja-tarangiṇî*, because it was liable to be flooded by the waters of the Mahâpadma Lake and was intersected by many streams. But during the reign of Avanti-varman (833—58) a phenomenal economic revolution was brought about so that the price of a *khâri* of rice fell from 200 to 36 *dinars*. This marvelous result is attributed by the Hindu historian to the engineering feats of the "illustrious" Sûyyâ, the *anna-pati* (lord of food).

Sûyyâ noticed that the water-locked tracts along the banks of the river Vitastâ were chiefly responsible for the calamities and famines of Kashmir. Accordingly he addressed himself first to the draining off of the water. Next he proceeded to dam up the river by a stone structure. Finally he removed the dam. Having thus given freedom to the stream Sûyyâ constructed several "new beds for the Vitastâ", i. e. canals, "wherever he knew inundation-breaches to occur during disastrous floods".

Sûyyâ's operations ultimately changed the very topography of the country. Through technical skill he succeeded in making the different streams "move about according to his will" "just as a snake-charmer does with the snakes". A new confluence of the Vitastâ with its most important tributary, the Sindhu, was artificially created by the engineer's genius, and "it will last" says Kalhana, "to the end of the world". Sûyyâ also constructed stone-embankments for about thirty miles along the Vitastâ and dammed in the waters of the Mahâpadma. Having "raised the land from the water" he founded several villages. As the water was kept by means of circular dykes the villages looked like round bowls. The previous dependence of the locality on rainfall was thus rendered unnecessary through an achievement of the human brain.

The activities of the Kashmirian officer did not stop at this point. The amount of water necessary for irrigation was calculated by him in an interesting manner. He began with an hygrometric examination of the different classes of land. All village lands were first subjected to a temporary inundation under certain conditions. Then he took some soil from each village and observed the time it took to dry up. The different periods within which irrigation would be required for the

[1] Kalhana, Book V, verses 68, 116—117, 72, 90—95, 97—98, 102, 106, 109—112.

different soils were thus ascertained. He then arranged accordingly on a permanent basis for the size and distribution of the watercourse for each village. The Ânula and other streams were utilized for the purpose.

The story of one irrigation-tank can be told for about eight centuries. The Sudarśana Lake at Girnar in Kathiawar near the Arabian Sea was constructed by Puṣya-gupta, a *râṣṭrîya* (governor) of the western prefecture under Chandra-gupta Maurya.[1] Sluices connecting the tank with the agricultural areas were opened out by Tuṣaspha, the viceroy of Asoka. About A. C. 150 repairs of an adamantine character were undertaken by Suviśâkha, assistant to Rudra-dâmana, a satrap probably of the Kuṣân Empire. In Skanda-gupta's time the dam had to be repaired a second time (458). The re-building was superintended by Chakrapâlita, a governor of the Gupta Empire.[2] Constitutionally speaking, *pax sârvabhaumica* has to be realized from the fact that both under the Mauryas and the Guptas Girnar was a remote corner of the empire, over 1,000 miles from Pâtali-putra, the capital.

The Sudarśana reservoir was built by damming up a small stream. The civil engineers of the Tamils conceived another idea in irrigation. Theirs was the plan of controlling a river at the head of its delta. The principle of anicuts is the distinctively original contribution of the Cholas to mankind's economic development. Their scheme of dealing with deltaic land has since been accepted everywhere. No nation has been able to improve upon it yet.[3] The hundred-mile embankments on the Kâverî and the main channels for irrigation were constructed by Kârikâla (*c* A. C. 150). Râjendra (1018—1035) excavated a large artificial reservoir at his new capital, Gangâikonda Śolapuram. The embankment was sixteen miles long and was provided with several substantial sluices.[4]

Equal, if not more, energy and funds were devoted by the civil service of Ceylon to the problem of irrigation. Parâkrama Bâhu I (*c* A. C. 1150) constructed 1470 tanks and 534 canals, and repaired 1395 large with 960 smaller tanks and 3621 canals. Today there is no part of the island, except the central mountain districts, in which the remains of canals and tanks are not to be found. And it appears on close investigation that almost all irrigation-works were links in a chain of large connected systems. There is, therefore, no hyperbole in the statement of Tennant that "excepting the exaggerated dimensions of Lake Moeris

---

[1] *Ep. Ind.*, 1905—1906, pp. 46, 47, 49.

[2] *Gup. Insc.*, pp. 56—65.

[3] Deakin, 252.

[4] Aiyangar, 185—188.

in Central Egypt and the mysterious basin of Al-aaram, the bursting of whose embankment devastated the Arabian city of Mareb, no similar constructions formed by any race, whether ancient or modern, exceed in colossal magnitude the stupendous tanks of Ceylon."[1]

6. *Pax Sârva-bhaumica and Pax Romana.*

The administrative history of the Ândhra, Kuṣân, Pâla, Châlukya and other Empires still awaits the minute scrutiny of epigraphists. The stray notice about the Sudarśana tank in the fifth century proves that the Gupta Empire at any rate was no less efficiently governed than had been that of the Mauryas. And what was their system of national government? The Hindu *chakravartis, châturantas, sârva-bhaumas* or world-rulers of the third and fourth centuries B. C., dictated duties to the governors of provincal capitals at Taxila on the Afghan frontier, Tosali in Orissa, Ujjayinî in the west and probably Suvarṇa-giri in the Deccan south of the Narmadâ. They knew how to command a net-work of fortresses situated at mathematically-calculated strategic points. They built up a bureaucratic hierarchy, which emanated from Pâtali-putra and filtering through the "district" jurisdictions administered by *sthânikas* came down to the village-nuclei under the *gopas.* Their financial organization embraced in its all-seizing sweep, as we shall see later on, the destination of every material resource and the destiny of every animal and human being. Evidently the Hindus of Maurya India were past masters in the art of nation-making i. e. centralized and unified rule.

The Oriental student of comparative politics may therefore legitimately ask: "What more was achieved by European imperialism, by the *pax Romana* of Diocletian and Constantine,[2] for instance? Were the efficiency and thoroughness of Maurya statesmen surpassed in any epoch of occidental polity?"

The evidences of the Tamil inscriptions of Southern India, the Sanskrit inscription of Rudra-dâmana, Asoka's Edicts, Megasthenes, and the *Artha-śâstra* in regard to Hindu imperial nationalism and provincial administration can be borne out by the accounts of empire-states given in epics like the *Mahâbhârata,*[3] and suggested in law-books like those of Gautama, Âpastamba, and Manu. The picture of nationalities that these literary sources exhibit is that of a centripetal tendency and homo-

---

[1] Deakin, 239—242. An account of Ceylonese civil service is furnished in Coomaraswamy's *Mediaeval*, pp. 19—20.

[2] Frank's *Roman Imperialism*, 353; Abbott's *Roman Political Institutions*, 334—340; Arnold, pp. 158—162, 188, 191.

[3] *J. A. O. S.*, 1889, p. 84.

geneous compacture of the kind systematically promoted by the Bourbons from Louis IX to Louis XIV.

7. *The Richelieus of India.*

Thus in Manu's[1] scheme every township or village was presided over by a vicegerent, who was subordinate to the ruler of ten townships. The ruler of ten was subordinate to the ruler of twenty; and the ruler of twenty to the ruler of a hundred, who, again, was subordinate to the ruler of a thousand villages. The civil service could be recruited from among the priestly, the military as well as the mercantile classes. The officers were responsible for the collection of revenue and preparation of reports relating to the area under supervision. And they had to protect their territories from robbers and criminals. It was the function of the village magistrate to keep his jurisdiction free from thieves to the distance of two miles in all directions. If the township were large, the police duties of the collector were more extensive. The distance that he had to guard against robbers was eight miles of the country surrounding his station. These officers were bound to repay to the loser whatever was stolen within their district.[2]

None of these magistrate-collectors of any grade had judicial functions. Institutionally, the judiciary of every rank appears to have been totally separate from the executive (i. e. the police and fiscal staff). In the gradually extended circle, based as it was on the decimal system, the lower grade magistrates collected revenues, received reports and passed them on to the higher grade men in succession, until the sinews of war and the news of the realm were finally focussed in the king or emperor, the lord of all.

If it may be allowed to combine this plan of imperial constitution laid down in the *smriti-śâstras, nîti-śâstras*, and the epic with the few epigraphic facts, if not as supplement, at any rate, as an illustration of the channels along which Hindu administrative *śakti* (genius) worked, we have in Maurya India (B. C. 322—185 B. C.) a picture of France organized under the *Intendants* of Richelieu for an area seven times as large.[3] How many such Maurya Empires can be credited to the political capabilities demonstrated in European history?

---

[1] Manu, VII, 115—117, 118—122, 123—125; *cf. Śukra*, I, lines 381—384, V, 162—169.

[2] *Âpastamba*, II, 10, 26, 6—8; *Gautama*, X, 46—47.

[3] Brissaud, p. 396. There is hardly any evidence to support Mookerji's contention that the Hindu empires were decentralized and minimum-functioned states (*cf. Local*, pp. 9—10). But see *Supra*, pp. 58—60; Sarkar's *Pos. Back*, Vol. II, 59—62.

Section 3.

The Judiciary.

1. *Early Conciliar Tribunals.*

Some of the earliest judicial tribunals among Hindus are those obtaining in the federated republic of the Vajjian States in Eastern India about the fifth century B. C. We have a picture of ultra-democratic judicial proceedings at the mote-hall of these United States. A succession of regularly appointed officers administered the criminal law. These were the justices, the lawyers, the rehearsers of the law-maxims, the council of the repesentatives of the eight clans constituting the union, the commander-in-chief, the vice-consul, and the *râjâ* (i. e. archon or consul) himself. The accused could be acquitted by each of these officers of the hierarchy. But if they considered him guilty, each had to refer the case to the next higher authority. The consul or president of the republic was the final judge as to the penalty in accordance with the law of precedents.[1]

The fountain-head of the judiciary of this and succeeding periods in Hindu administrative history has to be traced back to the *sabhâ*, council or soviet which formed the nucleus of the Vedic polity, and which figures conspicuously, although no doubt as a royal paraphernalia, among the institutions with which the poets of the *Mahâbhârata* and the *Râmâyaṇa* were familiar. It is out of this "homogeneous" gathering of the primitive tribes with its all-round functions that judicial tribunals of Śâkyan and post-Śâkyan India must have been "differentiated" through ages of evolution, in much the same manner as the modern courts of justice in West-European countries and in America are, historically speaking, descended from the folk-moot described by Tacitus in his *Germania.*[2]

The Hindu judiciary was essentially a system of assemblies or councils (*sabhâ*),[3] the "many" or the "few" sitting in judgment. By the end of the fourth century B. C. the institutions had attained a highly developed stage. And down to the thirteenth century imperial courts, original and appellate, with salaried judges and clearly defined jurisdiction over tribunals of lesser importance continued to be essential organs of the administrative machinery.

---

[1] *Buddhist India*, Ch. II; *Infra*, p. 148.

[2] Stubbs, Vol. I, 29; Jenks' *Law and Politics*, pp. 139—141.

[3] For the theory of judicial assemblies *vide* Manu XII, 110—112, 114.

2. *Maurya Judiciary.*

For the present, we know more about the Maurya than about other periods. The lowest courts of course were those of the village *panchâyat*. These were the councils of village elders, the "soviets of the *Mirs*", so to speak, and were presided over by the *gopa* or headman.[1] A thief or an adulterer could be deported by them out of the village. As a member of the village-court, the *gopa*, who was the fiscal and police head appointed by the Emperor, appears thus to have had some judicial function too. But the higher courts of Maurya India were presided over by officers thoroughly independent of the executive.

Such courts were of six ranks. First, there were courts at every town "forming the headquarters of villages". The next higher tribunals were the courts at every town which was the "headquarters of 400 villages". Next came those at every town, which was the "headquarters of 800 villages". The courts at places "centrally situated between every two provinces of the empire", and the tribunals at Pâtali-putra, the capital, constituted the next two successive rungs of the judicial ladder. Finally, came the keystone of the whole system, the highest court of judicature, at the capital, with the Emperor presiding in person over an assembly of judges. Louis IX's *Parlement* of Paris,[2] in so far as it was a court of justice, and exclusive of its legislative functions, could be modelled on this Supreme Court of the Mauryas as regards jurisdiction, authority, and control over the lower limbs of the hierarchy.

Excluding the lowest court of the *gopa* and the highest court of the Emperor, each of the five classes of tribunals comprised two courts of two distinct jurisdictions. The functions of one branch were *dharma-sthîya* or what may be described as "civil", the scope of the other was *kantaka-śodhana* (i. e. removal of the thorns of the state) or "criminal". Thus at every headquarter of villages, at every headquarter of 400 villages, and so on, there were two courts independent of each other. Pâtali-putra had therefore three courts including the Imperial Tribunal.

The *dharma-sthîya* courts were made up of three judges. They had power to inflict light fines. The cases involving validity of contracts, relation between master and servant, defamation, boundary disputes, damage to agriculture, pasture, and public roads, duties of man and wife, inheritance, succession and so forth fell within the cognizance of

[1] It is not clear if this headman is to be taken as identical with or distinct from the *gopa* of the civil service (who is in charge of five or ten villages). cf. Banerjea, pp. 291—294, and Majumdar, p. 59.

[2] Brissaud, pp. 432, 435, 441.

these tribunals. The *kantaka-śodhana* courts were likewise made up of three judges. They had power to inflict heavy fines and capital punishment. Within their jurisdiction came the suits relating to protection of artisans, merchants and peasants, measures against national calamities, robbery, mutilation of limbs, post-mortem examinations, etc.[1]

The judicial system of the Mauryas included of course the jury. But it is not clear as to whether the gilds were allowed to retain their privileges of self-legislation and self-adjudication. It is evident, however, that a millennium and a half before the Common Pleas ceased to follow the English king in his perambulations and began to be "held in some fixed place" through a reform initiated by the Magna Carta (1215) the principle of "fixed courts" had been well established among Hindus. And indeed the Maurya judiciary embodied in itself the same centralization from the rural unit up as was effected in the executive organs of administration.

3. *Itinerant Justices.*

One of the centralizing agencies in the judicial organization was the system of circuit judges. During the eleventh century, in Ceylon,[2] royal officials used to go out from the capital annually on circuit to administer justice in the country. The work of these itinerant justices was calculated to be an effective check on the irregularities of the local tribunals. They were to take to task the village elders in case they had transgressed any of the rules under which the *panchâyat* courts were constituted. Nor was this central control an unnecessary intermeddling; for the powers vested in the village judiciary were of a high order and needed careful supervision. In King Mahinda IV's time (1016—1042) the headmen and householders of the Dasagâma villages used to sit in session even in regard to the crimes of murder and robbery. The "proceedings of the inquiry having been so recorded that the same may be produced thereafter", the village court had the authority to inflict capital punishment on the murderer. The *gopa* and his assembly were also authorized to restore the identified property to the proper owners and hang the thieves who had perpetrated the violence. Similar judicial power was administered by the rural communes of the Chola Empire.[3]

---

[1] Law's *Hind. Pol.*, pp. 117—121.

[2] *Ep. Zeyl.*, Vol. I, no 21; The Ceylonese laws *Niti-nighanduva* are available in English (Colombo, 1888); *vide* Coomaraswamy's *Mediaeval*, p. 20; Jenks' *Law and Pol.*, Ch. IV, 131, 133.

[3] Infra p. 57. *Vide* Prahlad C. Divanji's "Judicial Administration in India in ante-Mohammedan Times" in the *Ind. Ant.* (July 1915) and "Ancient Hindu Law of Evidence" in the same journal (May 1920); Row's *Ancient Hindu Judicature*.

4. *Tribunals in Legal Literature.*

The characteristic features of this judicial organization were well reflected in the writings of the jurists.[1] In the six classes of courts of justice described in the *dharma-śâstras* and *nîti-śâstras* we find the same centripetal principles as in the actual institutions. Three of these are royal or imperial tribunals, beginning with the court of the sovereign, who is assisted by learned Brâhmaṇas as assessors. This tribunal is peripatetic, being held, like the English courts before the Great Charter, where the king abides or sojourns. Below this is the court of the *prâd-vivâka* or *dharmâdhyakṣa* i. e. chief judge. He is appointed by the sovereign and sits with three or more assessors not exceeding seven. The tribunal of the chief justice is a stationary court, being held at an appointed place. The next in order are the courts of the *puisne* judges appointed by the sovereign. Their jurisdictions are local. From their decisions an appeal lies to the *prâd-vivâka's* court and thence to the king in person.

The other three tribunals generally mentioned in all treatises on law and polity are what may be called the people's courts as distinguished from the royal courts. These represent the folk-element in Hindu judiciary. The highest of these popular tribunals are those of the *pûgas*. These are assemblies of townsmen, or soviets of persons (belonging to various tribes and following different professions but) inhabiting the same place. The next lower in importance are the courts of the *śreṇîs* (gilds). These are the organizations of traders or artisans, and conventions of persons (belonging to different tribes but) subsisting by the same profession. The third in the series are the *kulas*, or meetings of kinsmen, i. e. assemblies of relations connected by consanguinity.

The general tendency of the *dharma-śâstras* and *nîti-sâstras* is to treat these folk-tribunals as rather tentative courts.[2] They are not final organs of adjudication. The *kula's* decision may be revised by the *śreṇî*, if necessary, and the *śreṇî's* by the *pûga*. The authors consider the *pûga* (town) as less liable to partiality than the *śreṇî* (gild), and the *śreṇî* less than the *kula* (family). Appeals from the *pûga* lie to the *prâd-vivâka* or chief justice of the state. And the highest court of appeal is, of course, the tribunal of the sovereign himself.

---

[1] Colebrooke's "Hindu Courts of Justice" in the *Transactions of the Royal Asiatic Society of Great Britain and Ireland*, Vol. II (1828); *Mahâbhârata* (*Udyoga-parva*), LV, 58; Manu, XII, 111, Baudhâyana I, 1, 1, 8, Nârada, *Legal Procedure*, 7.

[2] Brihaspati I, 30; Śukra IV, v, lines 57—62; Nârada, I, 7; Yâjnavalkya II, 30.

Section 4.

National Finance.

Budget-making is an essentially modern institution. It is only since the time of Napoleon that regular estimates of receipts and expenditures have been yearly prepared in France.[1] And in spite of the comparative abundance of reliable data no ingenuity of modern research has been able to reconstruct the sheet of liabilities and assets for any period of the Roman Empire. But the administrative history of Hindu India is yet in its beginnings. It is out of the question therefore to attempt such wide guesses about the annual expenses even of the Maurya Empire (B. C. 322—185) for which information is more plentiful than for others as have been done in regard to the Athenian state by Bökh[2] or about the total revenues as have been done in regard to the Roman Empire by Gibbon and Guizot.[3] Nor of course is it possible to test the fiscal policy of Hindu states by the modern canons of taxation, especially on the complicated questions of justice, faculty, i. e. ability to pay, or equality of assessment.

1. *A Lay Balance-Sheet* (*c* 640 *A. C.*).

A contemporary account of the finances of the Vardhana Empire (606—647) is furnished by Hiuen Thsang, the Chinese state-guest of Harṣa's. It is said that forced labor was not exacted by the government. When the public works required it, labor was exacted but paid for in strict proportion to the work. Those who cultivated the royal estates paid a sixth of the produce as the share of the state. The river passages and the road barriers were open on payment of a small toll. In regard to public expenditure there are said to have been four charges on the private demesnes of the crown. The first charge was of course the management of the affairs of state and the provision for sacrificial offerings. The second was for providing subsidies for the ministers and chief officers of state. Honorariums for men of distinguished ability constituted the third charge, and the fourth was religious charity. Altogether, in the Chinese scholar-pilgrim's opinion, the taxes on the people were light, and personal service required of them was moderate.[4]

---

[1] Palgrave's *Dictionary* (Art. on "Finances-France"), Vol. II, p. 68; Leroy-Beaulieu's *Traité de la science des finances*, Vol. II, p. 11, 12.

[2] Schömann's *Antiquities of Greece*, p. 445.

[3] Ramsay and Lancian, p. 282.

[4] *Si Yu-ki*, Vol. I, pp. 87, 88.

Evidently we have here the material for a very elementary balance-sheet much too naive for an imperial organization[1] based as it was on the triumphs of *dig-vijaya* and military aggression[2] no less than on the victories of peace. The reporter was a lay-man and naturally failed to notice the "sinews of war" that operated the administrative machinery of *pax sârva-bhaumica* (peace of the world-state).[3] It is on such facile statements about "light taxes" and "religious charities", however, that students of comparative politics in the nineteenth century were used to founding their estimate of the Hindu political systems. In the publications on finance, as in the treatises on legislation and jurisprudence it has been the custom, therefore, to summarily dismiss the Oriental monarchies as primitive polities of the "patrimonial" type. Today the states of Old Asia are treated by scholars more or less in the same light as the feudal kingdoms of mediaeval Europe, i. e., as organizations modelled on a private household, the domestic establishment of the ruler.[4]

2. *South Indian Revenues* (*c* 900—1300).

But let us examine the imperialism of Hindu *sârva-bhaumas* (*Weltherrschern*) on the basis of their own charters, decrees and promulgations (*śâsanas*) that have been rendered accessible by the archeological investigations of recent years. The statesmen of the Chola Empire (900—1300) would appear to have been at their wits' end in devising new forms of revenue. No complete list of all the heads of government income is available for this south Indian (Madras and Mysore) state. But several Tamil inscriptions[5] describe the immunities from dues to the government enjoyed by certain villages through the grant of royal charters. From the schedule of these "privileges" we can automatically see a great part of the other side of the shield, viz. the normal contributions to the imperial treasury for which each village was ordinarily liable. Not all the items are, however, fully intelligible.

The available list indicates only the revenue from villages or village-unions. But it is questionable if we are justified in treating it exclusively as what should technically be a branch of "local finance". The village through its panchâyat was indeed responsible as a unit for the reali-

---

[1] See the extent of the Vardhana Empire on the map facing p. 340 of *Early Hist.*

[2] *Harṣa-charita*, p. 188.

[3] *Infra*, p. 223.

[4] Art. on Finance in the *Enc. Brit.*

[5] *South Ind. Insc.*, Vol. II, pt. i, no. 22; *Vide* H. Krishna Shastri's "Fiscal Administration under Early Cholas" in the *R. G. Bhandarkar Commemorative Essays* (Poona, 1917).

zation of all public income within its area.[1] But the heads of income do not seem to have been classified and specifically ear-marked as local and national. We need not, besides, attempt here a classification of the Chola revenues according to one or other of the accepted taxonomies. They can easily be brought down to the tripartite division into taxes, fees, and prices.[2]

a) *Sources other than Land.*

In the first place, there was a "tax in money".[3] It is not clear as to what should be meant by this item. It may have been a direct tax *per capita* like the poll tax of 1377—1380 in England during the Hundred Years' War or the *tributum* in Rome.

Something like "general property tax" has to be seen in several imposts. Like the horses and cattle taxed by mediaeval German states[4] "animals" were counted to contribute to the Chola exchequer. The furniture, clothing, and ornaments are not enumerated in the schedule of taxes on "personalty". But "movable" property as contrasted with the real estate was assessed in the form of "fixed capital" like looms and oil-mills. Tanks also were included in the list of property-dues.

A tax was realized on weights, whatever it might imply. But some light may be thrown on this item from the legislation of the Mauryas. In the *Arthaśâstra* of Kautilya (fourth century B. C.) we read that no trader was allowed to have his own weights and measures. Every day the business men had to have their scales and weights stamped afresh by the government.[5] The authorities realized a revenue from the stamps. Now if this custom of the first Hindu empire were followed by the Tamil *sârva-bhaumas*, we may consider this business tax on weights to be another property tax. The rate may have been small, but the total receipts of the empire under this head must have shown a high figure, as the number of taxable individuals including the pettiest retailer was obviously large.

It is doubtful if the business or license tax paid by the Tamil goldsmith should not be scheduled as a charge on property. But "unripe fruit" in the Kartigai month, though a levy in kind, must be regarded as such. Stocks, bonds and mortgages that are so prominent in modern economic life and necessarily occupy an important place in the taxation

[1] Aiyangar, pp. 161, 163, 164.

[2] Plehn's *Intro. to Pub. Fin.*, pp. 76—79, 92—100; Seligman's *Essays in Taxation*, pp. 430, 431.

[3] The list can be seen conveniently in Aiyangar, pp. 165, 166, 180—182.

[4] Seligman's *Ess.* p. 39. Cf. Aghnides' *Mohammedan Theories of Finance*, pp. 526, 527.

[5] Shamasastry's article on "Chânakya's Land and Revenue Policy" in the *Ind. Ant.* 1905, pp. 50, 51.

of property are not naturally to be looked for in Hindu finances of the eleventh, twelfth, and thirteenth centuries. But it is interesting to note that — the "sonship" was assessed among certain social classes, e. g. the "right hand" and "left hand" orders. The public income from the sonship dues was identical with that accruing from inheritance tax, or estate or "death duty", i. e. the charge made by modern governments on the transfer of property from the dead to the living.

None of these property dues were of course prices charged by the government for economic or other services rendered to the people. They were all deduced from the power of the state to obtain revenue by "compulsory dues and charges upon its subjects", i. e. taxes in the strictest sense of the term. None of them can moreover be regarded as income from "state property" and "state monopolies", the two sources that contribute about 25 per cent of French revenues.[1]

Taxes on consumption (*Aufwand-steuern*) were, besides, not neglected by the Chola Empire. There was a tax on bazars. The levy of tolls was common. The tax on trade or sales like the Athenian and Roman excise of 1 per cent[2] was another regular feature of the financial system. As taxes on the necessaries of life these excise duties could not but touch the community at every grade. They served, therefore, economically speaking, as real poll taxes though of an "indirect" denomination. We do not know if salt was a state monopoly as under the Roman republic[3] or as in Maurya India. But the French *gabelle*[4] was not to be forgotten by the Tamils who were too mindful of their revenues to overlook tapping this necessity of life that is bound to obey the law of "inelastic demand". We shall have details about Hindu salt tax in connection with Maurya finance.

A rent or license tax was realized from the fishers. Taxes on the collection of rents also are mentioned. Tax-"farming" may thus have been a fact in certain directions. Furthermore, the "penal power" of the state was effectively made use of to cooperate with its finance department. We do not have a long list of fines demanded of the delinquents by the Tamil Empire. It is known only that apothecaries were fined for "rotten drugs". An income of minor character is obvious in Kulot-tûnga's legislation (1070—1118) by which the state charged a seigniorage upon coining.[5]

---

[1] Palgrave, Vol. II, p. 69.

[2] Schömann, p. 449.

[3] Ramsay, p. 277.

[4] Brissaud, p. 505.

[5] Aiyangar, pp. 149, 150.

Income from the "services" of the state is mentioned in three connections. First, the villagers had to contribute their mite to maintain the watchman who was placed over the *vettis* (paths). This was for obvious reasons a regular rate or cess, though local, for one of the minimum functions of government. Secondly, the state seems to have supplied the *karman* to measure the paddy of the cultivators. He had to be paid for by the rural commune at a certain rate. Lastly, a water-rate or "tax on water-courses" for irrigation was an inevitable charge upon every peasant.

Mines, though they must certainly have been important sources of Chola revenues, are not mentioned in the inscriptions. Nor are the customs duties referred to. Of course neither of these could form part of the regular dues of a village to the government. But we are in a position to realize that when all these dues and others not enumerated in the inscriptions that happen to have been found are considered in their totality the income of the Tamil Empire would rise to a considerable amount.

b) *Collections from Land.*

We have now to add the revenue from property *par excellence*, the "real estate" as it is called. Not only in primitive communities but in Rome also even under the Empire land revenue was the mainstay of the government. And this land revenue was essentially a rent from "crown-land", *ager publicus*, i. e. public domain. It took the Romans long to get used to the idea of a non-land revenue. Taxes like the *tributum* were considered by the republic as "forced loans" to be repaid out of the loot of conquest, and these were resorted to only when the proceeds of the "domain" proved inadequate to meet the extraordinary expenses.[1]

Under the Tamils also south India's financial backbone must have been furnished by the realizations from land. The rate was not low. The Early Roman Empire used to levy land revenue at the rate of $^1/_{10}$th of the produce.[2] But in Chola India the government demand was $^1/_6$th. The high rate was indeed the normal *bhâga* or share of the government in land-produce according to the stereotyped "pious wish" of the *dharma-śâstras* (law books) and *nîti-śâstras* (political science).[3] And yet in

[1] Seligman's *Ess.* p. 35. The same Roman views are expressed in the sixteenth century by the French political philosopher Bodin in his *Les six livres de la république* (Bk. VI, Ch. II, *Des Finances*).

[2] Ramsay, p. 276.

[3] *Infra* pp. 155—160.

Realpolitik this conventional norm was but a fiscal camouflage that may deceive the academic student of financial history but did not fail to press the taxpayers themselves. For in Chola legislation the additional imposts on land, besides the tolls and octrois, were clearly defined as being $^1/_{10}$th of the yield. The total revenue from land was thus $^4/_{15}$ths or more than 25 per cent of the gross outturn in Râjâdhirâja's time (1035—1053).[1]

An interesting theoretical study in connection with the Chola revenue from real property would be that bearing on its precise character as to whether it was rent or tax. Incidentally it may be pointed out that communism in landownership is practically unknown in Hindu law-books.[2] The trend of ancient thought on land-tenure is to regard it as individual concern. But in *Tamil* inscriptions, while the individualistic tenure (the *ryotwari*, to use the British Indian term) is easily to be inferred, communal property in certain lands is also assured to village *panchâyats* by the legislation of Râja-râja the Great (985—1018).[3] We may take it that so far as the Chola Empire is concerned, land was owned both in severalty as well as in common.

This does not, however, settle the question as to how far, if at all, the crown was the legal proprietor of land, i. e. how far the "village community" (wherever it may have existed) or the individual cultivator were but "tenants" of the state-landlord (paying "economic" rents for the usufruct of public property) and how far their dues were "direct taxes" paid on their own immovable possessions. It is the tendency of modern indologists to postulate all lands as state property and the income from land necessarily as crown rent. But it is hardly possible to maintain this position on the strength of actual proprietary documents, *sâsanas* (laws or charters) and epigraphic records. For all practical purposes the presumption rather should be that Hindu India did not know of state-landlordism, i. e. land-nationalization[4] except of course in very limited areas. The land revenue of Hindu states was therefore generally speaking, a tax. But, as Giffen[5] explains away the distinction between rent and tax, "the fact of a government levying so general a charge may be held *ipso facto* to convert the charge into a tax having

---

[1] Aiyangar, pp. 181, 182.

[2] Jolly's *Recht*, pp. 93—96; Hopkins' *India* (Land Tenure), pp. 221, 225, 229; *Vedic Index*, Vol. I, pp. 245, 246.

[3] Aiyangar, pp. 161, 163, 164.

[4] See the discussion on "public lands" in Rau's *Finanzwissenschaft*, pp. 127—133; *cf*. Bodin, pp. 623—634.

[5] "Taxation" in the *Enc. Brit*.

much the same economic effects and consequences as a tax". For in strict theory, "where the government makes a charge, it levies a tax". The features of monopoly and compulsion on the taxpayer associated with all forms of land-revenue "make the charges difficult to distinguish logically from other taxes".

c) *The "Modern" Character of Tamil Finance.*

On the whole the Chola revenues were bulky in dimensions and the people of southern India heavily taxed. Only one ruler is spoken of as having slightly reduced the amount of the people's dues. Kulot-tûnga's name became a household word in Madras of the eleventh and twelfth centuries, for in 1086, the year of the Domesday Book, he abolished the tolls[1] after the completion of cadastral survey, — the second such survey of the Chola Empire. But the general story of *les nerfs de la république*, the nerves of the state, as Bodin puts it, under the Cholas was uniform. Like the governments of Europe in the days of Adam Smith,[2] the South Indian monarchs knew how to exact as much as they could "only desirous of finding the easiest means of doing so". The one redeeming feature seems to be that the Empire was conscious of the high price at which *pax sârva-bhaumica* was being enjoyed by the people. Râja-râja accordingly expressly instructed the finance officers to be elastic in the collection of revenues.[3] But no figures are available as to any of the heads of government income, and there is no means of making an estimate as to the probable national income. It is naturally impossible to form an idea as to the taxable capacity or "faculty" of the people. Nor is it convenient to hazard a conjecture as to the actual "burden of taxation", i. e. the proportion of the aggregate wealth of the people that the state demanded for all its functions and services.

Taxation as such was unknown in France previous to 1300.[4] As a function of the state and as an institution of "public law" it virtually ceased to exist with the destruction of the Roman Empire by the Teutons. In its place was substituted the "private claim" of customary dues, fines or tolls by landlords and barons.[5] The transition from this "feudal" to "modern" finance was a lengthy process in England.[6] It was not before the rise of nation-states in the fifteenth and sixteenth

---

[1] Aiyangar, pp. 149, 150.

[2] *Enc. Brit.* (Taxation).

[3] Aiyangar, p. 182.

[4] Brissaud, pp. 487—491; Leroy-Beaulieu, Vol. II, pp. 6, 7.

[5] *Enc. Brit.* (Finance).

[6] *Ibid.* (article on "English Finance").

centuries that the right of government to levy "taxes" became established or rather re-established in the western world. But, for purposes of comparative politics it is necessary to note that the Chola finances do not exhibit the features of the disintegrated feudal polity of mediaeval Europe. The revenues of the Chola Empire possessed the same variety in form as the Roman-Imperial and the modern French. They may be classified by students of *Finanzwissenschaft*, if required, according to the Latin *patrimonium*, *tributum*, and *vectigalium*, or the more popular *domaine*, *contributions directes*, and *contributions indirectes* of modern science. And of course the right of taxation was firmly planted in the political consciousness of Chola India.

3. *The Consumption-Schedule of Chola India.*

It is not difficult to explain why the imperial structures of the Hindus should have been heavily assessed organizations. The reasons are to be sought in the great variety and quantity of the state's "consumption". They are essentially identical with what economists like Nitti and Leroy-Beaulieu[1] have traced in the growth of public expenditures in modern times. The functions of Hindu governments were manifold. Consciously or unconsciously, whether backed by a definite theory of *nīti* (statecraft) like the late German empire or not, every state in India was a *Kulturstaat*. The invariable end of all Hindu polities was the protection and development of *dharma*. Like *Kultur* and Arnoldian "culture", *dharma* is a very comprehensive category. Exceedingly elastic in its significance, again, like the English term "law", the concept of *dharma* is the basis of distinction, the *fundamentum divisionis* between man and the brute. *Dharmeṇa hīnāh*, says the *Gītā*, *paśubhih samānāh*. In *dharma*, the analogue of the "virtue" in Plato's *Republic*, is to be found the *differentium* between the human world and that of *paśu*, or "beasts and birds" as Hobbes would have it. An agency for the promotion of humanism, i. e. for the advancement of all that lets "the ape and tiger die" and develops the people's material and moral interests, of anything, in short, that is conducive to national well-being was necessarily a multi-functional corporate organism. The *dharma-staaten* of India had therefore before them an almost unlimited range of what in scientific parlance is known as "developmental" activity. Not of an Arcadian character could thus be the "appropriations" of the Hindu empires.

---

[1] Leroy-Beaulieu, Vol. II, pp. 171—181. Hindu history is diametrically opposite to the picture suggested in Mookerji's statements about the functions of Indian states (*Local*, 3—4). *Vide Infra*, pp. 171—173 for the *nīti* theory of the scope of state activity.

We need not enumerate the duties of government stated in the *nîti-sâstras*. Let us note only the functions of the historic state-systems that may be gathered from the inscriptions and contemporary reports. The economic development of the country was undertaken by the Maurya, Gupta, Kashmirian, Tamil, and Ceylonese governments. Their care for irrigation[1] in different parts of the empire is a solid testimony to their recognition of the secular interests of the state. The construction of magnificent roads was another function along the same line.[2] The beautifying of cities and measures for street-cleaning, sanitation, etc were important items of state business in Chola territories.[3] The promotion of aesthetic as well as "productive" arts and crafts was a normal function of almost every Hindu state. The encouragement or "protection" of skilled workmen, the steady maintenance of shipbuilders and naval architects, and state employment of miners and other industrial artisans were among the duties of the Maurya civil service. Shipbuilding[4] and manufacture of arms and ammunitions were in reality crown monopolies. Wood-cutting, carpentry and smithery works came naturally therefore under state control. All governments undertook to lay out parks and grounds for recreation and pastime. Pharmaceutical gardens were treated as public necessities.[4] Palaces and public halls were likewise some of the "useful magnificences" that no state could dispense with. The Pândya rulers (*c* 100—300 A. C.) were patrons of *pariṣats* or academies of literature.[5] The Guptas[6] and the Pâlas[7] considered universities among important charges on the imperial exchequer. Temples and *vihâras* or monasteries were built at government expense both by the Vardhana and the Châlukya emperors of the seventh century,[8] indeed by all ruling houses. Not the conventional religion and morality of the time alone found an asylum in these institutions. The financial authorities must have regarded them as schools of higher learning as well. From the cultural standpoint these were at once the art-galleries and museums of the people. And as resorts for the relief of the sick,

---

1 *Ep. Ind.* 1905—1906, pp.46—49; *Gup. Insc.*, pp. 56—65; Kalhana, Bk. V, 68—117; Venkayya's "Irrigation in Southern India" in the *Arch. Sur. Ind. Ann. Rep.* 1903—1904; Deakin, 239—242; Aiyangar, 185—188.

2 Mc. Crindle's *Anc. Ind.* (Meg. XXXIV), p. 86; Arrian, III; Aiyangar, 188, 189; Law's *Hind. Pol.*, pp. 68—75.

3 Ayyar's *Town*, pp. 42, 44, 51.

4 Mc. Crindle's *Anc. Ind.*, p. 86; Strabo, XV, 46; *Ind. Ship.*, p. 192.

5 Aiyangar, pp. 70, 337, 359, 360, 379—382.

6 *Itsing*, pp. 65, 154, 177.

7 *Ind. Ant.* 1888, pp. 308—311.

8 *Si Yu-ki*, Vols I and II (See Hiuen Thsang's account of any of the states visited by him).

the distressed and the poor the ostensibly religious buildings discharged an important economic function like the Catholic institutions of mediaeval Europe. Add to all this the minimum functions of every state as state, viz. the protection of person and property, or national defense by army and navy as well as internal policing by adequate executive and judicial staff. The extent of these minimum functions can be realized from the fact that in the Maurya Empire the appropriations on this head absorbed 25 per cent of the total revenues.[1]

It is not necessary to compare the functions of Hindu states, item by item, as regards quantity and variety, with the long list of modern state activities, expanding daily as they have been under the impact of socialism. The socialistic trend of *dharma*-states is apparent enough. One must not surmise, however, that every public work among Hindus was the undertaking of the state. For, private effort i. e. the patriotism of citizens was responsible in every age for the founding and maintenance of useful institutions. In Gupta India hospitals[2] were built and endowed by the public-spirited townsfolk of Pâtali-putra, the Rome of the Hindus. Rudra-dâmana (*c* A. C. 150), a satrap of Gujarat, repaired the Sudarśana reservoir at his own expense, the ministers having refused to supply funds from the government treasury.[3] General Uṣavadâta's (*c* A. C. 100) endowments in the Andhra Deccan may serve as a standing example of the manner in which the people cooperated with the state and supplemented its activity along developmental or cultural lines.

One of the hill caves in Govardhana (Nasik District in the Bombay Presidency) was excavated at Uṣava-dâta's expense.[4] Among his numerous benefactions we read of the gift of 300,000 cows, the construction of the flights of steps on a river and the giving away of sixteen villages for religious purposes. This philanthropist used to maintain 100,000 scholars and priests with board. He bore the marriage expenses of eight Brâhmaṇas at Somnath in Gujarat. His quadrangles, public halls and halting places as well as gardens, tanks and wells were spread over the country from Broach and Bassein, the ports on the Arabian Sea coast, to Daśapura in Malwa, far inland in Upper India. Ferry boats were placed by him over six rivers in northern Bombay. Both sides of these rivers were also furnished with rest houses and equipped with arrangements for the distribution of water to travellers. Moreover, he founded

---

[1] *Ind. Ant.* 1909, p. 263.

[2] Beal's *Fa Hien*, p. 107.

[3] *Ep. Ind.* 1905—1906, *loc. cit.*

[4] *Nasik Inscr.* No. 17; *Early Hist. Dek.* sec. iv.

certain benefactions for the support of several academies of Vedic learning in various parts of the Maratha country.

Such private endowments for public purposes were undoubtedly numerous in every epoch of Hindu history. But none the less the financial burden of public administration weighed heavy upon the "pillars of the state". The government could not afford to depend solely upon local patriotism and voluntary contributions. The expenses of national house-keeping had to be met regularly from the resources of the empire. The finance department had therefore to raise the necessary revenue by hook or by crook.

Census[1] was an important institution of the Mauryas. It was used by the municipal corporation of Pâtali-putra as well as by the imperial civil service. The *gopa* or village magistrate, the *sthânika* or district magistrate, as well as the *nâgaraka* or mayor of the city were alive to the importance of vital statistics. The numbering of persons, houses and cattle, as well as the measurement of lands, pastures and gardens furnished the *samâhartâ* or collector-general with definite data for the valuation and assessment of the people's wealth.[2] The cadastral surveys organized by the Cholas[3] in 986 and 1086 were also calculated to ensure the same end. Both these instruments tended to bring about centralization and consolidation of the public revenues and were indeed together with the war office, the judiciary and the executive service the most effective means of establishing *pax sârva-bhaumica.* The financial organization aimed at by the Hindu empires was thus akin to the "integration" of national outlays and revenues that has been the steady achievement of modern Europe since the fifteenth and sixteenth centuries. And in classical times it is the system of the Roman Empire with its official tax-collectors who replaced the *publicani* or revenue-"farmers" of the republic that should be kept before the mind's eye while appraising the public expenditure, national resources or heads of income, and financial administration of Hindu India from B. C. 322 to A. C. 1300.

4. *Kautilyan Finances* (*c* 300 *B. C.*).

We shall now proceed to analyze the revenues of the Maurya Empire. One of the functions of the *gopa*, the officer at the lowest rung of the executive hierarchy, was to register the probable dues of the villagers in "working men"[4] along with taxes, tolls and fines. It is not clear

---

[1] Law's *Hind. Pol.* 106—114.

[2] *Ind. Ant.* 1905, p. 5.

[3] Aiyangar, 144, 149, 150, 175—177.

[4] *Ind. Ant. loc. cit.*

if we are to understand that the empire used to receive contributions in "services" like the Roman republic in its earlier stages,— such, for instance, as is recommended by Viṣṇu,[1] Manu,[2] or Śukra.[3] In Megasthenes's account of India, again, we read that one of the objects of the vital statistics kept by the census officials of the municipal corporation of Pâtaliputra was the levy of a tax.[4] If some particular tax is to be singled out because of this statement it was evidently a poll tax on the citizens per head.

The financial authorities themselves classified the revenues into seven principal groups according to the kind of resource tapped by them. "Fortified cities" constituted the first revenue jurisdiction. The *râṣtra* or "country" districts constituted the second. Mines were treated as a distinct source of public income. Gardens and forests also formed two independent groups. Quadrupeds like cows, buffaloes, sheep, goats, asses, camels, horses and mules likewise contributed their quota. The seventh head was traffic both by land and water.

Each of these sources is described in detail in the *Artha-śâstra*.[5] The several items of income from the "country", the second in the above grouping, comprised six heads. Crown-lands yielded the first revenue that was known as *sîtâ*. The second head was *bhâga* (share) or revenue in kind realized from private landlords. A special tax, *bali*, was demanded for religious purposes corresponding to the dues realized by Athens for the festivities. Sundry collections known as *kara* were made in money. *Târa* was the toll realized on boats, ferries and ships. The sixth item consisted of various dues, *vartanî* (road-cess), *śulka* (toll), etc. and was levied as a rate on all traffic.

The fortified cities contributed to the imperial exchequer under twenty different heads. These were toll, fines, weights and measures, jails, currency, passports, excise, slaughter-houses, oils, *ghî* (clarified butter), salt, goldsmiths, commerce, courtesans, gambling, house-building, artisans, gate-dues, and religious institutions. There were special taxes on a people called Bahârikas. They appear to have been mercenary soldiers or some wealthy community living at Nâlandâ, the famous university town of later ages. Like Jews in Europe this race was considered by the Hindu empire to be a good victim for fleecing.

Altogether, there were at least fifty different names under which

---

[1] Ch. III, 32.

[2] VII, 138.

[3] Ch. IV, sec. ii, line 241.

[4] Mc Crindle's *Anc. Ind.* 87—88.

[5] *Ind. Ant.* 1905, p. 47.

revenues flowed into the treasury. For our present purpose we shall classify them into eight modern categories: (1) land revenue, including the income from forests and gardens, (2) customs duties, (3) excise on sales, (4) "direct" property taxes of various denominations, (5) fines as penalties for all sorts of offence, (6) economic "earnings" or profits from the commercial undertakings of the naval department, (7) income from the crown monopolies in extractive (mine, salt, etc) and other industries, (8) miscellaneous collections like port-dues, etc.

a) *Land Revenue.*

As with the Roman Empire[1] the chief source of Maurya income was the receipt from land. In the West the process of fiscal reorganization from Hadrian to Diocletian led up to the system of assessment for fifteen years. But in regard to the Mauryas no information is available as to the period for which the valuations were made.

In Athens land belonged to the state. In Maurya India certain passages of the *Artha-śâstra* may lend color to the hypothesis as to the "public ownership" of the chief "agent of production". If Kautilya's statements may be taken as "positive law" on the subject, both land and water belonged to the government. The people could exercise their proprietary right in regard to all other species of property excepting these two.[2] But, on the other hand, this position will appear to be inconsistent with the fact noted above that two distinct items were enumerated as land-revenue from the *râṣtra* or country districts of the empire. The *sîtâ* was the income from the crown-lands, and was therefore rent. The other realization was specifically known as *bhâga,* the "share" of the state in the "produce" of the people's lands. The private proprietors were known as *sva-vîryopajîvinah.* Besides, the right of private property in real estate was clearly recognized in the law of sales. According to the legislation in the *Artha-śâstra,*[3] village lands were to be sold in the presence of forty neighbors who owned land in the vicinity. The state could demand only the legitimate excise on the sale. The same proprietary right is to be inferred from, though also limited by, the ruling that lands could be sold by cultivators only to cultivators, and that persons enjoying revenue-free lands could sell them only to persons who already possessed such lands. The distinction between crown-lands and private lands is also to be noted in the law of escheat. By the general

[1] Arnold, pp. 203, 204; Ramsay, 275—281; *Enc. Brit.* (Finance).

[2] *Artha* II, i, vi. Cf. the Mohammedan theory of public domain, Aghnides, pp. 500—521. Note the conditions of land tenure in Japan, Asakawa's *Early Inst. Life*, p. 73.

[3] *Ind. Ant.* 1905, p. 10; Law's *Hind. Pol.* pp. 161, 162.

law on the subject the rights of ownership over houses, fields, gardens, tanks and temples were forfeited if proprietors took no cognizance for a continuous period of five years.[1]

In the budget of the Maurya Empire as in that of the Roman we have therefore to look for two entries, theoretically considered, under land revenue. The first was rent paid by the *ryot* or tenant to the state-landlord, the second was a "direct tax" paid by the citizen to the government. The imperial demand from land was very high, higher even than what we have seen under the Cholas. For the land alone,[2] where irrigation was carried on by hands the due was $^1/_5$th of the yield; where irrigation was carried on by conveying water on shoulders or through water raised from tanks, lakes and streamlets the due was $^1/_4$th; and where irrigation was carried on by pumping (*sroto-yantra*) water from rivers, the due was $^1/_3$. An additional *udaka-bhâga* or water-rate was charged by the government at $^1/_4$th or $^1/_5$th of the produce. The total rates ranged therefore from $^2/_5$ths or 40 per cent to $^7/_{12}$ths or about 57 per cent of the gross outturn. Provisions for the remission of taxes are recorded. But it was not done on any *doctrinaire* principle. Abatements were graduated according to the difficulties and cost of improvement effected by cultivators.[3] Gardens were assessed at the same rates as cultivated lands. An additional one-sixth or $16^2/_3$ per cent had to be paid as excise on sales.[4]

b) *Taxes on Consumption.*

Important taxes of the Mauryas were twofold: customs and excise. Along with land revenue these must have constituted the mainstay of their finance. In Athens[5] under Pericles the policy of free trade appears to have been adopted as the city depended for its food supply on external sources. Its normal customs duty was therefore as low as 2 per cent. The Roman *portoria*[5] (customs dues) were higher, the earliest maximum being 5 per cent. The extreme maximum under Constantine was $12^1/_2$ per cent. But the Maurya tariff was high enough to verge on, if it did not actually establish, an economic "protection". Thus in regard to imported salt the empire demanded in the first place, one-sixth or $16^2/_3$ per cent of the entire commodity, and in the second place a 5 per cent as trade or sale tax on the remaining $^5/_6$ths.[6] Similarly foreign

---

[1] *Ind. Ant.* 1905, pp. 9, 105, 113.

[2] *Ibid*, p. 110. Note the 50 per cent in Islamic theory, Aghnides, 529.

[3] See details, *Ibid*, p. 9.

[4] *Ibid*, p. 114.

[5] *Enc. Brit.* (Finance). For a detailed account of Athenian finances see Schömann, pp. 432—464.

[6] *Ind. Ant.* 1905, p. 53.

liquors, wines and intoxicants had to bear heavy import duties which varied from one-fifteenth or $6^2/_3$ per cent to one-tenth or 10 per cent of their value.[1] In both cases, in addition to the tariff the government charged an extra duty in order to compensate the loss in the sale of local produce. The total maximum may have approached the British customs rate, which though down to 1700 not generally higher than 5 per cent rose to 25 per cent by 1759.[2]

The normal Maurya duty on foreign goods was one-fifth of their value, i. e. 20 per cent. One-sixth, i. e. $16^2/_3$ per cent was realized from fresh fruits, vegetables, pepper, dried fish, flesh and other perishable goods. The rates on conches, diamonds, pearls, etc were to be fixed at the custom house by experts. Silk garments, arsenic oxide, skins, carpets, etc were charged *ad valorem* from 6 to 10 per cent. The minimum rates on the tariff schedule were 4 to 5 per cent. In order to be consistent, of course, the Empire severely dealt with all cases of smuggling. The highest fine of 3,000 *paṇas* or $ 750 was the punishment prescribed for this offence by the penal code.[3] This was nothing extraordinary considering that the penalty for smuggling according to the latest law in the United States is a fine of $ 5,000 or imprisonment for two years or both. No figures are available as to the gross customs receipts. But it may be surmised that the 27 per cent of the total German Imperial revenues as accruing from customs alone would not have been envied by the Maurya chancellor.[4]

It might seem as if the Empire intended almost to place an embargo on foreign import. But there were certain tendencies in the fiscal policy of the Mauryas in regard to international trade that should indicate a different character of the tariff. The protective duties were high indeed but they were not intended to be "prohibitive". Rather, on the other hand, there was a deliberate attempt on the part of the authorities to encourage foreign imports. They regulated the prices[5] in such a manner that a reasonable profit was assured to the dealer in imported goods. And if necessary, special instructions were issued to the proper officials

---

[1] See details, *Ibid*, pp. 50, 55.

[2] Dowell's *History of Taxation and Taxes in England*, Vol. I, pp. 82—88, 145, 146, 163—167, 211—223; Vol. II, p. 37.

[3] *Ind. Ant.* 1905, pp. 49, 50; Higginson's *Tariffs at Work*, p. 112.

[4] Plehn, 184.

[5] *Ind. Ant.* 1905, p. 57. Note the seven distinct expenses of marketing, *śulka* (toll), *vartanī* (road-cess), *ativâhika* (conveyance-cess), *gulma-deya* (duty payable at military stations), *târa-deya* (ferry charge), *bhaktâ* (porter's wage), and *bhâga* (share of the state), that were calculated by the customs officials in fixing the price of the imported commodities.

to accord concessions in certain particulars to foreign merchants. Under these conditions it is doubtful if the Maurya tariff should be considered as "protective" in any significant sense. In any case its character as a measure for revenue purposes is unquestionable.

The duty of 1 per cent on all sales was a regular tax of the Roman Empire. Such an impost, call it market due, toll or octroi, was, as we have noted, prevalent in Athens also. The rates in Maurya India were much higher. Commodities sold by cubical measure were charged $6^1/_4$ per cent, those by weighing 5 per cent, and those by computation $9^1/_{11}$ per cent *ad valorem*.[1] This tax, known by the generic name of excise or inland trade revenue, was assessed by the Mauryas in two ways. In certain lines, e. g. salt, precious metals, etc they retained the monopoly of manufacture and sale for the government. But the general method of assessment was the grant of a license to the vendor or manufacturer.

The excise branch of the revenues was throughly centralized. The licensing procedure was most efficiently observed. Nobody was permitted to sell the goods at the places of growth or manufacture, e. g. fields, gardens, forests and mines.[2] All commodities had to be brought to the customs house or toll office near the city gate. These were then marked with the state stamp called *abhijnâna-mudrâ* (mark of identification) in *sindûra* (vermilion). The tax was levied, however, only after sale. The law was strict, as evasion of the excise was a capital offense. False statements to the officials made by merchants in regard to amount or price were moreover punished as cases of theft, i. e. by fine, mutilation or even death.[3]

It is evident that the customs and excise receipts of the Maurya Empire were much more voluminous than those of the Roman Empire. Analogues for this aspect of Hindu finance have to be sought in modern states like England, France, and Czarist Russia, where half of the national revenues is made up of the returns from customs duties and excises, or the United States where virtually the whole of "federal" revenues is derived from these two elements in the *Aufwand-steuern*.[4]

Recent authorities on the *Überwalzung* or "shifting" of taxation are for practical considerations inclined to do away with the formal or verbal distinction that economists have long drawn between the taxes on consumption (like customs and excise) and the taxes on property

---

[1] *Ibid*, *loc. cit.*

[2] See details, *Ibid*, pp. 50, 114.

[3] *Ibid*, pp. 48, 40. *Artha* II, xxi.

[4] *The Statesman's Year Book.*

or income.[1] But using the conventional nomenclature we have to mention that in addition to customs and excise, the so-called "indirect" taxes, the Maurya Empire levied "direct" taxes as well. It has already been pointed out, of course, that a great part of the land revenue was a direct tax on real estate in so far as land was the private property of citizens. The taxes on personalty or movable property have now to be enumerated.

c) *Direct Taxes.*

In Kautilya's list we do not have the taxes on looms, oil-mills, etc that are mentioned in the Chola inscriptions. Nor do the Tamil taxes on "sonship" or inheritance and succession appear in the Maurya statements. But, as we have seen, weights and measures were taxed.[2] Gamblers had to pay a license.[3] Dramatists, players, singers, and musicians were charged 5 *paṇas* ($ 1.25).[3] This figure does not, however, explain the rate. A tax was levied from prostitutes as in Athens[4] and in Rome under Caligula.[5] As a rule, cattle were not taxed *per capita.* They figured in the *samâhartâ's* (collector-general's) books only in connection with excise on sale. But under abnormal conditions, when an emergency finance was the problem, a special due was charged on domestic quadrupeds.[6] The same circumstances brought painters, sculptors, and artists generally within the tax-collector's grip.[7]

It seems, on the whole, however, that the Mauryas considered the taxes on property rather as a safety-valve to fall back on in dire necessity than as a normal source of regular imperial revenues. And when the necessity arose (e. g. through war conditions) the Empire did not hesitate to levy what were virtually "super-taxes" on both immovable and movable properties of the wealthier classes. In the first place, the rates of land tax were enhanced.[8] But regions barren or difficult to cultivate were exempted from this emergency taxation. And persons engaged in "essential industries", e. g. in agriculture, forestry, and elephant-training, were likewise granted a privilege. In the second place contributions in "services" were levied from "lacklanders", especially

---

[1] Giffen's art. on Taxation in the *Enc. Brit.* (*The Different Kinds of Taxes*); Seligman's *Shifting and Incidence of Taxation*, pp. 310, 311.

[2] See details, *Ind. Ant.* 1905, pp. 50, 51.

[3] *Ibid*, 58.

[4] Schömann, p. 449.

[5] Seligman's *Essays*, pp. 36, 37.

[6] *Ind. Ant.* 1905, p. 114.

[7] *Ibid*, p. 59.

[8] See details, *Ibid*, p. 115; also *Ind. Ant.* 1909, pp. 260, 261; *Artha*, V, ii.

from culprits and bad characters. The government in cooperation with the *samâhartâ* and the superintendent of agriculture was to improvise "war-farms" and "war-gardens" and induct such able-bodied persons into the work of cultivation.[1]

In the third place, persons rearing pigs and cocks had to contribute 50 per cent of their stock. Those who had sheep and goat farms were taxed $16\frac{2}{3}$ per cent, and herdsmen who reared cows and buffaloes 10 per cent.[2] In the fourth place, a special levy of 500 *paṇas* ($ 125) was raised from merchants in diamonds, horses, and elephants. Dealers in cotton goods had to pay 400 paṇas, dealers in grains and liquids 300, traders in glass and glassware 200, artisans and carpenters 100, and dealers in mud-pots, inn-keepers and small retailers 50.[2] In the fifth place, dramatists (and theater managers?) as well as prostitutes had to surrender half their annual earnings.[2] And lastly, as in Athens,[3] the government exacted extraordinary donations and gifts from temples and religious establishments.[4] The process might almost be described as a legalized looting of ecclesiastical property by the secular authorities.

Some of the war-taxes were described by Kautilya euphemistically as *praṇaya* or "love"-gifts.[5] The Empire used to pose as "beggar" and appeal to the "patriotism" of the citizens for "voluntary" subscriptions. And in order that the "modernism" of Maurya finance may be appreciated still further it has to be pointed out that titles of honor were conferred by the government on the patriotic contributors. Subscribers to the "liberty fund" were honored, for instance, with a rank in the court, an umbrella, or a turban or some ornaments in return for their gold.[6] Moreover, the government took special steps to advertise and give publicity to the donations of the patriots in order to create a spirit of rivalry among the rich in the acts of self-sacrifice.

It was not with an alleged Machiavellian wickedness but in quite the scientific methods of "high finance" that Kautilya approached the problem of financing a war or meeting an emergency. The financial experts of the Maurya civil service knew how to cause the rich to "vomit" (*vamana*) their accumulated wealth or otherwise deplete and

---

[1] See details, *Ibid*, p. 115; also *Ind. Ant.* 1909, pp. 260, 261; *Artha*, V, ii.

[2] See details, *Ibid*, p. 116. *Vide* Gupta's "Courtesanship in Buddhist India" in the *Hindustan Review*, Aug. 1919.

[3] Schömann, p. 454.

[4] *Ind. Ant.* 1905, p. 117.

[5] *Ibid*, pp. 115, 117; *Cf.* "benevolences" in British fiscal history, Dowell, Vol. I, pp. 155—157, 202, 203, 243, etc.

[6] *Ibid*, 1909, p. 261; *Artha*, V, ii.

drain (*karṣaṇa*) of their property.[1] Exploitation of "gold-lords" by the state was a process of expropriation that the *Artha-śâstra* does not hesitate to pronounce as the objective of the "ways and means" committee. Like the "liturgies" and *eisphora* of the Athenian-city state[2] high imposts of various denominations were therefore borne by people of large incomes in Maurya India. And the impact of war or emergency finance must have tended to make the demands of the government even in normal times "progressive" in spirit, if not mathematically so.

d) *Fines.*

We shall now consider the "non-tax" revenues of the Maurya Empire. These were principally of two classes: one derived from the penal (*danda*-inflicting) power of the state, the other from the economic activities of the government. The Empire as *danda-dhara* i. e. "sanction"-exercising organization must have realized an enormous amount from fines, as these were the usual penalties inflicted by the courts of justice. The list of "crimes" was lengthy. The arms of law could reach almost any individual. Dealers in foreign goods had as many chances of transgressing the *śâsanas* (commands of the state) as the butchers in municipal areas. The number of offenses against sanitary laws[3] was as large as that against the prescribed hours and places of fording rivers.[4] Persons committing nuisance on roads and other specified spots were fined one *paṇa* (twenty five cents). Travellers without passports (bearing government stamps) had to pay a fine of 12 *paṇas*.[5] Bearers of false or forged passes were fined 1,000 *paṇas*. No foreigners were admitted into the country without permit. Delinquents had to pay a fine of 3000 *paṇas*, the highest fine[6] sanctioned in Maurya legislation. This was the fine also meted out to those who tried to smuggle foreign goods in evasion of customs duties.[7] Negligence in having the day's government stamp fixed on weights and scales was fined $27^1/_4$ *paṇas*.[8] A fine of 600 *paṇas* was inflicted on the merchant who having imported foreign salt failed

---

[1] *Artha*, IV, iii.

[2] *Enc. Brit.* (Finance).

[3] See the list of fines in municipal areas in the *Ind. Ant.* 1905, pp. 51, 52, also in regard to the construction of buildings, pp. 58, 59. Note the fines realized from slaughter-houses, p. 55.

[4] See the ferry regulations, *Ibid*, p. 111.

[5] *Vide* the passport regulations in regard to travellers, *Ibid*, p. 54, and in regard to traffic in goods, pp. 47, 48.

[6] *Ibid*, pp. 51, 52.

[7] *Ibid*, pp. 48—50.

[8] *Ibid*, p. 51.

to compensate the government for the loss it might incur in not finding customers for its own salt.[1]

e) *Economic Earnings.*

The second head of non-tax revenue comprises the items of income that the Empire derived from its economic enterprises. Shipping lines[2] with fleets of boats for passengers and goods were operated by the state. The traffic by sea was large enough to render the undertaking a lucrative proposition. The Empire carried on another business under the supervision of the naval department. State boats were let out on hire by the *nâvadhyakṣa* or port commissioner for purposes of pearl fishery and the fishing of conch shells.[2] The ferry charges on rivers must also be considered in connection with the government's commercial ventures. These were regulated according to the size of rivers and the amount of freight carried.[3] Any load of commodities whether for sale or not was charged four *mâṣâs* (about six cents). One *mâṣâ* was paid by a traveller with a minor quadruped carrying some load. Two *mâṣâs* were demanded for a load carried on the head or on the shoulders, a cow or a horse. Double was the rate for transporting a camel or a buffalo. The ferry charge for a small cart was five *mâṣâs*, for one of medium size drawn by bulls six *mâṣâs*, and for a big cart seven *mâṣâs*. The ferry dues on large rivers were twice the respective rates.

But by far more important than these quasi-political commercial undertakings as sources of "sinews of war" or "roots of the army" were the industries owned and run or controlled by the government. Altogether three state-monopolies are mentioned in the Kautilyan schedule. The first monopoly was oil. The oil seeds were all brought to the government granary and pressed and made into oil by the state mills.[4] The administration of tobacco monopoly in France since the time of Colbert (1674) furnishes a modern analogue. The next monopoly was salt, as we have mentioned above. In order to "protect" this government industry the Empire legislated that purchasers of foreign salts must have to pay compensation to cover the loss sustained by the state.[5] Evidently foreign salt was not excluded altogether from the territory. There was, besides, the system of granting license by which private

[1] *Ibid*, p. 54.

[2] *Ind. Ship.* pp. 103, 106. Note *en passant* the regulations to protect passengers on ships operated by private companies, *Ind. Ant.* 1905, p. 113.

[3] *Ind. Ant.* 1905, pp. 53, 111, 112. Sixteen *mâṣâs* make one *paṇa.*

[4] *Ibid*, p. 55.

[5] *Ibid*, p. 54.

capitalists could manufacture and sell the commodity. In addition to the economic "profits" from the salt industry the government thus came to realize a large revenue from the customs, excise, and licenses.

The realization of salt *gabelle* was threefold. First, the importing merchant had to pay the regular $16^2/_3$ per cent as customs plus the 5 per cent on the remainder as excise. Secondly, the indigenous manufacturer purchased license from the government on the same terms. There was thus no economic discrimination against foreign salt. The effects of a countervailing excise duty were brought in operation, indicating the "fiscal" character of the tariff. And thirdly, it appears that the government charged $13^1/_3$ per cent as premium on the money that it received as price for the salt collected from the importer and the home manufacturer.[1]

The most important monopoly of the Maurya Empire was the mines and minerals. Indeed the manufacture of salt was scheduled in the *Artha-śâstra* under the category of mining. As defined by Kautilya mining was a comprehensive term, including as in mediaeval British law "wreck of the sea and royal fish".[2] There were therefore two branches of mining under the Mauryas: (1) ocean mining, i. e. pearl fishery, the fishing of conch shells and corals, and manufacture of salt, and (2) land mining.[3] The revenues from land mining were described as those accruing from gold mines, silver mines, mines of rubies, and metals such as iron, copper, etc.[4]

In ancient and mediaeval legislation or custom mines were "public" everywhere.[5] The silver mines at Laurium were owned by Athens. Mines were state property under the Roman Empire. Down to 1688 all English mines belonged to the crown. In 1568 the Exchequer Chamber stated the theory that the "king shall have the whole of the base metal."[6] Under the Mauryas also both land and ocean mines as well as the essaying of ores, coining, and commerce in minerals were *jura regalia*, or crown rights *sui generis*. But the mines were not worked by the government except when the operations needed small outlay. Modern advocates of modified *laissez faire* i. e. partial public ownership may quote the Maurya precedent as an instance of the "individualistic minimum" of state intervention in industry. As a rule, the Empire

---

[1] *Ibid*, p. 53.

[2] Palgrave, Vol. II, p. 765.

[3] Law's *Hind. Pol.*, pp. 5—10.

[4] *Ind. Ant.* 1905, p. 47.

[5] For a general discussion on "state mines" see Bastable's *Public Finance*, pp. 174—176.

[6] Palgrave, *loc. cit.*

let out the mines on royalty basis to private enterprise. The royalty included nine distinct items.[1] As usual, the rates were high. The rental for the Laurium mines was only 4¹/₆ per cent.[2] The French mines yielded 10 per cent.[3] The English rate on copper was 12¹/₂ per cent to the state plus 11¹/₉ per cent to the landlord.[4] But the Mauryas demanded 16²/₃ to 20 per cent as *vibhâga*, i. e. the government's "share" in the yield. In addition the capitalists had to pay 13¹/₃ per cent plus 5 per cent as sundry charges.[5]

There may have been some other industries similarly undertaken or let out on license with a view to augmenting the public income. The shipbuilding and munitions industries were of course state monopolies, as has been mentioned above. But obviously they are to be considered not so much from the standpoint of finance as of national defense.

f) *Miscellaneous Collections.*

Several miscellaneous taxes remain to be discussed as minor sources of income. The port duties[6] realized by the *nâvadhyakṣa* were distinct from both customs and excise. Villages on sea shores and on the banks of rivers and lakes were assessed at certain rates. The fishing license demanded by the state was one-sixth or 16²/₃ per cent of the actual haul. Merchants had to pay the customary tax of port towns. Another group of minor collections came from currency. A premium of 13¹/₃ per cent was regularly charged on coins of private or foreign mintage.[7] Besides, the same amount was realized by the government on every occasion that any body had to pay fine in cash.[8] Lastly, we have to mention the escheats. Houses, fields, gardens, tanks and temples lapsed to the state, as we have seen, if the proprietors neglected to exercise their rights of ownership for five years.[9] Similarly the Empire was the heir of prostitutes' property in the absence of daughters.[10]

No conceivable resource of the people appears thus to have been left untapped by the Maurya Empire. The all-reaching tentacles of Hindu finance lie on the surface. And if, as Adam Smith remarks, there

---

[1] *Ind. Ant.* 1905, p. 113.
[2] Schömann, p. 448.
[3] Brissaud, p. 487.
[4] Palgrave, *loc. cit.*
[5] *Ind. Ant. loc. cit.* Islamic law has 20 per cent, cf. Aghnides, 528.
[6] *Ind. Ship.* p. 106.
[7] *Ind. Ant.* 1905, p. 53.
[8] *Ibid.* p. 54.
[9] *Ibid.* p. 9; cf. Manu, VIII, 30.
[10] *Ibid.* p. 57.

be nothing in which governments are so prone to learn of one another as in the matter of new taxes, the first and the last empires of pre-Moslem India can still give points to the latest specialists in public finance. For, the methods and principles of statesmen from Kautilya to Kulottûnga were eminently matter-of-fact and realistic. Indeed, with the exception of stamp duties, national debt, postal receipts and a few others characteristically modern, the assets schedule of the first class powers of today can hardly exhibit any taxes and non-tax revenues in addition to what the Hindu *sumantra* (finance minister) and his board of experts hit upon pragmatically in the third and fourth centuries B. C. in order to "cover" the appropriations on the governmental machinery of what would hardly fall short of the largest and most extensive of all empires in the world's history.[1]

5. *The Ability to Pay.*

A study of the finances provokes naturally the correlated investigation into the general economic condition of the empire. But as yet it is hardly allowable to attempt a wide solution as to the "ability" of the people to meet the diverse demands of the government. In the first place, an enormous rise in prices may be postulated because of the high rates of customs and excise. This was sure to be felt by the entire community as consumers. In the second place, the normal land tax of 40 to 57 per cent, though it may not have shorn the landowning or agricultural classes to the skin, was certainly not a moderate levy. In the third place, the traders and the intellectual middle classes could not get scot-free from the imperial demand as the property tax was mercilessly applied to them especially in emergencies. And in the fourth place, the moneyed aristocracy, bankers, gilds and other wealthy groups had to "vomit" out their gold at the call of the empire.

Economically speaking, then, we have no grounds for believing that there was any class-discrimination of the type to which France, for instance, was a victim during the *ancien régime*. The Mauryas maintained no privileged class on anything like an appreciable scale. Nor would the government demands, though heavy, appear to have been oppressive

---

[1] See the map of the Maurya Empire in the third century B. C. facing p. 162 of Smith's *Early Hist.* Compare the area with that of any of the European Empires in Freeman's *Hist. Geo.* (with Atlas), or specifically with that of the Roman Empire at its greatest extent (third century A. C.) in the *Atlas of Ancient and Classical Geography.* Note, in comparison, that India is all Europe *minus* the Russia of the Czars, and that Maurya India, although it excluded the southern fringe of the peninsula in a condition of semi-dependent autonomy, included the whole of Afghanistan and Baluchistan. *Vide supra*, p. 26.

or likely to sap the economic foundations of the society. On the contrary, there were certain distinctive services by which the state sought to develop the "staying power" and taxable capacity of the *prakriti*. We have spoken above of the socialistic trend of Hindu states as *dharma-staaten*, in so far as the sphere of their activity was coextensive with the range of human interests. It is necessary now to add that the same tendency is noticeable in two other directions.

First, the Maurya Empire owned several industries and controlled the production of wealth in certain lines. Government supervision of some sort or other brought the economic functions of the people within the compass of partial "public ownership." The consequent abolition of *entrepreneurs* or middlemen in a few channels of business was a positive advantage to the community. Secondly, the Empire sought to regulate by legislation the more important branch of a nation's economic life, viz. distribution and exchange, i. e. value. The maximum rate of interest was determined by the government.[1] The market was protected from the ravages of "profiteers". Reasonable prices and fair profits were fixed by official experts after calculating the legitimate expenses of production including the cost of marketing.[2] The government scheduled likewise the rates of wages and fees for laundrymen, painters, dramatists, singers, and artists.[3]

Such an imperial intervention in the *prakriti*'s economic activity, or what is the same thing, such "state socialism" under "enlightened despots", must have been appreciated at least by the common laborer. The rate of wages in Maurya India was 5 *paṇas* a month or 15 dollars a year.[4] It is interesting to observe that in Chola India in the eleventh and twelfth centuries a temple janitor earned $8^1/_2$ Rupees per month, i. e. $30 a year.[5] These rates, howsoever low by the present day American standard, were much above the Ricardian "iron law of wages" when compared with the current prices and the purchasing power of money during the two periods.[6]

And as for the salaries paid by the government they were liberal enough to satisfy the officers' appetite. They were indeed, humanly

[1] The rate was 15 per cent per year (Law's *Hind. Pol.* pp. 171—177). The usual rate at Athens was 12 to 18 per cent (Schömann, p. 435).

[2] See details in the *Ind. Ant.* 1905, pp. 55—57.

[3] *Ibid*, p. 59.

[4] *Ibid*, p. 53.

[5] Aiyangar, p. 181.

[6] *Ind. Ant.* 1905, p. 53. One Rupee in Maurya India bought 49 *sers* (Madras) of rice. In British India one Rupee today buys not more than 8 *sers*. *Cf.* Aiyangar, p. 183.

speaking, calculated to prevent the desire for "squeeze".[1] The common soldier of the Maurya Empire received 500 *paṇas* ($ 125) per year. The highest salary in the third and fourth centuries B. C. e. g. that for the generalissimo was 48,000 *paṇas* ($12,000) a year. The *samâhartâ* (collector-general) was paid at half this rate. The earning of a middle class man e. g. of an accountant in southern India under the Cholas was 16²/₃ Rupees per month, i. e. 60 dollars a year.[2] Payments were either in kind or in money. The Cholas used to pay even handicraftsmen often in land for customary work. Under the Mauryas payment in gold might be commuted for that in kind at fixed rates.[3]

We are not concerned here with "index numbers" or the statistics of wages and prices nor with the manner in which the tariff, if it was really protective to some extent, may have affected the course of investments, commerce and industries. The stray figures for the third and fourth centuries B. C. and the eleventh and twelfth centuries may be taken for what they are worth. Only, it is necessary to bear in mind that in British India today the average *per capita* income is 20 Rupees or 6²/₃ dollars *per annum*. On the whole, then, it may reasonably be concluded that the financial burden[4] of *pax sârva-bhaumica*, howsoever heavy it might be whether absolutely or relatively, was easily borne by a contented peasantry and working class, a prosperous industrial and commercial aristocracy, and last but not least, a well-paid civil service and army, especially in view of the fact that under Chandragupta and Asoka the people of India had the conscious satisfaction of being citizens of the first and greatest power of the world.

---

[1] *Vide* the list of salaries in the *Artha*, V, iii. (*Ind. Ant.* 1909, pp. 263, 264).

[2] Aiyangar, p. 181.

[3] *Ind. Ant.* 1909, p. 264. For 5 *paṇas* one obtained 165 *sers* (Madras). *Ind. Ant.* 1905, p. 53.

[4] For a Hindu theory of state housekeeping see *Pos. Back*. Vol. II, pp. 111—126.

Chapter VI.

Gaṇas or Republics of the Hindus

(*c* B. C. 600—A. C. 350).

The aspects of the Hindu constitution described thus far open up the norm in the *Realpolitik* of monarchical India. The rights of the people and their democratic achievements under Hindu royalties were generically on a par with those of the nations ruled by *le grand monarque* and such "enlightened despots" as Peter, Frederick and Joseph. The political psychology that lay behind the Hindu institutions was not different in any way from that of the French under the Bourbons or of the Germans until the War of the Liberation.

India's institutional experience was not, however, confined to the monarchical sphere. The Hindu constitution grew along republican or non-monarchical lines also.[1] Let us exclude from our present consideration the patriarchal-democratic "crowned republics" of Vedic India,[2] the *kula-samghas* (family-soviets or communal republics) referred to in the *Artha-śâstra*[3] as "invincible", or the *gaṇas*, described in the *Mahâbhârata*[4] as nationalities constituted on the principle of "equality". Epigraphy and numismatics are now in a position to safely declare that there were at least three periods in the early history of India during which Hindus developed the *gaṇa* or *samgha* polity of the Hellenic and pre-Imperial Roman type.

---

[1] *Vide* Law's "Forms and Types of Hindu Polity" in the *Mod. Rev.* for Sept. 1917; Jayaswal's "Introduction to Hindu Polity" in the same journal, May-July, 1913, and "Republics in the Mahâbhârata" in the *Journal of the Bihar and Orissa Research Society*, 1915, pp. 173—178; Mookerji's *Fundamental Unity*, 74—75, and *Local*, 31, 215; Banerjea, 42—46; Majundar, pp. 87—122. The attention of scholars was first drawn to this subject by Rhys Davids in his *Buddhist India*, Ch. II, cf. Lal's "Republican Tradition etc." in the *Mod. Rev.* (January 1920); *Pos. Back*, Vol. II, 46—51.

[2] *A. P. S. R.* Nov. 1918, pp. 592—595; Basu's *Indo-Aryan Polity*.

[3] I, 35.

[4] *Śânti-parva*, Ch. CVII, 23—24, 30—32.

Section 1.

Republicanism in the Occident.

But before proceeding to describe the republics of the Orient, it is desirable to have an estimate of the political mentality of republican peoples in the Occident. For, Eur-American scholars are likely to attribute the least undesirable incidents in the East to the alleged inherent defects of the so-called Oriental character. But they need only remember that the course of republic has not run smooth even in Occidental France.

France was declared a republic in 1792. Napoleon, the first servant of the people, became emperor in 1804. His empire lasted till the occupation of Paris by the allies in 1814. The Bourbons were then restored to the French throne, and reigned till 1830. Thus, for the first twelve years of this period there was a republic (if the regime under Napoleon as First Consul after the overthrow of the Directory in 1799 should still be called republican), and for the next twenty five years there was the *ancien régime.*

The July revolution of 1830 dethroned the Bourbon Charles X, and set up in the Duke of Orleans a "citizen king". Louis Philippe did not, however, play the president of a republic, as had been expected. In reality he extented for another eighteen years the one-man-rule of the preceding Restoration. In 1848 he was forced to abdicate, and the second French republic was established. This lasted for four years.

In November 1862 Louis Napoleon, the president of the second republic, "managed" to have himself elected emperor. The second Napoleonic Empire went on till 1870. It was the defeat and capture of Napoleon at Sedan by the Prussians that led to his dethronement and the establishment of the third republic by the infuriated mob.

The form of government at home often depends on the success or failure of a foreign policy. Under our very eyes William II's miserable failure in the attempt to wrench "world-dominion" from Great Britain's hands has led not only to a phenomenal democratization of the German constitution but to the subversion of monarchy itself. During the middle of the fifth century B. C. the Confederacy of Delos under the leadership of Athens, which had been at first organized against Persian aggressions, transformed itself into an Athenian empire; and Pericles, the first citizen of Athens, worked his way up to a virtual despot. But the demos of this the most perfect of ancient European democracies tamely submitted to Periclean autocracy because it was triumphant abroad and spread the reputation of Athens far and wide. Similarly the French advocates of "liberty, equality, and fraternity" cast their democratic principles to the winds while Napoleon Bonaparte was laying out suburbs of Paris and French "spheres of influence" in every country of Europe. Their cry then was *Veillons au salut de l'empire.* And if Napoleon III could defeat the Prussians at Sedan, it may be surmised not without reason that France would have continued till today to be a monarchy, no matter whether constitutional or despotic.

However, it is the third republic that has been existing in France since 1870. But royalists have not yet disappeared from the society. Until 1875 the republic had to pass through great storm and stress. The Bourbonists, the Napoleonists, and the Orleanists were actively engaged in anti-republican agitation. Since then indeed the career of the republic has been rather peaceful. But this is chiefly because the three royal dynasties have become extinct. The last Napoleon died in 1879, the last Bourbon in 1883, and the Orleanist candidate in 1894. The agitators have not found other suitable candidates for the crown. But even today in the Chamber of Deputies there are parties which call themselves "monarchists" and "Bonapartists". A section of journalism in France has always been pro-monarchic (cf. *L'Action Française* of Paris), and strangely enough, the constitution of 1875 does not definitely provide for the perpetuation of the republican form of government.

The political tendencies of the French people under the Third Republic are anything but democratic. The French are probably the most high-handed of all the colonial powers in Asia and Africa. This republic was not less despotic than were the monarchical nations in the treatment of the late Manchu-Chinese empire. Nor is it more considerate to the Chinese republic. The Lao-hsikai (Tientsien) affair of 1916 is a recent incident. And in spite of the solemn conferences and mutual assurances of the Powers at Madrid (1880) and Algeciras (1906) in regard to the integrity and independence of Morocco, France systematically pursued an aggressive policy in that Sultanate by which finally Germany was exasperated to bring about the Agadir crisis of 1911. Besides, "the tyranny exercised by the army, the alleged influence wielded over the army by the clergy, the fact that military organization is used as a means of propaganda for royalism, the vicious opposition on the part of the majority of the press to all truly liberal ideas and motives of action, the unscrupulous distortion by the same press of all facts opposed to its own ideas of patriotism, all these may be regarded as portents and symptoms of social retrogression".[1]

---

[1] Reinsch's *World Politics*, p. 73. In regard to the earlier phases of American *swa-raj* see the chapter on "Sham Democracy" in Walter Weyl's *New Democracy*.

Such being the facts, it may not be quite fanciful to guess that if in August 1914 the Germans had succeeded in capturing Paris, as they had planned to do, probably the first thing that the French mob would have done after the defeat would have been to raise the cry, "Down with the republic", "Back to the Crown". That, however, is an open question. But it is a most undisputed phenomenon that none of the greatest thinkers and writers of France were advocates of a republic. Voltaire, the great intellectual protagonist of the eighteenth century was not decidedly anti-monarchical. Montesquieu was not an advocate of the kingless polity. His idealization of the English limited monarchy, as the system in which the alleged separation of the legislative, executive and judicial powers is wrongly believed to ensure the freedom of the people, is perhaps the most widely known fact in the literature of political science. Among the post-Revolutionary men of letters Thiers, though a critic of Napoleon III's absolutism, was a staunch believer in the principles of constitutional monarchy. And his rival and colleague, Guizot, the philosopher and historian, was the right hand man of Napoleon III in his almost Pisistratean "tyranny". And about the same time (1834) Victor Hugo was in a mood to idolize the first Napoleon. The cult found expression in lines like the following:

> Toujours lui! Lui partout! ou brûlante ou glacée
> Son image sans cesse ébranle ma pensée
>
> Napoléon, soleil dont je suis le Memnon . . .
> . . . Napoléon, ce dieu dont tu seras le prêtre.

Truly, the general and enlightened sentiment of the people in this first republic born in a monarchical country is thoroughly unrepublican. It cannot then be maintained that European temperament is normally congenial to republican theories or institutions.

It is in the background of such facts that Hindu experiments in republican polity must have to be appraised.

Section 2.

Three Periods of Hindu Republics.

(a) *Third Period* (*c B. C.* 150—*A. C.* 350).

To begin with the latest epoch of *gaṇas*. The period of about five hundred years (*c* B. C. 150—*c* A. C. 350) between the fall of the Maurya and the rise of the Gupta Empires witnessed the growth and development not only of two powerful monarchies, the Kuṣâns in the Northwest and the Andhras in the Deccan, as we have noticed in a preceding chapter, but also of a number of non-monarchical states that were considerable enough to leave a mark on diplomatic history. It is difficult as yet to describe definitely the duration or extent of sovereignty of these states, but numismatic finds clearly point to the fact that the republics which struck coins in the name of the respective peoples covered in their entirety the territory separating the southern from the northern power. And in the middle of the fourth century A. C. they served to furnish the *ultima thule* of the Gupta Napoleon's ambitions in the western direction. Geographically, therefore, all the independent republics enjoying full sovereignty were located in the Southern Punjab, Rajputana and Malwa.

The northernmost were the Audumbaras[1] of the Punjab with jurisdiction over the Ravi valley. They began to issue coins as a sovereign state during the first century B. C.

1. *The Yaudheyas.*

To their south came the Yaudheyas who were known in their heyday as the "heroes among the Kṣatriyas", i. e. the "heroes of heroes". They were an independent power by about B. C. 100.[2] Their territories comprised both banks of the Sutlej with spheres of influence occasionally extending to the banks of the Jumna on the east and the regions of Rajputana on the south.

In the second century, A. C., Rudra-dâmana[3] (125—150) inflicted a defeat on them, but centuries earlier they had come out brilliantly in India's resistance to Alexander. The *mahârâja* or "great chief" (lit. great king) of this *gaṇa* was elected by the people, and he was also the *mahâ-senâpati* (commander-in-chief).

To the south of the Yaudheyas came the Arjunâyanas.[4] During the first century B. C. and after they were thus in possession of northern Rajputana.[5]

2. *The Mâlavas.*

Further south, between the Chambal and the Betwa, were settled the Mâlavas.[6] Their status as an independent republic began sometime

---

[1] The coins of these *gaṇas* are fully described with illustrations in a chapter of Banerji's comprehensive numismatic volume in Bengali, *Prâchin Mudrâ* (Ancient Coins), I. (c B. C. 1000—A. C. 1300), pp. 102, 104, 109—120.

[2] Cunningham's *Coins of Ancient India*, p. 66, 75—79.

[3] *Ep. Ind.* 1905—06, pp. 44—47; *Gup. Insc.*, p. 252.

[4] Rapson's *Indian Coins*, p. 11.

[5] Banerji's *Prâchin*, p. 109.

[6] *Ibid*, p. 113—117, Majumdar 116.

during the second century B. C. In the first century A. C. they had to encounter a punitive expedition under General [illegible]vadâta,[1] the officer of Satrap Nahapâna, for having entered into an aggressive war with his feudatories, the Uttama-bhadras.

The western neighbors of the Mâlavas were the Sibis.[2] Their earliest coins also belong to the end of the second century, B. C.[3]

The Kunindas had their territory most probably adjoining to that of the Yaudheya republic in the east. They held the upper doab of the Ganges and the Jumna, in close proximity to the foot of the Himalayas.[4] Their earliest coins as an independent state were probably issued in the second century B. C. A neighboring race, the Vrisnis,[5] was likewise a power in the second century, B. C.

3. *Pluralism in Constitutional Life.*

During the first century, B. C., therefore, it was possible for the merchants of *Madhyadeśa* (the "middle countries" of Northern India) travelling in the Deccan to tell the subjects of the Ândhra Empire that the "form of government" was diverse in the north. On being asked by Kapphina *le Grand* as to the name of their ruler, as we read in the *Avadâna-śataka*[6] they had to offer in their reply a distinction between the states ruled by *ganas* i. e. "*gouverné par une troupe* (*état republicain*)" and those ruled by kings. The story of the international relations or constitutional changes of the period is not at all clear, really a blank. We know only that in the teeth of Samudra-gupta's *digvijaya*, "conquest of quarters" (330—50), all these republican nations succeeded in maintaining their autonomy by doing homage and paying tribute.[7] That is; they lost their sovereignty and became feudatories or protectorates of the Gupta Empire.

b) *Second Period* (*c. B. C.* 350—300).

These last republics of India were not freaks of Nature on Hindu soil. They were but continuing the political heritage of their great predecessors. Probably the greatest period of Hindu republics lay between the fourth and the sixth centuries B. C. Those republican nation-

---

[1] *Ep. Ind.* 1905—06, p. 79.

[2] Rapson, 14.

[3] *Arch. Surv. Rep.* VI, pp. 200—207.

[4] *Ibid*, XIV, pp. 134—138, 146; Rapson, 12.

[5] Majumdar, 119.

[6] No. 88. See Feer's French transl. p. 337.

[7] *Gup. Insc.*, p. 14.

alities were thus contemporaneous with Sparta, Athens, Thebes, and Rome. And their ultimate extinction through the establishment of the Maurya Empire (B. C. 323) almost synchronized with the annihilation of the Greek city-states by Philip of Macedon at the battle of Cheronoea (B. C. 338).

Megasthenes records the Hindu tradition prevailing in his time (B. C. 302) that during a period of 6042 years from the time of "Dionusos to Sandrokottos" a "republic was thrice established" in India.[1] Certain cities are also mentioned by him where "at last the sovereignty was dissolved and democratic government set up".[2] The Maltecoroe, the Singhoe, the Moruni, the Marohoe and the Rarungi were, as he says, free nations with no kings. They occupied mountain heights where they had built many cities.[3] This is the earliest foreign report about the existence of republican states among Hindus.

Nor had republics passed into the domain of legend towards the end of the fourth century B. C. For the India that was encountered by the Greeks who had preceded Megasthenes by about 20 years, i. e., who belonged to Alexander's hordes, previous to Chandra-gupta Maurya's establishment of the empire and expulsion of Seleukos the Greco-Syrian from Aghanistan (B. C. 303), was a land of republics and commonwealths, used to assemblies or senates and leaders or presidents.

1. *Patala.*

In the estimation of Greek soldiers, Patala was the Sparta of the Hindus. It was a famous city at the apex of the delta of the Indus. In this community, as Diodorus tells us, the ,,command in war was vested in two hereditary kings of two different houses, while a council of elders ruled the whole state with paramount authority".[4]

2. *The Ârattas.*

Large indeed in Alexander's days was the number of democratically governed peoples, with the institutions of *sva-râj* (self-rule), though often of an oligarchic character. One of the most important of these nations was the Ârattas (*Arâṣtrakas*, i. e. kingless) with their kinsmen, the Kathians. Justin calls them robbers and they are condemned as such in the *Mahâbhârata*. But they proved to be a powerful military aid to Chandra-gupta in his successful wars against Macedonians and Greco-

[1] Fragment L.

[2] Fragment I.

[3] Fragment LVI.

[4] Mc. Crindle's *Invasion of India*, p. 296.

Syrians. It was the splendid assistance rendered by the Ârattas[1] that to a great extent enabled the Hindu commoner to easily clear the Indian borderland of the *mlechchha* (unclean, barbarian) Europeans, and push the northwestern limits of his empire to the "scientific frontier", the Hindukush Mountains.

3. *The Mâlava-Kṣudraka Entente.*

Two other nationalities that have a pan-Indian reputation as having figured in the army of the Kurus in the armageddon of the *Mahâbhârata* happened to strike the imagination of the Greeks in an interesting way. These were the Mallois (Mâlavas) and the Oxydrakai (Kṣudrakas).[2] The former are described by Arrian simply as "a race of independent Indians". But the latter are singled out by him as by far the most attached to freedom and autonomy. From the military standpoint, both were very powerful peoples. But like Athenians and Spartans they had always been used to flying at each other's throats.

Alexander, however, had to count on a formidable opposition from them. For, as it happened, on this occasion parallel in Hindu annals to the Persian invasion of Greece, the Mâlavas and the Kṣudrakas "resolved to forget old enmities and to make common cause against the invader". The alliance was cemented, as Diodorus narrates, by "wholesale intermarriage, each giving and taking ten thousand young women for wives". The strength of the combined army was 90,000 fully equipped infantry, 10,000 cavalry and about 900 chariots.[3]

4. *The Sarbacae.*

Among the other republican nationalities of the time we know about the Sambastai[4] (the Sabarcae ?), on the statement of Diodorus, that they dwelt in cities with democratic form of administration, and about the Cedrosii (Gedrosioi),[5] on the report of Curtius, that they were a "free people with a council for discussing important matter sof state". Another race is mentioned by Curtius, probably the Sabarcae (?) of Diodorus, as a powerful Indian tribe whose "form of government was democratic and not regal". They had no king but were led by three generals[6] who owed office to election. Their army consisted of 60,000 foot, 6,000 cav-

---

[1] *Ibid*, pp. 38, 406.

[2] *Ibid*, p. 140.

[3] Diodorus, XVII, 98 in Smith's *Early Hist.*, pp. 94—95.

[4] Mc Crindle's *Invasion*, pp. 252, 292.

[5] *Ibid*, 262.

[6] *Ibid*, 252.

alry and 500 chariots.[1] Similarly, the Oreitai, the Abastanoi, the Xathroi (the Kṣatriya), and the Arabitai are four peoples whom Arrian calls "independent tribes with leaders".[2] Of these the Kṣatriyas were expert naval architects. They supplied Alexander with galleys of thirty oars and transport vessels.[3]

5. *The Agalassois.*

Two other nations came to have close touch with the troops of Alexander. These are the Agalassoi and the Nysaians. The former, as Curtius says, put up a strong resistance to the Greek invaders, and may be taken to have been the first historic protagonists of Hindu *Bushido* or Kṣatriyaism. For when they were defeated by the enemy, these gallant patriots preferred death to dishonor and national humiliation. Accordingly they "set fire to the town and cast themselves with their wives and children into the flames".[4] Thus, in the pride of nationalism, which was subsequently fostered also on the occasion of Moslem invasions in the Middle Ages, has to be sought one of the feeders of the custom that in subsequent ages came to be practised exclusively by women, viz., the *sati* (the self-immolation of widows on the funeral pyres of their husbands).

6. *The Nysaians.*

The Nysaians[5] are described by Arrian as a free commonwealth. They had a president, but the government of their state was entrusted to the aristocracy. This aristocratic element was represented by the council of three hundred wise men. One hundred of these senators were called for by Alexander. "How, o King !" was the reply of the president of the Nysaian Republic to this suggestion of the Macedonian, "can a single city, if deprived of a hundred of its best men, continue to be well governed ?" The reply was characteristic of the political mentality of the republican Hindus of the Punjab and Northwestern India who presented single or united fronts against Alexander's Indian adventure (B. C. 327—324).[6]

---

[1] *Early Hist.*, p. 98.

[2] Mc Crindle's *Invasion*, pp. 167, 169, 155, 156.

[3] *Early Hist.*, p. 99.

[4] *Ibid*, p. 93.

[5] Mc Crindle's *Invasion*, pp. 79, 80, 81; Arrian, v, ii.

[6] Smith's "Position of the Autonomous Tribes of the Punjab" in the *Journal of the Royal Asiatic Society*, 1903, pp. 685—702.

7. *Republicanism Militant.*

This militant republicanism was no less troublesome·a thorn in the side of the contemporary Indian adventurer. The task of achieving imperial nationalism that lay before the commoner Chandra-gupta Maurya was not an easy job. For in addition to subjugating the kingdoms and lesser empires that had been in existence since the days of Ajâtaśatru, the "new nationalist" of the fourth century B. C. had to make a clean sweep of the powerful republican states that enjoyed absolute sovereignty here and there and everywhere throughout Northern India.

Pax Sârva-bhaumica could not be attained until the diplomacy[1] of his finance minister had extirpated the democratic *gaṇas* of the Madrakas (of the Central Punjab) and the Kukuras (of the lower Indus), the Kurus and Pânchâlas (of the Upper Gangetic Valley), and the Vrijjikas, Lichchhavikas and Mallakas of the eastern provinces.[2] It was not exclusively by methods of "open war" that these republics were crushed. For, like the latest expert in his profession in Eur-America, Kautilya was too proud a master of the "human nature in politics" to advise the use of "blood and iron" in season and out of season. The Macedonian "wiles" which made the oracles of Greece to "philippize" and Demosthenes to wrangle with Aeschines over a lump of the enemy's gold were accordingly reproduced in the politics of the East.

c) *First Period* (*c B. C.* 600—450).

1. *Eleven Republics.*

This cluster of republics represented evidently the survival of a type of polity thad had been more or less uniformly distributed throughout the Hindu world, at least in the Indo-Gangetic plains. An older link in the chain of India's political evolution is furnished by the commonwealths of the fifth and sixth centuries B. C. And it is to the eastern regions of Northern India, roughly speaking, to the modern province of Bihar, that we have to turn our eyes for these oldest historical specimens of Hindu republics.

These republican peoples were eleven in number.[3] In regard to eight of them there is hardly any information of political importance. The Bhaggas had their headquarters in Sumsumâra Hill, the Bulis in Allakappa, and the Kalamas in Kesaputta. Pipphalivana was the territory of the Moriyâs, and Râmagâma of the Koliyas. There were three branches

[1] *Artha*, Bk. XI, Ch. I.

[2] *Ibid*.

[3] Rhys Davids gives ten.

of the Mallas, one with sovereignty in Kusinârâ, the second in Pava, and the third in Kâsi.[1] The most important of these eleven nations were the Sâkiyas of Kapila-vastu, the Videhas of Mithilâ and the Lichchhavis of Vesâli. The last two were amalgamated and went by the name of Vajjians.

Readers of the *Kunâla Jâtaka*[2] are aware that the Sâkiyas had a fight with their neighbours, the Koliyâs. The *casus belli* was economic. Each state wanted to monopolize the Rohinî River for irrigating its own agricultural lands. Princes of monarchical states often entered into matrimonial relations with the leaders of these *gaṇas*. The *Bhadda Sâla Jâtaka*[3] narrates the story of King Pasendi's proposal to the Sâkiyas to give him a daughter in marriage. We know from the same *Jâtaka* that the Lichchhavis had a fracas with the generalissimo of the Kosala monarchy. The cause was the violation of a republican sentiment. The wife of the general had bathed in the waters of their holy tank at Vesâli, and thus defiled the reservoir that was consecrated to the investiture of the republic's legislators. The "marvellous prosperity" of the Lichchhavi capital is referred to in the *Ekapanna Jâtaka*[4] which also describes the "triple wall" of the city, "each wall a league distant from the next", — with the usual gates and watch-towers.

2. *The Sâkiyas.*

No republic in mankind's ancient history can surpass the Sâkiya republic in the magnitude of its influence on world-culture. For, the region over which it had authority has for two thousand and five hundred years remained the Jerusalem of Buddhism, the *Tien-chu* ("Heaven") of the Chinese and the *Tenjiku* of the Japanese. Sâkya the Buddha (or Awakened) was, as the name implies, a citizen of the commonwealth of the Sâkiyas. His father Suddhodana and cousin Bhaddiya were archons of this state. The common tradition that Sâkya renounced princedom is erroneous. For he was not a prince at all but only the son of a president.[5]

The Sâkiyas numbered one million strong. Their territory lay about fifty miles east to west and extended thirty or forty miles south from the foot of the Himalayas. The administrative and judicial business of

---

[1] This is the eleventh. Jacobi's *Jaina Kalpasûtra*, p. 65. Vide Pandey's "Vajji Country and the Mallas of Pava" in the *Hind. Rev.* (May-June 1920).

[2] No. 536.

[3] No. 465.

[4] No. 149.

[5] *Buddhist India*, pp. 19, 22, 41.

this republic was carried out in a public assembly, the Senate. The civic center of Kapila-vastu, the capital, as that of other cities, of the nation, was the *santhâgâra* or the mote-hall. The young and old alike took part in the deliberations as to the government of the country. The chief was elected by the people. He used to preside over the sessions as chief judge. The title of the president was *râjâ* (literally, king).[1] It corresponded in reality to the consul in Rome and the archon in Athens. And if the emissaries that Pyrrhus of Epirus sent to republican Rome (B. C. 280) could not describe the Roman Senate except as an "assembly of kings" there was nothing specifically undemocratic in the honorific title of *râjâ* for the chief executive of a Hindu republic.

3. *The United States of the Vajjis.*

The republic of the Vajjians was a United States of ancient India. It was a federation formed by the union of eight nations[1] that had formerly been distinct and independent of one another. Vesâli was the headquarters of this federal republic. The two most prominent of the members in this union were the Videhas and the Lichchhavis. The Videhas had once been citizens of a monarchical state, and their original territory covered 2300 miles. The Lichchhavis of a certain period used to elect a triumvirate of three archons to conduct their administration.[1]

The Senate or general assembly of the Lichchhavi *gaṇa* appears to have been a very large body. In the stories of the *Ekapanna Jâtaka*[2] and the *Chulla-Kalinga Jâtaka*,[3] the conventional number of congressmen or senators, known usually as *râjâs*, is given as 7707. Evidently the "young and old" are to be included in the huge membership of this folk-parliament. These *râjâs* were not only legislators, but seem to have been "viceroys" (vice-presidents?), generals and treasurers" as well. In other words, they were "given to argument and disputation" not only over the questions of custom or law, but also over those affecting the bureaucratic administration, national defense or peace and war, and public finance. All the interests of the state must have been publicly discussed by the central council of the republic.[4] The cabinet of this mammoth assembly was however quite a manageable body. It consisted of nine *gaṇa-râyâṇas*[5] (i. e., ministerial chiefs or kings) to rep-

---

[1] *Buddhist India*, pp. 19, 22, 41. [2] No. 149. [3] No. 301.

[4] The interpretation offered here is substantially different from that given by Majumdar (pp. 92—94). Here as in the Tamil rotation of offices (*Supra*, p. 54) we have to observe *l'amateurisme démocratique* of which Joseph-Barthélemy speaks in *Problème de la compétence*, pp. 11—12, 16—17.

[5] Jacobi, p. 65.

resent the entire state. Corresponding to the *Yajnas*[1] or sacrifices and anointments of all monarchies, Hindu and Christian, the Lichchhavis had an investiture ritual too. A sprinkling[2] of the senators with the waters of the tank at Vesâli was apparently an incident in the political ceremonial of the *gaṇa*.

Quite in keeping with the almost mobocratic consitution of the Lichchhavi Senate the organization of the judiciary was democratic to the nth term of utopian idealism. The Vajjian Confederacy acquired from the Lichchhavis their system of judicial proceedings described in the *Atthakathâ*.[3] In order to be convicted as criminal the defendant had unanimously to be found guilty by seven tribunals of the hierarchy in succession, but if innocent, could be discharged by each of them. The officers who tried him in the first instance were called *vinichchiya mahâmâtta* (chief judicial officers). If proved innocent, he might be acquitted forthwith. But if guilty in their finding, he had automatically to face a second trial by the *vohârikas* (i. e. *vyavahârikas* or lawyers). The next higher courts to examine the evidence as to guilt were those of the *sutta-dhara* (maintainers of the Canonical *Suttas*), *attha kulaka* (council of judges from the eight clans), *senâpati* (commander in chief) and the *upa-râja* or vice-president. The highest court was that of the *râjâ* or president who alone had the authority to declare the accused guilty and was the final judge also as to the penalty. The sentence had to be passed, however, according to "case-law" recorded in the *paveni-pustaka*, i. e. the book of precedents.[4]

4. *Division of Power.*

It is evident that few, if any, of these republics had their jurisdiction confined to single villages or cities like the ordinary commonwealths of Greece or the town states of Hansa. The *gaṇas* have, generally speaking, to be treated not in terms of thousands of citizens, but of millions and not in terms of scores of square miles, but of hundreds or thousands. The Sâkiya and Vajji states should accordingly have to be understood as bearing resemblance to the Athenian republic of Attica (or the Periclean "empire" of Athens) and the "dominion of a city over cities"

---

[1] *Infra* p. 225.

[2] *Bhaddasâla Jâtaka* (No. 465).

[3] Turnour's "Examination of the Pali Buddhistical Annals" in the *Journal of the Asiatic Society of Bengal*, 1838, pp. 993—994.

[4] The alleged Tibetan (Mongolian) origin of the Lichchhavi judiciary has been examined by Hemchandra Ray Chaudhuri in the article on the "Lichchhavis of Vaisali" in the *Mod. Rev.* for July, 1919

known as the republic of Rome, or to the extensive oligarchies of mediæval Italy named after prominent cities like Florence, Venice, Genoa, and so forth.

The question of "local government" was therefore an important one to the *gaṇa-râyâṇas* of Buddha's time (B. C. 623—543). It is interesting to observe that the management of affairs of the rural areas of these republics was not the monopoly of the male sex. The laying out of parks, the erection of communal halls, rest-houses and reservoirs, and the construction and mending of roads between village and village were undertaken by men and women in joint committees.[1]

5. *Śakya, the Anti-Monarchist.*

The principles of the Sâkiya republic, nay, the entire philosophy of democratic republicanism found an able exponent in Śâkya, the Buddha, who, though he renounced the family-ties, remained an active propagandist all his life. And the propaganda embraced lectures[2] as much on constitutional law, trial by jury, *res judicata*, government by the majority, the importance of public meetings, and all other branches of civic life, as on the pathway to salvation and the elimination of misery from the world of men.

He had great interest in the welfare of the Vajjian Confederacy and was almost the political and spiritual adviser of its council of elders. During the last days of this republic, while it was singing the swan-song of its sovereign existence owing to the threat of Ajataśatru, King of Magadha, that he would extirpate the Vajjians "mighty and powerful though they be", it was Śâkya's anti-monarchism and republican fervor that kept up the spirit of resistance among the Senators sufficiently high to enable them to accept the royal challenge. For they were heartened by Sâkya's judgment that the Vajjians could not be overcome by the king in battle as long as their federation was unbroken.[3]

6. *The Civilization of Republican India.*

The cultural achievements of republican India might easily be belittled. But let students of the history of civilization compare the contributions of the age of Hindu republics with the values of European culture from Pythagoras to Plato, and from the expulsion of the Tarquins to Augustus Caesar, such as Dopsch, for instance, describes in *Wirtschaft-*

[1] *Supra*, p. 52.

[2] *Supra*, pp. 37—40.

[3] *Dialogues of the Buddha*, Vol. II (*Mahâ-pari-nibbâna-suttânta*).

liche und Soziale Grundlagen der europäischen Kultur. In an inventory of India's contributions[1] to the spirit of inquiry and the progress of mankind the epoch of republics (*c* B. C. 600—A. C. 350), interspersed no doubt with monarchies, must be recognized as responsible for the anatomy, therapeutics and medicine of Charaka's academy, the linguistics and methodology of Pâṇiṇi and his scholars, the metallurgy and alchemy that found patron-saints in Patanjali and Nâgârjuna, the philosophical speculations of the atomists (*Vaiśeṣika*), monists (*Vedânta*), sensationalists (*Chârvâka*), and sceptics (*Lokâyata*), the schools of political science that came to be finally absorbed in the systems of Kautilya and Śukra, the legal and sociological theories associated in the long run with the *nom-de-plumes* of Manu and Yâjna-valkya, the elaboration of the *Jâtaka* folklore and of the *Râmâyaṇa* and *Mahâbhârata* epics, dramaturgy and fine arts of the Bharata[2] and Bâtsâyana[3] cycles, the mystical militarism and *niṣkâma karma* or "categorical imperative" of the *Gîtâ*, and last, but not least, the *sarva-sattva-maitrî*[4] (humanitarianism and universal brotherhood) of Sâkya, the preacher of *appamâda* (strenuousness) and apostle of *viriya* (energism).

Section 3.

Valuation of India's Democratic Attainments.

Intensive researches will no doubt in the future furnish a more realistic and detailed history of the popular institutions of the Hindus. It is not improbable that one day we shall know, age by age, and country by country precisely to what extent the peoples actually participated in the work of government.

But already we are in a position to conclude, first, that despotism is not the sole message of the East, and secondly, that the West also has been the prolific parent of despotism. On the other hand, the democratic elements in the Oriental polities must not be interpreted too liberally so as to imply the "referendum", the "initiative", "gild-socialism" and so forth of the latest constitutional developments.[5]

---

[1] Seal's *Positive Sciences of the Ancient Hindus*, Mitra's *Indian Mathematics*, Ray's *History of Hindu Chemistry*, Sarkar's *Hindu Achievements in Exact Science*.

[2] *Annales du Musée Guimet*, Vols I and II; Text in the *Kâvya-mâlâ Series;* Sylvain Levi's *Theater Indien*.

[3] cf. Jolly's *Recht*, 46, 50, 53, etc. See also his "*Kollektaneen zum Kautilya Arthaśâstra*" in the *Zeit. deut. morg. Ges.* (1914).

[4] *Saddharma-pundarika* (Lotus of the True Law), p. 234; *S. B. E.* Vol. XXI, p. 222.

[5] Dicey's *Law of the Const.*, xci—c; Oberholtzer's *Referendum in America*, pp. 1—44, 471—513.

First, it need be observed that in monarchical India there was no *organic* connetion between the people and the council of ministers, and the council itself had its tenure under royal pleasure. The Oriental Richelieus and Bismarcks were, *in law*, no better than the "king's men" as had been the ministers of England previous to the introduction of the Cabinet system, e. g. in the seventeenth and eighteenth centuries. Hindu ministers may sometimes have been king-makers and often virtually the rulers of the country; altogether, the monarchy may thus have been tempered by the counsels of the wise, the "virtuous" "guardians" of Plato's *Republic*. But the good government enjoyed by the people in a benevolent "aristocracy" or the enlightened despotism, say, of a Kautilyan *râjarṣi* must not be compared with the rights of individuals as modern constitutional law understands them. Despotism was no doubt modified by the councils, but they could not place "legal" restraints on the exercise of royal power.

Secondly, the so-called village communities, those "little republics", were not independent of the kingdoms and empires. They did not enjoy the rights of "sovereignty" in historical times. In Vedic India they may have been conterminous with the autonomous tribes. Subsequently they may have continued for some time as urban or rural republics. But during the period under survey they remained normally but the lowest rungs of the ladder in a system of imperialism, i. e. of centralized national administration.

Thirdly, it would be wholly misunderstanding the local and county administration of modern times, on the one hand, and the independent city-states and clan-republics of the ancient and mediaeval world, on the other, if one were to proceed to interpret the negative advantages of *laissez faire* due to imperial weakness as identical with the conscious assertion of authority by the people in the provinces. Compulsory non-interference on the part of the central government whether through lack of facilities for communication or through military incompetency does not imply such positive exercise of political power by the districts, cities and villages as is possible or at any rate as is being sought in modern nation-states.

The development of *śreṇîs*, *gaṇas*, folk-moots, ministerial councils and the like should not therefore be seriously adduced as evidence of qualification to meet the problems of the republican polity with which Young Asia has to grapple today. Even in Greece the people have chosen to subvert the *gaṇa* and restore Constantine to the throne (1921). Asia's past political experience is of no greater value for present purposes than Greek, Roman and feudal attainments can possibly be to the modern

Latins, Slavs or Teutons.[1] For, the modern republic, not to speak of its recent sovietic phase, was utterly unknown to the Occident until very late times. It is an essentially new phenomenon in world politics comparable to the steam engine, the parent of the "Great Society". To take an extreme instance, the novitiate through which the Orient has been passing in China since 1912 is not qualitatively different from that through which France had to pass.

It is well to remember how the very idea of a republic stank in the nostrils of Europeans when the American republic was born. The general antipathy to the first French republic was as notorious as is today the sentiment against anti-propertyism and sovietic *svarâj*. The whole Napoleonic war was really a war of self-defence on the part of the trustees of republicanism against the enemies of popular government who were financed and directed by England. The Holy Alliance of 1815 also under the leadership of Russia was a union of monarchies, organized to put down democratic upheavals and help the crowned heads. It was to withstand the effects of this "league of nations" that the Monroe Doctrine was launched in 1823 on behalf of the republics of the New World. In the history of the constitution, President Monroe's message belongs to the same category as the military challenge of revolutionary France to the ruling dynasties of Europe. Similarly the struggles of 1830 and 1848 had to be fought on every inch of European soil on the question of republicanism (at any rate, democracy or consitutionalism) *vs.* absolute monarchy. All these facts indicate the enormous opposition in the teeth of which the modern republic has had to grow up. They point also to the profoundly novel character of the theories and institutions associated with it.

---

[1] In the controversy raised by the Montagu-Chelmsford Report the nationalist sentiment is officially represented by Sir C. Sankaran Nair, who quotes Rhys Davids, Havell, Aiyangar, Banerjea, Bhandarkar, and Jayaswal in the *Minute of Dissent to the Government of India's Despatch* of March 5, 1919, secs. 2, 3, 4 (*Indian Review*, July 1919), while the Anglo-Indian opinion is non-officially voiced by Mr. Vincent Smith in *Indian Constitutional Reform viewed in the Light of History*, pp. 18—21. According to the methodology followed in the present treatise both these viewpoints, in so far as they have bearing on the political *tradition* or genius of India, are fallacious extremes. The English historian of Hindu and Mohammedan politics manages, as usual, to ignore the despotism in occidental tradition and forget the fact that down to 1789 European masses, no less than the Indian, were as innocent of "elective councils and diarchies" as is the man in the moon of the binomial theorem. On the other hand, the Hindu *svarâjist* is almost inclined to minimize the unprecedented character of the cumulative assertion of the human spirit in politics from the American revolution to the Russian revolution. The problem before the descendants of Vajjians and Yaudheyas is today as easy or as difficult as that before the inheritors of Greek and Roman democracies. An appeal to history at the present juncture is irrelevant and useless.

The modern republic is, in the first place, a country-state and not a mere city or clan. Secondly, and as a consequence of this, it is not a "direct" democracy of all the people sitting in legislative sessions. The system has its life in the principle of representation. Thirdly, it is not part of a larger whole, not a "home-rule" territory, but an absolutely independent organism, a fully self-determined or *selbständig* political unit, an unconditioned *sva-râj*.

Only one republic of this type existed in the world at the time of the French Revolution. But the example of Switzerland seems to have played no part in the evolution of modern republicanism. The Girondist demagogues used to illustrate their lectures not so much from contemporary or mediaeval history as from ancient Greece and Rome. But these Classical republics were not republics in the modern sense of the term.

Athens was but a city-state. It was, besides, based on a fundamental injustice. Under Pericles the number of free citizens was only 25,000. The number of slaves was then 300,000. Moreover, Pericles was all but imperator in name.

Rome also had originally been a city-state like Athens, Sparta and Thebes. Subsequently, she became mistress of Italy. The Roman Senate was a republican aristocracy during the period of conquests — "an assembly of kings" as it appeared to the emissaries of King Pyrrhus of Epirus. But Rome did not merge herself in an "Italian" republic. Roman Italy was essentially the empire of a republican city-state over other cities. The "Roman franchise" was granted to the subject cities very sparingly. Further, with extra-Italian expansion the republic was converted into a formal empire.

The Middle Ages produced several types of republican states, aristocratic, oligarchic, and even democratic. The chartered towns of England and France, the Hanseatic cities of north Germany, and the Italian cities like Florence, Venice or Naples, are the best examples of such republics. But the English and French cities never claimed "sovereign" rights; the German cities were formally "free" but actually semi-dependent, as they had to acknowledge more or less the jurisdiction of feudal lords, markgrafs, or emperors; it was only the Italian cities that may be said to have approached the ancient Hellenic city-states in real autonomy and independence. "North Italy is the only region in medieval Europe where the greater part though not the whole of a continuous territory is divided up into the domains of a number of city states just as the more civilized portion of ancient Greece was."[1]

---

[1] Sidgwick's *Development*, 277.

On the whole, however, the mediaeval cities, because of their partial or complete sovereignty, were the greatest stumbling blocks in the evolution of nationality in Italy and Germany. It is on the graves of these republics that modern Italy and Germany had to be raised. It is evident therefore that these are not the prototypes of the republic as understood today.

Towards the end of the eighteenth century, the Americans and the French had thus no precedent, ancient or mediaeval, to go by in the constitution of their republics. They were the first to break the ice. Not in a worse or more helpless condition is Asia placed today. Like the occidentals, Asians also cannot get any help from their own past tradition. Naturally, therefore, it is the examples of the United States and of France that have inspired Asia in the nineteenth century, as they have done the Latin Americans, in new political experiments. The constitutional monarchy of Japan, the limited Shahnate of Persia, the parliamentary regime of the "Union and Progress" party of the Young Turk, Chinese republicanism, and the nationalist movements from Calcutta to Cairo, are thus so many links in the chain of thousand and one influences that the East has been imbibing from the West in modern times. This spiritual conquest of Asia by Eur-America from Washington and Adam Smith to Karl Marx and Lenin indicates, therefore, the absolute limit[1] of the extreme claims that may be advanced on behalf of ancient Hindu achievements in politics.

---

[1] Uyehara's *Pol. Dev. Jap.*, pp. 78, 79, 113, 114; Bland's *Li Hung-chang*, pp. 251—260; Macdonald's *Turkey and the Eastern Question*, 53—55; Vambery's *Western Culture in Eastern Lands*, 324—354.

PART II

THE CONCEPTS OF HINDU POLITICS.

CHAPTER VII.

Hindu Literature on Politics.

Section 1.

Political Speculation in Ancient India.

It is with reference to all this *milieu* in life and institutions that Hindu political thought has to be understood. Unfortunately the impression has got abroad since Max Müller[1] wrote the *History of Ancient Sanskrit Literature* and *India: What Can It Teach Us?* that the literature of the Hindus deals mainly with vague idealism, unpractical mysticism, and other-worldly absurdities, — at best, with metaphysical philosophizing. Besides, a few alleged pessimistic passages from one or two Buddhist books in the Pali language are erroneously taken to be the watchword of all Hindu speculation.

A complete history of Hindu literature whether in Sanskrit[2] or the Prakrit languages it is impossible yet to attempt. A catalogue of catalogues, the *Catalogus Catalogorum*, has been compiled by Aufrecht. It contains the shortest possible notices of about twenty five thousand manuscripts in Sanskrit. Thousands of other manuscripts remain still to be explored, tabulated and indexed. In the meantime a hasty glance at Aufrecht's volumes is enough to convince us that Sanskrit literature is the literature of every human activity from cooking, dancing, painting, cattle-breeding, gardening and grooming to erotics, thieving, warfare, navigation, and manufacture of military implements, in other

---

[1] *His. Sans. Lit.* (ed. 1860), pp. 18, 25, 29—31; *India* (ed. 1883), 97—101, 105, 107, 117. *Vide* the author's "Hindu View of Life" in the *Open Court* for August, 1919, "Comparative Literature from the Hindu Standpoint" in the *Hindustan Review* (July 1919). *Hindu Art: Its Humanism and Modernism.*

[2] *Vide* Haraprasad Sastri's "Educative Influence of Sanskrit Literature" in the *Collegian*, 1916, for a concise but comprehensive account.

words, of *dharma*, *artha*, *kâma*, and *mokṣa*. Needless to observe, economic, political and legal treatises occupy a great deal of space.[1]

For obvious reasons, in India as in Europe accounts of socio-political life and theory are to be met with in almost every branch of literature, prose and verse. Even literary epics like the *Raghu-vamśa* and the *Kirât-ârjunîya*, and story-books like the *Pancha-tantra* and the *Daśa-Kumâra-charita* can be exploited by sociological art-critics for the political message of the authors exactly in the same way as Virgil, Dante, Vondel and Milton have been used as interpreters of their ages. And of course in the two so-called epics, the *Râmâyaṇa* and the *Mahâbhârata*,[2] which according to the *Sâhitya Darpaṇa* ("Mirror of Literature"), a mediaeval work on rhetoric, are not poems at all but books of history, especially in the latter the serious student of politics would not have to labor hard in order to find rich material. To the same category belong also the *Purâṇas*, the storehouses of every conceivable information about India and Hindu culture. Nor would the *Brihat-Samhitâ* of Varâhamihira, the *Natural History* of the Hindu Pliny, fail to furnish important facts about polity and political speculation compiled, as they were, for a manageable *Encyclopedia Sanskritica*, by a distinguished scientist of Gupta India. Similarly the treatises on archery known as the *dhanur-vedas* and the sexological works like the *Kâma-sûtra* of Bâtsâyana may be consulted for the subject matter of economics and politics, and of secular knowledge generally.

But it is not solely among *belles lettres* and books comprehended in the *trivium* or *quadrivium* of mediaeval European universities that the student of Hindu politics has to rummage. Law, public finance, constitution, town-planning, national defense, sovereignty, these and allied problems constituted in themselves the basis of two special literary categories. The first category is that of the *smriti-śâstras*, *dharma-śâstras* and *dharma-sûtras*,[3] and the second is that of the *artha-śâstras* and *nîti-śâstras*. These two groups of *śâstras* (*Wissenschaften*) exhaust within them the entire range of Hindu social science. It is therefore to these treatises on *dharma* (law) and *smriti* (tradition) as well as *artha*

---

[1] Aufrecht's volumes have been used extensively in the author's *Positive Background of Hindu Sociology*, Vol. I.

[2] For an almost exhaustive study of the general politics of the *Mahâbhârata vide* Hopkins' article in the *Journal of the American Oriental Society*, 1889. But Book XII (*Śânti*) needs a separate special treatment.

[3] For the status of these *śâstras* in the "grammar" of Hindu science *vide* Oldenberg's *Grihya-sûtras of Gobhila etc.* (S. B. E. Series), Introduction, xxxiii—iv. See the section on the "Autonomy of Political Śâstra" in *Pos. Back*, Vol. II, pp. 12—18.

(desired-for objects, i. e. human interests) and *nîti* (*mores*, or social duties) that we have to turn for the topics of a Montesquieu's *Esprit des Lois* or for what Aristotle would call "politics", i. e. the science of *samgha* or *samûha* (group) life. There is a difference, however, between these two classes of sociological literature. The *smriti* sciences are more social and religious, while the *artha* sciences are more, or rather exclusively, political and economic.

The *dharma-śâstras* which, like the Japanese *Kojiki* and *Nihongi*, incidentally treat of legal, economic and political matters in connection with socio-religious topics are named after about a score of promulgators[1] such as Manu, Atri, Viṣṇu, Hârîta, Yâjnavalkya, Uśanas, Angiras, Yama, Âpastamba, Samvarta, Kâtyâyana, Brihaspati, Parâśara, Vyâsa, Śamkha, Likhita, Dakṣa, Gautama, Śatâtapa, and Vaśiṣtha. The well known *Manu Samhitâ* and the *Institutes* of Yâjnavalkya are thus *smriti* or *dharma* books. All treatises on Hindu law (and custom) naturally fall within this group.

It was to this legal literature of the Hindus, especially to the section bearing on inheritance and partition of property that the interest of European scholars was first directed. The plain reason was the exigencies of the newly imposed British administration about the time of the partition of Poland (1772). It is Manu and Yâjnavalkya, therefore, and subsidiarily the "law-books" of Brihaspati, Nârada, Gautama, Âpastamba, Viṣṇu, and Vaśiṣtha, popularized through the *Sacred Books of the East Series*, that obtained currency in the general culture of the nineteenth century. To students of comparative politics these so-called "sacred" books failed necessarily to furnish much data. Rather, on the contrary, this *Series* served to divert the attention of scholars from Hindu achievements in institutional (*samûha*) life, public law, social service and civic administration. All the same, some use of the oriental data has been made by Gomme for folklore and anthropological investigations; Gibelin and Maine succeeded in gleaning a few ideas for comparative jurisprudence; and Nietzsche[2] threw a new light on sociology by championing the claims of the *Manu Samhitâ* as against the *New Testament* of Christianity.

In this connection it is desirable to mention several treatises in the Pâli language which, although they stand apart from the general Sans-

---

[1] The list varies with different authorities. *cf.* Sris Chandra Vasu's *Yâjnavalkya Smriti*, Book I, Ch. I, Introduction, 4—5. Jolly's *Recht und Sitte* offers the most comprehensive study of the material embodied in the law-books. See chapter I (*Die Quellen*).

[2] *The Twilight of Idols*, p. 46; *The Will to Power*, Vol. I, Book II, p. 126; *The Anti-Christ*, pp. 214—215.

krit category, deserve a high rank as documents of Hindu public law. These are the statute-books of Buddhist monastic life and belong to the group of Śâkya's *sîla* (conduct) teachings known as *Vinaya* (i. e. discipline, organization, government). Up till now Pâli literature has absorbed the attention of scholars solely from the standpoint of theological doctrines and psychological dogmas. But certain sections of it are rich in the material of civic and juristic institutions and ideals. The *Mahâvagga* and the *Chulla-vagga*,[1] no doubt treatises on ecclesiastical polity, may be singled out for studies in politics[2] similar to those which have been bestowed by European scholars on the Canon Law[3] systematized by Gratian of Bologna (1150) in the *Decretum*, or on the writings of the Jesuit Fathers[4] and the literature of the Oxford Movement.[5] Buddhist compilations throw special light on constitutional law, conciliar (*samgha*) administration and republican nationalism, and are thus invaluable sources for an analysis of the democratic philosophy obtaining in pre-Maurya India.

Section 2.

Nîti-Śâstras.

The second class of Hindu sociological literature, viz., the *artha* and *nîti śâstras*, has been arresting the attention of scholars only for the last decade or so. As Kautilya tells us, many were the writers on politics[6] in ancient India, though the works of very few are extant. There is a book that passes for the work of one Ghata-karpara. A second *nîti śâstra* is by tradition fathered on Vidura, a statesman of the *Mahâbhârata*. The sage Vaiśampâyana is credited with a third, viz. the *Nîti-prakâśikâ*.[7] Somodeva's *Nîti-Vâkyâmrita* is another such book. And there is a treatise, entitled the *Yukti-kalpa-taru*,[8] attributed to king Bhoja of Dhârâ in Malwa (in the Middle West of India). This Bhoja may have

[1] English translations in the *S. B. E. Series*.

[2] Figgis' *Fellowship of the Mystery*, V, VI; *Divine Right of Kings*, 219—220

[3] Carlyle, II, 94, etc.; Taylor's *Mediaeval Mind*, Vol. II, 265—275.

[4] Figgis' *From Gerson to Grotius*, Lect. VI.

[5] Laski's *Studies in the Problem of Sovereignty*, Ch. III.

[6] A complete list of these books based on Aufrecht is to be seen in Law's articles in the *Mod Rev.*, 1916—1917. Another list specifically on arts and crafts has been prepared by the same author for his article on "*Vârtâ* or Hindu Economics" in the *Ind. Ant.*, 1918—19. See a brief summary in Bhandarkar's *Anc. His. Ind.*, pp. 87—113.

[7] Edited by Oppert for the Madras Government. Banerjea cites a few passages from the *Nîti-vâkyâmrita* (*Public*, pp. 12, 72, 75, 98, 100, 103, 107, 111, 189, 190, 193, 271, 275).

[8] *Yukti* has been edited by Ishvara Chandra Shastri for the Sanskrit Press Depositary, Calcutta (1917). For *A Brihaspati Sutra* by F. W. Thomas see *Le Museon*, March 1916.

been identical with Mihira Bhoja (*c* 840—90), the Napoleon of the Gurjara-Pratîhâra Empire. Finally, a *sûtra* or aphoristic treatise dealing with *nîti* topics is credited to Brihaspati, the same perhaps of the *Smriti* fame.

But the only historically authentic, and for the present the most important *nîti* work is a volume of the late fourth century B. C., the *Artha-śâstra*[1] of Kautilya, the finance minister of Chandra-gupta Maurya. This treatise combines the theory of Machiavellian *Realpolitik* with the "blood and iron" statecraft of Bismarck. The dissertations of pre-Kautilyan philosophers seem to have been swallowed up in this volume and it proved· be the bible not only of Asoka the Great's imperialism, but also of the chauvinists of the Vikram-âdityan epoch; for Kâmandaka's abridgment[2] of Kautilya's principles, entitled the *Nîti-sâra*, appears to have been in circulation about the fourth century A. C. And as such it acquired a position like that of the *Prince* of the Florentine diplomat which used to be consulted by every English and Continental statesman of the "New Monarchy" period. The influence of the *Artha-śâstra* is accordingly to be noticed as much in the activities of Premier Bhandi the "king-maker" of the Vardhana House (seventh century) as in those of the Bengali premiers Darbha-pâṇi and Kedâra-miśra (eighth and ninth centuries), through whose *nîti*, as the inscriptions assert it, the Pâla Dynasty became for a time the paramount power in Northern India.

Curiously enough, however, in the history of Hindu political speculation it is not the historic Kautilya but a *nom-de-plume*, that of Śukra, a "sage" like Manu, that happened to become the patronymic of *nîti-śâstras*. The volume attributed to this *âchârya*, "learned doctor" or professor, viz., the *Śukra-nîti*[3] (Śukra's *Laws* on *Politics*) is almost synonymous with *Staatswissenschaft* or political philosophy in the scientific tradition of India. In its present form it is evidently a later compilation than the *Kâmandakî-nîti*, but it contains materials that go back to the earliest epochs of Hindu history.[4]

---

[1] Discovered, edited and translated by R. Shamashastry, of Bangalore, Mysore; *Ind. Ant.* 1905, p. 5.

[2] Sanskrit text edited by Rajendralal Mitra for the *Bibliotheca Indica Series;* English translation by Manmathanath Dutt. See the prefaces to both editions. Kâmandaka acknowledges the Kautilyan origin of his book (I. 2—8).

[3] Sanskrit text edited by Gustav Oppert for the Madras Government, English translation by B. K. Sarkar for the Panini Office, Allahabad. The text edited by Jivânanda Vidyâsâgara of Calcutta is different from the Madras text at various points.

[4] For a discussion of the date of the *Śukra-nîti* see the author's *Pos. Back.*, Vol. II, pp. 63—71.

The birth of *nîti-śâstra*, i.e., political science (science of punishment, "sanction" and sovereignty, or *danda-nîti* as it is sometimes called) is, like the origin of all other Hindu *vidyâs*[1] (sciences, known to be thirty two in number) and *kalâs* (arts, known to be sixty four), obscurely believed to be Minervan, or, in other words, divine. The conjectural account of its dim beginnings brings it down to Dr. Śukra as the last of the *riṣis* (sages) who cared to set his seal on civic, economic and political studies. Formerly, says the *Mahâbhârata*,[2] for the protection of creatures the science of polity was delivered by the Lord Himself. As it happened to be a huge volume Siva (a god) epitomized it in ten thousand sections. His work is known as the *Vaiśâlâkṣa* from his name *Viśâlâkṣa* (the "large-eyed"). An abridgment in five thousand sections was afterwards made by Indra (another god) and in three thousand by Brihaspati, a super-man or *riṣi*. This last was further boiled down to one thousand by Śukra. All this reduction in size was necessary because art is long and "life is short". The story of this abridgment following abridgment is told by the compiler of the *Śukra-nîti*[3] also. "For the good of men", as we read, "Brahmâ" (the highest God) had spoken that treatise which contained ten million verses. By a process of selection the essence (*sâra*) of that *nîti-śâstra* has been abridged by Vaśiṣtha and others like myself for the increase of prosperity of the rulers of the earth and of others whose life is of short span".

It is clear, therefore, that in stead of comparing Aristotle, the father of European political science, with Ganeśa, the God of Success in Hindu mythology, who is invoked by priests at the commencement of all religious ceremonies Pollock should have commenced his *Introduction to Politics* with the name of Śukra, who in the estimation of India has monopolized the credit of systematizing and propagating *nîti-śâstras* among mankind. For the present, however, the real historic pioneer is Kautilya, the "guide, philosopher and friend" of the first Hindu Alexander, whose place may be compared to that of the chief justice of Bagdad, Mawerdi (972—1058), author of the Arabic *Artha-śâstra, El Akham es Soulthaniyah* (*Les Statuts Gouvernementaux*).

---

[1] Śukra, Ch. IV, sec. iii, lines 45—200. For the significance of the term *danda-nîti vide Pos. Back*, II, pp. 29—31.

[2] *Śânti* LIX, 76—86.

[3] Ch. I, lines 4—7; *Vide Pos. Back*, Vol. II, pp. 12—18, 21—29.

Section 3.

Scope and Province of *Nīti-śâstra.*

Chronologically the latest book is, as we have seen, the *Yukti-kalpa-taru.* It treats of taxation, expeditions, espionage, siege, diplomacy, peace, embassies and city administration, besides other topics.[1] The *Śukra-nîti* deals with the duties of princes, functions of the crown-prince and state officials, characteristics of friends and allies, sinews of war, fortresses, army, general rules of statecraft, and social customs and institutions. In the *Kâmandakî-nîti* we have a summary of the entire Kautilyan system, except that it omits a discussion of the departments of state, civil and criminal laws and a few other items.

In addition to these themes, Kautilya's *Artha-śâstra* in its 150 sections grouped in 15 chapters deals with the training and personal safety of kings and ministers, relations between government servants and the monarch, the rise and growth of states, the "sixfold policy", the vices and calamities of kings, military affairs, and measures for the promotion of peace and opulence. The doctrine of *mandala* i. e. "sphere" of influence or of international activity is elaborately discussed in twenty sections (chapters VI and VII). Republics (*gaṇas*) form the subject matter of a separate chapter (XI); and to *aikaiśvarya* (one-man-rule) is devoted the section on consolidation and absolute sovereignty (Ch. V, sec vi).

To a certain extent Kautilya's book may be used as an Imperial Gazetteer[2] of Maurya India, as it furnishes descriptive information on subjects like the following: Working of mines, operating of irrigation works; establishment of factories; maintenance of preserves and grazing grounds; the laying out of highways of commerce, waterways, land-routes, and other facilities for communication; establishment of markets and stores; construction of embankments, dams and bridges; planting of fruit and flower trees, of medicinal plants and herbs; protection of the disabled, the helpless and the infirm, and also of beasts; famines; census; central and municipal government; livestock. These treatises will thus bear apt comparison with the political chapters of the Arabic

[1] *Vide* the summary of its contents from a manuscript in Bengali character in the *Pos. Back. Hind. Soc.*, Vol. I, pp. 12—14. The dates of *Śukra* as of *Yukti* are open questions.

[2] Law's *Studies in Ancient Hindu Polity*, Vol. I, is based on the *Artha-śâstra*. Jacobi's German article (1912) on the authenticity of Kautilya has been translated for the *Ind. Ant.* (June, July, 1919). Jolly's date for Kautilya in the *Zeit. Deut. Morg. Ges.* (1914, p. 355) is disputed by Jacobi in the same journal (*vide "Ist das Daśakumâracharita gleichzeitig mit dem Kautilya Arthashâstra?"*). See also Mookerji's introduction to Law's book, and Keith's article in the J. R. A. S. (1916).

Prolégomènes Historiques, viz. Ibn Khaldoun's (1372—1406) *Mokaddemah* (section III), or with the Persian *Traité du Gouvernement, the Siasset Nameh* by Nizam-oul-Moulk (*c* 1063).

But we need not depend on the topical analysis of the contents of these volumes for an estimate of the Hindu conception of political philosophy. For, the proper sphere or function of *nîti-śâstra* was discussed by some of the writers themselves. According to Śukra[1], *nîti-śâstra* is to dictate policies about allies, enemies and neutrals. It is expected to suggest the art of winning over the hearts of men. It is, besides, to be efficacious in diplomacy and international measures. While, on the one hand, its practical character as a manual of guidance for rulers is thus emphasized, Sukra, on the other hand, takes special care to bring out its universal importance as a *sarvopajîvaka* (useful to all) body of knowledge.[2] "*Nîti-śâstra*", says he, "ministers to the interests of all and hence is followed and respected by all. It is also indispensable to the prince since he is the lord of all men and things".[3]

How is it possible that a *śâstra* should be serviceable to all the orders in a community unless it is a science of all sciences, i. e. encyclopedic in its scope? The claims of *nîti-śâstra* are therefore presented by the utilitarian theorist on the strength of such a "synthetic" approach to human interests. "Other sciences" are *ekaika-deśa-bodhi*, i. e. they treat only of singled-out or specialized aspects of man's life, and are limited as a matter of course.[4] As Śukra observes, one can do without a knowledge of grammar,[5] for the study of grammar is not a *sine qua non* for the mastery of words and their meanings. Similarly the study of logic[5] may be dispensed with by one who wants to acquire a knowledge of material substances. By like arguments can the comparative "uselessness" of Jaimini's *Mimâmsâ*[5] dealing with the rituals and ceremonies of religion, and of Vyâsa's *Vedânta* philosophy[5] which treats of the "eternal verities" of the universe, be easily demonstrated, as is done in the *Śukra-nîti*. But the one science which nobody can afford to ignore is the *nîti-śâstra*. "Without *nîti* the stability of no man's affairs can be maintained just as without food no man's physical body can be preserved."[6] Political philosophy is thus the very basis of social *sthiti* or *equilibrium* furnishing, as it does, the spiritual foundations of human existence.

[1] Ch. I, lines 11—13, 25—26.
[2] *Ibid*, 9.
[3] *Ibid*, 23—24.
[4] *Ibid*, 8, 18—19.
[5] *Ibid*, 14—17.
[6] *Ibid*, 21—22.

A *vidyâ* or science that seeks to impart knowledge calculated to foster the "preservation of human society" and provide the man-in-the-street with skill and intelligence becomes necessarily comprehensive and all-embracing in its topics. *Nîti-śâstra* in the hands of Śukra assumes thereby the proportions not of ethics or politics in the circumscribed sense, but of sociology in the wide sense of Aristotle's "architectonic" or dominant science. The extensive range of the subject matter of the *śâstras* on *danda-nîti* is adumbrated in the *Mahâbhârata*[1] and the *Daśa-kumâra-charita*[2] also, and may on the whole be easily comprehended by students familiar with the multiplicity of topics in Montesquieu.

Section 4.

Relativity of Political *Śâstras* to Politics.

Neither merely pedagogic-ethical nor purely descriptive-anthropological are these political *vidyâs* of Sanskrit literature. As manuals of *râja-dharma* or duties for princes the *nîti-śâstras* have their natural analogues in Elyot's *Boke named the Governour* (1531), and in the works of John of Salisbury (twelfth century), Aquinas (thirteenth century), Occleve (fourteenth century), Patrizi (fifteenth century), and the like.[3] For certain purposes, again, they may be slightly compared to treatises of the type of Fortescue's *Governance of England* (1476). Moreover, like the Arab encyclopaedist Al Farabi's (*c* 950) *Model City*, based as it was on Plato, and like the *Prince* and the *Utopia* the writings of Kautilya, Kâmandaka, Śukra and Bhoja are contributions to political "ideals" as well.

But, and here lies the chief difficulty in regard to every branch of Hindu thought including even psychology, logic and metaphysics, the machinery of "sociological criticism" is hardly applicable because of the paucity of "external evidences" with which to bear out, interpret or militate against, the "internal". In regard to the ancient and mediaeval works of political theory in the West modern scholarship has almost successfully decided as to which portions of which texts are descriptive-historical and which are normative, utopian or idealistic. This has been possible owing to the wealth of archeology. The evidences of literature

[1] *Sânti*, Ch. LIX, 139—143.

[2] Pt. II, Ch. viii. The importance of this book in the antiquarian study of the *Artha-śâstra* will be evident from a single word *idânim* which has given rise to the Jolly-Jacobi controversy in the Z. D. M. G. (1914).

[3] Croft's *Elyot's Governour*, Vol. I, pp. lxiii—lxvi; Plummer's *Governance of England* (text introduction, notes).

have been systematically checked and appraised by reference to actual facts. "Pious wishes" of theorists have thus been disentangled from photographic accounts of institutions.

The discrepancy between theory and practice, paradoxical though at first sight, is today almost a postulate in the history of European political speculation. Marsiglio of Padua in his *Defensor Pacis* (1324) is known to have anticipated Martin Luther and Machiavelli in the thorough-going secularization of politics. According to this writer, as Bluntschli explains it in the *Geschichte der neueren Staatswissenschaft*, the supreme institution is the state, the Pope has no right to the election of prince or emperor, and the *plenitudo potestatis* or omnipotence of the Pope is a myth. But this anti-theocratic theorizing was, as Sullivan remarks in his essay on *Marsiglio and Ockam*, the exact antipodes of the facts of the political world.

Again, the Carlyles[1] have traced the *ideas* of natural equality, freedom, and justice, back to Cicero (first century B. C.) through Canonists and Church Fathers of the Middle Ages, and Roman jurists like Ulpian and Gaius. But during all this period slavery was recognized as a lawful and legitimate institution, privileges and inequalities in property were the rule, and the divine right of the king was an established fact. It was not until the French Revolution that legal effect was given to the doctrine of natural equality which had been promulgated ages ago by Stoics in opposition to the theory of the Aristotelians.

Further, according to the *theory* of the lawyers, e. g. Ulpian (second century A. C.), the source of political authority was the people. But from Hadrian to Justinian (sixth century) the emperor's will was law. And in the fourteenth century Bartolus, the "prince of jurists", was but maintaining the jurisprudence of traditional *Realpolitik* when he affirmed that the Roman Emperor was *Deus in terris* and *sempiternus* and that to dispute him was sacrilege.[2]

Thus has the "historical school" of criticism established in Eur-America a distinction between the face-value of the political shibboleths and their real worth. But as yet, in spite of a legitimate presumption, there is not much rational ground for scientific scepticism in regard to the tenets of the political *śâstras* of India. Because, facts about the institutional environment of the Hindus can be gleaned only inadequately

---

[1] *Med. Pol. Theory*, Vol. I, pp. 9, 48, 114, 199; Vol. II, p. 118; Vol. III, p. 89; Vol. I, pp. 75, 76, 86, 116, 264; Vol. II, pp. 119, 120, 129; Vol. I, p. 70.

[2] Woolf's *Bartolus*, p. 24. See Figgis' *Divine Right*, pp. 343—372, for an estimate of Bartolus in the history of European political philosophy.

from indigenous sources. Nor do the contemporary accounts of Greek, Roman and Chinese writers on India afford much help in this direction.

Not a single event has yet been discovered for the whole century from 230 to 330 A. C. The history of the Deccan for three hundred years between the Ândhra and the Châlukya periods is a blank, as also that of Northern India during the latter half of the sixth century. The name of Samudra-gupta (A. C. 330—375), the "Indian Napoleon", was unknown to historians before 1904. Other *digvijayî* or "world-conquering" empire-builders like Govinda III, the Râṣtrakûta (795—815), and Bhoja (*c* 840—890) of the Gurjara-Pratîhâra House have come into prominence since then, — but practically as mere names however. Not even by name are more than half a dozen of the distinguished premiers, generals, finance-ministers and viceroys known today.

Nobody could yet attempt a systematic history of Pâtali-putra, the Rome of the Hindus off and on for over a thousand years. Authentic information about gilds and other public associations of economic or constitutional importance is all but negligible. Fiscal and military institutions can rarely be described for any period excepting that of the Mauryas, thanks to the epoch-making discovery of the *Arthaśâstra*. A study of the Vikramâdityan empire in comparison, say, with the system of Roman imperialism from Constantine to Justinian, the contemporaries of the Guptas, the historic prototypes of Kâlidâsa's legendary Raghu, or with the Bourbon monarchy from Louis XI to Louis XIV is out of the question for a long time to come.

It is superfluous to add that the conditions are not ripe yet for "intensive" works like Vinogradoff's *English Society in the Eleventh Century*, Brissaud's *History of French Public Law*, Abbott's *Roman Political Institutions* or Dopsch's "Economic and Social Foundations of European Culture"[1] being undertaken on the history of Hindu polity. Nay, what may be called the "extensive" researches of Guizot in the origins and growth of representative government among the Teutonic peoples await the patient toil of a long roll of spade-workers in Indian coins, inscriptions and excavations.

Details of social and economic environment and of the actual secular life in ancient and mediaeval India have however been coming out recently. But, as would have appeared from the preceding chapters, they are so very scrappy that the Spencerian doctrine of the "relativity" of philosophy to institutions can hardly be made use of for the satisfactory

---

[1] *Vide* Ulrich Wilcken's "*Alexander der Grosse und die Hellenistische Wirtschaft*" in *Schmoller's Jahrbuch* for 1921.

explanation of the epochs of Hindu culture. And, of course, a history of Hindu political theories, like that of European by Bluntschli, Janet, Dunning or the Carlyles, is not a problem of the near future.

The difficulties of appreciating the *nîti-śâstras* at the present moment can be understood if one were almost to imagine what would have been the value of Plato's *Republic* if only one of his *Dialogues* were accessible to modern scholars as the sole document of a period of, say, two hundred years, for which no other evidence of a political, economic, literary or numismatic character were available, or how much of the Renaissance in Europe would be intelligible today, if the sole evidence for it were More's *Utopia.* In the absence of trustworthy historical data, indologists, both Hindu and foreign, supposing that they were unbiased, have been led to understand or rather misunderstand a complex and varied culture-history of several thousand years from the popular verses of a few poets, or the traditional sayings of one or two religious teachers. But at least during the last ten or fifteen years archeology has been able to cry halt to this sort of uncritical over-valuation or under-valuation of India's achievements; for, the "positive background" of Hindu sociology is becoming clearer every day.[1]

[1] And yet two otherwise excellent publications of recent date, Banerjea's *Public Administration in Ancient India* (1916) and Havell's *History of Aryan Rule in India* (1918), are vitiated by a fundamental fallacy because they have made no distinction between political theory and political institutions. They have, besides, accepted the statements in the *śâstras* at their face-value without discriminating between "pious wish" and *Realpolitik.* On the other hand, the fallacy of an opposite character is equally manifest in Smith's *Oxford History of India* (1919) because the author has made it a point to disparage the *śâstras* in a sweeping manner without trying to evaluate them in the perspective of European writings of the same class. In an article on "Oriental Monarchies" in the *Mod. Rev.* (March 1917) J. N. Sarkar points out the merits of K. V. R. Aiyangar's *Considerations on Some Aspects of Ancient Indian Polity* (Madras, 1916); but the book has not reached the present author yet.

CHAPTER VIII.

The Theory of the Constitution in Hindu Political Philosophy.

Section 1.

The Doctrine of *Saptâmga* (Seven Limbs).

The seven categories, *svâmin* (sovereign), *amâtya* (minister), *surhit* (ally), *koşa* (finance), *râştra* (territory), *durga* (fortress), and *vala* (army) constitute the basis of all political speculation among Hindu philosophers. They form the *saptâmga*,[1] or the "seven limbs" of the body politic. The theory of the constitution is epitomized in the doctrine of *saptâmga*. An analysis of each of these seven constituents of a state, as well as their mutual relations, is the specific theme of all *nîti-śâstras*, from the *Artha-śâstra* of Kautilya to the *Yukti-kalpa-taru* of Bhoja. Necessarily subsumed under this fundamental investigation is the discussion of *samaya* (compact) as the origin of the state, *dharma* (*droit*, *Recht*, justice, law, duty, etc.) as the end of government, *bali* (offerings) as the *rationale* of taxation by the state for its services to the community, *aparodha* (expulsion of tyrant), *mandala*, and other concepts of *Staatswissenschaft* in Sanskrit literature.

Now, to modern historians of political science, single phrases, even single words of Plato and Aristotle loom unduly large. This extravagance of interpretation is not without its justification. Every age interprets its past in the light of its own experience and conscience. Classical Hellas has thus been reborn in the modern West, since Aquinas (1225—1274)[2] raised his theological superstructure on Aristotelian foundations, almost as many times as there have been Machiavellis, Bodins, Montesquieus, Francks, Janets and Barkers[3] to consult the ancient encyclopedias of

---

[1] Vişņu, III, 33; Śukra, I, lines 121—122, V, 1—2; Kâmandaka, I, 16, IV, 1; *Pos. Back*, Vol. II, pp. 34—39; cf. Coker's *Organismic Theories of the State*.

[2] Article on "Aquinas" in the *Enc. Brit.*; Dunning's *Political Theories*, Vol. I, 189—213; Franck's *Reformateurs et publicistes de l'Europe*, Vol. I, pp. 63—70.

[3] Bluntschli's *Geschichte des Allgemeinen Staatsrechts und der Politik*, pp. 6—46, 258—276; Barker's *Plato*, pp. 146, 176, 389, 390; Dunning, Vol. I, p. 54; Willoughby's *Political Theories of the Ancient World*, pp. 128—130.

culture. The values of every political thinker and theory in Europe have in this cumulative way been fixed definitely and in relation to one another. And the momentum is being accelerated with the sundry new experiences of recent times from Hegel and Austin to Liebknecht and Duguit,[1] the two poles of the theory of sovereignty. The political futurists of today are indeed awaiting the issue of Bolshevik versions not only of the *Plato-Samhitâ* but even of the *Aristotle-nîti* to meet the demands of the new *Novum Organum* of the current régime of the "discredited state."

It is not intended here to apply this "right of interpretation" to the doctrine of *saptâmga* or to the other auxiliary doctrines of the *nîti-śâstras*, whether from the conservative, liberal, or radical view-point. Only a few dicta are being gleaned at random from the texts bearing on the *theory* of the constitution, without any comment as to its impact, if any, on *Realpolitik*. These would be enough, however, to bring out, first, that if man is a "political animal", he is equally so in the East and in the West, both in ancient and modern times, in spite of the differences created by steam, electricity, and air-navigation, and secondly, that notwithstanding the diversity of technical terminology, it is well-nigh impossible to distinguish the methods and results of Hindu Aristotles, Senecas, Alcuins, and Hobbeses from those of their western colleagues.

But it is necessary to remember at the outset that in the whole range of Hindu political thought there is to be found no trace of theocracy[2] as embodied in the social philosophy of Augustine's *De Civitate Dei* (The City of God) or of Aquinas' *De Regimine Principum* (Government of a Prince). For no period could the political ideas of the Hindus be treated as a branch of ecclesiastical history as Figgis considers it right in regard to European political speculation during the fifteenth and sixteenth centuries.[3] No *śâstra*-writer ever preached that some "high priest" or even the king is God's viceroy on earth, or that the religious association, e. g., a *samgha* or temple-government, is a "self-sufficient" *svarâj*, independent of or coordinate with, nay, superior to, the secular organization of the *râṣtra*. There is no touch of the conflicts between canon

[1] Laski's *Studies in the Problem of Sovereignty*, pp. 20—24, 65—68; *Authority in the Modern State*, pp. 113—114; 363.

[2] Bluntschli's *Geschichte der neueren Staatswissenschaft*, pp. 3—7; Poole's *Illustrations of the History of Mediaeval Thought*, pp. 226—255; Mc Cabe's *Augustine and His Age*, pp. 375—410; Taylor's *Mediaeval Mind*, Vol. I, 61—87; Gierke's *Political Theories of the Middle Age*, pp. 104—115 (notes).

[3] *From Gerson*, p. 31.

law and civil law[1] in the treatises on *nîti* and *dharma or smriti*, and the doctrine of *saptâmga* is absolutely undisturbed by the rivalry of the Byzantine conception (Justinian's) of the church as subservient to the state with the antithetic Gregorian doctrine of the supremacy of *sacerdotum* over *imperium*.[2] But all the same, for purposes of historical perspective, it will be advisable in the present discussion to have an adequate orientation to the subject matter of Poole's *Illustrations of the History of Mediaeval thought* and Littlejohn's *Political Theory of the Schoolmen and Grotius*.

Section 2.

A Moslem Review.

In the sixteenth century Abul Fazl, a Mohammedan minister of Akbar the Great, compiled an Imperial Gazetteer of India in Persian under the title of *Ayeen-i Akbari*[3] (the "Instutites of Akbar"). He devoted certain sections of his book to Hindu laws (*Beyhar*, i. e. *vyavahâra*), and gave a summary of current political notions.

The monarch should be "ambitious",[4] according to the traditional *râja-nît* (state-craft), "to extend his dominions. No enemy is so insignificant as to be beneath his notice". A wise prince, as we read in the Persian resumé, should banish from his court all corrupt and designing men. The king's functions are described as being "similar to those of a gardener", who plucks up the thorns and briers and throws them on one side, whereby he beautifies his garden, and at the same time raises a fence which preserves his ground from the intrusion of strangers. Accordingly the king should "detach from the nobles their too numerous friends and dangerous dependents". An important maxim teaches, besides, that "in affairs of moment it is not advisable to consult with many".

In these political recipes we have the German idea of "self-defence", the American conception of "preparedness", the Greek theory of ostracism and the universal custom of deporting undesirables. And those who are familiar with the "secret clauses" of all treaties, and who watched the course of events leading to the great war of 1914 as well as to its close would surely ditto the Hindu dictum: "In affairs of moment it is not advisable to consult with many". For even today, in spite of universal literacy, power of the press, manhood suffrage,

---

[1] Woolf's *Bartolus*, p. 14, Carlyle II, p. 94.

[2] Woolf, pp. 55, 60; Figgis' *From Gerson*, Carlyle, II, 148, 198.

[3] Smith's *Akbar*, pp. 4, 459.

[4] Gladwin's translation, Vol. III, pp. 194—213.

referendum, and ministerial responsibility to the people, all nations do really

> "Leave all God gave them in the hands of one, —
> Leave the decision over peace and war
> To king or kaiser, president or czar."

And in international affairs the "Big Three" or even the "Big Two" decide the destiny of millions, e. g. of the Germans in Silesia (1921).

The Persian synopsis of the Sanskrit texts has something to say on international relations. According to Hindu statecraft, if any monarch is more powerful than oneself, one should continually strive to sow dissension among the rival's troops, and in case of failure should prudently purchase his friendship. "The prince whose territory adjoins to his", Abul Fazl tells us further, obviously reproducing the Kautilyan doctrine of *mandala*,[1] "although he may be friendly in appearance, yet ought not to be trusted; one should be always prepared to oppose any sudden attack from that quarter. With him whose country lies next beyond the last-mentioned he should enter into alliance". In these remarks there is nothing essentially Hindu, oriental or mediaeval, nor anything distinctively Machiavellian or Bernhardian. It is substantially on this elementary psychology of international relations that the *ententes*, conventions, and interchange of diplomatic visits in the modern world are based. "Human, all too human" are these precepts of the *Artha-śâstra* popularized for the "sons of Adam" through the *Manu-Samhitâ*,[2] and they did not need the special pleading of a Nietzsche's *Will to Power*[3] to make them current coin for the present generation of statesmen.

Among other Hindu ideas the following is quoted by Abul Fazl: "If he finds it necessary to attack his enemy he should invade the country during the time of harvest". This was Napoleon's military method too. He wanted the war to pay its own way as far as possible. And of course strategic necessity and cosiderations of "high politics" may justify any measure from the desecrating of the tomb of Al Mahdi in Egypt to the declaration of war by Germany against neutralized Belgium.

We shall now proceed to single out a few of the more important tenets in the *nîti-śâstras*, without attempting, however, to be either comprehensive in treatment or exhaustive in reference. The object

---

[1] *Infra*, pp. 214—221.

[2] VII, 158.

[3] Vol. II, Book IV, p. 183.

is only to throw light on the trend of political thinking among Hindus in the perspective of Eur-American speculation. The "personal equation" of the theorists as well as the differences in the *milieu* will be ignored in the present discussion. It is evident that no "historian" of political theory should be excused who passes without comment from the *Sabhâ-parva* to the *Śânti-parva* of the *Mahâbhârata* and from either to the *Śukra-nîti* or from *Kautilya* to *Manu* as if he were moving in the same world and speaking of the same age. But for some time yet indology will have to content itself more with the psychological analysis of the categories and concepts of political science than with the historical presentation of the growth of doctrines such as one finds in Atger's *Histoire des doctrines du contrat social.* The following sections are being offered, therefore, subject to the fundamental fallacy implied in this "limiting condition" of archeological data.

Section 3.

The *Prakriti* (People) and the State.

John Stuart Mill in his *Representative Government* has discussed the characteristics which make a race fit for the popular institutions of self-government. One of his criteria is that the people must be able not only to appreciate and profit by such institutions but must have to be actively interested in all that relates to public life. Śukra also is strongly of opinion that it is the duty of the *prakriti*, the people, not only not to commit certain wrongs, but also to hand over to the police, or otherwise disclose to the state the existence of, the men who are in any way undesirable to the society. The whole community is thus enjoined to be an information-and-vigilance committee and an association for public safety. The demands of the state on the *prakriti* are necessarily manifold in Hindu thought.

In Kautilya's[1] analysis of the duties of the people we are familiar with the notion that the citizens should be on the lookout in the streets as to whether a trader has paid the toll on his commodities at the custom office. This principle of active cooperation with the state as contrasted with the passive obedience to and observance of the laws promulgated by it is laid down in the *Śukra-nîti*[2] in such general terms as the following: "You should never keep screened, or give protection to, men of wicked activities, thieves, bad characters, malicious and

[1] *Supra*, p. 66.

[2] Ch. I, lines 595—596.

offensive persons as well as other wrong-doers". More comprehensive touch of the people (i. e. the "society") with the state is indeed contemplated by the theorist. For, the Śukra polity is essentially an omnipresent all-inclusive agency for the advancement of human welfare, — a *Kultur-staat*, in short. The *kâla*,[1] i. e. age or epoch (*Zeitgeist*) is as much the making of the state as its fundamental function is the promotion of *dharma*[2] (law, justice, duty, culture, and what not) i. e. the "virtue" of the Greek theorists, which is as encyclopedic or extensive as life itself.

Such doctrines of the *nîti-śâstras* have important bearing on the problems of political philosophy in regard to the limits of state control or the sphere of governmental activity. The new type of 100 per cent socialist state in Bolshevik Russia is undoubtedly bound to have a deep influence on the theory of the proper functions of the state. But it is questionable if Sidgwick's "individualistic minimum" of state interference may not still be regarded as the last word, academically speaking, on rival claims between the two extremes that may be urged for the state and the individual. So far as pure theory is concerned, the issues between *laissez faire* and intervention may indeed be taken to have been finally settled in Mill's *Liberty*. Now, the Hindu thought on the subject is quite elastic. It is not a minimum-functioned state that Kautilya and Śukra have before their imagination. Hindu theorists are no *doctrinaire* individualists. As champions of *dharma* they have extended the functions of the state so wide as to include whatever should be deemed expedient according to social needs, as readers of the *Sabhâ-parva* (Canto on "Council") of the *Mahâbhârata* are aware.

The theory of old age pensions is not indeed stated by any of the Hindu theorists. But the widows of soldiers killed in battles are to receive pension according to Vaśiṣtha.[3] The *Mahâbhârata*[4] suggests that the state should support the wives and children of men who have sacrificed their lives for it or otherwise been in distress while serving it. Protection of the weak and afflicted persons is insured in the *Artha-śâṣtra*.[5] Kautilya would legislate also to forbid trade in dangerous goods,[6] as he would likewise forbid "profiteering", high rates of interest and so forth. The social and economic legislation[7] recommen-

---

[1] Ch. I, lines 43—44, IV, i, 116—117.

[2] Ch. I, 45—51; IV, iii, 849. cf. Chinese and Japanese conception of "virtue" in Asakawa, [p. 325.

[3] XIX, 20.

[4] *Sabhâ*, Ch. V, 54, *Śânti*, Ch. LXXXVI, 24.

[5] Book I, pp. 38—39.

[6] *Ind. Ant.* 1905, p. 49;

[7] Ch. I, lines 587—626.

ded in the *Śukra-nîti* is sweepingly vast and wide. It leaves very little to the caprices of the individual's civic sense and patriotism. Tanks, wells, parks and boundaries must not be obstructed by the citizens. Nor must the use of religious houses, temples and roads be hindered in any way. The movements of the poor, the blind and the deformed similarly call forth the solicitude of Śukra legislators.[1]

Besides, among the *śâsanas* or positive laws conceived by Śukra we read that without the sanction of the state the following things are not to be done: gambling, drinking, hunting, use of arms, sales and purchases of cows, elephants, horses, camels, buffaloes, men, immovable property, silver, gold, jewels, intoxicants and poisons, distillation of wines, the drawing up of deeds indicating a sale, gift or loan, and medical practice.[2] The important professions and economic activities which involve public safety and the future interests of the individuals concerned are thus not left to the discretion and common sense of the *prakriti* (the society). In Śukra's conception the *râjya* (the state) has to function as the Platonic „guardian" even of the citizens' self-interest.

Municipal by-laws and regulations relating to patents, licenses and charters are in this manner provided for in the theory of the *nîti-śâstras*. The logic of such control exercised by the *dharma-staaten* over the economic and social life of the people is essentially the same as that at the back of German state-socialism and modern "nationalization" schemes which have culminated in the "public ownership" movement. And this is all the more evident in the enumeration of the crafts and industries that the Śukra state seeks encourage.[3] The list of productive and aesthetic arts that demand the "developmental" attention of the government according to the *Śukra-nîti* together with the schedule of duties[4] that Kautilya, Manu and the *Mahâbhârata* recommend for the king furnishes the Hindu theory of "enlightened despotism" with its hydra-headed bureaucracy. Whether the *prakriti* exercise the initiative and sense of responsibility for their material and moral development or not, the state of the *nîti-śâstras* must address itself to the problem of national culture. As the promoter of *dharma*, and the creator of *kâla* (time or epoch) the state is necessarily the or-

---

[1] *Ibid*, lines 601—602.

[2] *Ibid*, lines 603—608.

[3] Ch. I, lines 734—741; Ch. II, lines 390—411.

[4] *Mahâ*, *Sabhâ*, Ch. V (whole), 53, 76—79. *Vide* the references in Law's article in the *Mod. Rev.* for Feb., 1917.

ganizer of patriotism and the pioneer of civilization, — indeed, the chief dynamo of social engineering. French *étatisme* is identical in spirit.

Section 4.

Kingship a Public Office.

While "*l'état c'est moi*" embodied the prevailing bible of European despots from Alexander and Augustus Caesar to Louis XVI the political philosophers were adumbrating the gospel of justice, natural equality, and sovereignty of the people. Mediaeval political theory in the West, as one can gather from Gierke's and Poole's investigations and the more "intensive" researches of the Carlyles, Figgis and Woolf, was essentially a philosophy of "pious wishes", no matter whether conceived by the Stoics, the Roman lawyers or "civilians", or church fathers and canonists. It is interesting to observe that such "ideals" found expression also, though under different categories, in the *śástras* on *níti* and *dharma* from Kautilya to Bhoja.

The poet's definition of the king as one who ministers to the well-being of the *prakriti* was lifted up by Śukra into a plank of radical philosophy. In one passage of his *Politics* about the position of the king we seem to read the Bolshevistic lines of Robert Burns:

> "The rank is but the guinea's stamp,
> . . . .
> Though hundreds worship at his word,
> He's but a coof for a'that."

For, "does not even the dog look like a King", asks Śukra,[1] "when it has ascended a royal conveyance? Is not the king justly regarded as a dog by the poets?" The sentiment is certainly much more extremistic than that in the cry of the first English socialists, the Lollards, viz., "When Adam delved and Eve span, who was then a gentleman?" Śukra wants us to understand that the King is great only from his station, but that as an individual he is just a mortal among mortals. The office of kingship, if at all, may be conceded to be sacred, but not the person who happens to hold it. As a human being he is not distinct from other men. In order that the king can command awe and reverence of the people, he is therefore advised by the philosopher to be attended by his retinue of officers. Verily, the regal insignia and paraphernalia, the royal seal,[2] and not the King himelf is the real sovereign. American individualism does not go any further.

---

[1] Ch. I, lines 745, 746.

[2] Ch. II, line 587.

This conception of the dignity of man is evident, again, in the principles of recall and *plebiscite* that the *Śukra-nîti* advocates. In cases of conflict between the king's officers and the subjects the king is advised to take the side of the people. He is to "dismiss the officers who are accused by one hundred men."[1] The truth *vox populi vox dei* was thus known to Hindus also. They have here given expression to the Confucian *mores* preserved in the *Shu-king*.[2] "The great God", said the super-man of China, "has conferred *even on the inferior people* a moral sense, compliance with which would show their nature invariably right."

The supreme importance of the *prakriti* is never lost sight of in the speculations of Śukra. The king is a master only in the sense that he is to protect the people's interests and punish the offenders.[3] Like Seneca the Stoic philosopher of the first century A.C. the Hindu theorist would accordingly exhort the ruler to remember his responsibility as "one out of all mankind who has been chosen to act in the place of the gods."[4] The king is therefore not to enjoy any prerogatives or treat the people in any way he likes.

In all *nîti-sâstras*, as in the writings of Alcuin and Jonas, the *rationale* of kingship is the promotion of *dharma* or justice. This dispensing of justice is to be administered by the king not only between subjects and subjects but also between himself and the subjects. He is to appoint spies as much to get secret information about the people's activities as also against his own conduct. He is to find out in what light his policies are being taken by the *prakriti*. And if the unpleasant truth comes out, viz., if his intelligence department tells him "People dispraise you, O King", it would be "un-kingly" or "un-philosohic" as Plato would have remarked, to get angry and punish the persons who condemn him.[5] Rather, he should follow the ideal of the *Râmâyaṇa* and the spirit of Kâlidâsa's *Raghu-vamśa*, or that of the French epic of the twelfth century, *Le Couronnement de Louis*,[6] which taught in quite the *nîti* style of the Hindus that the purpose of God in making the king is not to enable him to satisfy his appetite but that he should tread down all wrongs under his feet.

Śukra certainly goes far beyond the poets, when he declares categorically that the king's position is really one of *dâsyatva*, i. e. servitude

---

[1] Ch. I, lines 754, 755.

[2] Part IV, Book III, Ch. II (Legge's translation).

[3] Ch. I, lines 27—28, 239, 245—248.

[4] Carlyle I, pp. 31, 224; III, 109.

[5] Ch. I, lines 255—269.

[6] Carlyle III, p. 32; cf. Asakawa's *Early Inst. Jap.*, pp. 40—42.

"The ruler has been made by Brahmâ (the highest God) a servant of the people. His revenue is the remuneration for his services. He is sovereign or master solely in order that he may protect."[1] The king of the *nîti-śâstras* is thus a trustee for the *prakriti*. He is a mere wage-earner in Baudhâyana's *Institutes*[2] also, and is logically liable to fines according to Manu,[3] for his duty is, as Hincmar (805—882)[4] would say in Carolingian Europe, to "govern according to laws". This conception is the farthest removed from the message of Bodin and Bossuet with their doctrine of absolute monarchy as a *gouvernement de droit divin*.

Quite consistently with the position of the king as a *dâsa* or servant is the right of petition by the subjects postulated in Hindu thought. The king, says Sukra, must personally inspect every year the villages, cities and districts. "He must investigate which subjects have been pleased and which oppressed by the staff of officers and deliberate upon matters brought forward by the people."[5] Altogether, then, the state of the Śukra school of politics is a people's *râjya* under royal supervision. The majesty of the people is their political slogan. Such ideas about the dignity of the *prakriti* or *droits de l'homme* bear apt comparison with those of Azo (1150—1230), the Italian jurist, who in spite of the autocratic *milieu* of the Middle Ages wrote on the sovereignty of the *populus* or *universitas*.[6]

Section 5.

Ministry the Pivot of National Life.

The doctrine of the sovereignty of the *prakriti* is in the thought of the *nîti-śâstras* invariably connected with that of the *amâtya* (ministry) as a check on the possible autocracy of the *svâmin*. One of the earliest landmarks in the history of this doctrine is to be noticed in Vedic writings, the *Aitareya Brâhmaṇa*[7] and the *Śatapatha Brâhmaṇa*.[8] In that body of literature the people are "worshipped" by the king at "election"

---

[1] Ch. I, lines 375—376, IV, ii, 259.

[2] I, 10, 18, 1.

[3] VIII, 336.

[4] Article in the *Enc. Brit.*; Carlyle I, 234.

[5] Ch. I, lines 751—752; *cf.* Kâmandaka's Confucian dictum in regard to the importance of the people (XIV, 15). The *Great Learning* says: "By gaining the people the kingdom is gained, and by losing the people the kingdom is lost" (Chang's Commentary, Ch. X).

[6] Carlyle, Vol. II, 63—66; Gierke, 30—37, 45—48.

[7] VIII, 175.

[8] III, 4, 1, 7; III, 22, 18; V, 3, 1, 6; V, 3, 5, 31—37.

in and through their representatives, the *Ratnins*,[1] among whom the head of the village elders is one.

The *Mahâbhârata*[2] maintains this tradition in so far at least as it considers the priests to be the "non-official" mouth-pieces of the people, and the councillors as their "natural leaders", the Platonic "guardians". Finally, in a discussion of the *Artha-śâstra* it is even established that the state has its "sole prop" in the ministry (*mantri-pariṣat*).[3] The *amâtya* of the Kautilyan theory is in essence an organ through which the folk-will can be brought to bear on the constitution.

In a very elementary manner the *Agni Purâṇa*[4] and the *Matsya Purâṇa*[5] advise the king "not to decide on the policies alone". The arguments against one-man-rule or exclusive "personal" government are based in the *Śukra-nîti* on the conception that the monarch is not *infallible.* "Even if the work be a trifling one", aruges Śukra, "it can be done with difficulty by only one individual". "What can be performed by an unfriended person for a kingdom that is considerable?" is therefore his natural query.[6] Hence his deliberate advice that "even the king who is proficient in all the sciences and a past master in statecraft should never by himself study political interests without reference to ministers. The wise ruler, the ideal "philosopher-king", or the *râjarṣi* as Kautilya would say, should ever abide by the well-thought-out decisions of councillors, office-bearers, subjects, and members attending a meeting, — never by his own opinions."[7]

This hypothetical case of an "all-knowing" sovereign is well known to students of European political philosophy from Plato to Mill. But the utilitarian creed of the "greatest happiness of the greatest number" on which is erected the legislation of the present day is not prepared to trust itself to the discretion of such an ominiscient benevolent individual. For according to modern political conscience the physical magnitude, if not anything else, is too much for one man. The logic of the *Śukra-nîti* is thus essentially modern. Besides, Śukra is conscious also of the complexity of moral and social relations, as well as of the diversity[8]

---

[1] Jayaswal's "Constitutional Aspects of Rituals at Hindu Coronation" in the *Mod. Rev.*, Jan. 1912.

[2] *Âdi*, Ch. LXXXV, 19—22; *Śânti*, Ch. LXXXIII, 48—50, XCI, 29.

[3] Book V, Ch. IV.

[4] Ch. CCXXV, verse 18.

[5] Ch. CCXX, verse 37.

[6] Ch. II, lines 1, 2.

[7] *Ibid*, lines 3—6.

[8] *Ibid*, lines 9, 12, 13.

of intellectual attainments among the members of a community, — facts which make it all the more improbable that any single intellectual giant should be competent enough to manage a whole state.

Such also are some of the considerations on which Kautilya, Kâmandaka, Manu and others seek to institute a council of experts as the permanent advisory instrument of monarchical polities. And in regard to their position in the state Śukra's idea is definite and clear. "If the king fears their control", says he, "they are good ministers". It is inconceivable to him that "there could be prosperity in a territory where ministers are not feared by the king".[1] The *amâtyas* in constitutional theory are thus not mere "king's men" like the ministers of England before the introduction of the Cabinet system. They must have an individuality and independence of character in order that they may control the whims and caprices of the monarch and systematically govern the course of the *râjya*. Nay, by the strength of their wisdom they are expected to "deliver a king who has gone astray".[2] And the acid test of their statesmanship is the "improvement of the state in extent, population, efficiency, revenue and administration".[3]

The *nîti*-philosophers have not neglected to consider the other side of the shield. The contingency of an arbitrary Charles I, the Chow of the Mencian radicals in ancient China, the Veṇa of Hindu tradition, has not been ignored either by Kautilya or by Śukra. The evils of "personal government", with their natural and necessary reactions, have been discussed in all the *śâstras*.[4] If the monarch follows his own will, say, against the advice of Jâjnavalkya[5] or of the *Purâṇas*, he will tend to be the cause of miseries, says the *Śukra-nîti*.[6] He is likely to "get estranged from the kingdom and alienated from his subjects", in other words, to provoke a revolution. Indeed, he is no longer a "legitimate" king, for by ignoring or defying the counsels of ministers he has made himself into a "thief in the form of a ruler", an "exploiter of the people's wealth", a persecutor, a tyrant.[7] In all respects, both negatively and positively, the ministry is thus a constitutional check in the Hindu theory of monarchy.

---

[1] *Ibid*, lines 163—164.

[2] *Ibid*, lines 14—18; cf. Kâmandaka, IV, 44—45, 48—50.

[3] *Ibid*, line 166.

[4] Kautilya, Book I, vii; Kâmandaka, II, 60, 64, 71, 73; XI, 75.

[5] I, 312.

[6] II, lines 7—8.

[7] *Ibid*, lines 515—516.

Section 6.

Right to Revolt.

The limitations of the king as ruler are fully admitted in the theory of the *nîti-śâstras*. Kâmandaka,[1] Manu,[2] and Śukra[3] are never tired of moralizing, like Elyot in his *Gouvernour*, as to the failings to which the monarch as much as all other human beings is naturally liable, especially because of his high position. Moreover, the restraints on his authority implied in the conception of kingship as a public service and in that of the ministry as a body of overseers and controllers are the two checks that the philosophers offer to the doctrine of the *saptâmga*.

It has to be observed that both these restrictions are distinct from and in addition to the moral and spiritual checks that are binding upon all men as men according to normal Hindu pedagogics. The king therefore is not sacred. As a consequence Hindu thought does not seem to have ever recognized any "divine right" of kings, just as Hindu history does not know of any theocratic state, except in the Khalsa of the latter-day Sikhs.

This secular idea of monarchy is not however inconsistent with the conception of the ruler as a "god in human form".[4] The divine character of royalty is described in the *Manu Samhitâ* and the *Mahâbhârata* and is stated also in the *Śukra-nîti*. Royalty is indeed superhuman energy embodied in a human institution, exactly as every activity and *élan* or *śakti* of life is godly or divine in the mythological imagery of Hindu heinotheism.

But the king is not "vicar of God" as understood by mediaeval western philosophers, imperial as well as anti-imperial.[5] The divinity that hedges the monarch is the glory and importance of the functions that he has to perform as *svâmin*. By analogizing the marks of *aiśvarya*, i. e. sovereignty with the attributes and *śakti* of the gods (or powers of nature) Śukra wants the people to understand nothing more than the fact that kingship consists in protection of person and property,[6] administration of justice,[6] diffusion of culture and *dharma*,[6] philanthropy and charity,[6] and last but not least, realization of revenues.[6]

---

[1] I, 23, 37, 56—57; IV, 46, 48; XIII, 19; XIV, 1.

[2] VII, 39—41; 45—53.

[3] I, lines 181, 183—185, 197—198, 243—244.

[4] Manu VII, 4—8; *Mahâ, Vana*, CLXXXV, 27—31; Śukra, I, lines 141—143.

[5] Carlyle, I, 147—160; III, 115, 117—123; Figgis' *Divine Right of Kings*, pp. 219—226.

[6] I, lines 144, 151; 147; 145, 146; 149; 148.

Not even the thinkers of Manu's school by any means contemplate the "patristic" dogma of the state or the monarch as divine in a theological sense. Their metaphor is meant only to bring to the forefront the supreme character of Bodin's *majestas* as an abstract attribute in civil society. In order to appreciate Hindu political theory it is essential to remember this materialistic view of sovereignty (*aiśvarya*) which, so far as Eur-America is concerned, is absolutely un-Christian or pre-Christian, i. e. "modern" and Greek.

In any event, the metaphorical sacredness of sovereignty does not carry with it, according to *nîti* philosophers, the infallibility and inviolability of the holder of the sceptre, the *danda-dhara.* Not any prince and every prince is "made out of the permanent elements" of the gods of fire, air, water, light, wealth and so forth. It is "only the king who is virtuous that is a part of the gods". How to know such a ruler? The marks of the "god in human form" are fully described in the *Kâmandakî-nîti*, *Śukra-nîti*, and the *Manu-Samhitâ.*[1] He must practise self-restraint and be valorous and skilled in the use of arms and weapons. He must be well up in statecraft and diplomacy and must be able to crush the foes. He must be learned in the arts and sciences. And he must have long-period statesmanlike views. But "otherwise, i. e. if he happens to be the enemy of *dharma* (*Kultur* or Platonic "virtue") and oppressor of the people the king is a part of the demons". Such notions are diametrically opposite to the creed of Augustine[2] that even Nero was ruler by divine right.

One must not consequently look for a Gregory the Great in India to preach on the exemplary conduct of a "good subject" like David who would not criticize the tyranny even of a Saul. The radical tendencies of the *nîti-śâstras* are developed on postulates which are as the poles asunder to the axioms of the church fathers. In *nîti* thought the King *can* do wrong as any other mortal. The person, property and family of the ruler are therefore not exempt from punishment (*danda*) by the people, e. g. the fine of the *Manu Samhitâ.* The bed-rock of Hindu political philosophy in the analysis of Kingship is accordingly furnished by the differentiation of the king as "a part of the gods" from the king as "a part of the demons". This is the basis of the distinction between "legitimate Kingship" and its contrary, i. e. tyranny. In the treatises on *smriti* and *nîti* Kingship automatically ceases to be legitimate as it

---

[1] Kâmandaka, IV, 3—8; Śukra I, lines 139—140, 167—170; *cf.* Manu VII, 25, 26, 27—29, 30—32, 33—34.

[2] Augustine's *City of God*, Book V, 19, 21 (Dods' transl., Vol. I, pp. 216, 219).

ceases to promote justice (*dharma*), and the drastic remedy suggested is revolution and tyrannicide.

Kautilya observes that *prakriti-kopo hi sarva kopebhyo garîyân*, the wrath of the people is the supremest or most dangerous of all wraths. This is the Hindu counterpart of the Confucian proverb, "Of all who are to be feared, are not the people the chief?" In other words, the "fear of the people is the wisdom of the lord". Like Mencius,[1] the Rousseau of ancient China, and Manegold of Lautenbach, the most radical anti-imperialist of mediaeval Europe, Manu has described in no uncertain terms as to the form generally taken by this "wrath of the people". "The King who through foolishness arbitrarily tyrannizes over his own state is very soon deprived of his kingdom and life together with his kith and kin. As the lives of living beings perish through torture of the body, so the lives of kings also are lost through torturing the Kingdom."[2] Such a "torturer" or persecutor is known as "ruiner" or "destroyer" in the *Mahâbhârata*. And according to its teachings he is to be executed (*nihantavyah*) by the people.[3]

It is thus not the Gregorian doctrine of non-resistance championed by Hobbes in the *Leviathan* or by his junior French contemporary *Bossuet* in the *Politique* that could have found an echo in Hindu political thought. The Stuarts of England and *le grand monarque* would have been thoroughly disappointed with the *nîti* theory in regard to the status of the king. The right of resistance to the King's "demonical", i. e. autocratic and arbitrary (or "Satanic", to employ Mohandas Karamchand Gandhi's expression in 1921) rule is taken for granted, and the doctrine of explusion of the tyrant one of the A. B. C.'s in Hindu political *Weltanschauung*. The student of the *nîti-śâstras* is thus constantly reminded of Languet's (1518—1581) queries in the *Vindicae contra Tyrannos*[4] as to whether it is "lawful to resist a prince who violates the laws of God and lays waste his church" and "whether one might resist a prince who oppresses and ruins the state and how far".[5] And the conclusion that is advanced by the European advocate of tyrannicide is identical with that of the protagonists of *dharma*.

The *tyrannos* of the Western political theory is the "mere fellow"

---

[1] *The Book of Mencius* (Legge's transl.), Bk. I, pt. II, Ch. VIII, 2, 3. *Vide* the author's "*Democratic Background of Chinese Culture*" in the *Scientific Monthly*, January, 1919. cf. Dawson's *Ethics of Confucius*, 241—247.

[2] Manu VII, 111, 112.

[3] *Anuśâsana*, Ch. LXI, 32—34.

[4] Dunning Vol. II, 46—55.

[5] Chs. II, III.

(and not a "sovereign") of the Chinese Mencians and "the monarch who follows his own will",[1] "a thief in the form of a ruler",[1] "the enemy of virtue, morality and strength",[1] etc. of the Hindu radicals. The *Śukra-nîti* is quite at one with the *Politics* of Aristotle in its investigation of the "abuses" to which monarchy degenerates under "abnormal" conditions. And neither Isidore of Seville under the influence probably of Stoic teachings nor John of Salisbury[2] in the *Policraticus* makes out a more pronounced antithesis between the king and the tyrant than does Manu or Śukra.

The unequivocal enunciation of the doctrine of resistance, i. e. of the rights of the *prakriti* as against the "demon" in human form is as manifest in Śukra as in Manu. Quite in keeping with the spirit of the *Mahâbhârata* Śukra gives the verdict that the people should "desert the tyrant as the ruiner of the state".[3] The "alienation from the subjects"[4] because of "repression" leads ultimately to his ruin.[4] The "discontent" may assume larger proportions and "destroy the monarch with his whole family".[5] The overthrow and execution of Vena and Nahûṣa, the tyrants of Hindu legends, are therefore justified as a matter of course.[6] Only, the *Śukra-nîti* and the *Manu Samhitâ* are not explicit as to the methods of doing away with tyrants, if, for instance, as approved in England by the author of the *Policraticus*, the "poisoning" of a Tiberius could be resorted to by the people.[7]

As a natural corollary, however, the right to "cashier kings for misconduct" is in Śukra's theory backed by the right to "elect" a ruler. In the place of the deposed tyrant the priest with the consent of the ministry should install one who belongs to his family and is qualified.[8] This advice of the Hindu philosopher is of a piece with Menicus' commendation of the conduct of the rebel minister I Yin,[9] and is organically related to the general theory of popular sovereignty in Asian political philosophy.

---

[1] *Śukra-nîti*, II, lines 7—8, 515—516, 549—550.

[2] Poole (*John of Salisbury*), 201—225, 238; Carlyle III, 111, 113, 137—140, 145; for a general account of Isidore see Brehaut's *Encyclopedist of the Dark Age, Isidore of Seville*.

[3] II, 550.

[4] II, 8, I, 319—320; *cf.* the effects of the mal-administration of justice in Kâmandaka, XIV, 13—14.

[5] IV, ii, 49.

[6] I, 135—138.

[7] Figgis' From *Gerson*, p. 170; Carlyle, III, 145.

[8] II, 551, 552.

[9] Book VII, pt. I, XXXI. Vide "the doctrine of resistance in Hindu thought" (*Pos. Back*, II, pp. 43—46).

Section 7.

Taxes (Bali) as Wages and Prices.

The right of the *prakriti* to revolt is essentially derived from the conception of *samaya* or compact, and this again is integrally connected with the theory of *koṣa* or public finance.

On election, according to the *Mahâbhârata*,[1] the ruler makes a *pratijnâ*, vow or oath that he will protect the people, and the people reciprocate by promising to help him with the "root of the army",[2] i. e. the "sinews of war" or *les nerfs de la république*. Kingship is by very nature a public office, and the masters of the king are the people who have the power of the purse. From the standpoint of the sovereign, then, as Śukra makes it clear, the revenues are but the wages for his labor, and from the standpoint of the people they are the prices offered for the service of protection.[3]

Taxation, according to this theory, is the "cash nexus" binding the king and the people in the *râjya*. It represents in reality the material basis of the contract between two parties who have an eye to the equalization between compensation and the benefit rendered. The right to levy a tax is dependent on the duty of protecting the people. Should, however, the taxes be ever so unjust in the realization or in the disbursement, the "discontent of the people would destroy the king with his whole family."[4] The right of resistance is a natural weapon of the people in Śukra's theory of finance. Recourse is had to it as the ruler ceases to discharge his functions according to the terms of the compact.

For normal times, however, i. e. as long as the people are paying the piper and the piper is willing to play the tune called for, Kâmandaka and other Hindu theorists have made provision for a considerable amount of revenue. It is not a slight Theocritean burden of taxation that the *niti-śâstras* have in view, for the state conceived by them is not a primitive polity with functions of an idyllic character. Manifold are the services, as we have seen, rendered by the state in Hindu theory;

---

[1] *Sânti*, Ch. LIX, 106—107; Ch. LXVII, 18, 24—28. Passages bearing on this subject may be seen in Kumaraswamy's "Hindu Theories of State and Social Compact" in the *Hindustan Review*, May-June, 1918.

[2] Śukra, IV, ii, 28.

[3] *Supra*, p. 176.

[4] Śukra IV, ii, 49.

the revenues (*bali*, *bhâga* or *kara*) i. e. the prices or wages therefore are necessarily varied and considerable.[1]

Manu[2] and Śukra[3] recommend a levy on almost every taxable resource of the people. Indirect taxes on commodities are to be paid by traders. No sale is to be left unassessed, from cattle and gold to fruits and flowers. Land of course contributes its quota. The right of preemption is also to be enforced. One day's service per mensem and per fortnight the state is allowed, by Manu[4] and Śukra[5] respectively, to exact from artists, craftsmen, menial workers and independent laborers.

The only limit that the *Manu Samhitâ* knows is the absolute limit furnished by the sound economic doctrine, "as far as the market will bear." It lays down the golden rule of realizing the maximum possible without inflicting the least annoyance. For the state that shears the sheep to the skin really kills the goose that lays the egg. In Manu's language, "excessive imposts" would lead but to the "destruction of one's own roots."[6] We are told indeed that the levy is be *alpâlpa*, i. e. in small quantities. But the camouflage of these alleged negligible doses can not impose on anybody, for the theorist takes care to point out that the people are to be sucked dry in the manner in which "leeches, calves and bees" help themselves upon their food.[7] The process of steady and patient although slow and imperceptible drain is thus suggested. Statesmen are in short to be guided by the principle analgous to the one well known in the investors' world, viz. that of "small rates" but "quick returns."

We find this hint of Manu's fully elucidated in the *Arthaśâstra*. "Just as fruits are gathered from a garden," says Kautilya,[8] "as often as they become ripe, so revenue shall be collected as often as it becomes ripe." This principle of continuous levy might be indiscriminately observed in a suicidal fashion. Hence the sober advice that the collection of revenues or fruits must not be allowed "while they are unripe," for there is a danger lest their "source be injured" to the immense peril of the state. In the *Mahâbhârata's* phraseology the *râṣtra* must not be "over-milked."[9]

---

[1] *Supra*, pp. 172—173, *cf.* Kâmandaka's "eightfold" sources of public income (V, 78—79), and list of appropriations (XIII, 31—32).

[2] VII, 127, 130, 131, 132.

[3] IV, ii, lines 212—258.

[4] VII, 138.

[5] IV, ii, 241.

[6] VII, 139.

[7] VII, 129.

[8] Bk. V, Ch. ii, *Ind. Ant.* 1909, p. 264.

[9] *Śânti* LXXXVII, 20—22.

The fear of injuring the source or killing the goose, or "spoiling the market", as economists would say, haunts likewise the financiers of the Śukra school. The cultivator is to pay the dues to the state but the state must take care that he "be not destroyed."[1] Land revenue is to be realized, as we read in the *Śukra-nîti*, in the fashion of the "weaver of garlands" and not of that of the charcoal merchant.[2] The latter sets fire to the woods to make charcoal and thus destroys the whole property. But the weaver of garlands plucks from the trees only such flowers as are full blown and preserves the rest as well as the trees for future use. Fortified with this much discretion the finance minister is to test the "faculty" or taxability of the people at every conceivable point. He is to "enjoy fruits everywhere" and "collect funds by hook or by crook."[3]

No resource is then left untapped in Hindu fiscal thought, and "taxes, more taxes, still more taxes" appears to be the slogan popularized by the *Kâmandakî-nîti*.[4] But the theory of such a heavy assessment is redeemed by the postulate that the people are normally in a position to bear the burden and maintain the "root of the army." The philosophers of finance have therefore seen to it that the state promotes by all means the economic prosperity of its members.[5]

The *Sabhâ-parva* of the *Mahâbhârata* is explicit about the development of agriculture by the government to such an extent as to render it independent of the monsoons. Kâmandaka wants the state to patronize the commercial classes. The people's interests are looked after in Śukra's suggestion that if "new industries be undertaken or new lands brought under cultivation" no taxes are to be demanded until the new ventures "have realized profit twice the expenditure."[6] Such remissions of taxes or suspensions of revenue for certain periods are however not to be permitted by Kautilya on *doctrinaire* grounds.[7] The difficulties in the improvement effected by the peasants are to be carefully considered in fixing the rate of remission. Likewise is the wealth of the land sought to be augmented by protective duties, e. g. on foreign salts and wines.[8] Kautilya would also recommend legislation against "profiteering."[8] Consumers may thereby be protected from ruinously high pro-

---

[1] IV, ii, 222. The complete account of Śukra's theory of public finance is to be found in *Pos. Back*, Vol. II, pp. 111—126.

[2] IV, ii, 35—36, 223.

[3] IV, ii, 3, 259.

[4] V, 87.

[5] *Ibid* IV, ii, 3—6, 15—16, 29—30; *Sabhâ*, V, 76—79; Kâmandaka, V, 80.

[6] IV, ii, 242—244.

[7] *Supra*, p. 124.

[8] *Supra*, pp. 124—125.

fits and a general level of moderate prices would encourage saving. But on the other hand Śukra does not want to be unjust to the seller.[1] The excise on sales is not to be realized if the trader receives what is less than or just equal to the cost.

Development of national resources being thus provided for in diverse ways, the Hindu theory of taxation automatically finds its own safety-valve. This principle of replenishment or recuperation is clearly stated by Śukra in the dictum that the "collector of taxes is to be like the gardener who plucks flowers and fruits after having duly nourished the trees with care."[2] Kâmandaka's idea is similar.

The financiers' solicitude for the people's material prosperity is brought out in bold relief by the special arrangements they seek to devise for "hard times" in state housekeeping. Emergency finance is treated by them as something distinct from normal finance. Fines, land revenues, excise, etc., must not be enhaced, says Śukra,[3] in normal times. Nor should holy places, religious establishments or properties consecrated to the gods be assessed as sources of public income under peace conditions. Extraordinary duties and fines may be levied when the state is preparing to maintain an army on war-footing.[4] While the community at large is to be drawn upon for war-finance by regular enhancements of the rates, the pressure of the state is to be borne more distinctively by the rich. And the doctrine is laid down that loans are to be floated by the government to which the wealthy classes should be invited to contribute. The "public debt" is to be redeemed, however, with interest when the national danger is over.[5]

Section 8.

Militarism and *Machtpolitik* (*Śakti-Yoga*).

"A joy is it to be killed in war," says the *Mahâbhârata*,[6] "painless is the soldier's death, and heaven is his goal." The poets of the Great Epic were but continuing the tradition of the *Vedas* pervaded as they had been by *śakti-yoga*, the spirit of *pouvoir* or *Machtpolitik*. For, nothing short of a world-conquest was the ideal of Young India of the Vedic period. "Mighty am I," as the earliest Hindu political philos-

---

[1] IV, ii, 218.

[2] *Ibid* II, 345—346; *Kâmandaki*, V, 84.

[3] IV, ii, 17—18.

[4] IV, ii, 19—20.

[5] IV, ii, 21—22.

[6] *Karṇa-parva*, XCIII, 55—59.

ophers set the creed of life for man, "Superior by name, upon the earth, conquering am I, all-conquering, completely conquering every region."[1] Thus began the conception of war as a "categorical imperative" in Hindu thought, which found its most complete expression in the doctrine of *niskâma karma* preached by Krişņa in the *Gîtâ*.[2] And naturally the militaristic philosophy of the *Gîtâ* was further popularized by works like the *Agni Purâņa*[3] for mediaeval India, when we find that the *Gîtâ* is virile enough to be cited even in 1911 by an English general in the introduction to Clausewitz's German classic on War.

Manu also is a champion of this Kşatriyaism (militarism) of the Hindus. But probably modern war-lords would recognize in the Indian Śukra their own kin. "Even Brâhmaņas (the most intellectual order of people)," says he, "should fight if there have been aggressions on women and on priests or if there has been a killing of cows (which are held inviolable by Hindu religion)."[4] According to the *Śukra-nîti*, the death of Kşatryias (warriors) in the bed is a sin. "The man who gets death with an unhurt body by excreting cough and biles and crying aloud is not a Kşatriya."[5] The military morality is categorically stated thus: "Death in the home except in the fight is not laudable. Cowardice is a miserable sin."[6] And "the Kşatriya who retreats with a bleeding body after sustaining defeat in battles and is encircled by members of the family deserves death." Further, what is there to regret in the death of the brave man who is killed at the front? It is a blessing in disguise. For, "the man is purged and delivered of all sins and attains heaven."[7] Nay, who would not invite such a death? For, "the fairies of the other world vie with one other in reaching the warrior who is killed in action in the hope that he be their husband."[8] Nothing indeed could be more tempting in view of the notion that "the rascal who flies from a fight to save his life is really dead though alive, and endures the sins of the whole people."[9]

The "sanction" inculcated here would be called *Bushido* in Japan. This seems to be a chip from the Lycurgan creed followed in the public

---

[1] *Atharva Veda* (Bloomfield's version), XII, i, 54.

[2] Section II (Telang's transl. in the *S. B. E.*), pp. 46, 47, 48.

[3] Ch. CCXXXII, 52—56, CCXLIV, 8.

[4] IV, vii, 599.

[5] IV vii, 608—609.

[6] IV vii, 612—613, 614—615.

[7] IV vii, 620—621.

[8] IV vii, 622—623.

[9] IV vii, 656—657.

barracks of Sparta. Or, is it a spark from the *Politics* of Heinrich von Treitschke, or from the British militarist Maude, according to whom "war is an indispensable necessity of human progress," and in whose psychology. the slogan, "first in peace" carries with it as a necessary corollary, the motto "first in war"?

Let us now look to the other side of the shield. The international jurists of the world and peace-propagandists of America had for some time previous to the World-War (1914—1918) been devising ways and means to render warfare more humane and less barbarous. On several occasions before the outbreak of the War resolutions were passed by the "Concert of Europe" at the Hague Conferences regarding the kind of arms and ammunitions to be avoided out of consideration for human suffering. But the Hindu thinkers of Manu's school have handed down a tradition of chivalrous "ideals" probably as old as the sixth century B. C. The *Manu Samhitâ's* resolution reads thus in verse:[1]

> "Let the soldier, good in battle, never guilefully conceal,
> (Wherewithal to smite the unwary) in his staff the treacherous steel;
> Let him scorn to barb his javelin — let the valiant never anoint
> With fell poison-juice his arrows, never put fire upon the point.
> In his car or on his war-horse, should he chance his foe to meet,
> Let him smite not if he find him lighted down upon his feet.
> Let him spare one standing suppliant, with his closed hands raised on high,
> Spare him whom his long hair loosen'd blinds and hinders from to fly,
> Spare him if he sink exhausted; spare him if he for life crave:
> Spare him crying out for mercy, 'Take me for I am thy slave'.
> Still remembering his duty, never let the soldier smite
> One unarm'd, defenceless, mourning for one fallen in the flight;
> Never strike the sadly wounded — never let the brave attack
> One by sudden terror smitten, turning in base flight his back."

These sentiments and pious wishes may be useful even today. We notice once more that the mentality of Hindu political thinkers is quite of the same stuff as that of the modern Eur-American phrase-makers. For the Orientals also knew how to lecture on making the world safe for "civilization and humanity."

[1] Griffith's rendering; Manu, VII, 90—93 *cf.* also Śukra, IV, vii, lines 716—721.

Section 9.

Caste and Public Service.

The gospel, "*Durch Nacht und Blut zum Licht*", i. e. the *dharma* of *puissance* or militarism is not intended exclusively for the so-called military (Kṣatriya or Samurai) caste. In Hindu thought army service has always been held to be national, i. e. the duty of every order of citizens. Brâhmaṇas (priests) can be soldiers according to the *Mahâbhârata*,[1] as well as according to the lawbooks of Gautama[2] and Vaśiṣtha.[3] The *Manu Samhitâ* also recommends recruitment from the priestly caste.[4] And, as noticed above, Śukra's opinion is quite clear. Baudhâyana is in favor of enlisting the Vaiśya[5] (the so-called artisan and mercantile classes). They are eligible as soldiers in the *Mahâbhârata* also.[6]

No distinction is likewise made in the *Artha-śâstra* between castes (or hereditary and personal occupations) in the matter of inducting troops for national defense. The regulating principle is nothing but fitness or qualification as fighting material. In Kautilya's book there is a discussion as to the relative bravery of the different castes. "My teacher says," as we read, that "of the armies composed of Brâhmaṇas, Kṣatriyas, Vaiśyas or Śudras (lower orders), that which is mentioned first on account of bravery is better to be enlisted than the one subsequently mentioned." But to this Kautilya makes an objection on the ground, rather too idealistic for his usual commonsense attitude, that the Brâhmaṇas might be won over by prostration, because as priests they are likely to be sentimentally weak to those who are submissive. Hence the army of Kṣatriyas trained in the art of wielding weapons is better, or the army of Vaiśyas or Śûdras having greater numerical strength."[7] Thus while Kautilya does not make the calling of arms the exclusive preserve or monopoly of any section of the community, he would exempt the Brâhmaṇas, if at all, on the sole ground of military incompetency.

Further, the theory of national service on the question of castes is explicitly stated in the *Śukra-nîti*. According to this treatise caste is to play no part in the consideration of a person's qualifications for offi-

---

[1] *Śânti*, Ch. LXXVIII, 34.

[2] VII, 6.

[3] II, 22.

[4] X, 81; Śukra, IV, vii, 599, 664—667.

[5] Baudhâyana, II, 2, 4, 18.

[6] *Karṇa* XLVII, 19, *Śânti*, CLXV, 34.

[7] Bk. IX, II.

cership. No officer in the army hierarchy from *âjutika* (general in command of ten thousand troops) down to the *gaulmika* (head of thirty) and *pattipâla* (head of five or six) is to be selected from any privileged class, tribe or race. Only such persons as are well up in *nîti-śâstras*, in the use of arms and ammunitions, the manipulation of battle arrays, and in the art of management and discipline, as are not too young but of middle age, as are brave, self-controlled, able-bodied, always mindful of their own duties, as are devoted to their superiors and hate their enemies should be made commanders and soldiers, no matter whether they are Śûdras, Kṣatriyas, or Vaiśyas or even descended from *Mlechchhas* (or unclean barbarians).[1]

But since the warrior caste is likely to specialize in valor, the *Śukranîti* would give the preference to a Kṣatriya, and failing him, to a Brâhmaṇa.[2] As a rule, it would not confer commission on the mercantile or agricultural classes, the Vaiśyas, because their service is needed in other fields. They can not be spared from attending to the normal economic interests of the state. And as for the Śûdras, they are usually to be held incompetent or unfit to take the lead, because like the ancient Greeks, the Hindu thinkers also postulated the existence of a class of "natural" slaves,[3] born only to serve. Under ordinary circumstances, therefore, a Śûdra is not to be in command of troops. But even these conventional arguments against Vaiśyas and Śûdras are overridden by the supreme consideration of valor. Since fighting is treated as "the duty of the four pure as well as of mixed castes",[4] the commander may be selected from any caste,[5] for, after all, says Śukra finally, it is bravery that is to be looked for in a commander. The only persons against whom the theoretical injunction is absolute are the cowards, even though they be Kṣatriya by caste.[6]

This principle of indifferentism to caste regulates Śukra's thought not only in regard to the officers and privates of the army but to every branch of the public service. As usual, the Śûdra is normally declared ineligible for a seat on the council of ministers and the traditional preference is accorded to the Brâhmaṇa, failing him to the Kṣatriya, and failing that, to the Vaiśya.[7] But this stereotyped order of selection for

---

[1] II, 276—285. For Śukra's theory of caste in society see *Pos. Back*, Vol. II, pp. 89—95.
[2] II, 865—866.
[3] Manu VIII, 413—414.
[4] Śukra II, 868.
[5] *Ibid* II, 867.
[6] *Ibid* II, 866.
[7] II, 859—861.

the ten *prakritis* or councillors is thrown overboard in the general discussion on the subject. We are told that only those who are versed in politics and are men of good deeds, habits and attributes, and who are gentle in speech and old in age "should be made members of council irrespective of caste."[1] In making appointments to offices "one should not notice only the caste or race or only the family,"[2] though the "accident of birth" is of course an important consideration. "Work, character and merit, — these three are to be respected — neither caste nor family.[3] Neither by caste nor by family can superiority be asserted." The importance of caste is relegated in the *Śukra-nîti* only to social functions, such as marriages and dinner parties.[4]

Further, among the six officers[5] to be appointed in each village as representatives of the Crown, it is interesting to observe that the chief executive may come even from the priestly caste, and that even the warrior caste can contribute men to the department of revenue.[6] Thus according to Śukra, the Brâhmaṇa need not always have to pursue the religious avocation, nor the Kṣatriya always to be a soldier. In political theory, therefore, caste (birth-affiliation) is not the supreme factor in an individual's occupation or professional activity, as it has been alleged to be by the scholars in indology.[7]

Incidentally, it may be pointed out that the Hindu theory of social orders did not treat the castes as water-tight compartments even in regard to marital relations. Inter-caste marriages were held valid by Kautilya, Manu, Yâjnavalkya and Viṣṇu.[8] Race-fusion or blood inter-

---

[1] II, 333—336.

[2] II, 110.

[3] II, 111—112.

[4] II, 113.

[5] II, 242—245.

[6] II, 862—863.

[7] A rare exception is Hopkins. *Vide* his article in the J. A. O. S., 1889, p. 185.

[8] Kautilya LXIV; *Mahâbhârata, Anuśâsana-parva*, xlvii, 17, 28, xlviii, 4, 7, 8; Manu, III, 13, X, 6—7; Viṣṇu, XXIV, 1—4; Baudhâyana, I, viii, 2—6, I, ix, 3, 5; Yâjnavalkya, I, 57, 91, 92, II, 125. These references are borrowed of Vanamali Vedantatirtha's *Bengali* article in the *Prabâsî* (Calcutta) for Vaiśâkha, 1326 (April, 1919).

Enough data are not available yet for an epigraphic study of the caste system. But already it might be shown that the *râjâs* of the ruling dynasties and of the *gaṇas* (republics) belonged very rarely to the so-called Kṣatriya caste, as the theory of water-tight compartments would lead one to presume. Similarly generals and officers of the army were contributed by the priestly, trading and Sûdra classes. *Cf.* Mookerji's *Local*, 59—62, Majumdar, 146—149, 160, 164, 171, 172. A "military interpretation" of Hindu history with special reference to the ethnic elements has been suggested in Sarkar's *Chinese Religion*, pp. 195—208 (A Melting-pot of Races). Note the cephalic index

mixture, both horizontal and vertical, was therefore accepted as a normal phenomenon of actual life in the legal investigations of those sociologists who interested themselves in the problems of inheritance, succession, and partition of property.

---

tests as well as legends and inscriptions on the strength of which Rama Prasad Chanda maintains that Brâhmaṇas of the "outer countries" were "outlandic" in stock, and that Brâhmaṇas and non-Brâhmaṇas are of common origin (*The Indo-Aryan Races*, 163, 167, 180, 182, 188—191, 194).

CHAPTER IX.

The Theory of Sovereignty in Hindu Political Philosophy.

The state (*râjya*) as an entity is grounded in the pheno menon of *aiśvarya* or *svâmitva* i. e. sovereignty. The theory of the state, therefore, is fundamentally the philosophy of sovereignty.

No matter whether it is exercised by the one or the few or the many, no matter whether it is vested in the long run in the legislature or the executive or the judiciary, no matter whether it is identical with the despotism of custom or the rule of positive law, no matter whether it manifests itself in and through a single organ as the *primum mobile* embracing all organized spheres or is exhibited simultaneously in several coexistent coordinate corporations of a pluralistic universe, and finally, no matter whether it is the monopoly of the bourgeoisie or of the proletariat, it is *svâmitva* that ushers into being the phenomena called politics in social existence. In political speculation the central problem obviously is the analysis of this great *śakti* (force) that constitutes the core of "political" relations, i. e. the *élan* of *samûha* life.

"What is sovereignty?" is then the moot question to be attacked by all political philosophers. Let us proceed to examine how the problem was grasped by the *smriti* and *nîti* theorists of India. It is to be remembered, however, that we are here concerned with the thought which prevailed in the world ages before the ideas discussed in Merriam's *History of the Theory of Sovereignty since Rousseau*, Scherger's *Evolution of Modern Liberty*, Michel's *L'Idée de l'Etat*, Barker's *Political Thought in England from Spencer to the Present Day*, Joseph-Barthélemy's *Role du pouvoir exécutif dans les républiques modernes* or *Problème de la compétence dans la démocratie*, and Laski's *Studies in the Problem of Sovereignty*.

Section 1.

The Theory of the State.

a) The Doctrine of Mâtsya-nyâya

(The Logic of the Fish)

At the back of political thinking in India there was the process of dichotomy at work. Hindu thinkers tried to understand the state by differentiating it from the non-state. Their method was logical as well as historical. That is, in the first place, they tried to investigate in what particulars the state analytically differs from the non-state; and in the second place, they tried to picture to themselves as to how the pre-statal condition developed into the statal, i. e. how the state grew out of the non-state. The chief solution of both these problems they found in the doctrine of *mâtsya-nyâya* or the logic of the fish.

What, now, is the non-state according to Hindus? The same question was asked by the philosophers of Europe thus: "What is the state of nature?" And the Hindu answer was identical with the European.

According to Hooker (1554—1600) in the *Ecclesiastical Polity* the state of nature is a state of strife. The *Leviathan* of Hobbes (1588—1670) declares similarly that the state of nature is a state of war and of no rights. In Spinoza's (1632—77) opinion also, in the *Tractatus Theologico Politicus*, the state of nature is a state of war and a state of the right of might. The non-state is thus conceived to be a war of "all against all", an "anarchy of birds and beasts", or a regime of vultures and harpies as John Stuart Mill would have remarked.

It is interesting to observe that in China also the state of nature was analyzed by Moh-Ti (*c* 500—420 B. C.) in almost self-same terms. In the non-state, as Su Hu explains it in *The Development of Logic in Ancient China*, "each man has his own notion of right. Therefore one man has one notion of right, two men have two notions of right, and ten men have ten notions of right. The more men there are, the more conceptions of right will there be. Consequently each man approves his own notion of right and denounces every other man's. So they denounce one another".

This Hobbesian "law of beasts and birds" or the *Naturprozess* of Gumplowicz is the logic (*nyâya*) of the fish (*matsya*) in India. Should there be no ruler to wield punishment on earth, says the *Mahâbhârata*[1] (*c* B. C. 600—A. C. 200), "the strong would devour the weak like fishes in water. It is related that in days of yore people were ruined through sovereignlessness, devouring one another like the stronger fishes preying upon the feebler". In the *Manu Samhitâ*[2] likewise we are told that "the strong would devour the weak like fishes" if there be a virtual reversion to the non-state (if, for example, the king is not vigilant in

[1] *Ŝânti-Parva*, LXVII, 16—17; LXVIII, 11—12. The history of the theory of *mâtsya-nyâya* in European sociology from Heracleitus to Gumplowicz is clearly summarized in Barnes' article on "The struggle of races and social groups" in the *Journal of Race Development* (April, 1919), pp. 394—400. For Protagoras' conception of the origin of the State after primeval chaos *vide* Barker's *Plato*, p. 130.

[2] VII, 20.

meting out punishments to those that should be punished). The *Râmâyaṇa*[1] also describes the non-state region as one in which "people ever devour one another like fishes". And a few details about the conditions in this non-state are furnished in the *Matsya-Purâṇa.*[2] "The child, the old, the sick, the ascetic, the priest, the woman and the widow would be preyed upon", as we read, "according to the logic of the fish" (should *danda* or punishment fail to be operative at the proper time).

The idea of the fish-like struggle for existence or self-assertion was thus a generally accepted notion in the "floating literature" of Hindustan. It found an important place in the exclusively political treatises also. It was exploited as early as the latter half of the fourth century B. C. by Kautilya, one of the first, as we have seen, among the historical names in political science. According to him in the *Artha-śâstra*[3] the logic of the fish prevails while the state is unformed. "In the absence of the wielder of punishment the powerful swallows the powerless". And Kâmandaka also, who several centuries later generally follows Kautilya, writes in his *Nîti-sâra*[4] (Digest of Politics) that in the absence of punishment (*danda*), the destructive or ruinous logic of the fish operates through mutual animosities of the people and leads to the disruption of the world.

Nor was the doctrine confined within the circle of academicians and theorizers. We find it prevalent even among diplomatists and practical statesmen, e. g. of the ninth century. In the declarations of the Bengali emperor Dharmapâla[5] we are informed that his illustrious dynasty owed its origin to an "election" by the people. We are told further that it was "in order to escape from the logic of the fish", i. e. in order to escape from being absorbed into another kingdom, or to avoid being swallowed like a fish that the people of Bengal "made his father Gopâla accept the sovereignty". The mediaeval Hindu monarch was here using almost the same metaphor as has been employed in the nineteenth century by Mill in his essay on *Liberty* when he explains how "in order to prevent the weaker members of the community from being preyed upon by innumerable vultures it was needful that there should be an animal of prey stronger than the rest, commissioned to keep them down".

This theory of the non-state or the state of nature has had important bearings on other doctrines of Hindu political philosophy. For the

---

[1] *Ayodhyâ-Kânda*, LXVII, 31.

[2] CCXXV, 9.

[3] I, 4.

[4] II, 40.

[5] Banerji, Vol. I, pp. 147—149.

present we have only to note that in India political speculation was not divorced from the general intellectual currents in the society. The political philosophers kept themselves abreast of the contemporary thought in other branches of inquiry. The logical apparatus and dialectical machinery used in political discussions were familiar instruments in the cultural *milieu* of the scientific world.

Mâtsya-nyâya, for instance, is an expressive technical term in India's legal phraseology. In Raghu-nâtha's (fifteenth century) *Laukika-Nyâya-Samgraha*[1] (Compilation of Popular Legal Maxims) we find the "logic of the fish" coupled with the "logic of the monsters". The logic of the monsters is known as *Śundopaśunda Nyâya*. Śunda and Upaśunda are two monster-brothers, like Pyrochles and Cymochles in Spenser's *Faerie Queene*. They are said to have quarrelled over the nymph Tilottamâ and destroyed each other in the contest. Thus when two contradictory facts are equally strong, they neutralize each other. But when they are of unequal strength, i. e. when the one can overpower the other, there is generated a field for the operation of the logic of the fish and the survival of the fitter.

The logic of the fish arises, as Raghu-nâtha explains it, under a double set of conditions. First, there must have to be a conflict between a powerful and a comparatively powerless unit. And secondly, the latter must have been crushed and obliterated by the former. It is frequently referred to, says he, in the *Itihâsas* (treatises on history) and the *Purâṇas*, and he quotes the following passage from Vaśiṣtha:[2] "By this time that Rasâtala region had become extremely sovereignless, i. e. an anarchic non-state, characterized by the ignoble logic of the fish." Vaśiṣtha's verse is elucidated by Raghu-nâtha with the gloss that "strong fishes began to make an end of the weaker ones".

The non-state is then a state of anarchy, one in which the "tyranny of robbers" has full play, "justice is non-existent", and the "people prey upon one another". It is "the greatest evil".[3] "Enjoyment of wealth and wives is impossible" under it.[4] Only the robber is then happy. Even his happiness is precarious, because "the one is deprived of his loot by two, the two are robbed of theirs by several combined".[5] "A free man is made a slave" and "women are raped".[6]

---

[1] Kishori Lal Sarkar's *Rules of Interpretation in Hindu Law*, Lecture VI.

[2] Cited in Maitra's *Gauda-lekha-mâlâ* (Inscriptions of the Bengali Imperial Dynasty) in Bengali, p 19.

[3] *Mahâ.*, *Sânti*, LXVII, 1—3.

[4] *Ibid*, *Ibid*, LXVII, 12.

[5] *Ibid*, *Ibid*, LXVII, 14.

[6] *Ibid*, *Ibid*, LXVII, 15.

The psychology of men in the state of nature is brought out in the Book on *Śânti* (Peace) of the *Mahâbhârata* according to the following causal nexus: "Then foolishness or stupidity (*moha*)[1] seized their minds. Their intelligence being thus eclipsed, the sense of justice (*dharma*) was lost. Cupidity or temptation (*lobha*) overpowered them next. Thus arose the desire (*kâma*) for possessing things not yet possessed. And this led to their being subjugated by an affection (*râga*) under which they began to ignore the distinction between what should and what should not be done.[2] Consequently there appeared sexual license, libertinism in speech and diet, and indifference to morals. When such a revolution[3] set in among men, *Brahman* (the idea of Godhead) disappeared, and with it, law (*dharma*)".

It is thus with the negation of morals and manners, the nullification of property, the very antithesis of law and justice that the non-state is identified. And this appears to have been the fundamental position of Hindu theorists on the state. From this negative analysis it requires but a logical "conversion" according to the law of "contraries" to establish positively the philosophy of the state. To this we shall now address ourselves.

b) The Doctrine of Danda
(*Punishment, Coercion, Sanction*).

Two "inseparable accidents" of the Hindu theory of the state are, first, the doctrine of *mamatva* ("mine"-ness) or *svatva* (*suum*), i. e. "one's own"-ness, *proprium*, *Eigentum* or property, and secondly, the doctrine of *dharma* (i. e. law, justice and duty). And behind them both lies the doctrine of *danda* (punishment, restraint, or sanction). Herein is to be sought the nucleus of the whole philosophy of sovereignty.

A state is a state, argue Hindu philosophers, because it can coerce, restrain, compel. Eliminate control or the coercive element form social *(samûha)* life, and the state as an entity vanishes. *Danda* is *überhaupt* the very essence of statal relations. No *danda*, no state. A *danda*-less, i. e. sanctionless state is a contradiction in terms.

We have noticed above that the absence of *danda* is tantamount to *mâtsya-nyâya* or the state of nature. It is clear also that property and *dharma* do not exist in that non-state. These entities can have their roots only in the state. The theory thus consists of two formulae:

---

[1] *Śânti*, LIX, 15.

[2] *Ibid*, LIX, 18—19.

[3] *Ibid*, LIX, 20—21.

I. No *danda*, no state;
II. (a) No state, no *dharma*, and
(b) No state, no property.

What, then, is the *rationale* of this *danda*?[1] What is it that makes coercion the *sine qua non* of the state? Why is it that the very idea of government should imply a restraint, a check, a control, a sanction? In Hindu political philosophy the answer to these questions is to be found in the "original nature of man".

The phenomena of government are founded on the data of human psychology. And in regard to them the general trend of thought all the world over seems to have been the same. In ancient China Hsun Tze (B. C. 305—235?) strongly condemned the doctrine of Mencius (B. C. 373—289) who had postulated the "original goodness" of human nature. For, according to his counter-theory (Book XXIII)[1] "man is by nature wicked, his goodness is the result of nurture". "A curved twig", to cite again from Su Hu's unpublished thesis (IV, iii), needs straightening and heating and bending in order to become straight.** And man who is by nature wicked needs teaching and discipline in order to be right and requires the influence of *Li* and *Yi* (*Sittlichkeit*) in order to be good. The ancient rulers understood the native viciousness of man,** and therefore created morals, laws and institutions in order that human instincts and impulses might be disciplined and transformed".

Let us now turn to the western world. Seneca, the Stoic philosopher of the first century A. C., "looked upon the institutions of society as being the results of vice, of the corruption of human nature. They are conventional institutions made necessary by the actual defects of human nature". The philosophical "anarchists" of modern times will not accept this doctrine. Men indeed had known a previous period of innocence; but after a time, according to this Roman thinker, they became avaricious. "Avarice rent the first happy society asunder. It resulted that even those who were made wealthy became poor, for desiring to possess things for their own, they ceased to possess all things. The rulers grew dissatisfied with their paternal rule; the lust of authority seized upon them."[2]

This doctrine of human depravity and the natural wickedness of man was entertained by the Church Fathers also. St. Irenaeus (second

---

[1] In regard to *danda* see the section on the "psychological premises of Hindu Politics" in the *Pos. Back*, Vol. II, pp. 31—34.

[2] Carlyle, Vol. I, p. 24. In Aristotle's language, "men are easily spoiled, and not every one can bear prosperity" (cf. Dunning, Vol. I, 89).

century A. C.) in discussing the causes which have made government necessary holds the view that "men departed from God and hated their fellow men, and fell into confussion and disorder of every kind; and so God set men over each other imposing the fear of man upon man, and subjecting men to the authority of men, that by this means they might be compelled to some measure of righteousness and just dealing".[1]

The idea that "the institution of government was made necessary by sin and is a divinely appointed remedy for sin" was continued and developed by St. Augustine and St. Gregory the Great. It was "emphatically restated by the ecclesiastical and political writers" of the period from the ninth to the thirteenth century, and found a champion in Pope Hildebrand, Gregory VII (1073—1085).[2]

The verdict of Hindu thinkers on the nature of man is identical. According to Kâmandaka,[3] men are by nature subject to passions and are covetous of one anothers' wealth and wives. "Rare", says Manu,[4] "is the man pure or sinless" (by nature). *Durlabho hi śuchirnarah.* The lower ones tend to usurp the places of the higher. People are prone to interfering with the rights of others[5] and violating morals and manners.[6]

Not that there was no Saturnian golden age of pristine purity and bliss. For, says the *Mahâbhârata*[7] anticipating by over a millennium the dogmas of Father Lactantius and others, "at first there was neither state nor ruler, neither punishment nor anybody to exercise it. The people used to protect one another through innate righteousness (*dharma*) and sense of justice". But, as among Stoics and Canonists, the "fall" of mankind is accounted for by Hindus also on the basis of a postulate of sin, loss of true religion, *moha,* stupidity, and what not.

On the whole, therefore, it is not a roseate romantic conception of human tendencies and instincts that the *Mahâbhârata* offers. The dictum, "spare the rod, and spoil the child", proverbial in western pedagogics, might be dittoed by the Hindu thinkers. For, as we read in the Book on *Śânti*, by nature "men tend to overthrow[8] one another. Left to itself the "whole world would be in a mess" like a devil's workshop. As a rule, men are used to behaving like "the creatures[9] that cannot

[1] *Ibid*, Vol. I, p. 129.
[2] *Ibid*, Vol. II, 143—146, Vol. III, 97, 105, 187.
[3] II, 42.
[4] VII, 22.
[5] *Manu* VII, 21.
[6] *Ibid*, VII, 24.
[7] *Śânti* LIX, 14.
[8] *Ibid* LXVIII, 8.
[9] *Ibid*, LXVIII, 10—12.

see one another when the sun and the moon do not shine", or like the "fishes in shallow waters", or "birds in places safe from molestation where they can fly at each other's throats in a suicidal strife".

Men, we are told, normally acknowledge only one right and that is the right of might. Those who do not part with their property for the asking run the risk of being killed.[1] Wives, children and food of the weak are liable to be seized perforce by the strong. "Murder, confinement and persecution constitute the eternal lot of the propertied classes".[2] The very phrase, 'This is mine' (*Mamedam*), may be lost from the vocabulary, and *mamatva* or property become extinct", — an ideal which is being anxiously sought for in the contemporary Utopia of Soviet Russia.

The natural tendency of human relations,[3] again, according to the *Mahâbhârata*, is toward sexual promiscuity (*yonidoṣa*). The formation of marriage alliances or of stable societies is not instinctively prompted to man as he is . And if possible, he would shirk even agriculture, commerce, and other means of livelihood, preferring a state of slothful ease and "primrose path of dalliance".

Such is the man natural, or man as nature made him, in the political anthropology of the *Mahâbhârata*. This state of license is the furthest removed not only from a Wordsworthian "Nature's holy plan" but also from the picture of original man governed by a law of "reason" as exhibited in Locke's treatises on *Civil Government*. Nor is it anything but antipodal to the Rousseauesque faith in man's natural impulses and idealization of the "human heart by which we live". Instead, therefore, of postulating with the writer of the *Emile* that "all things are good as their Author made them, but everything degenerates in the hands of man", or finding "reason to complain what man has made of man", the Hindu students of political theory set a high premium on the institutions and conventions that make up the artificial thing called civilization. In fact it is to "educate" man out of the deplorable mire of primitive license and beastly freedom that government has been instituted, say they. The state is designed to correct human vices or restrain them and open out the avenues to a fuller and higher life. And all this is possible only because of *danda*.

In all discussions of political theory, therefore, the doctrine of *danda* occupies a foremost place. Some writers have even called their treatises

[1] *Ibid.* LXVIII, 14.
[2] *Ibid.* LXVIII, 19
[3] *Ibid.* LXVIII, 21–22

on politics and statecraft *Danda-nîti* (Laws of Sanction, or Science of *Danda*). In the *Manu Samhitâ*, at any rate, no other category is calculated to command greater attention. For, is not *danda* "divine, God's own son, the protector of all beings, and as powerful as law itself?"[1] Indeed, it keeps all created beings to their respective duties (*sva-dharma*) the "virtues" of Plato or the "functions" of Bradley and other neo-Hegelians, and makes them cooperate to the enjoyment (*bhoga*) or happiness of mankind.[2] Nay, it is in reality "the king, the male (compared with which all other things are female), the manager of affairs, the ruler, the surety for the four orders pursuing their own duties in life".[3] Further, it governs, protects, watches; and, last but not least, is identical with law.[4] To crown all, the whole world is rectified by *danda*[5] and even the gods and demigods are subject to its authority.[6]

Danda, as interpreted by Manu, is obviously the very principle of omnipotence, comparable to the *majestas* of Bodin or the *summa potestas* of Grotius. It is the abstraction of that power whose concrete embodiment is *aiśvarya, svâmitva* or sovereignty in a state, which is explained by Figgis as the real "divine right" of kings. It is absolute, with jurisdiction over all, uncontrolled by any entity.

A ruler *in office* personifies this *danda*, but the ruler *as a person* is subject to it as every other individual is. Hence the inevitable dilemma of kingship in the Hindu theory of the state. It is by wielding this terrible weapon that the king is to preside over and regulate the state. He is the *danda-dhara* i. e. holder or bearer of the instrument of sovereignty, but he is himself liable to be scorched by it, may be one of its first victims for he is not "infallible".

In Hindu political thought, therefore, *danda* is a two-handed engine and cuts both ways. On the one hand, it is a terror to the people and is a corrective of social abuses. It is a moralizer, purifier, and civilizing agent. As Kâmandaka[7] observes, it is by the administration of *danda* that the state can be saved from a reversion to the logic of the fish and utter annihilation, as well as the people set right. It is through fear of punishment, according to the *Śukra-nîti*,[8] that people become "vir-

[1] *Manu*, VII, 14.

[2] *Ibid*, VII, 15; cf. Carr's *Philosophy of Benedetto Croce*, pp. 127 etc.; Bosanquet's *Some Suggestions in Ethics*, pp. 43—44, 64—65; *Pos. Back*, Vol. II, p. 28.

[3] Ibid, VII, 17.

[4] *Ibid*, VII, 18.

[5] *Ibid*, VII, 22.

[6] *Ibid*, VII, 23.

[7] II, 40—42.

[8] IV, I, lines 92—97.

tuous" and refrain from committing aggression or indulging in untruths. *Danda* is efficacious, moreover, in causing the cruel to become mild, the wicked to give up wickedness, and the garrulous to beware of loquacity. It can subdue even beasts, and of course it frightens the thieves and terrifies the enemies into submission as tributaries, demoralizing all those that are wayward. Nay, it is good also for preceptors and can bring them to their senses, should they happen to be addicted to an extra dose of vanity or unmindful of their own avocations.[1] Finally, it is the foundation of civic life, being the "great stay of all virtues"; and all the "methods and means of statecraft" would be fruitless without a judicious exercise of *danda.*[2] Its uses as a beneficent agency in social life are, therefore, unequivocally recommended by Śukra.[3]

But, on the other hand, *danda* is also a most potent instrument of danger to the ruler himself, to the powers that be. For, "unweary lies the head that wears the crown", in more sense than one. The mal-administration of *danda*, says Kâmandaka,[4] leads to the fall of the ruler. If the ruler is wise enough to manipulate it carefully, as Manu observes,[5] it is surely conducive to the greatest good of the people. But what is the guarantee that the holder of the weapon would not bungle with it and handle it thoughtlessly or arbitrarily? Should that be the case, the *danda* would lead to the ruin of the state. And would the office-bearer, the king, got scot-free? By no means. Manu is an advocate of regicide. He does not hestitate to declare that *danda* would smite the king who deviates from his duty,[6] from his "station in life". It would smite his relatives too together with his castles, territories and possessions. The common weal depends, therefore, on the proper exercise of the *summa potestas*, the *aiśvarya*.

Danda thus carries with it its own nemesis, and we are at once reminded of Mill who says in his *Liberty* that "as the king of the vultures would be no less bent upon preying on the flock than any of the minor harpies it was indispensable to be in a perpetual attitude of defence against his beak and claws". It is a like bulwark of people's rights as against the ruler that is furnished by the Hindu doctrine of *danda*, in so far as its efficacy is attributed to the careful handling of it. In the first

[1] IV, I, lines 99—100.
[2] IV, I, lines 101—102.
[3] IV, I, line 98.
[4] II, 39.
[5] VII, 19.
[6] VII, 28—29.

place, Manu would not allow any ill-disciplined man[1] to be the administrator of the *danda*. In the second place, the "greatest amount of wisdom", e. g. that accruing from the "help of councillors and others"[2] is held to be the essential pre-condition for the handling of this instrument. And here is available the logical check on the possible absolutism of the *danda-dhara* in the Hindu theory of sovereignty.

By the doctrine of *danda*, then, the state is conceived as a pedagogic institution or moral laboratory, so to speak, not necessarily a Lycurgan barrack, of course. It is an organization in and through which men's natural vices are purged, and it thereby becomes an effective means to the general uplifting of mankind. Hindu theorists therefore consider the state to be an institution "necessary" to the human race if it is not to grovel in the condition of *mâtsya-nyâya* ruled by the law of beasts. Man, if he is to be man, cannot do without political organization. He must have a state, and must submit to sanction, coercion and punishment, — in a word, to *danda*.

Section 2.

The Theory of Property, Law, and Social Order.

a) The Doctrine of Mamatva (Property).

According to the *Mahâbhârata, Manu Samhitâ, Śukra-nîti* and other texts of Hindu political theory, government is by nature coercive because man is by nature vicious. The state can thus be born only in and through *danda*, i. e. punishment or sanction. It is out of a condition of the "logic of the fish" (*mâtsya-nyâya*) or the Hobbesian and Spinozistic „state of nature", that *danda*[3] brings into existence a well regulated civil society called the state. In Aristotelian terminology *danda* would be the "efficient cause" of the state.

What, now, are the marks of the state? How does it declare its existence? What are its functions? In what manner does it make itself felt among the people? In Hindu theory the state, as soon as it crystallizes itself into shape, conjures up *mamatva* ("mine"-ness, *Eigentum, proprium*) or *svatva* (suum) i. e. property, and *dharma* (law, justice and duty) out of primitive chaos or socioplasmic anarchy. Both these institutions are creations of the state. The state functions itself by gene-

[1] VII, 28.

[2] VII, 30.

[3] *Manu*, VII, 20; Kautilya, I, iv.

rating them, and people recognize it in its activities fostering their nurture. *Mamatva* and *dharma* are therefore two fundamental categories in the political speculation of the Hindus.

Property does not exist in the non-state[1] (*mâtsya-nyâya*) i. e. in the condition of men left to the pursuit of their "own sweet will". In the non-state, of course, men can possess or enjoy, but they do not "own". Property, however, is not mere *bhoga* i. e. enjoying or possessing, its essence consists in *mamatva* or *svatva* i. e. ownership.[2] It is "one's own"-ness that underlies the "magic of property". To be able to say *mamedam*[3] (This is mine) about something constitutes the very soul of owning or appropriation.

This proprietary consciousness is created in men for the first time by the state through its sanction, the *danda*. For it enjoins[4] that vehicles, apparel, ornaments, and jewels must be "enjoyed by those to whom they belong", and that one's wife, children, and — food "must not be encroached upon by others." And it is only through *bhaya*[5] or fear of the state that the people observe these injunctions, and the sanctity of property is kept entire.

A distinction is here brought out between mere *bhoga* and *mamatva* as the basis of the difference between the non-state and the state. In Europe the identical discrimination has been made by Rousseau in his *Social Contract*. "In the state of nature," says he, "there is but possession which is only the effect of the force or right of the first occupant"; whereas "ownership which is founded only upon a positive title" is an incident of "civil society".

Property (*bhoga* plus *mamatva*), then, is a *differentium* between the non-state and the state. And juridically speaking, the property taken cognizance of by the state is *laukika* i. e. worldly, material, or secular, as the *Mitâkṣarâ*, the *Sarasvatî-vilâsa*, and other law-books[6] make it clear. Thus considered, it is necessarily also a *differentium* between the state and the extra-state, e. g. a Sukhâvatî,[7] the transcendental Land of Bliss in Buddhist metaphysical lore. For, in that super-sensual region "beings are not born with any idea of property even with regard to their

[1] *Mahâ.*, *Śânti*, LXVII, 12—14.

[2] *Ibid*, LXVIII, 19.

[3] *Ibid*, LXVIII, 15.

[4] *Ibid*, LXVIII, 16.

[5] *Ibid*, LXVIII, 8.

[6] Cited in Jolly's *Recht*, p. 91: *Svatvam laukikam (das Eigentum ist weltlich)*; *Sarasvatîvilâs "geht vielleicht am weitesten in dieser Richtung" "in dem es die Entstehung des Eigentums aus rein weltlichen Akten betont"*.

[7] *Buddhist Mahâyâna Texts*, Part II, pp. 13, 43, 55.

own body." Besides, according to the *Gîtâ*, property is not to be aquired by ascetics and monks who desire to live, like the Senecan "wise man" or the Catholic Capuchin, an extra-statal or super-political life, in which, as the proverb goes, man is either a beast or a god.

We are not concerned here, however, with property, *laukika* as it is, in its bearings as a legal institution. The Hindu analysis of the distinction between real and personal property or discussion of the right to use, destroy, transfer, bequeath and sell each species of property, need not therefore detain us. We are interested for the present in the concept of property as a political category only, i. e. as influencing the theory of the state. But it may be remarked, in passing, that it is the state backed by *danda* that gives validity to the "seven modes"[1] of acquiring property and to its "three titles"[2] as well as to other legal incidents.[3]

Nor does it fall within our scope to discuss the concept of property as an economic entity. Obviously, of course, the property generated by the state is Aristotelian in its exclusiveness, as the phrase *mamedam* signifies. It does not contemplate the communism of Plato or of More. "A field," says Manu,[4] "belongs to him who cleared away the forests, and a deer to him who first wounded it". This is individualistic tenure and jurisdiction in their primitive form.[5] But no matter whether held in common or private, it is pertinent to observe that the sacredness of property can be established only by the state through its *danda*.

Two miraculous changes are effected in social life, once private property is thus ushered into existence. First, people can sleep at night without anxiety "with doors open."[6] And secondly, women decked with ornaments may walk without fear though "unattended by men".[7]

This sense of security as regards property is therefore the first great achievement in the humanization of Caliban. This is the first item in the civilizing of man by *danda* out of the *mâtsya-nyâya* or "law of beasts and birds".

b) The Doctrine of Dharma.

(Law, Justice, and Duty).

Property is the first acquisition of man through the state. His second acquisition is *dharma*. The doctrine of *dharma* is like the doctrine of

[1] *Manu*, X, 115.

[2] *Vaśishtha*, XVI, 10.

[3] Jolly, 90—92.

[4] IX, 44.

[5] Letourneau's *Property: Its Origin and Development*, p. 72.

[6] *Mahâ, Śânti*, LXVIII, 30.

[7] *Ibid*, LXVIII, 32.

mamatva an essential factor in the theory of the state, and both have their foundations in the doctrine of *danda.*

There is no *dharma* in the non-state,[1] i. e. in the condition of men left to themselves.[2] It comes into existence with the state. *Dharma* is created by the state or rather by its sanction, *danda.*[3] No state, no *dharma. Dharma* does not flourish where "politics" is not, it flourishes only as long as there is the state. In other words, *dharma* appears as *mâtsya-nyâya* disappears, and *dharma* ceases to exist with the extinction of the state. Logically, therefore, a people can have no *dharma* when its statal life is abolished, e. g. through loss of freedom, revolution or anarchy.

We shall now proceed to analyze this *dharma.* What is that category in Hindu thought which, besides property, serves to differentiate the state from the non-state? What is that characteristic, shorn of which, as shorn of *mamatva,* the state would revert to the condition of *mâtsya-nyâya?* The answer to these questions lies in the doctrine of *dharma.*

Dharma is a very elastic term. Like *jus, Recht* and *droit* it has more than one meaning. It really admits of almost all the ambiguities associated with the term "law" as analyzed by Holland in his *Jurisprudence.* Thus there are at least five senses in which *dharma* is used both in scientific treatises as well as in common parlance; viz.,

1. religion, a category of theology, e. g. Confucian *dharma,* Mohammedan *dharma,* Christian *dharma,* Hindu *dharma* etc.,
2. virtue, as opposed to vice or sin, a category of ethics,
3. law, as a category of jurisprudence,
4. justice,
5. duty.

For purposes of political theory we have to neglect 1. and 2. and confine ourselves to the import of *dharma* as law, justice, and duty. The doctrine of *dharma* then enunciates three propositions: — first, that the state differs from the non-state as a law-giving institution; secondly, that the state differs from the non-state as a justice-dispensing institution; and thirdly, that the state differs from the non-state as a duty-enforcing institution.

In the *mâtsya-nyâya* there is no law, no justice, no duty. The state is the originator of law, justice and duty.

---

[1] *Ibid,* LXVII, 1.

[2] *Ibid,* LXVIII, 22.

[3] *Manu,* VII, 14, 15, 18.

A. *Dharma* as law.

Dharma (law) is the creation of the state, and the state, as such, has the sanction of *danda*. Theoretically, therefore, every *dharma*, if it is nothing but *dharma*, is *ipso facto* what should be called "positive" in the Austinian sense. *Dharma* is obeyed as *dharma*, only because of the coercive might of the state. All *dharma-śâstras*, i. e. the legal text books e. g. those of Manu, Yâjnavalkya, Nârada, Brihaspati, and others, would thus automatically acquire the character of "statute"-books simply because their validity, provided they have any validity, depends on the authority of the state. The Yâjnavalkyas and Manus would obviously have no "sanction" in a condition of *mâtsya-nyâya*.

But probably, so far as actual practice is concerned, the *dharma-śâstras* of India had no greater sanctity than as treatises embodying the "positive morality" of the different ages. Let us therefore examine how the nature of *dharma* (as law) was understood by the theorists themselves. As is well known, law as a category of jurisprudence, has passed through two stages in European thought. The same two concepts we notice in Hindu political philosophy also.

In ancient European theory law is the embodiment of eternal justice. Thus according to Demosthenes (fourth century B. C.) laws are the gifts of the gods and the discovery of the sages. In Aristotle's conception law is the rule of god and reason. Stoics like Cicero and Seneca believed that law lies in the hearts of all men.

This doctrine of "natural law", of law as the "king of all things", was maintained by the jurists such as Gaius and others whose views are codified in the *Digest* of Justinian. It was the theory also of Celsus and other Church Fathers. In medieval European (Teutonic)[1] theory, so far as there was any theory independent of the tradition of Roman jurisprudence, law was not something "made" or created at all, but something which existed as a part of the national, or local or tribal life.

The modern theory of law in Europe may be said to have originated in the sixteenth and seventeenth centuries with Bodin and Hobbes in their analysis of sovereignty. It has since become classical, however, as the handiwork of Austin,[2] the father of analytical jurisprudence. According to this view, law is the command of the sovereign enforced by a sanction.

Thus there are two theories of law, — first, law as uncreated or original, existing either as a part of the universal human conscience, taught by "natural reason", or as a custom among the people; and

---

[1] Carlyle, Vol. I, p. 235; Mackenzie's *Studies in Roman Law;* Gomme's *Folklore*, 84—100.

[2] *Lectures on Jurisprudence*, VI.

secondly, law as created by the fiat of a law-maker, as something which is to be obeyed not because it is just, good or eternal, but because it has been enacted by the state. Both these conceptions are to be found among the speculations of Hindu political philosophers. The distinction between positive law and ethics is clearly set forth by Vijnâneśvara (eleventh century) in his notes on the text of Yâjnavalkya[1] in regard to the judicial duties of the King.

The ethical conception of law as the dictate of conscience, i. e. as *jus naturale* has a long tradition in Hindu thought. In the *Brihadâraṇyak-opaniṣat*[2] law is identical with truth and is as powerful as king. It is of course the creation of God. Brahman (God), we are told "was not strong enough." So he "created still further the most excellent *dharma.**** There is nothing higher than law. Thenceforth even a weak man rules a stronger with the help of the law, as with the help of a king. Thus the law is what is called the true. And if a man declares what is truth, they say he declares the law; and if he declares the law, they say he declares what is true. Thus both are the same."

According to Âpastamba,[3] law is what is "unanimously approved in all countries by men of the Aryan society who have been properly obedient to their teachers, who are aged, of subdued senses, neither given to avarice nor hypocrites". In the *Manu-Samhitâ*,[4] again law is whatever is practised and cherished at heart by the virtuous and the learned, who are devoid of prejudices and passions. Vaśiṣtha[5] and Baudhâyana[6] also hold the view that law is the practice of the *śiṣtas* i. e. those whose hearts are free from desire." The *śiṣtas* or *riṣis*, i. e. passionless and unavaricious persons of India are obviously the "sages" of Demosthenes.

And in Yâjnavalkya's Code[7] accordindg to which law is *sadâchâra* i. e. the "practice or conduct of good men", what "seems pleasant or good to one's self", and the "desire that springs from mature consideration," as well as in the *Vyavahâra Darpaṇa*, where law is described as something "eternal and self-existent, the king of kings", far "more powerful and right" than they, we have once more the Oriental counterpart of the Greek, Stoic, Roman and Patristic conceptions of law as morality.

---

[1] Mitra, pp. 32—33; K. L. Sarkar, Lect. IX, p. 116.

[2] I, 4, 14, *The Upaniṣads*, Vol. II, p. 89.

[3] I, 7, 20, 8.

[4] II, 1.

[5] I, 5—6.

[6] I, 1, 1, 4—6.

[7] I, i, Introduction, 7.

In Hindu analysis *dharma* came to be defined as positive law also The conception of law as *râjnâm âjnâ* in Kautilya's language i. e. as. command enforced by sanction finds clear expression in the writings of Nârada, Śukra, Jaimini and his commentator Śabara Svâmi. In Nârada's *Smriti*[1] we are informed that the performance of duty having fallen into disuse, positive law (*vyavahâra*) has been introduced, and that the king as superintending the law is known as *danda-dhara* or wielder of *danda* (the power to punish). The sanction is definitely mentioned in the *Śukra-nîti*,[2] according to which the sovereign should categorically state in his commands that he would "surely destroy by severe punishment those offenders who after having heard these his decrees would act contrary to them."

In order that the law may be seriously recognized as command Śukra stipulates that the greatest amount of publicity should be given to it. For instance, it is the duty of the sovereign to have the laws announced by the state drum[3] or have them inscribed in esplanades as written notices. The documents embodying these commands (*śâsana-patra*)[4] are to bear the king's signature, date, etc. Laws thus being the promulgations of the state, we read further in the *Śukra-nîti*[5] that the king is the "maker of the age", the "cause of time" and of the good and evil practices, and that since the ruler is the dictator of virtues and vices, people make it a point to practise that by which he is satisfied. Besides, as law is upheld by sanction we can easily understand why Śukra advises the sovereign to make use of his terrible weapon[6] in order to maintain the people each in his proper sphere.

The same idea of positive law is expressed by Jaimini in the very definition of *dharma*. As we find in his *Mimâmsâ-Sûtra, chodanâlakṣaṇohrtho dharmah.*[7] *Dharma* is that desired-for object (*artha*) which is characterized by command (*chodanâ*). Jaimini has also examined the reason as to why that which is determined by a command should be obligatory. He analyzes the reason as lying in the fact that "the relation between the word of command and the purpose to which it is directed is eternally efficacious."[8]

---

[1] Introduction, I, 2.

[2] I, lines 623—624.

[3] *Śukra*, I, 625—626.

[4] *Ibid*, II, 607—608.

[5] IV, I, lines 116—119.

[6] *Ibid*, I, 120.

[7] Ganganath Jha's *"Shabara Swami's Commentary on Jaimini's Mimamsa"* in the *Indian Thought* for 1910.

[8] K. L. Sarkar, Lect. I, pp. 23—24.

The doctrine of *dharma* as law introduces into the theory of the state the cardinal element of *aiśvarya* or *svâmitva*, i. e. sovereignty. Whether *dharma* be taken as equivalent to the dictates of a moral sense, or as the observance of a tribal or some other established usage, or as the deliberate order issued by an authority with threat of punishment in case of violation, it is clear enough that *dharma* is like *danda* the most awe-inspiring fact in the state's life. *Danda* and *dharma* are indeed the two faces of the political Janus, so to speak, the one looking to the failures, the other to the triumphs. Or, to express the same thing in a different way, *danda* is the root of a tree which flowers in *dharma*. The state can be recognized positively by *dharma* which is in evidence, while *danda* maintains its vitality from behind.

B. *Dharma* as justice.

We have now to understand the doctrine of *dharma* as justice in its bearing on the theory of the state. Justice does not exist in the *mâtsya-nyâya*; if therefore a reversion to *mâtsya-nyâya* is to be avoided i. e. if the state is to be maintained, justice must not be tampered with. Justice is necessarily as integral a limb of sovereignty in Hindu conception as law.

The dignity of justice has been declared by Manu[1] in the following terms: "If justice is violated, it destroys the state, if preserved, it maintains the state. Therefore justice must not be destroyed". Such sentiments in the *Manu Samhitâ* could be bodily incorporated in the writings of a Jonas or an Alcuin of the ninth century and other mediaeval European theorists[2] with whom the maintenance of justice is the *sine qua non* of the state and kingship.

But what is justice? It is a most practical or pragmatic definition that Hindu theorists offer. According to Manu[3] justice consists in the application of law to the cases arising between the members of the state. And that law is to be known from the customs and from the *Institutes*, e. g. those of Gautama, Yâjnavalkya and others.

Justice, as interpreted by Śukra,[4] consists of two elements. First, it consists in a discrimination of the good from the bad (of course, according to the laws). Secondly, it has a utilitarian basis in as much as it is calculated to minister to the virtues of the rulers and the ruled and promote the common weal.

---

[1] VIII, 15.

[2] Carlyle, III, 109.

[3] VIII, 3.

[4] IV, v, lines 7—11.

The doctrine of *dharma* as justice is thus organically connected with the theory of the state as contrasted with the non-state.

C. *Dharma* as duty.

Mâtsya-nyâya is a condition in which duties are nil. Men left to themselves tend even to persecute[1] their mothers, fathers, the aged, the teachers, the guests and the preceptors. It is the fear of *danda* that brings about an order among men, each man minding his own duty (*sva-dharma*).[2] The doctrine of *dharma* as duty is thus like that of *dharma* as justice naturally a doctrine of the conservation of the state. It is only from this standpoint that the theory of duties has a bearing on the theory of the state.

The doctrine of duty as stated in the *Gîtâ*[3] runs thus: "One's own duty, though defective, is better than another's duty well performed. Death in performing one's own duty is preferable; the performance of the duties of others is dangerous". The passage here has no mere metaphysical significance. This theory of *sva-dharma* (one's own duty) or "My station and Its Duties" as Bradley would define it, has a political significance as well. It has the sanction of the state behind it; for, says Manu[4] "neither a father, nor a teacher, nor a friend, nor a mother, nor a wife, nor a son, nor a domestic priest must be left unpunished if they do not keep within their duty". According to Śukra[5] also, the people should be kept each in his proper sphere by a "terrible use" of the weapon of sovereignty.

Duties are thus enforced by *danda*, which also backs the laws. Indeed from the angle of the *prajâ* or *prakriti* (the people in the state), *dharma* as duty is but the obverse of *dharma* as law. What the state calls "laws" are recognized as "duties" by its members as a matter of course. The doctrine of duty is thus identical with that of law turned inside out.

Altogether, then, the doctrine of *dharma* in its entirety imparts to the state the character of an institution for the advancement of "culture". The state elevates man out of the law of beasts by instituting legislation, adjudication, and enforcement of duties. The functions of the state are thus in keeping with the ideas involved in the doctrine of *danda*. The state as a pedagogic or purgatorial or moral-training institution is not

---

[1] *Mahâ, Śânti*, LXVIII, 16.

[2] *Ibid*, LXVIII, 8; *Manu*, VII, 21, 22, 24; *Śukra*, I, lines 45—51.

[3] ch. III; cf. Bosanquet's *Philosophical Theory of the State*, pp. 204—207; Barker's *Plato*, p. 176.

[4] VIII, 335.

[5] I, line 120; IV, iii, 15.

merely a *mamatva*-insuring instrument i. e. a property-securing agency, but a *dharma*-promoting *samûha* (public association) i. e. a *Kultur-Staat* or the "virtue"-state of Plato. And herein the Hindu theory meets Aristotle's conception of the state as the means to the furtherance of the "highest good" of man.

c) The Doctrine of Varṇâśrama (Classes and Stages).

Out of *mâtsya-nyâya* evolves *dharma* through the fiat of *danda*. Now *dharma* has need to be embodied, i. e. the *Kultur-Staat* must have to materialize itself in space and time. This is accomplished in the *râṣtra*, which provides *aiśvarya* (sovereignty) with "a local habitation and a name". It is in and for the *râṣtra* that the state institutes *mamatva* and *dharma*. Property, law, justice and duty are concretely realized through this medium. The doctrine of *râṣtra* thus furnishes the crowning arch in the Hindu theory of the state.

What is this *râṣtra*? It signifies "the country". Both "movable and immovable things" are indicated by the term.[1] It is a territorial concept comprehending an aggregate of human beings and material possessions and thus constitutes the "physical basis" of the state. It may be taken almost as equivalent to *res publica*. The doctrine of *râṣtra* would therefore naturally consist of two parts: (1) the doctrine of property and (2) the doctrine of *prajâ*, *prakriti* or population. The doctrine of property has already been investigated. Let us now examine the doctrine of population in its bearing on the theory of the state.

In the *mâtsya-nyâya* condition there is the people, but no state, because there is no *danda* to enforce *dharma*. If the *prajâ* is not to remain *ad infinitum* an amorphous mass of *selbstandig* atoms, it must have to follow *sva-dharma*, i. e. the members of the society must perform their respective "duties", which, as we have seen, are really "laws" turned inside out. The observance of these duties would necessarily imply the organization of the people into a unified state, a *samûha* or a *polis*.

Now, communally speaking, the *prakriti* or members of a society naturally fall into economic and professional groups, classes or orders, the so-called castes of India. The alleged classification of a society into four occupational groups, e. g. Brâhmaṇa, Kṣatriya, etc. is however a conventional myth, at best, a legal fiction. Students of *Realpolitik* like Śukra[2] are aware that the actual number of these orders or castes is "unlimited". The reason, as may be guessed, is stated in the *Śukra-nîti*

[1] IV, iii, line 2.

[2] IV, iii, lines 22—23.

to be the "intermixture of blood through marriages". These orders of *prajâ* or classes of members of the state are known as *varṇas*[1] i. e. colors, probably designated after some typical (or hypothetical?) ethnic complexion. Further, from the standpoint of the individual, we have to notice that people pass through well-marked physiological stages, e. g. infancy, adolescence, etc. These stages or periods of life in every person are called the *âśramas*.[2] They are arbitrarily known to be four in the span of human existence.

The total population with all its interests and problems of all the different periods of life is then comprehended by the two categories, *varṇas* (classes) and *âśramas* (stages). If therefore the people is to constitute a state, every member of each of the *varṇas* (no matter what their number and what their occupations) must have to perform the duties (*sva-dharma*) of his "station" at each of the four *âśramas* or periods of life. Thus, the soldier at the front must "do or die", the young man while at school must not marry, the king must keep to the coronation oath, and so forth. This is the doctrine of *varṇâśrama*,[3] the counterpart of the Platonic correlation of "virtue" and status (*Republic*, II, III, IV).

As soon, therefore, as the *prajâ* is organized into a state, be it in any part of the world or in any epoch of history, a *varṇâśrama* spontaneously emerges into being. It is inconceivable, in this theory, that there should be a state and yet no *varṇâśrama*. To say that the state has been born and yet the various orders or classes of the people do not follow *dharma* would indeed be a contradiction in terms, a logical absurdity. *Sva-dharma* leads inevitably to *varṇâśrama*, the two are "relative" terms. They indicate coexistent phenomena in the social world. In other words, the doctrine of *varṇâśrama* is a corollary to that of *dharma* as duty, *varṇâśrama* is but *sva-dharma* "writ large".

The non-existence of *varṇâśrama* is possible only under conditions of non-performance of duty. Suppose the *varṇas* do not follow *dharma*, e. g. the soldier flies from the enemy in a cowardly manner, the husband does not maintain the wife, the judge encourages the fabrication of false evidence, the king violates the *samaya* or compact with the *prakriti*, and so forth. According to Śukra[4] the offenders are to be rectified by the *danda* of the state. This is the supreme moment for the exercise of *aiśvarya* (sovereignty). Why, even the king is not immune from penalty.

---

[1] Kâmandaka, II, 18—21.

[2] *Ibid*, II, 22—31.

[3] Kâmandaka II, 35; *Pos. Back*. Vol. II, p. 90.

[4] IV, iv, 6, 82—83.

Rather, as Manu[1] declares "the settled rule", where "a common man would be fined one *kârṣâpaṇa*, the king shall be fined one thousand". Really, a state is no state unless it can enforce as duty the *dharma* that it has enacted as law. This should be postulated in the irreducible minimum of the state's functions. One can therefore easily understand with Kâmandaka[2] why if *dharma* is violated by the members of the state there is bound to be a *pralaya* or dissolution of the world. Verily, with the extinction of *varṇâśrama* there is a reversion to *mâtsya-nyâya*. The violation of *sva-dharma* and of *varṇâśrama* brings back the "state of nature", and the state automatically ceases to exist.

Varṇâśrama, though obviously a socio-pedagogic and ethnico-economic term, is thus fundamentally a political concept. It is an indispensable category in an organic theory of the state. It is identical with *râṣṭra* from the demographic (*prajâ* or population) aspect. The doctrine of *varṇâśrama* is therefore the doctrine of *râṣṭra minus* the doctrine of property; and further, the doctrine of *dharma* (as law and duty) applied to the total *prakriti* (or members of the state) coincides with the doctrine of classes and stages. The doctrine of *varṇâśrama* then is clearly an integral part in a consistent philosophy of politics.

Section 3.

The Theory of International Relations.

a) *The Doctrine of Mandala (Sphere of Influence).*

The conception of "external" *aiśvarya* (sovereignty) was well established in the Hindu philosophy of the state. The Hindu thinkers not only analyzed sovereignty with regard to the constituent elements in a single state. They realized also that sovereignty is not complete unless it is external as well as internal, that is, unless the state can exercise its internal authority unobstructed by, and independently of, other states.

"Great misery", says Śukra, "comes of dependence on others. There is no greater happiness than that from self-rule". This is one of the maxims of the *Śukra-nîti*[3] bearing on the freedom of the *râṣṭra*, or the

[1] VIII, 336.

[2] II, 34.

[3] Ch. III, line 646. It is not the object of this section to describe the Hindu laws of peace, war and neutrality, for which see Visvanath's "International Law in Ancient India" in the *Mod. Rev.*, April-November 1918, and Pramatha Nath Banerji's "International Law and Custom in Ancient India" in the *Journal of the Department of Letters*, Vol. I (Calcutta University), 1921.

land and the people in a state. Kautilya also in his remarks on "foreign rule" expresses the same idea in a negative manner. Under it, we are told in his *Artha-śâstra*,[1] the country is not treated as one's own land, it is impoverished, its wealth carried off, or it is treated "as a commercial article". The description is suggestive of John Stuart Mill's metaphor of the "cattle farm" applied to the "government of one people by another."

The doctrine of independence (*svârâjya, aparâdhînatva*) implied in this conception of external sovereignty was obviously the foundation of the theory of the state in relation with other states. And it gave rise to certain categories of *droit des gens* or *jus gentium* which normally influenced Hindu political thinking from at least the fourth century B. C. These concepts can more or less be grouped under the doctrine of *mandala*, that is, sphere or circle (of influence, interests, ambitions, enterprise, and what not).

This doctrine of *mandala*, underlying as it does the Hindu idea of the "balance of power," pervades the entire speculation on the subject of international relations. It is hinted at by Śukra[2] and referred to by Manu.[3] Kâmandaka[4] has devoted a whole chapter to the topic. It has been exhaustively treated by Kautilya.[5] We are not concerned here with the doctrine as such; we shall only study it in its bearing on the theory of sovereignty.

In the first place, the doctrine of *mandala* is essentially the doctrine of *vijigîṣu* (aspirant to conquest) or *Siegfried*. It is the cult of expansion. Now, the *Mahâbhârata*[6] inculcates the ethics of "manliness as the highest thing" and characterizes it as consisting in a ceaseless "upward striving". The same aspiration to "press only up" and "bend not" or "elect glory even at the cost of life" can influence each and all of the states on earth. The doctrine becomes necessarily a spur to the struggle for existence, self-assertion and world domination among the *Siegfrieds*. The conception is thus altogether a dynamic factor calculated to disturb the equilibrium and *status quo* of international politics.

First, then, in regard to the doctrine of *vijigîṣu*. According to Kau-

---

[1] Book VIII, ch. II, *Ind. Ant.*, 1910, p. 83. For older uses of the concept of *sva-râj* (self-rule) *vide* the *Atharva-Veda*, XVII, I, 22, 23, also Macdonell and Keith's *Vedic Index*, Vol. II, p. 494; the *Mod. Rev.* March 1919.

[2] IV, I, lines 39—43.

[3] VII, 154, 156, 207.

[4] Ch. VIII.

[5] Book VI, ch. II.

[6] Book XII, ch. 56, verse 15; V, 127, 19—20; V, 134, 39; *J. A. O. S.*, 1889, pp. 156, 187—189.

tilya,[1] it is the ambition of each state to acquire "strength and happiness" for the people. The *élan vital* of a ruler in Kâmandaka's conception[2] also lies in the "aspiration to conquer". The king, says he, should establish in himself the *nâbhi* (or centre of gravity) of a system. He should become the lord of a *mandala*. It is part of his duty to try to have "a full sphere around him" just as the "moon is encircled by a complete orb". The "full sphere" is, of course, the circle of states related to the *Siegfried* as allies, enemies and neutrals. Perpetual "preparedness" must therefore be the first postulate of *Realpolitik* in Hindu theory. "One should be ever ready with *danda*" (the "mailed fist"), declares Manu[3] naively, "should always have one's might in evidence and policies well-guarded, as well as be ever on the look out for the enemy's holes". Further, one should "bring to subjection all those elements that are obstacles to the career of triumph".[4]

The *rationale* of this preparedness is very simple indeed. It is as elemental as human blood itself. It goes without question in *Śukra-nîti*[5] that "all rulers are unfriendly", nay, they are "secret enemies to those who are rising, vigorous, virtuous and powerful". "What wonder in this?" asks Śukra, and his solution is given in another query which carries its own answer: viz., "Are not the rulers all covetous of territory?" Such being the data of international psychology, Kâmandaka[6] frankly suggests that "in order to do away with one's enemies their kith and kin should be employed" whenever possible. For, is not poison out-done by poison, diamond cut by diamond, and the elephant subdued by the elephant? "Fishes, again, swallow fishes, similarly relatives relatives." The *Râmâyaṇa* is cited in the *Kâmandakî-nîti* for a corresponding precedent in diplomatic tactics. The fact is well known that in order to overthrow Râvaṇa his brother Vibhîṣaṇa was exploited by Râma.

The *vijigîṣu*, then, cannot by any means afford to indulge in pious wishes or have faith in the Utopian statecraft of idealistic dreamers. What under these conditions are likely to be the relations between the hypothetical Siegfrieds of the *nîti-śâstras*? These firebrands are normally endowed with a war-mentality and a bellicose attitude. The world in their eyes is a theater of warfare and equipment for warfare, as it has really been since the Chinese philosopher Sun Tzu's *Art of War*; and they

---

[1] *Ind. Ant.*, 1909, p. 284.
[2] VIII, 1, 3, 6.
[3] VII, 102.
[4] *Manu*, VII, 107.
[5] IV, I, lines 15—17.
[6] VIII, 58, 67.

proceed on the assumption that nothing can be unfair in war. The student of political science must therefore have to make almost the same remarks about the "aspirants" of Hindu political speculation as those of Grotius in the prolegomena to his epoch-making *Laws of War and Peace* (1625). "I saw prevailing throughout the Christian world", writes the father of international law, in regard to the European international politics of the early seventeenth century, "a license in making war of which even barbarous nations would have been ashamed. Recourse was had to arms for slight reason or no reason, and when arms were taken up, all reverence for divine and human law thrown away, just as if men were henceforth authorized to commit all crimes without restraint".

The *vijigīṣu* would think like Maude of the British War-office that the "surest means of keeping the peace is war", or like Stockton, the American militarist, that "the army and the navy is not a burden during peace, but if properly maintained is but a paying business proposition". He can also have the idealism of a Hegel in order to support his *sâdhanâ* or *Streben* to win the place in the sun, and if necessary may as well induct the ancient Greek sophists in his service to prove that might is right.

The theorists who propounded the cult of *vijigīṣu* would have been in good company with the philosophers of ancient Greece. In Aristotle's postulate of "natural" slaves, "natural" masters, "natural" wars, and so forth, the writers of the *nīti-śâstras* could easily find a place for the "natural" aspirations, "natural" allies and "natural" enemies of their doctrine of *mandala*. The *Politica* assumes that the "barbarians", or non-Greeks, were intended by nature to be slaves[1] and ruled by the Greeks. And since slaves are "property" like "other things", warfare with the object of making slaves and thus acquiring wealth is a legitimate and "naturally just" occupation.[2] This Aristotelian justification of warfare can be easily recognized as forming the theoretical basis and psychological background of all wars from the conquests of Alexander and the Roman Caesars down to the Thirty Years' War.[3] Furthermore, the methods and tactics of the Christian *vijigīṣus* who are responsible for the expansion of Europe in Asia, Africa and America, can all be traced to the dicta of the father of political science, though as a rule moralists are apt to associate them with the teachings of Machiavelli's *Prince* (1513).

---

[1] Book I, chs. ii, vi.

[2] Book I, ch. viii.

[3] Lawrence's *Essays on Modern International Law*, IV. *Vide* Machiavelli's *Discourses*, Bk. II, xxi, Willoughby, pp. 77—78, Lilly's *First Principles in Politics*, p. 56, Hobhouse's *Metaphysical Theory of the State*, pp. 100—103, Stockton, p. 203.

The opinions adumbrated in the *nîti-śâstras* are in any case neither exclusively oriental nor exclusively medieval or primitive. Nor need they be dubbed exclusively Machiavellian. For, has not the *Prince* furnished the fundamental logic of statesmen from the Athenian Pericles and Macedonian Philip down to the Metternichs, Bismarcks and Cavours of our own times? "Also it must be recognized", as Figgis, justifying the methodology of Machiavelli, says in his volume on political theory, *From Gerson to Grotius*,[1] "that in a state of things like international politics, where there is no recognized superior, and even International Law is but the voice of public opinion, the condition of affairs is very much more nearly akin to the state of nature as imagined by Hobbes than it is in the relation of individuals". It is on such considerations that, like Machiavellism, the doctrine of *vijigîṣu* maintains its legitimate place in a theory of international relations. It provides an unvarnished statement of the only hypothesis which can satisfactorily explain the innate militarism that the human world inherits from "beasts and birds".

Let us now examine the other aspect of the doctrine of *mandala*, that of the struggle for existence and "place in the sun" among the states. To a *vijigîṣu*, as Bhîṣma[2] declares, "right is that which a strong man understands to be right"; and the international *mores* of the *Mahâbhârata*[3] is summed up in the dictum that "victory is the roo. of right", just as its creed of life for the individual appraises "death as better than lack of fame". How, then, is this quest of fame, victory or world-domination to be regulated by each state in competition with the others? Are there any rules or methods by which the competing states may guide themselves in this conflict of aspirations? These constitute in substance a natural corollary to the doctrine of *vijigîṣu*.

The "proper study" of the *vijigîṣu*, a Kaiser Wilhelm *in posse*, is, according to the *Manu Samhitâ*,[4] his own and his enemy's spheres. And how are these spheres located in his imagination? Śukra gives a brief summary of the Siegfried's investigations as to the "balance of forces" or "conjuncture of circumstances" with a view to the "Next War." We are told that the enemies diminish in importance according as they are remote from the "centre of the sphere." First to be dreaded by the *vijigîṣu* are those who are situated around or very near his own state, then those who live farther away,[5] and so on. With the remote-

[1] Page 101.

[2] *Mahâ.*, Book II, ch. 69, verse 15.

[3] *J. A. O. S.*, 1889, pp. 187—189.

[4] VII, 154.

[5] *Śukra-nîti*, IV, 1, lines 39—41.

ness of location, enmity, hatred or rivalry naturally declines. Whether a state is to be treated as inimical, indifferent or friendly depends *per se* on its propinquity or distance. The geographical distribution of states influences their psychology in regard to their neighbors as a matter of course in such an order that the positive antipathy of the nearest dwindles into tolerable apathy of the next and gives way to active sympathy and even friendliness of the farthest distant. This, however, is not the only possible grouping of powers in a *vijigîṣu's* estimation. The *Śukranîti*[1] gives another order in which the states may be distributed. According to this computation, first are situated the enemies, then come the friends, next the neutrals, and the most remote on all sides are the enemies again.

These are the elementary principles of international dealings of which élaborate accounts are given in the writings of Kautilya and Kâmandaka. The theory holds that there is a hypothetical tug-of-war always being fought between the *vijigîṣu* and his *ari* (the enemy). These two are the combatants or belligerents. Along with these are to be counted another two states in order to furnish a logical completeness to the hypothesis. The *quadrivium*[2] consists of the following members:

1. The *vijigîṣu*: the aspirant, e. g., an Alexander "mewing his might," bent on "conquering and to conquer;"

2. The *ari* (the enemy): the one that is situated anywhere immediately on the circumference of the aspirant's territory;[3]

3. The *madhyama* (the mediatory): the one (located close to the aspirant and his enemy) capable of helping both the belligerents, whether united or disunited, or of resisting either of them individually;[4]

4. The *udâsîna* (the indifferent or the neutral): the one (situated beyond 1, 2, and 3) very powerful and capable of helping the aspirant, the enemy and the mediatory, together or individually, or resisting any of them individually.[5]

These four states, then, constitute the smallest onit of international grouping. From the standpoint of the *vijigîṣu* all other states are either his own allies or the allies of his enemy. Such states are held to be eight

---

[1] *Ibid*, IV, i, lines 42—43.

[2] *Kâmandakî*, VIII, 20; *Manu*, VII, 156.

[3] *Artha*, Book VI, ch. ii, in the *Ind. Ant.* for 1909, p. 283. For a fuller account of the Kautilyan *Mandala* see Law's *Inter-state Relations in Ancient India*. He suggests new terminology for states 3. and 4. in the *quadrivium* (*vide*, pp. vi, 13). But so far as the problem before the *vijigîṣu* is concerned the new terms do not seem to introduce any new point of view (p. 31).

[4] *Ibid*. According to Law, *madhyama* — "medium power" state, cf. *Inter-state etc.*, p. 10.

[5] *Ibid*. Law describes *udâsîna* as the "super-power" (*Ibid*, pp. 9—13).

in number according to the hypothesis. How, now, is the "aspirant" to pick up his own allies from the crowd? He need only study the geographical position of these states with reference to the belligerents, i. e., to himself and to his enemy.

The *madhyama* (the mediatory) and the *udâsîna* (the neutral) may be neglected by the Siegfried, for the time being, in his calculation of the possible array of forces directly allied or inimical to his career of conquest. The two belligerents, with the eight others (divided in equal proportion as their allies *in potentia*), are then located in the following order of *entente cordiale* by Kâmandaka[1] and Kautilya.[2]

The "aspirant" occupies, of course, the hypothetical centre. Next to his front is the "enemy." Now we have to calculate frontwards and rearwards. Frontwards: next to the "enemy" is situated (1) the aspirant's ally, next to that is (2) the enemy's ally, next (3) the ally of the aspirant's ally, and last (4) the ally of the enemy's ally. Rearwards from the aspirant: First is situated (1) the rearward enemy, next is (2) the rearward ally, then comes (3) the ally of the rearward enemy, and last (4) the ally of the rearward ally.

There is nothing queer, archaic or unworkable in this conception of international relations. A simple illustration would show how humanly the political theorists of India approached the foreign policy of nations. Thus, for instance, according to the Kautiliyan doctrine of *mandala*, the "natural enemies" of France engaged in studying the *modus operandi* for "the next war" would be Spain, England and Germany, and her "natural allies" Portugal, Scotland, Ireland and Russia. A French *vijigiṣu*, e. g., a Napoleon, embarking on a war with Germany, should begin by taking steps to keep his "rear safe." With this object he should have Spain attacked by Portugal, and manage to play off the anti-English forces in Ireland and Scotland in such a manner that England may be preoccupied at home and unable to attack France in support of Germany. As Germany, on the other hand, is likely to have China as her natural ally (supposing there is no other state between Russia and the Far East), the French *vijigiṣu* should set Russia against China, and so on. It is obvious that the diplomatic feats conceived by the Hindu political philosophers could be verified almost to the letter by numerous instances in European and Asian history, especially in ancient and medieval times when Eur-Asia was divided into numberless nationalities.

[1] VIII, 16, 17.

[2] Book VI, ch. II, *Ind. Ant.*, 1909, p. 284.

Nay, the principle of Kautilyan *mandala* is in operation even now in the numerous states carved out of the old Germanistic empires (1918). For instance, the manner in which Poland is being bolstered up by France against Germany on the one hand and Soviet Russia on the other is in keeping with the adumbrations of the Old Asian Richelieu. Italy's pro-Hungarian sentiments as against Jugo-Slavia (1921) are also explicable quite easily by the *nîti* theory of political geography.

Be this as it may, we have to observe that the group of ten states or a *decennium* constitutes one complete *mandala*. The *vijigîṣu* is the centre of gravity of this sphere. Now each state can have the same legitimate aspiration, that is, each can be fired by the same ambition to form and figure out a sphere of its own. The inevitable result is a conflict of interests, a pandemonium of Siegfrieds united in discord. The problem of statesmen in each state is to find out the methods of neutralizing the policies of others by exploiting the enemies of its rivals in its own interests. The doctrine of *mandala* thus makes of *nîti-śâstra* or political science essentially a science of enmity, hatred, espionage and intrigue, and an art of thousand and one methods of preparedness for "the next war."

We need not go into the details of the *Machtpolitik* conceived in Kautilya's *Artha-śâstra* or in the sections on warfare in the *Śukra-nîti*. But it is already clear that the doctrine of *mandala* has launched us at last into *mâtsya-nyâya*,[1] the logic of the fish, the Hobbesian law of beasts, anarchy. The doctrine assumes and is prepared for a world of eternally warring states. While "internal" soverignty dawns as the "logic of the fish" sets, "external" sovereignty postulates the existence of the same logic as a fact in international relations. In one instance *danda*[2] or punishment, that is, "sanction" of the state, is exercised to crush anarchy, but it is apparently in order to maintain a world-wide anarchy that *danda* or *Faust-recht* is employed by one state against another. The theory of the state is thus reared on two diametrically opposite conceptions:

1. The doctrine of *danda*, which puts an end to *mâtsya-nyâya* among the *prajâ* or members of a single state;
2. The doctrine of *mandala*, which maintains an international *mâtsya-nyâya* or the civil war of races in the human family.

From one anarchy, then, the state emerges only to plunge headlong into another. This is the dilemma that pervades the political philosophy of the Hindus.

---

[1] Kautilya, I, iv; Kâmandaka, II, 40.

[2] Manu, VII, 20; Śukra, I, line 45.

b) The Doctrine of Sârva-bhauma (World-Sovereign).

The Hindu theory of sovereignty did not stop, however, at the doctrine of a universal *mâtsya-nyâya*, that is of a world in which each state is at war with all. It generated also the concept of universal peace through the establishment of a *Weltherrschaft* as in Dante's *De Monarchia.*[1] The doctrine of *mandala* as a centrifugal force was counteracted by the centripetal tendencies of the doctrine of *sârva-bhauma* (the ruler over the whole earth). With this theory of the world-state and *Pax Sârvabhaumica* we shall conclude our present study.

In Europe the idea or ideal of a universal empire took most definite shape towards the beginning of the fourteenth century "exactly when the actual development of the modern nationalities was rendering it practically impossible."[2] This crisis and this transition in Western political thought are best represented in Bartolus (1314—1357), the "prince of jurists," for he began[3] by seeing a single universal empire, but he ended by recognizing a miniature empire in every *de facto* independent power. The same conception of a world sovereignty or a *federation de l'empire* is however as old in India as the political philosophers of the earliest Vedic period.

"Monarchy at its highest," we read in the *Aitareya Brâhmaṇa,*[4] "should have an empire extending right up to natural boundaries, it should be territorially all-embracing, up to very ends uninterrupted, and should constitute and establish one state and administration up to the seas." The ancient theorists were evidently thinking of the Indian continent as identical with the entire world. The achievement of a pan-Indian nationality was in their eyes the equivalent of a world federation just as in medieval European theory the unification of western Christendom was tantamount to the constitution of one state for all mankind, or as in the Eur-American world-peace movements of today "the world" is postulated to be the territories inhabited by albinoes or white races.

This theory of a world-nationalism (or, what is the same thing, a United Indianism) exercised a powerful influence on the political speculations of the Hindus. It grave rise to set formulae and slogans that fired the imaginations of the Alexanders, Charlemagnes and Fredericks of India through the ages. The *Aitareya Brâhmaṇa*[5] records some of

---

[1] I, 4, I, 8, I, 10, etc.

[2] Carlyle, Vol. III, 179. But the concept of Dantesque universal monarchy is as old as Cicero. *Vide* Atger's *Histoire des doctrines du Contrat Social*, p. 26.

[3] Woolf, 45, 109, 196.

[4] VIII, 4, 1, in Mookerji's *Fundamental*, p. 89.

[5] VIII, 1, 39.

the ambitions and ideals of the Young India of the sixth century B.C. and beyond. "I want to attain to lordship over all rulers," proclaims one aspirant, "I want to achieve the conquest of both space and time . . . I want to be *sârva-bhauma* . . . and be the *eka-rât* (sole monarch) of the earth up to the skies."

Hindu political thought produced several other categories to express the same idea of the world-state or universal sovereignty. We have, first, the doctrine of *chakravarti.* It indicates that the *chakra* or wheel of the state-chariot rolls everywhere without obstruction. The wheel is the symbol of sovereignty. Or, if *chakra*[1] be taken as denoting a country from sea to sea, the *chakravarti* would be the ruler of a state from sea to sea (i. e., extending to the farthest limits). It is this conception of a political "dominion," of a secular overlordship, that is employed metaphorically with a spiritual significance in the conception of the Lord Buddha as *Chakkavatti.* "A king am I, Sela," says Buddha[2] using the language of his contemporary imperialists, "the king supreme of righteousness. The royal chariot-wheel in righteousness do I set rolling on— that wheel that no one can turn back again."

Secondly, we have the doctrine of *sârva-bhauma* expressed in the more popular and conventional conception of *samrât.* The *Mahâbhârata,* for instance, uses this category in order to convey the idea of a world dominion. "There are *râjâs* (kings) in every home (state) doing what they like," we read in the Book on *Sabhâ,*[3] "but they have not attained to the rank of *samrât*; for that title is hard to win." And this rank is at last won by Yudhisthira in the epic. Yudhisthira would thus be the *Veltro* of the *Divine Comedy.*

Another category in which the doctrine of *sârva-bhauma* is manifest is that of *châturanta,* of which Kautilya[4] availed himself in order to establish his ideal of imperial nationalism. The *châturanta* state is that whose authority extends up to the remotest *antas* (limits) of the *chatur* (four) quarters. The ruler of such a state *ananyâm prithivîm bhumkte,* i. e., enjoys the whole earth with none to challenge his might. In the *Artha-śâstra,* he is known also as *chakravarti,* for the territory of such a *châturanta* is called *chakravarti kṣetra* (dominion of a *chakravarti*).

The *sârva-bhauma, chakravarti, samrât,* or *châturanta* of Hindu political theory is identical with the *dominus omnium,* or lord of *univer-*

---

[1] Monier Williams' *Dictionary.*

[2] *Sela-sutta* in *Sutta-nipâta,* III, 7, 7; Hardy's *Manual of Buddhism,* p. 126.

[3] *Mahâ, Sabhâ* XV, 2.

[4] *Artha,* I, v, vii.

sitas quaedum in Bartolus's terminology,[1] the *hwangti* of the Chinese.[2] He is "the monarch of all I survey." He rules a state whose limits extend from sea to sea (*âsamudra-kṣitīśa*), and his chariots have free passage up to the skies (*ânâka-ratha-vartma*), as Kâlidâs, the Virgil of India, puts it in his *Raghu-vamśa* ("The House of Raghu"). The pretensions of the doctrine of *sârva-bhauma* thus bear close analogy with the universal authority claimed by Hildebrand (*c*1075) for the Papacy, or with that rival conception of his opponents, the Ghibelline imperialism of the Hohenstaufens. Herein is to be perceived the Hindu counterpart of the doctrine, albeit from the monarchical angle, of a single state for entire humanity, the futurist version of which has embodied itself from time to time in diverse forms, — in the visions of "permanent peace," or in the pious wishes for a "parliament of man" or for the now almost discredited "league of nations," or for its antithesis, the communist "Third International" of the proletarian world.

The doctrine of *sârva-bhauma* does not stand alone in Hindu political philosophy. It is backed up by several other concepts which may be regarded as its logical feeders. First is the concept of the gradation of rulers in the scale of *aiśvarya* (sovereignty). The *Rig Veda*,[3] the *Śatapatha Brâhmaṇa*,[4] and other ancient documents recognize a hierarchy or graded rank of states from the lowest unit up. According to the *Aitareya Brâhmaṇa*[5] the smallest nationality is a *râjya*. From this rung the ladder gradually takes us through higher or larger "powers" like the *sâmrâjya*, *svârâjya*, *vairâjya*, and *mahârâjya* up to the greatest power, known as the *âdhipatya*.

Another scale of small nationalities, medium states, and great powers is furnished in the following schedule of the *Śukra-nīti* thus:[6]

Title	*Annual Income in Silver Karṣa*[7]
1. *Sâmanta*	1 to 3 hundred thousand
2. *Mâṇḍalika*	3 hundred thousand to 1 million
3. *Râjâ*	1 million to 2 million
4. *Mahârâja*	2 million to 5 million
5. *Svarâṭ*	5 million to 10 million
6. *Samrâṭ*	10 million to 100 million
7. *Virâṭ*	100 million to 500 million
8. *Sârva-bhauma*	500 million and up

[1] Woolf, pp. 22, 196.

[2] Hardy, p. 126.

[3] IV, 21, 1.

[4] XI, 3, 2, 1, 6

[5] VIII, 4, 1.

[6] Ch. I, lines 365—374. *Vide* Rao's "Kings, Crowns, and Thrones in Ancient and Mediaeval India" in the *Mod. Rev.*, Feb. 1917.

[7] A little more than 25 cents in present United States currency.

The *sârva-bhauma* is further described as being that ruler "to whom the earth with its seven islands is ever bound."

This concept of a scale of nationalities or a rank of states, as "first class powers" or "great powers" and "small nations" or the like, according to income and title, is essentially linked up in Hindu theory with the concept of political *yajnas*, sacrifices and rituals, which are fully described in the *Brâhmaṇas*. The *Gopatha Brâhmaṇa*[1] says that Prajâpati became *râjâ* by *râjasûya* sacrifice, *samrât* by *vâjapeya*, *svarât* by *aśvamedha*, *virât* by *puruṣamedha*, and so forth. We need not go into the details of these rituals. We have only to note that not every ruler is entitled to perform any and every sacrifice. Each sacrifice has its own value or mark of sovereignty attached to it; the dignity, might and rank of states being dependent on the character of the sacrifice performed.

According to the *Śatapatha Brâhmaṇa*,[2] again, the office of the king is the lower and that of the emperor the higher, and therefore one becomes king by offering the *rajâsûya*, and by the *vâjapeya* one becomes emperor. But the *râjasûya* is known to be the highest sacrifice in the *Taittirîya Brâhmaṇa*,[3] for according to this work, it can be performed only by universal monarchs exercising sovereignty over a large number of princes as the lord of an imperial federation. The *Aitareya Brâhmaṇa*[4] also says that by virtue of the *râjasûya*, *Janamejaya*, *Saryâta* and ten other rulers, "subdued the earth" and became "paramount sovereigns." In the *Âpastamba Śrauta Sûtra*,[5] however, *aśvamedha* (horse-killing) sacrifice possesses the greatest dignity, for it can be performed by a *sârva-bhauma* (the ruler of the whole earth).

It is obvious that authorities differ as to the relative importance of the political sacrifices, but all are united in the concept that the rituals have a state-value on their face, and that it is the greatest power or the largest nationality alone that is entitled to the highest sacrifice (be it the *râjasûya* or the *aśvamedha*, or what not). The concept of *yajna*, like that of the scale of the states, is therefore an important element in the theory of *Weltherrschaft*, world-monarchy or federated universe embodied in the doctrine of *sârva-bhauma*.

Last but not least in importance as a foundation for the doctrine

---

[1] Part I, pp. 77, 78, in the *Bibl. Ind.*; *vide* Law's "Forms and Types of States in Ancient India" in the *Mod. Rev.*, Oct., 1916.

[2] V, 1, 1, 13.

[3] Rajendralal Mitra's *Indo-Aryans*, Vol. II, p. 2, 3.

[4] VIII, 21—23.

[5] XX, 1, 1.

of *sârva-bhauma* is the concept of *dig-vijaya*[1] or conquest of the quarters. It implies that there is no longer a mere *vijigîṣu* or aspirant, awaiting his chance, mewing his might, or watching the conjuncture for "the next war." The Siegfried has conquered the quarters of the globe, he has realized his highest ambitions. The wheel of his chariot has rolled to the very extremities of the world, and there is none to question his power and prestige. All rival states have been subdued by him. He has brought them to subjection almost in the manner that Napoleon wished when he said in 1804: "There will be no rest in Europe until it is under a single chief, an emperor who shall have kings for officers, who shall distribute kingdoms to his lieutenants, and shall make this one king of Italy, that one of Bavaria; this one ruler of Switzerland, that one governor of Holland, each having an office of honor in the imperial household." *Dig-vijaya* has conferred on the *vijigîṣu* the chiefship of such a Napoleonic league of nations.

It is under these conditions of a "conquest of the quarters" that the hero of the *Raghu-vamśa* is authorized to celebrate the *viśva-jit* (indicating world subjugation) sacrifice at the end of his Alexandrine exploits. *Dig-vijaya* brings about a situation in which there is absolutely no scope for the doctrine of *mandala* or international *mâtsya-nyâya*. The world is at peace under the undisputed sway of the lord of the *universitas quaedum*, the *sârva-bhauma*. The unstable equilibrium of a *vijigîṣu's* hypothetical *mandala* has given way to the *pax sârva-bhaumica* established by the *de facto* monopoly of world control through *dig-vijaya*.

A natural concomitant of the concept of *dig-vijaya* is the idea that the *sârva-bhauma* has all the other rulers related to him not as to the *vijigîṣu* of a *mandala*, that is, not as to the ambitious storm-centre of an international sphere, but bound as to a *râja-râja* or king of kings, to whom allegiance is due as overlord. With the rise of the *sârva-bhauma*, the *mandala* necessarily disappears. The old order of the "enemy," the "neutral" and other states has vanished, the new order of the world-state has arisen. An epoch of universal peace has replaced the age of warring nationalities, conflicting *ententes*, armed neutralities, and militant attitudes. The doctrine of *sârva-bhauma*, as the concept of federal nationalism, imperial federation, or the universe-state, is thus the keystone in the arch of the Hindu theory of sovereignty. The message of *Pax Sârva-bhaumica*, in other words, the doctrine of unity and concord is the final contribution of *nîti-sâstras* to the philosophy of the state.

---

[1] *Aitareya Brâhmaṇa*, VIII, 4, 1; for instances of *dig-vijaya* in Hindu political tradition *vide* Mookerji's *Fundamental*, p. 87.

INDEX.

(The footnotes are not indexed)

I. Indian.

A) Terms.

adhikârin 57, 98.
âdhipatya 224.
aikaiśvarya 161.
aiśvarya 179, 180, 193, 201, 210, 212, 213, 214, 224.
âjnâ 72, 76.
âjutika 190.
amâtya 167, 177, 178.
anumati-kappa 39.
aparodha 167.
aparuddha 85.
ari 219.
artha 156—158, 209.
âśrama 213.
aśvamedha 225.
âyudha-jîvi 31, 32.
bali 122, 167, 184.
beyhar 169.
bhâga 115, 122, 123, 184.
bhûyiṣṭhâh 69.
chakkavatti 223.
chakravarti 25, 99, 105, 223.
châturanta 25, 105, 223.
chodanâlakṣaṇohrtho dharmah 209.
danda 75, 129, 180, 195, 197, 198, 200—207, 209—213, 216, 221.
danda-dhara 129, 180, 201, 203, 209.
danda-nîti 160, 163.
dâsyatva 175.
dharma 32, 33, 74, 79, 118, 156, 157, 167, 169, 172—174, 175, 179—181, 189, 197—199, 203, 205—214.
dharmâdhyakṣa 110.
dharma-śâstra 73, 110, 115, 156, 157, 207.
dharma-states 118, 120, 134, 173.
dharma-sthîya 108.
digvijaya 14, 15, 17, 89, 91, 112, 165, 226.
drohin 57.
droṇa-mukhya 97.
durga 167.
eka-rât 223.
gaṇa 32—34, 40, 44, 45, 50, 51, 136, 140, 141, 145—148, 151, 161.
gaṇa-râyâṇa 147, 149.
gaulmika 190.
gopa 58, 67, 73, 100, 101, 105, 108, 109, 121.
grâma 32, 33, 50, 51.
janapada 71.
jânapada 71, 72.
jetthaka 46.
kantaka-sódhana 108, 109.
kara 122, 184, 224.
karṣaṇa 129.
kârṣâpaṇa 42, 214.
khârvâtika 97.
koṣa 167, 183.
kula 33, 110.
kula-samghas 136.
mahâdanda-nâyaka 89.
mahârâjya 140, 224.
mahâ-sabhâ 50, 98.
mahâ-senâpati 140.
madhyama 219, 220.
mamatva 197, 200, 206, 212.
mamedam 200, 204, 205.

mandala 161, 167, 170, 215—218, 220, 221, 222, 226.
mândalika 224.
mantri-parisat 51, 69, 177.
mantri-sabhâ 51.
mâtsya-nyâya 16, 22, 26, 194, 196, 197, 203—207, 210—212, 214, 221, 222, 226.
mukhya 46, 48.
nâbhi 216.
nâgaraka 65, 67, 73, 121.
naigama 32, 33, 41.
nau-vala 91.
nâvadhyaksa 77, 96, 130, 132.
nigama 32, 50, 51.
nigama-sabhâ 36, 51, 62.
nîti 118, 157, 159, 162, 169, 174, 175, 178, 180, 181, 193, 221.
nîti-sâstra 23, 70, 73, 89, 106, 110, 115, 119, 156, 158, 159, 160, 162, 163, 166, 167, 168, 170, 172, 173, 175, 176, 179, 180, 181, 183, 190, 216—218, 221, 226.
olai-nâyakam 69.
paṇa 66, 78, 127—129, 134.
pancha-vara 53.
panchâyat 50, 52, 53, 55—59, 64, 57, 68, 75, 98—100, 108, 109, 116.
parisat 34, 36, 70, 119.
paveni-pustaka 148.
pattipâla 190.
pax sârva-bhaumica 25, 26, 97, 102, 104, 112, 117, 121, 135, 145, 222, 226.
prâd-vivâka 110.
prajâ 211, 214, 221.
prakriti 85, 134, 171, 173—176, 181—183, 191, 211—214.
pratijnâ 84, 183.
pûga 31—33, 44, 50, 51, 110.
pura 33, 50.
purusamedha 225.
râjâ 32, 37, 107, 147, 148, 168, 223, 224.
râja-dharma 163.
râja-drohin 57.
râja-nît 169.
râjarsi 151, 177.
râjasûya 225.
râjya 173, 176, 178, 183, 193, 224.
râjnâm âjnâ 72, 74, 76, 209.
râstra 122, 123, 167, 212, 214.
râstrîya 104.
ratnin 177.
ryot 124.
ryotwari 116.
sabhâ 40, 44, 48, 50—52, 54, 55, 56, 58, 67, 71, 99, 107, 223.
samâhartâ 67, 73, 100, 121, 127, 128, 135.
sâmanta 224.
samaya 84, 167, 183, 213.
sambid 44.
samgha 30—33, 34, 37, 38, 39, 42, 49, 67, 81, 82, 136, 157, 158, 168.
samgrahaṇa 97.
samiti 40, 52.
sâmrâjya 224.
samrât 223, 224, 225.
samsad 52.
samûha 2, 32, 33, 34, 37, 39, 44, 45, 48, 67, 74, 157, 193, 197, 212.
sangam 35, 60.
santhâgara 52, 147.
saptâmga 168, 169, 176, 179.
sârva-bhauma 15, 19, 23, 25, 35, 49, 62, 78, 91, 92, 99, 105, 112, 113, 222, 223—226.
sarva-sammati 45.
śâsana 49, 72, 73, 112, 116, 129, 173.
śasana-patra 209.
senâpati 92, 98, 148.
sitâ 122, 123.
smriti 32, 33, 106, 156, 157, 159, 169, 180, 193, 209.
śreṇi 32, 40, 41, 44—48, 67, 110, 151.
sthânika 67, 73, 105, 121.
sthanîya 97.
strîdhana 28, 29.
śulka 122.
sumantra 133.
surhit 167.
sutta-dhara 148.
svadharma 201, 211, 213, 214.
svâmin 167, 179.
svâmitva 193, 201, 210.
svarâj 25, 33, 48, 49, 51, 53, 54, 58, 59, 143, 152, 153, 168, 224.
svarât 224, 225.
svatva 197, 203, 204.
târa 122.
târika 90.

ubbahika 82.
udâsîna 219, 220.
udaka-bhâga 124.
upa-râja 148.
vahavah 82.
vairâjya 224.
vâjapeya 225.
vala 167.
vamana 128.
varga 45.
varṇa 213.
varṇâśrama 213, 214.
vartani 122.
vibhâga 132.
vijigîṣu 23, 59, 92, 215, 217—221, 226.
vinichchiya mahâmâtta 148.
virât 224, 225.
viśva-jit 226.
vohârika 148.
vrâta 31, 32.
vyavahâra 169, 209.
vyavyhârika 148.
vyûha 94.
yajna 148, 225.

B) Persons.

Abul Fazl 169, 170.
Ajâta-satru 84, 145, 149.
Ajitâ 81.
Angiras 157.
Âpastamba 105, 157, 208, 225.
Ârya-râja 70.
Asoka 14, 34, 58, 70, 76, 77, 79, 99, 100, 104, 105, 135, 159.
Atri 157.
Avanti 92.
Avanti-varman 103.
Bâlâditya 34.
Bâṇa 61, 84, 92.
Bâtsâyana 150, 156.
Baudhâyana 176, 189, 208.
Bhaddiya 146.
Bhandi 85, 159.
Bharadvâja 69.
Bharata 150.
Bhîṣma 218.
Bhoja 73, 158, 163, 165, 167, 174.
Bilhana 73.
Brihadratha 84.
Brihaspati 41, 44, 45, 47, 48, 73, 157, 160, 207.
Buddha (Śâkya) 30, 37, 52, 81, 145, 149, 223.
Chakrapâlita 104.
Chakrâyudha 90.
Chandeśvara 45.
Chandra-gupta 21, 32, 58, 59, 77, 95, 104, 135, 159, 142, 145.
Charaka 150.
Dakṣa 157.
Danuja-mardana 18.
Darbha-pâṇi 90, 159.
Daśaratha 60.
Deva-pâla 35, 90.
Devapi 85.
Dharma-pâla 14, 17, 90, 195.
Dhritarâṣtra 86.
Eran Sattan 41.
Gautama 28, 40, 41, 43, 48, 105, 157, 189, 210.
Ghatakarpara 158.
Gopâla 85, 195.
Gotami-putra 15.
Govinda III, 165.
Hari-ghoṣa 97.
Hari-sena 89.
Hârîta 157.
Harṣa-vardhana 14, 16, 60, 85, 92, 111.
Jaimini 162, 209.
Janamejaya 225.
Jîmûta-vâhana 28.
Jîvanta 42.
Kalhana 73, 103.
Kâlidâsa 16, 89, 165, 175, 224.
Kâmandaka 159, 163, 178, 179, 183, 186, 195, 199, 201, 202, 214—216, 219, 220.
Kâniṣka 15.
Kapphina le Grand 141.
Kârikâla 104.
Kassapa 75.
Kâtyâyana 32, 33, 45, 48, 157.
Kautilya 31, 32, 43, 47, 51, 58, 67—69, 72, 74, 77, 80, 82, 90, 97, 113, 123, 127, 128, 130, 131, 133, 145, 150, 151, 158—161, 163, 167, 170—174, 177, 178, 181, 184, 185, 189, 191, 195, 209, 215, 219, 220, 221, 223.
Kedâra-miśra 159.
Khankha 70.
Khâravela 71.

Kirti Nissamka Malla 75.
Krişņa 187.
Kulot-tûnga 17, 59, 74, 75, 101, 102, 114, 117, 133.
Kumâra-gupta 42.
Kuntala 92.
Kuru 85.
Laksmaņa-sena 17.
Likhita 157.
Mahâ Kassapa 38.
Mahâpadma 103.
Mahinda 109.
Manu 28, 41, 44, 50, 73, 80, 81, 105, 196, 122, 150, 157, 159, 171, 173, 176, 178—182, 184, 187, 188, 191, 199, 201, 203, 205, 207, 210, 211, 214—216.
Mihira Bhoja 17, 159.
Mitra Miśra 33, 45, 48.
Nâgadasako 84, 85.
Nâgârjuna 150.
Nahapâna 141.
Nahûşa 182.
Nârada 33, 44, 46, 157, 209.
Narasimha-gupta 34, 87.
Pâņiņi 30—32, 50.
Parâkrama Bâhu 104.
Parântaka 53.
Parâśara 157.
Pasendi 146.
Patanjali 150.
Poros 94.
Prajâpati 225.
Pratâpâditya 69.
Prithu 84.
Prithvi-râja 19.
Pulakeśi 16, 92.
Puru 86.
Puşya-gupta 104.
Puşya-mitra 15, 21.
Râdhâ-gupta 70.
Raghu 89, 165.
Raghunâtha 196.
Râjâdhirâja 116.
Râja-râja 17, 53, 57, 69, 75, 91, 98, 101, 102, 116, 117.
Râjaśekhara 17.
Râjendra-chola 15, 41, 69, 91, 104.
Râma 216.
Râvaņa 216.
Revata 81.
Rudra-dâmana 70, 85, 104, 105, 120, 140.
Sabara Svâmi 209.
Sabbas 87.
Śâkya (Buddha) 30, 31, 37—39, 52, 81, 83, 100, 107, 149, 150, 158.
Samkha 157.
Samudra-gupta 15, 59, 87, 89, 90, 141, 165.
Samvarta 157.
Sandhimati 70.
Sandhyâkara 73.
Sandrokottos 142.
Śântanu 85.
Saryâta 225.
Satâtapa 157.
Sela 223.
Simhanâda 92.
Śiśunâga 23, 84, 85.
Skandagupta 42, 87, 92, 97, 104.
Someśvara 90, 97.
Subandhhu 61.
Suddhodana 146.
Śukra 41, 74, 81—83, 122, 150, 159, 160, 162, 163, 171—179, 182, 187, 189—191, 202, 209—216, 218.
Śunda 196.
Suviśâkha 104.
Sûyyâ 103.
Tilottamâ 196.
Tiru-valluvar 35.
Tusaspha 104.
Udaya 23.
Udayibhaddako 84.
Ugra-Peruvalludhi 35.
Upaśunda 196.
Uśanas 157.
Uşavadâta 36, 42, 51, 62, 120, 141.
Vaiśampâyana 158.
Vallâla-sena 97.
Varâhamihira 61, 156.
Vaśiştha 157, 160, 172, 189, 196, 208.
Veņa 84, 178, 182.
Vibhişaņa 216.
Vidura 158.
Vijnâneśvara 28, 32, 33, 208.
Vikrama-chola 41.

Vikramâditya 16, 19, 23, 70, 159, 165.
Vîra-deva 35.
Vîra-sena 97.
Visâlâkṣa 160.
Viṣṇu 44, 122, 157, 191.
Vyâsa 157.
Yadu 86.
Yajna-śrî 15, 93.
Yâjnavalkya 28, 32, 33, 44, 45, 48, 50, 51, 73, 150, 157, 178, 191, 207, 208, 210.
Yama 157.
Yayâti 86.
Yudhiṣṭhira 223.

C) Dynasties, Races or Nations.

Abastanoi 144.
Agalassoi 95, 144.
Ândhra 15, 42, 53, 62, 93, 105, 120, 140, 141, 165.
Âratta 142, 143.
Arjunâyana 140.
Assakenoi 94.
Bahârika 122.
Bengali 17, 18, 31, 35, 62, 90, 159, 195.
Bhagga 145.
Buli 145.
Cedrosii 143.
Ceylonese 119.
Châlukya 16, 17, 74, 92, 93, 102, 105, 119, 165.
Chola 15, 17, 26, 43, 53, 55, 57, 59, 67, 69, 72, 75, 78, 80, 91, 98, 101, 104, 109, 112—119, 121, 124, 127, 134, 135.
Gangaridae 89.
Gedrosioi 143.
Gujarâti 36, 42.
Gupta 16, 19, 23, 26, 33, 34, 41, 42, 52, 61, 71, 78, 80, 89, 99, 104, 105, 118, 120, 139, 141, 156, 165.
Gurjara-Pratîhâra 17, 18, 21, 61, 91, 159, 165.
Hoysâlâ 17.
Kalama 145.
Kalingoe 89.
Karkota 70.
Kashmirian 103, 118.
Kathian 142.
Koliya 145, 146.
Kṣudraka 95, 143.
Kukura 145.
Kuninda 141.
Kuru 143, 145.
Kuṣân 15, 16, 70, 104, 105, 139.
Lichchhavika 32, 145, 148.
Mâlava 33, 95, 140, 141, 143, 145.
Mallaka 145.
Malla 146.
Malloi 95, 143.
Maltecoroe 142.
Mârâthâ 18, 59, 92, 120.
Marohoe 142.
Maurya 14, 15, 17, 23, 26, 41, 43, 46, 47, 50, 52, 56—62, 64, 66—68, 72, 74, 77, 80, 82, 84, 93, 95, 97, 99—102, 104—106, 108, 109, 111, 113, 114, 119—121, 123—129, 131, 132, 134, 135, 139, 142, 158, 161, 165.
Mlechchha 190.
Moriya 145.
Moruni 142.
Nanda 89.
Nysaian 144.
Oreitai 144.
Oriya 89.
Oxydrakai 143.
Pâla 17, 23, 78, 85, 91, 105, 159.
Panchâla 145.
Pândya 60, 61, 62, 67, 88, 119.
Peshwa 18.
Prasii 89.
Râjput 17.
Rarungi 142.
Râṣṭrakûta 15, 17, 91, 165.
Sabarcae 143.
Sâkiya 146, 148, 149.
Sambastai 143.
Sena 17, 91.
Sibi 141.
Sikh 14, 18, 179.
Singhoe 142.
Sunga 15, 23, 97.
Tamil 35, 41, 55, 56, 60, 63, 68, 91, 99, 104, 105, 112, 116, 119, 127.
Uttama-bhadra 141.
Vajjian 37, 107, 146, 149.
Vardhana 16, 26, 61, 72, 80, 92, 97, 99, 111. 119 159.
Videha 145—146.
Vrijjika 32, 145.

Vrișṇi 141.
Xathroi 93, 144.
Yâdava 17.
Yaudheya 33, 140, 141.

D) Places.

Ajantâ 61.
Akesines 94.
Allakappa 145.
Ânula 104.
Assam 89.
Ayodhyâ 60.
Bâdâmi 16, 61.
Bankipore 14, 61.
Bengal 17, 28, 61, 73, 85, 89, 91, 93, 97.
Betwa 140.
Bhattiprolu 51.
Bihar 34, 61, 62, 89, 145.
Bijapur 16, 61.
Bombay 61, 90, 120.
Broach 120.
Calcutta 154.
Ceylon 15, 53, 55, 56, 62, 69, 75, 91, 103, 104, 105, 109.
Chambal 140.
Chenub 94.
Chera 63, 67, 91.
Chola-mandala 99.
Comorin 102.
Conjeeveram 55, 91.
Coromandel Coast 61, 102.
Daśagâma 109.
Daśapura 42, 120.
Deccan 15—18, 36, 53, 62, 73, 91—93, 105, 120, 140, 141, 165.
Delhi 18, 23, 60.
Desert Cathay 16.
Devagiri 17.
Dhârâ 158.
Dvârakâ 60.
Dvâra-samudra 17.
Ganges (Gangetic Valley) 14—17, 61, 62, 88—90, 94, 97, 141, 145.
Girnar 70, 104.
Gokarṇa 90.
Govardhana 36, 42, 62, 67, 120.
Gujarat 42, 47, 53, 60, 88, 103, 120.
Gwalior 63.
Hâthigumphâ 71.
Himâlayas 88, 90, 141, 143, 146.
Hydaspes 94.
Indo-Gangetic 94.
Indraprastha 60.
Indrapura 42.
Indus 62.
Jhelum 94.
Jumna 140, 141.
Kalyan 17.
Kanara 90.
Kanauj 16, 17, 61, 90.
Kapilavastu 146, 147.
Karur 63.
Kashmir 17, 69, 53, 103.
Kâsî 146.
Kathiawar 70, 104.
Kâverî 104.
Kâverî-pumpattinam 61, 63.
Kedâra 90.
Kerala 15.
Kesaputta 145.
Khâlimpur 90.
Kośala 146.
Kottaru 102.
Kuśinârâ 146.
Lamkâ 75.
Madhyadeśa 141.
Madras 41, 56, 63, 69, 91, 93, 103, 112, 117.
Mâdurâ 35, 60, 63.
Magadha 89, 95, 149.
Mahânadî 102.
Mahâpadma Lake 103.
Mahârâṣtra 53.
Malabar Coast 60.
Malkhed 17.
Malwa 61, 90, 120, 140, 158.
Massaga 94.
Mithilâ 146.
Mysore 91, 112.
Nâlandâ 34, 35, 122.
Narmadâ 16, 92, 97, 105.
Nâsik 16, 36, 42, 51, 62, 120.
Orissa 91, 102, 105.
Patala 142.
Pâtaliputra 14, 16, 23, 34, 41, 61, 62, 64—67, 72, 90, 100, 102, 104, 105, 108, 120—122, 165.
Pava 146.

Peshawar 15.
Pipphalivana 145.
Protalis 89.
Pukar 61.
Punjab 18, 60, 62, 90, 93—95, 140, 144, 145.
Puri 92.
Puruṣapura 15.
Râjagaha 38.
Rajputana 17, 90, 140.
Râmagâma 145.
Rawalpindi 60.
Rohini River 146.
Satyaputra 15.
Sindh 90.
Sindhu 103.
Solapuram 104.
Somnath 120.
Srâvasti 70.
Sudarśana 70, 104, 105, 120.
Suṁsumâra 145.
Sutlej 140.
Suvarṇa-giri 65, 105.
Tâmralipta 61.
Tamluk 61.
Tanjore 57.
Taxila 60, 65, 67, 88, 105.
Tosali 105.
Ujjayini 61, 65, 67, 105.
Vanji 60, 63.
Vâtâpi 16, 61.
Vesâli 39, 81, 146—148.
Vijaya-nagara 18.
Vindhya 76, 93.
Vitastâ 103.
Woraiyur 60.

E) Books.

Agni-Purâṇa 69, 177, 187.
Aitareya Brâhmaṇa 84, 222, 224.
Artha-śâstra 3, 43, 58, 67, 68, 72, 73, 77, 80, 82, 97, 98, 105, 113, 122, 123, 129, 131, 136, 156, 159, 161, 165, 167, 170, 172, 177, 184, 189, 195, 215, 221, 223.
Atthakathâ 148.
Avadâna-śataka 141.
Ayeeni Akbari 169.
Bhadda-Sâla Jâtaka 146.
Brihadâraṇyak-opaniṣat 208.
Brihat Samhitâ 156.
Chulla Kalinga Jâtaka 147.
Chullaka-setthi 41.
Chulla-vagga 38, 39, 82, 158.
Daśa-Kumâra-charita 156, 163.
Dâya-bhâga 28.
Ekapanna Jâtaka 146, 147.
Epic of the Anklet 35.
Gitâ 118, 150, 187, 205, 211.
Gopatha Brâhmaṇa 225.
Harṣa-charita 61, 84, 92.
History of Ancient Sanskrit Literature 155.
India What Can It Teach Us? 155.
Jâtakas 19, 41, 43, 46, 52, 60, 150.
Jewel Belt 36.
Kâmandakî-nîti 69, 73, 159, 161, 180, 185, 216.
Kâma-sûtra 156.
Karpûra-manjarî 17.
Kirâtârjunîya 156.
Kunâla Jâtaka 146.
Kural 35.
Laukika-Nyâya-Samgraha 196.
Mahâ-vagga 38, 158.
Mahâbhârata 19, 33, 46, 47, 51, 60, 69, 70, 84, 85, 86, 88, 98, 105, 107, 136, 142, 143, 150, 156, 158, 160, 163, 171—173, 177, 179, 181—186, 189, 194, 197, 199, 200, 203, 215, 218, 223.
Manu Samhitâ 74, 98, 157, 170, 173, 180, 184, 188, 189, 194, 201, 203, 208, 210, 218.
Matsya-Purâna 177, 195.
Mimâmsâ 162, 209.
Mitâkṣarâ 28, 204.
Nîti-prakâśikâ 158.
Nîti-Vâkyâmrita 158.
Pancha-tantra 156.
Purâṇa 156, 178, 196.
Raghu-vamśa 16, 156, 175, 224, 226.
Râja-taranginî 69, 73, 103.
Râma-charita 73.
Râmâyaṇa 46, 51, 60, 70, 86, 107, 150, 156, 175, 195, 216.
Rig Veda 224.
Sabhâ-parva 171, 172, 185.
Sacred Books of the East Series 157.
Sâhitya Darpaṇa 156.
Sânti-parva 171.

Sarasvati-vilâsa 204.
Śatapatha Brâhmaṇa 224, 225.
Silavanâga 43.
Srauta Sûtra 225.
Suppâraka 41.
Śukra-niti 69, 73, 83, 159—162, 171, 173, 175, 177—180, 182, 185, 187, 189—191, 197, 199, 201, 203, 209, 212, 214, 216, 219, 221, 224
Vaiśeṣika 150.
Valahassa 41.
Vâsavadattâ 61.
Vedânta 150.
Vedic 19, 50—52, 56, 59, 64, 71, 79, 85, 107, 121, 136, 151, 186, 222.
Vinaya 31, 38, 50, 158.
Vîra-mitrodaya 32, 45.
Vivâda-ratnâkara 45.
Vyavahâra-Darpana 208.
Yukti-Kalpa-taru 73, 158, 161, 167.

F) Miscellaneous.

Akbar the Great 18, 169.
Aryan 208.
Aurangzib 19.
Baji Rao 19.
Banerjee 29.
Brahmâ (god) 84, 160, 176.
Brâhmana 85, 110, 120, 187, 189, 190, 191, 197, 208, 212, 225.
Buddhist 14, 19, 22, 30—32, 38, 39, 41, 50, 52, 60—62, 146, 155, 158, 204.
Catalogus Catalogorum 155.
Chârvaka 150.
Chatterji (Bankim Chandra) 31.
dinar 103.
Gandhi (Mohandas Karamchand) 181.
Ganeśa (god) 160.
Greater India 16.
Haider Ali 19.
Islam 18.
Jaina 14, 19, 32, 39.
Jayaswal 71, 72.
Kâli (goddess) 18.
Khalsa 179.
Kṣatryia 93, 147, 170, 187, 189, 190, 191, 144, 212.
Kumbha Melâ 36.
Lakṣmi (goddess) 92.
Lokâyata 150.
Mahmud 93.
Modern Review 71.
Moghul 18, 19, 23, 59.
Mohammedan (Moslem) 9, 19, 25, 93, 169
Pâli 62, 155, 157, 158.
Pâśupata 48.
Pillar Edict 76, 77.
Prâkrit 72, 155.
Provincials, Edict 76.
Rock Edict 76, 77.
Sanskrit 36, 50, 72, 73, 89, 97, 105, 155, 157, 163, 167, 170.
Shah Jahan 19.
Śiva (god) 160.
Shivaji 18.
Śûdra 189, 190.
Sukhâvati 204.
Vaiśya 189, 193.
Young India 3, 19, 87, 223.

II. Oriental.

Afghan 35, 60, 87, 102, 105.
Afghanistan 15, 32, 87, 90, 94, 95, 142.
Africa 138 217.
Al-aaram 105.
Al Iarabi 103.
Algeciras 138
Al Mahdi 170.
Andaman 91.
Arab 163
Arabian Sea 70, 88, 92, 104, 105, 120.
Arabic 160, 161.
Assyrian 9, 93.
Bagdad 160.
Baluchistan 15, 95.
Bassein 120.
Bay of Bengal 91.
Buddhist Asia 37.
Burma 91.

Bushido 144, 187.
Cairo 27, 35, 154.
Caliphate 20.
Central Asia 16, 22, 87.
China 15, 19, 25, 40, 42, 61, 73, 79, 152, 175, 178, 181, 194, 198, 220.
Chinese 9, 16, 34, 35, 40, 48, 62, 67, 79, 80, 111, 146, 154, 165, 182, 216, 224.
Chow 178.
Confucius 9, 80, 81, 175, 206.
Development of Logic in Ancient China 194.
Egypt 9, 15, 61, 100, 105, 170.
El Akham es Soulthaniyah 160.
El Azhar 35.
Fa Hien 34, 62, 79, 80, 99.
Genro 38.
Greater Asia 22.
Greco-Syrian 142.
Han Empire 15.
Hiuen Tsang 35, 61, 63, 70, 72, 80, 92, 99, 111.
Horiyuji 35.
Hun 21, 87.
Hsun Tze 198.
hwangti 224.
Ibn Khaldoun 162.
Indian Ocean 87.
Islam 18, 21.
Itsing 62.
I Yin 182.
Japan 5, 6, 16, 35, 76, 154, 187.
Japanese 38, 146, 157.
Jerusalem 146.
Kojiki 157.
Khusru 16, 61.
Laccadives 91.
Lake Moeris 104.
Lao-hsikai 138.
Maldives 91.
Manchu-Chinese 138.
Mareb 105.
Mawerdi 160.
Meiji 76.
Mencius 91, 178, 181, 182, 198.
Mikado 76.
Moh Ti 194.
Mokaddemah 162.
Mongolia 37.
Mongol 22.
Morocco 138.
Moslem (Mohammedan) 14, 15, 17, 18, 20, 22, 23, 133, 144, 206.
Mutshuito 76.
Nara 35.
Nearchos 93.
Nicobar 91.
Nihongi 157.
Nizam-oul Moulk 162.
Pegu 91.
Persia 9, 16, 21, 61, 93, 137, 143, 154, 162, 169, 170.
Prolégomènes Historiques 162.
Prome 91.
Samurai 189.
Sassanian 16, 61.
Scythian 21.
Semiramis 93.
Shamanist 9.
Shahnate 154.
Shu 73.
Shu-king 175.
Siasset Nameh 162.
Su Hu 194, 198.
Sultanate 138.
Sun Tzu 216.
Tai-tsung 16.
Tang 16.
Tartar 9, 21.
Tenjiku 146.
Tibet 37.
Tien chu 146.
Tientsien 138.
Tokyo 27.
Tsin 19.
Union and Progress 154.
Young Asia 25, 151.
Young Turk 154.

III. Eur-American.

Abbott 165.
Adams 84.
Adolfus 17.
Aeneid 16.
Aeschines 145.
Agadir 138.
ager publicus 115.
agora 52, 71.
Alcuin 74, 168, 175, 210.
Alexander 15—17, 19, 21, 32, 60, 87, 88, 90, 93—95, 140, 142—144, 160, 174, 217, 219, 222, 226.
Alsace-Lorraine 23.
America 6—8, 10, 27, 107, 169.
American 6, 10—13, 98, 152, 154, 174, 188, 217.
ancien régime 9, 58, 133, 137.
Angle 22.
Anglo-Saxon 81.
Apollo 36.
Aquinas 163, 167, 168.
Arcadian 59, 118.
Argentina 13.
Aristotle 157, 160, 163, 167, 168, 182, 207, 212, 217.
Aristotelian 164, 203, 205.
Arrian 95, 143, 144.
Art of War 216.
Assize 82.
Atgers 171.
Athenian 111, 114, 129, 134, 137, 143, 148, 218.
Athens 9, 24, 65, 122—124, 126—128, 131, 137, 142, 147, 148, 153.
Attica 24, 148.
Aufrecht 155.
Aufwandsteuer 114, 126.
Augustine 74, 168, 180, 199.
Augustus 35, 65, 95, 149, 174.
Aurelian 65.
Austin 1, 74, 75, 168, 207.
Austria 11, 12, 23.
auxilia 95.
Azo 176.
Balkan 22.
Barker 167, 193.
Bartolus 164, 222, 224.
Bastille 2.
Bavaria 226.
Beaumanoir 74.
Bebel 29.
Beccaria 8.
Becquerel 6.
Belial 8.
Belgium 170.
Bernhardian 170.
Bismarck 3, 7, 74, 151, 159, 218.
Blanc (Louis) 7.
Bluntschli 164, 165.
Bodin 1, 20, 117, 167, 176, 180, 201, 207.
Boke named the Governour 163.
Bökh 111.
Bologna 35, 158.
Bolshevik 2, 23, 24, 47, 80, 168, 172, 174.
Bossuet 176, 181.
Bourbon 59, 71, 106, 136—138, 165.
Boutmy 20.
Bracton 74.
Bradley 201, 211.
Brazil 13.
Brisaud 165.
British 10, 58, 80, 116, 125, 135, 157, 188, 217.
Browningite 2.
Buckle 20.
Burns 174.
Bury 23.
Byzantine 14—16, 19, 169.
Caesar 17, 174.
Caesar-Pope 23.
Caesaro-papism 14.
cahier 11.
Calhoun 30.
Caliban 205.
Caligula 127.
Canonist 158, 164, 199.
Capitula 86.
Capuchin 205.
Carlyle 164, 165, 174.
Carolingian 176.
Carpathian Mountains 22.

Catholic 37, 120, 205.
Cavour 218.
comitia 51.
concilium 51.
Celsus 207.
Consuetudines Feudorum 74.
Central Europe 23.
Champs de Mai 70.
Champs de Mars 70.
Chamber of Deputies 138.
Charlemagne 7, 16, 17, 23, 26, 85, 87, 222.
Charles 8.
Charles I. 178.
Charles the Fat 17.
Charles V. 19, 26.
Cheronea 142.
Christian 11, 19—22, 25, 33, 35, 42, 53, 60, 67, 148, 157, 180, 206, 217, 222.
Christian Topography 62.
Church Fathers 196, 207.
Cicero 74, 164, 207.
Civil Government 200.
civitas 33, 52, 71.
Clausewitz 187.
Code Justinian 73.
Code Napoleon 29.
Colbert 130.
Cologne 40.
comitia 50.
Common Pleas 109.
Confederacy of Delos 137.
Congress of Versailles 22.
Constantine 13, 16, 17, 34, 105, 124, 151, 165.
contributiones directes 118.
contributiones indirectes 118.
Convention 11.
Cosma 62.
Coutumes de Beauvoises 74.
Council of Toledo 70.
Council of Trent 36.
Crime and Punishment 8.
Curtius 143, 144.
Curzon 24.
Czar 24.
Czarist Russia 126.
Dane 22.
Dante 9, 13, 23, 156, 222.
Danton 11.
Das Nationale System der politischen Ökonomie 22.
David 180.
De Civitate Dei 168.
Decretum 158.
Defensor Pacis 164.
De Legibus et Consuetudinibus Angliae 74.
De Monarchia 23, 222.
Demosthenes 145, 207, 208.
De Ortu et Fine Romani Imperii 25, 26.
De Regimine Principum 168.
Der Rassenkampf 26.
Desmoulins 11.
Dialogues 166.
Diet of Worms 12.
Digest 73, 207.
Diocletian 105, 123.
Diodorus 94, 142, 143.
Divine Comedy 223.
domaine 118.
Domesday Book 101, 117.
dominus omnium 223.
domus 33.
Dopsch 149, 165.
dos 29.
dot 29.
Draconian 79.
droit 167, 206.
droit des gens 215.
droits de l'homme 176.
Duke of Orleans 137.
Dunning 165.
Duguit 2, 168.
Dutch 12.
Ecclesiastical Polity 194.
Edward 84, 101.
Egyptian-Greek 62.
Egypt 170.
eisphora 129.
Elyot 163, 179.
Emathian 71.
Emile 200.
English 12, 25, 29, 46, 71, 83, 85, 101, 109, 110, 118, 131, 132, 139, 153, 159, 174, 187, 220.
English Society in the Eleventh Century 165.
Epirus 147, 153.

Esprit des Lois 157.
Essai d'une psychologie politique du peuple anglais au XIXe siècle 29.
Essay on Milton 7.
Eur-America 1, 5—9, 13, 20, 24, 25, 30, 74, 145, 154, 164, 171, 180, 188, 222.
Eur-Asia 9, 220.
Evolution of Modern Liberty 193.
Faerie Queene 196.
Fehmic Courts 83.
Figgis 45, 168, 174, 201, 218.
Finanzwissenschaft 118.
Florence 40, 149, 153, 159.
Fortescue 163.
France 6, 7, 10, 11, 21, 22, 24, 25, 74, 85, 106, 111, 117, 126, 130, 133, 136—139, 152—154, 220, 221.
Franck 167.
Frankish 70, 81.
Frederick 18, 25, 87, 136, 222.
Frederick Barbarossa 17.
Frederick the Great, 3, 18.
Freeman 20.
French 10—12, 25, 30, 58, 114, 118, 132, 137, 139, 152—154, 164, 175, 181, 220.
French Academy 35.
From Gerson to Grotius 218.
Fronde 25.
Frontiers 24.
gabelle 114, 131.
Gaius 73, 164, 207.
gemot 52.
Genoa 149.
George III, 79.
German 3, 11, 23—25, 29, 81, 85, 113, 118, 125, 136, 137, 139, 153, 169, 170, 173, 221.
Germany 6, 20, 138, 153, 154, 170, 220.
Geschichte der neueren Staatswissenschaft 164.
Ghent 40.
Ghibelline 7, 23, 157, 224.
Gibbon 111.
Gierke 33, 45, 174.
Giffen 116.
Girondist 153.
Goethe 6, 31.
Gomme 157.
Goth 22.
Götz 31.
Gouvernance of England 163.
Governour 179.
Grand Assize 82.
Gratian 158.
Great Charter 110.
Greater Rome 65.
Greco-Roman 61.
Greco-Syrian 95.
Greece 13, 15, 19, 21, 22, 63, 143, 145, 148, 151, 153, 217.
Greek 19, 21, 30, 32, 62, 64, 67, 71, 77, 86, 87, 93, 142—144, 151, 165, 169, 172, 180, 190, 208, 217.
Gregory the Great 99, 169, 180, 181, 199.
"Greyhound" 23.
Grotius 201, 217.
Guelph 7, 23.
Guizot 47, 111, 139, 165.
Gumplowicz 26, 194.
Gustavus Adolphus 19, 25, 97.
Hadrian 15, 73, 123, 164.
Hague 188.
Hanniballan 88.
Hansa 19, 40, 148, 153.
Hapsburg 9, 13, 25.
Hegel 1, 20, 168, 201, 217.
Hellas 21, 31, 167.
Hellenic 21, 38, 136, 153.
Hellenistic 15, 32, 87.
Henry II, 82.
Herder 3.
Hildebrand 25, 199, 224.
Hincmar 176.
Histoire des doctrines du contract social 171.
Historical Geography of Europe 20.
History of French Public Law 165.
History of the Roman Conquest from B. C. 88, 146—264.
History of the Theory of Sovereignty since Rousseau 193.
Hobbes 1, 16, 18, 26, 118, 168, 181, 194, 203, 207, 218, 221.
Hohenstaufen 224.
Hohenzollern 13.
Holland (author) 12, 206, 226.
Holy Alliance 152.
Holy Roman Empire 14, 23, 25.
Homeric 20, 52.

Hooker 194.
Hugo (Victor) 139.
Hundred Years, War 25, 113.
Hungarian 221.
Huntington 20.
idola 4, 9, 79.
Illustrations of the History of Mediaeval Thought 169.
Inferno 23.
Inquisito Eliensis 101.
Inquisition 79.
Institutes 29, 73, 176.
Intendants 106.
Introduction to Politics 160.
Ireland 25, 220.
Irenaeus 198.
Isidore 14, 182.
Italian 13, 23, 25, 30, 47, 153, 176.
Italy 13, 21—23, 149, 153, 154, 221, 226.
James II, 8, 83.
Janet 165, 167.
Janus 26, 210.
Jonas 74, 175, 210.
Jesuit 158.
Jew 122.
John of Salisbury 163, 182.
Joseph 136.
Joseph-Barthélemy 30, 193.
Jugo-Slavia 221.
Jura regalia 131.
Jurisprudence 206.
Jus 206.
Jus gentium 215.
Jus naturale 208.
Justinian 16, 17, 29, 73, 74, 164, 165, 169, 207.
Jute 22.
Kaiser Wilhelm 218.
Korzybski 3.
Kultur 118, 180.
Kultur-Staat 118, 172.
Lactantius (Father) 199.
L'Action Française 138.
Lafayette 11.
laissez faire 1, 48, 59, 131, 151, 172.
La Marseillaise 11.
Languet 181.
Laski 193.
Later Roman Empire 23.
Latin 13, 19, 30, 118, 152.
Latin-American 13, 154.
Laurium 131, 132.
Laws of War and Peace 217.
Le Couronnement de Louis 175.
l'état c'est moi 8, 71, 174.
le grand monarque 136, 181.
les nerfs de la république 117, 183.
Lenin 2, 24, 154.
Leroy-Beaulieu 118.
Les six livres de la république 116.
Les Transformations du Droit Public 2.
Leviathan 24, 181, 194.
Le Vote des Femmes 30.
Lewis 86.
liber burgus 40, 49.
Liberty 172, 195, 202.
L'Idée de l'Etat 193.
Liebknecht 2, 168.
Life of Alexander 89.
List (Frederick) 22.
Littlejohn 169.
Lives 87.
Locke 200.
Lollard 174.
Lombard 74.
London 40.
Lothair 86.
Louis IX, 106, 108.
Louis XI, 165.
Louis XIV, 8, 19, 59, 71, 106, 165.
Louis XVI, 11, 174.
Louis Philippe 137.
Lowie 28.
Luther (Martin) 164.
Lycurgan 187, 203.
Macaulay 7.
Macedonian 21, 88, 94, 95, 142, 144, 145, 218.
Machiavelli 13, 47, 128, 159, 164, 167, 170, 217, 218.
Madrid 138.
Magna Carta 109.
Maine 3, 20, 29, 74, 157.
majestas 180.
Manegold of Lautenbach 181.
Marat 11.
Marathon 21.

Married Women's Property Act 29.
Marsiglio and Ockam 164.
Marx (Karl) 154.
Maude 188, 217.
Maurice 17.
Mazzini 7, 13, 24.
Mediterranean 19, 21.
Megasthenes 64, 65, 72, 77, 86, 88, 93, 96, 100, 103, 105, 122, 142.
Menander 15, 21, 87.
Merriam 193.
Messiah 2, 23.
Metternick 218.
Mexico 13.
Michel 193.
Middle Ages 20, 22, 71, 153, 164, 176.
Mill J. S. 6, 29, 171, 177, 194, 195, 202, 215.
Milton 156.
Minervan 160.
Mir 108.
Mirabeau 11.
Model City 163.
Moloch 8.
Monroe Doctrine 152.
Montesquieu 20, 139, 157, 163, 167.
More 205.
Morgarten 12.
Müller (Max) 3, 20, 155.
municipium 31, 50.
Naples 153.
Napoleonic 3, 6, 12, 16, 23, 26, 29, 78, 90, 99, 111, 137, 138, 140, 152, 159, 165, 170, 220, 226.
Napoleon III, 138, 139.
Napoleon (Louis) 137.
National Assembly 11.
Natural History 62, 89, 145, 146.
Nero 180.
New Monarchy 159.
New Testament 157.
Newton 6.
Nietzsche 157, 170.
Nitti 118.
Norman 22, 74, 84, 101.
Northampton 82.
Novum Organum 4, 168.
Occleve 163.
Officium palatinum 70.
Ordinatio Imperii 86.
Orleanist 138.
Ottoman 22.
Oxford 35.
Oxford Movement 158.
Padua 164.
Palatine Hill 65.
Papacy 224.
Paracelsus 4.
Paradiso 23.
parapherna 29.
Paris 35, 40, 108, 137, 138, 139.
Parlement 108.
pater familias 29.
patrimonium 118.
Patrizi 163.
pax Romana 26, 105.
Pericles 9, 24, 124, 137, 148, 153, 218.
Periplus of the Erythraean Sea 62.
Peter 19, 25, 136.
Philip 47, 142, 218.
Pippin 86.
Pisistratean 139.
Plato 118, 149, 151, 166—168, 173, 175, 177, 180, 201, 205, 212, 213.
Pliny 60, 62, 89, 93, 95, 156.
Plutarch 87, 88, 89, 94.
Poland 22, 157.
Policraticus 182.
polis 30, 32, 34, 63, 212.
Politica 217.
Political Theory of the Schoolmen and Grotius 169.
Political Thought in England from Spencer to the Present Day 193.
Politics 182.
Politique 181.
Politische Geographie 22, 24.
Pollock 160.
Polybius 88.
Poole 169, 174.
portoria 124.
Portugal 220.
Portuguese 13.
Prince 7, 21, 163, 218.
Problème de la compétence dans la démocratie 193.
Problem of Sovereignty 193.
Protestant 25.

Prussian 11, 137, 138.
Ptolemy 62.
publicani 121.
Purgatorio 23.
Pyrrhus 147, 153.
Pythagoras 149.
quadrivium 156, 219.
Ratzel 22.
Räuber 31.
Reform Bill 7, 12.
regnum 33.
Renaissance 4, 166.
Representative Government 171.
Republic 118, 151, 166, 213.
res publica 212.
res judicata 149.
Rhine 81.
Ricardian 134.
Richard II, 83.
Richelieu 35, 58, 74, 101, 106, 151, 221.
Role du pouvoir executif dans les républiques modernes 193.
Roman 8, 21, 23, 25, 26, 29, 62, 63, 68, 79, 88, 93, 96, 114, 115, 122—124, 126, 136, 151, 153, 164, 165, 174, 198, 207, 208, 217.
Roman Empire 15, 26, 60, 111, 117, 118, 121, 131.
Roman Political Institutions 165.
Rome 3, 15, 19, 23, 25, 64, 65, 88, 95, 99, 102, 103, 115, 120, 127, 142, 147, 149, 153, 165.
Romulus 65.
Rousseau 6, 181, 200, 204.
Russian 1, 12, 21, 23, 24, 80, 152, 172, 220.
sacerdotum 169.
Salamis 21.
Saracen 21.
Saturnian 199.
Saul 180.
Saxon 22, 74.
Scandinavian 22.
Scherger 193.
Schiller 31.
Schwyz 12.
Science and Art of Human Engineering 3.
Scipio 88.
Scotland 22, 25, 220.
Second Punic War 88.
Sedan 137, 138.
Seeley
Seleukos 21, 87, 95, 142.
Seneca 74, 168, 175, 198, 205, 207.
Servius 65.
Shelley 2.
Sicily 21.
Sidgwick 172.
Siegfried 23, 59, 215, 216, 218, 220, 221, 226.
Sièyes 11.
Silesia 170.
Slav 152.
Smith (Adam) 20, 117, 132, 154.
Social Contract 204.
Social History of the American Family 30.
Soviet Russia 200, 221.
Spain 13, 21, 22, 26, 70, 220.
Sparta 142, 143, 153, 188.
Spencerian 165.
Spenser 196.
Spiegel 74.
Spinoza 194, 203.
stadia 100, 102.
Stockton 217.
Stoic 164, 174, 182, 198, 199, 207, 208.
Stuart 181.
Subjection of Women 29.
Sullivan 164.
Summa de legibus 74.
summa potestas 201, 202.
Supan 24.
Swabian 74.
Sweden 22, 25.
Switzerland 12, 153, 226.
Tacitus 52, 107.
Tarquin 149.
Tennant 104.
Tennyson 12.
Teutonic 38, 71, 81, 117, 152, 165, 207.
Thebes 142, 153.
Theocritean 183.
Thiers 139.
Third International 224.
Third Republic 138.
Thirty Years, War 25, 217.
Tiberius 95, 182.
Tirol 13.
Treitschke 6, 188.

Trajan 15.
Tractatus Theologico Politicus 194.
Trebia 88.
tributum 113, 115, 118.
trivium 156.
Turkey 25.
tyrannos 181.
United States 10, 13, 30, 76, 107, 125, 126, 147, 154.
Ulpian 73, 164.
Unterwalden 12.
Uri 12.
Utopia 163, 166, 200, 216.
vectigalium 118.
Vehm-Gerichte 81.
Veltro 23, 223.
Venice 149, 153.
Vienna 9, 22, 25.
Vindicae contra Tyrannos 181.
Vinogradoff 165.
Virgil 156, 224.
Visigoth 70.
Voltaire 139.
Vondel 156.
Wales 22, 24, 25.
Walpole 47.
War of the Liberation 136.
Washington 6, 10, 154.
Weser 81.
West-European 14, 107.
Westphalia 12, 22, 81, 83.
Western Roman Empire 16.
Whitman 6.
Will to Power 170.
Wenceslaus 17.
William II, 137.
William the Conqueror 101.
Wirtschaftliche und soziale Grundlagen der europäischen Kultur 150.
witan 71.
Woolf 174.
Wordsworthian 200.
Yankee 10.
Young (Arthur) 6.